The Meaning
of Working

ORGANIZATIONAL AND OCCUPATIONAL PSYCHOLOGY

Series Editor: PETER WARR
MRC/ESRC Social and Applied Psychology Unit, Department of Psychology,
The University, Sheffield, England

A list of books in this series is available from the publisher on request.

The Meaning of Working

MOW International Research Team

1987

 ACADEMIC PRESS

Harcourt Brace Jovanovich, Publishers
London   Orlando   San Diego   New York
Austin   Boston   Sydney   Tokyo   Toronto

ACADEMIC PRESS INC. (LONDON) LTD.
24/28 Oval Road
London NW1

United States Edition published by
ACADEMIC PRESS INC.
Orlando, Florida 32887

British Library Cataloguing in Publication Data
is available

ISBN 0-12-509360-8

Phototypeset by Katerprint Typesetting Services, Oxford
Printed by St Edmundsbury Press, Bury St Edmunds, Suffolk

Preface

The MOW research project investigates, within industrialized nations, the meanings people attach to one of their most important life roles: working. It assesses these meanings of working in eight countries (Belgium, Britain, the Federal Republic of Germany, Israel, Japan, Netherlands, USA, Yugoslavia) by using both national representative samples of the work force and specifically chosen socially important target groups. In total close to 14,700 individuals provided work meaning data. It represents a collaborative research effort of 14 team members and an even greater number of supporting institutions over a period from 1978–1984.

This volume provides a first analysis and summary of findings from the MOW research project. The first three chapters describe the reasons, theoretical bases, and methodological approaches utilized in the Meaning of Working (MOW)-study. Chapters 4–13 provide the body of major findings. They deal with an analysis of the main dimensions of the empirically identified work meanings (e.g. centrality of working as a life role, the significance of societal norms regarding working, valued working outcomes), their interrelationships and patterns, their sociographic and individual developmental antecedents and consequences in terms of preferences regarding specific jobs and working in general. This part of the volume also contains an analysis of characteristics people tend to refer to in defining an activity as being "work". The data analysis tries to do justice to the need to compare national representative samples, to analyze specific occupational effects as reflected in target groups across countries, and to evaluate possible interactive effects of country and target group. The concluding Chapter 14, apart from summarizing the main findings, explores possible action and policy implications in the light of presently promoted and discussed policy options regarding work in industrialized societies.

March 1987   MOW International Research Team

To
Makoto Takamiya

With his death our team lost
an invaluable colleague.

Foreword

The collaboration of several national teams engaged in joint comparative research usually requires some central support throughout the lifetime of a project to facilitate coordination, standardization, the development of concepts and methods, data analysis and integrated reporting. Such central support was not available for MOW. In consequence, we also lacked a permanent center of coordination. These severe handicaps could be overcome only through mustering of support from many different sources and by extraordinary commitments of team members. This makes for a long list of acknowledgements.

The International Institute of Management (IIM) of the Science Center Berlin was crucial in enabling us to carry the MOW-research at least to a take-off stage. By granting an extensive research fellowship to G. W. England in 1978 it enabled the first intellectual grounds to be laid in a preliminary research proposal (England and Wilpert, 1978) which served as a discussion basis for four IIM-funded international workshops—which allowed the formation of the team and the joint development of basic concepts and procedures.

A large number of other institutions gave support during subsequent stages of the research by partially supporting plenary or committee meetings of the MOW-team:

- Institut für medizinische Dokumentation und Systemforschung (MEDIS), Munich, Federal Republic of Germany
- Ghent State University, Ghent, Belgium
- Free University of Amsterdam, Netherlands
- The University of Oklahoma, Norman, Oklahoma, USA
- Osaka University, Osaka, Japan
- Maison des Sciences de l'Homme, Paris, France.

In view of the lack of a permanent center of coordination we had to assign certain critical functions to various institutions:

- The development of a codebook for standardized data treatment was supported by the Free University of Amsterdam.
- The creation of the international MOW-data bank, data bank documentation and the major part of international comparative analysis was performed at the Ghent State University.
- The typing of the final manuscript was shared by the Free University of Amsterdam and the University of Oklahoma.

The national studies of this research were decentrally funded by various academic institutions and national funding agencies.

- Belgium: Laboratory of Socio-Psychology of Work and Organization of the Ghent State University; Fonds voor Kollektief Fundamental Onderzoek; Ministerie voor Tewerkstelling en Arbeid (BTK)
- Federal Republic of Germany: Pädagogische Hochschule Berlin (Pilot Study); Technical University Berlin (Target Group Study); Volkswagen Foundation (Representative Survey)
- Great Britain: Work and Society, Taylor Nelson Associates Tavistock Institute
- Israel: United States–Israel Binational Science Foundation (BSF), Jerusalem, Israel
- Japan: Japan Institute of Group Dynamics, Fukuoka; Japan Ship Building Industry Foundation, Tokyo; Faculty of Human Sciences, Osaka University
- Netherlands: Netherlands Organization for the Advancement of Pure Research
- USA: University of Minnesota, University of Oklahoma (College of Business Administration and President's Associates), AT&T Network Systems, Oklahoma City Works
- Yugoslavia: Institute of Sociology, University Edvard Kardelj, Ljubljana; Slovenian Research Foundation

Collective responsibility for this publication is shared by the 14 members of the International MOW-Team:

- Dr J. H. T. H. Andriessen, Institute for Social Research, Tilburg, Netherlands
- Vojko Antončic, Director of the Institute of Sociology, Ljubljana, Yugoslavia
- Dr Pol Coetsier, Professor of Socio-Psychology of Work and Organization, Ghent State University, Ghent, Belgium
- Dr Pieter J. D. Drenth, Professor of Work and Organizational Psychology, Free University of Amsterdam, Netherlands
- Dr George W. England, Professor of Management, Director, Center for

Economic and Management Research, University of Oklahoma, Norman, Oklahoma, USA

- Dr Itzak, Harpaz, Lecturer of Human Resources, University of Haifa, Haifa, Israel
- Dr Frank A. Heller, Director, Centre for Decision Making Studies, Tavistock Institute of Human Relations, London, Great Britain
- Lic. Marnix Holvoet, Research Fellow for Data Analysis, Ghent State University, Ghent, Belgium
- Dr Rob N. van der Kooij, Work and Organizational Psychologist, Netherlands Railways Ltd, Utrecht, Netherlands
- Dr Jyuji Misumi, Professor of Social Psychology, Osaka University, Osaka, Japan
- Dr S. Antonio Ruiz Quintanilla, Assistant Professor of Work and Organizational Psychology, Technical University Berlin, Berlin (West), Germany
- Dr Rie Spoelders-Claes, Associate Professor of Sociopsychology of Work and Organization, Ghent State University, Ghent, Belgium
- Dr William T. Whitely, Associate Professor of Management, University of Oklahoma, Norman, Oklahoma, USA
- Dr Bernhard Wilpert, Professor of Work and Organizational Psychology, Technical University Berlin, Berlin (West), Germany.

Collective responsibility in complex tasks such as international comparative research does not negate but presupposes division of labor:

- The individual country studies were carried out under joint responsibility of the team member(s) of each respective country.
- Rob van der Kooij took the main responsibility for the development of the Codebook.
- An analysis committee met several times to prepare guidelines for international data analyses. Its members were V. Antončic, P. Coetsier, P. J. D. Drenth, M. Holvoet, R. van der Kooij, A. Ruiz Quintanilla and W. T. Whitely.
- The creation of the international MOW-data bank, its documentation and data processing of most of the international analyses were taken on by M. Holvoet. Additional analyses for particular purposes were carried out in most other member countries on the basis of the international data files distributed to all country teams.

Although the International MOW-Team collectively authors this volume, its development must be seen as a process of many interactions of individual or subgroup drafting, written comments from individual team members, and plenary review and approval. This process was utilized to draw as much as possible on the talents in the group. In consequence, it would be almost impossible in most cases to identify a particular concept or idea with a specific individual in the team. However, the diversity of intellectual styles and approaches will certainly show itself as a consequence of the set of individuals who accepted the main responsibility to draft—and several times redraft—a given chapter. This is at the same time an asset of this volume—in terms of its intended richness of approaches—and a liability—in terms of the challenge to the reader to adapt to divergent styles. Acceptance of the responsibility to draft and redraft a given chapter was influenced partly by individual preference and affinity to a theme, partly by mild pressures from the team, and partly by English language fluency. Hence, the following division of labor ensued:

Chapter 1: B. Wilpert, W. T. Whitely
Chapter 2: W. T. Whitely
Chapter 3: P. J. D. Drenth, M. Holvoet
Chapter 4: G. W. England, W. T. Whitely
Chapter 5: G. W. England, P. Coetsier, R. Spoelders-Claes
Chapter 6: P. Coetsier, R. Spoelders-Claes, G. W. England
Chapter 7: G. W. England, I. Harpaz
Chapter 8: V. Antončic
Chapter 9: I. Harpaz, R. Spoelders-Claes, P. Coetsier
Chapter 10: R. Spoelders-Claes, P. Coetsier
Chapter 11: R. N. van der Kooij, A. Ruiz Quintanilla
Chapter 12: W. T. Whitely, G. W. England
Chapter 13: J. Misumi with the assistance of T. Sugiman
Chapter 14: G. W. England, F. A. Heller, B. Wilpert

An Editorial Committee consisting of G. W. England, F. A. Heller, W. T. Whitely and B. Wilpert was charged to tie up loose ends, streamline and integrate the whole manuscript in terms of language and structure before submitting it for final approval to the whole International Team and, finally, to the publisher.

While the MOW-Team suffered terribly from the sudden death of its colleague Makoto Takamiya in 1981 and from missing his important and significant impacts in the early phases of the project, the Team took comfort in the continued emotional and spiritual support from his father, Susumi Takamiya.

March 1987   MOW International Research Team

Contents

Preface   v

Foreword   vii

1. Why Study the Meaning of Working?   1
   Introduction   1
   The historical and philosophical significance of work   3
   The individual significance of working   5
   The significance of the meaning of working as a causal
       variable in social or institutional change   7
   The changing context of working: societal trends affecting
       the meaning of working   8
   The significance of the meaning of working as a topic
       in current comparative research   11
   The focus of meaning of working (MOW)   12

2. Meaning of Working/Model and Concepts   15
   The model   15
   Work centrality   17
   Societal norms   19
   Valued working outcomes and work goals   24
   Relationship between meaning of working concepts   25
   Antecedents of the meaning of work   27
   Macrosocietal influences   34
   Consequences of the meaning of working   36
   General summary   37

3. Meaning of Working/Design and Methods   39
   Introduction   39
   Considerations in cross-national or cross-cultural research   40

Nature of the study   42
Development of instruments   49

4. The Structure of Meaning of Working   63
   Introduction   63
   Measurement of meaning of working   64
   The sample utilized   66
   Empirical structure of meaning of working   67
   Qualitative similarity of meaning of working structures
       found in each country   74
   Summary   75

5. Work Centrality   79
   Introduction   79
   The concept of work centrality   80
   The measurement of work centrality   81
   Work centrality and involvement with working and
       commitment to working   89

6. Societal Norms about Working   91
   Introduction   91
   Entitlement and obligation norms toward working   94
   The influence of sex, age, and educational level on
       the societal norms about working   105

7. Valued Working Outcomes and Work Goals   111
   Introduction   111
   A broad assessment of the functions of working   111
   Work goals   115
   Summary of valued working outcomes   128

8. The Meaning of Working in Terms of Preferences   133
   Introduction   133
   Preferability of intrinsic work   135
   Preferability of leisure   148
   Summary   156

9. Definitions of Working   161
   Introduction   161
   International comparison of definitions of working   163
   Target groups' definitions of working   163
   Identification of work definitions clusters   165
   Conclusions   170

10. Meaning of Working Patterns 173
    Introduction 173
    Developing meaning of working patterns 174
    Procedure for the formation and validation of MOW patterns 174
    Identification of MOW patterns 175
    Distribution of national representative samples on the
        MOW patterns 179
    MOW patterns among target groups 180
    Summary 181

11. Antecedents of Meaning of Working Patterns 186
    Introduction 186
    Biographical variables 186
    Work history, job, and organizational characteristics 193
    The present job 195
    Conclusions 199

12. The Consequences of the Meaning of Working 201
    Introduction 201
    Meaning of working and involvement with work for
        national labor force samples 202
    Valued working outcomes and preferences for jobs/national
        labor force comparisons 206
    Complex man: patterns of work meanings and patterns
        of consequences 212
    Summary 217

13. International Comparison of the Relationships
    between MOW Variables 221
    Introduction 221
    Quantification on response pattern 222
    Relationships among sex, age, education, occupation,
        status, and MOW variables 239
    Inclusion of question items from survey on National
        Character (Japan) 241
    Characteristics of people with high, medium, and
        low work centrality 242
    Summary 244

14. The Meaning of Working; Overview and Implications 247
    Introduction 247
    The general structure of MOW 248
    Individual variability in meaning of working 250

Attachment to working   251
Normative expectations about working   252
The nature of a desirable working life   253
Meaning of working patterns   255
Definitions of working   257
Working and societies   259
Alternative interpretations   261

Appendix A3.0   265

Appendix A3.1   325

Appendix A3.2   357

Appendix A8   365

Appendix A9   367

Appendix A13   373

References   381

Index   393

Chapter 1

Why Study the Meaning of Working?

Introduction

Once again, the topic of working has raised its Janus head. Mankind's age-old archetypal longing to be freed from labor's toil and trouble is instantaneously contradicted by the unshaken conviction (with its similar historical persuasiveness) that it is working, in particular, that creates, defines, and guarantees human existence. Today, for the first time in recorded history, we seem to come quite close to realizing the dream to enter "the realm of freedom where laboring stops" (Marx, 1933: 873). Decades ago, Arendt (1958: 4–5) anticipated the paradox that epitomizes the ambivalence about working:

> The modern age has carried with it a theoretical glorification of labor and has resulted in a factual transformation of the whole society into a laboring society. The fulfillment of the wish, therefore . . . comes at a moment when it can only be self-defeating. It is a society of laborers which is about to be liberated of the fetters of labor, and this society does no longer know of those other higher and more meaningful activities for the sake of which this freedom would deserve to be won . . . What we are confronted with is the prospect of a society of laborers without labor, that is, without the only activity left to them. Surely, nothing could be worse.

In viewing the loosening ties of the individual to his or her family, country, and traditions in modern, industrialized society, Durkheim (1960) concluded that it is mainly work and the division of labor that provides the social connections between man to man and creates the basis of societal integration. Anthony (1980: 424) asks:

> But what is to be the course and the foundation of moral order when work ceases for many or diminishes for most? If men enter society through work what will be left of society if work ends? And if work has formed the logic of the relationship between man in industrial society how is their relationship to

be explained if that society is changed? Is it possible that man will become truly alienated from other men only when he is released from work which was said to have alienated him?

In a nutshell, these queries raise, at the same time, the philosophical, the anthropological, the societal, and the individual significance of working. In the following sections, we attempt to answer the question "Why Study the Meaning of Working?" by reviewing five answers provided in the literature:

1. The historical and philosophical significance of working.
2. The individual significance of working.
3. Work meanings as a causal variable in social and organization change.
4. Societal trends that affect the meaning of working.
5. The importance of the meaning of working as shown by the current comparative research interest in the topic.

However, before reviewing these five answers, we would like to provide the broad definition of working that guided our study. We define working as paid employment (including self-employment). In doing so, we exclude other work referents such as housework, voluntary work, school work and other forms of working where there is no exchange of labor services for pay.

The major reasons for this definition can be traced to the significant and recent (at least historically) phenomena of the institutionalization of working and the trend away from working as an activity involving the entire family. The institutionalization of working is an ever present fact of life in industrial or service economies. Working today occurs within the context of large internal and external labor markets. Working is increasingly an activity circumscribed by rules and laws that govern practices in almost every area of the employment relationship. Laws govern the age at which people can begin working, hours of work and age of retirement. Further, the trend away from agrarian economies has truncated and separated working as an activity so that it is no longer inextricably intertwined with other life roles.

With these trends, working began to emerge as activities occurring within the context of a formalized process in which labor is exchanged for pay. This is a process frequently conceptualized as part of the employment contract. As discussed elsewhere in this and subsequent chapters many of the meanings of working we study have origins that stretch back through the centuries. However, it is the institutionalization of working and its altered relationship to other life roles that shapes much of the current meaning assigned to it. Paid employment in exchange for purposive defined and coordinated activity, and the altered relationship of this activity with other parts of life are two of the assumptions from which we launch our investigation. They are surely two major phenomena that shape the contemporary meaning of working for our respondents.

The historical and philosophical significance of working

In her incisive and brilliant analysis of the human condition Arendt (1958) distinguishes *labor* from *work*, the former denoting the often painful efforts of our body "necessitated by its needs," the latter referring to the work of our hands which fabricates "the sheer unending variety of things whose sum total constitutes the human artifice." Labor, thus, is seen as serving the immediate needs for the maintenance of life through products of short durability and for immediate consumption. It constitutes "man's metabolism with nature." Work, on the other hand, creates objects of longer use and durability through often violent intervention in natural settings, life processes, and through the modification of man's physical environment (Udy, 1970).

Both—labor as the basis for the maintenance of human life and work as the continuous process of the creation and perpetuation of material (reified) culture—appear to be necessary conditions of human nature. While the use of instruments and machines (i.e., products of work) tend to progressively eliminate labor, specialization and division of work, as well as its intrinsic utilitarianism, may tend to transform work into a mode of labor (Arendt, 1958: 174).

Notwithstanding its refinements, Arendt's (1958) perspective is clearly rooted in Western, particularly Judeo-Christian, traditions that frequently show an ambivalence towards working. In the Old Testament (Genesis 3: 17–19), working is clearly considered as the punishment for man's original sin. The redeeming value of working is of a secondary order: through sharing the fruits of working with people in poverty and distress. The Reformation, while still continuing to accept the retributional character of working, developed a new evaluative discussion: Men and women's work became an obligation or duty of particular value due to its contribution to God's creation. Religious pronouncements "considered (working) as helping to build God's kingdom—working was good, hard working better" (Drenth, 1983: 9). This was the notion which Weber (1922) could easily appropriate in his seminal treatise, *The Protestant Ethic and the Spirit of Capitalism.*

For Thomas Aquinas, working was considered a "difficult good" (*bonum arduum*), difficult because of its taxing character, and good, in part, because of its feature of being full of hardship. The challenge was to transform nature and thus fulfill God's command to subjugate nature and enable man's self-realization according to God's image (Genesis 1: 26–27). The social doctrine of the Catholic Church as reflected in the encyclicals of the popes for the past century (especially Leo XIII, *Rerum Novarum*, 1891; Pius XI, *Quadragesimo Anno*, 1931; John Paul II, *Laborem Exercens*, 1981) deliberately links up to this notion that working is the central means of subjugating nature. The theme of man's dominance over nature is most expressly taken up by John Paul II (*Laborem Exercens*). He, more than his predecessors, developed a differentiated picture of working in its "objective" meaning, that is, the use of technology as a part of working in subjugating nature, and its "subjective" meaning, that is, man's self-realization through working in the social context of his family and his socio-cultural ethnic. This dual role of working is seen as crucial for man's "personalization."

In summary, Judeo-Christian views include working as a form of punishment, as a duty or obligation to God and society, as a difficult process pitting men and women against nature with character development as the product, and as an instrument contributing to the progressive realization of the Kingdom of God. Non-occidental, religious, or cultural traditions seem to place a different emphasis on working, less subjugating nature and more fulfillment of social obligation to receive rewards. In Islamic teachings, working appears as a critical human activity to make man pleasing and acceptable to God. Some of the Sayings of Muhammad may illustrate this (from Allama Sir Abdullah Al-Mamun Al-Suhrawardy, 1949):

> He who neither worketh for himself, nor for others, will not receive the reward of God.
> Who is able and fit and doth not work for himself, or for others, God is not gracious to him.
> Those who earn an honest living are the beloved of God.
> God is gracious to him that earneth his living by his own labour, and not by begging.

In Buddhist thinking, the attainment of Nirvana is tantamount to liberating oneself from one's passions that constrain and impede its attainment (Sugita, 1983). According to Dôgen (1200–1253), the founder of the Sôtô sects of Zen Buddhism, the road to Nirvana is to properly execute the most simple and banal daily activities—drink tea, eat rice, carry water. The Zen priest, Suzuki Shôsan (seventeenth century), extended this notion to the proper conduct of professions which he contrasted to the passion-reviving influence of idleness: "When one carries out arduous and difficult tasks and when one suffers from it, one is not constrained by passions. One then practices a Buddhist activity." Hence, Nirvana can be reached through hard professional work: "Farming is a Buddhist activity." Physical labor, spiritual advancement, and character formation are conceived as elements of one unified underlying process. In summary, these non-Western religions tend to view working as an activity harmonizing men and women with nature and an activity that develops personal character.

The individual significance of working

It is, however, a different question from these historical religious consider-ations to ask how, empirically, working people experience labor or work, and what significance and meaning working has for them personally. Can the significance of working be reduced to the intrinsic expressive dualism of goals? Is working only a means where *goal* implies the "potentially enrich-ing experience through which men can develop their aptitudes and abilities, enjoy the satisfactions of achievement and find an outlet for their creative capacity" (Korpi, 1978: 111)? That is, is working largely instru-mental and viewed primarily as a means to other goals with economic returns as the main purpose" (Korpi, 1978: 110)? Or is it necessary to emphasize the future implications of "changing meaning of work as poss-ibly resulting in: (a) a shift in the definition of good citizenship from that of being a productive individual to that of being a socially relevant consumer; (b) a significant modification in the function of educational institutions to the function of socializing for the new society; and (c) a redefinition of work in the life-cycle of the individual" (Dublin, 1976: 26–27)?

Some clues about the individual significance working may have for people can be derived from the simple observation of absolute time individuals spend working. In most industrialized countries, the average working person spends nearly one-third of his or her waking activities at work. In addition, the time one spends in planning, training, and preparing for work (socialization to work and its meaning) appear to begin at a rather early age (Goldthorpe, Lockwood, Bechofer and Platt, 1968; Sewell, Haller and Ohlendorf, 1970). Further, the time one invests worrying about being out of work extends over a large segment of a person's life.

Other clues about the expressive significance of working for individuals are provided by experiences such as "unemployment and retirement" that disengage people from work. The numbers and statistics on redundant labor often obscure much of the human dimension of unemployment. Studs Terkel (1972: 44) captured these comments from an unemployed 45-year-old construction worker as he expressed his frustration and dis-couragement: "Right now I can't really describe myself because . . . I'm unemployed . . . So, you see, I can't say who I am right now . . . I guess a man's something else besides his work, isn't he? But what? I just don't know."

Wilensky (1960, 1961) uses the concept of career as an integrative device between the work and non-work spheres of life. But when the person experiences unemployment, career perspectives are destroyed and the various spheres of life become fragmented (Aiken, Ferman, and Sheppard, 1968). Wilensky studied the degree of alienation from work of 1156 male professionals. Alienation was defined as the "disassociation of self from work and a loss of capacity to express one's self in work." Wilensky (1960, 1961) found that the best predictor of alienation was chaotic career experiences including unemployment. Similarly, Israeli (1935) found that Lancashire and Scottish unemployed, as compared with employed groups, were more negative and more depressed in the sense that they expected greater failure in various situations in the future. The traumatic and often catastrophic effects of unemployment on individuals is evidenced from consistent findings over more than 5 decades, from the classic Marienthal study in the 1930s (Jahoda, Lazarsfeld, and Zeisel, 1960) to more recent research (Jahoda, 1979).

Warr (1985), in reviewing the thrust of empirical evidence of a large number of cross-sectional and longitudinal studies on the relationship between unemployment and health, concludes that unemployment clearly impairs psychological well-being in terms of, e.g., happiness, present life satisfaction, experience of pleasure and strain, self-esteem, anxiety, distress, and depression. However, since not every unemployed person reports and displays the same levels of deteriorated well-being, we must assume that specific additional factors mediate or moderate the unemployment-health relationship, such as employment committment (centrality or salience of one's work), biographic age, length of unemployment, financial strain, low ensuing activity levels, social class, sex, and country of origin (due to differences in social security systems and unemployment benefits).

The ultimate consequence of unemployment may be reflected in one correlate: death. Brenner (1980) estimated that a 1% increase in U.S. unemployment rate results in approximately 37,000 additional deaths, with more than half of those fatalities caused by increased incidence of heart attack and other cardiovascular diseases. Since Durkheim's (1897) pioneering work on suicide, there have been several studies that have observed a relationship between unemployment and suicide (Stearns, 1921; Cavan, 1928; Dayton, 1940; MacMahon, Johnson, and Pugh, 1963). However, as Warr (1985) points out, although research results on the impact of unemployment on both mortality and suicide rates are rather suggestive and intriguing, they must be considered with some methodological caveats. Studies as widely spaced from Eisenberg and Lazarsfeld (1938) to Dooley and Catalano (1980) summarize extensive bodies of research conducted in the United States and Europe, indicating relationships between economic conditions and behavioral disorders, changes in political attitudes, and emotional effects on children. As the period of unemployment lengthens, biographical accounts describe a progression from optimism through pessimism to fatalism with adaptation to this final state resulting in a narrowed range of interests and behavior. Apathy sets in along with increased inferiority feelings, destruction of family relationships, and a weakened interest in politics and organizations (Brunngraber, 1933; Jahoda et al., 1960; Beales and Lambert, 1934; Gatti, 1937).

These early accounts differ very little from more recent accounts of ecosystem distrust, or the distrust of people, things, and institutions in one's environment (Triandis, Feldman, and Weldon, 1975). Triandis goes on to describe the components of ecosystem distrust as less trust in people, suspicion of the motives of others, rejection of authority figures and institutions of the establishment, and seeing the environment as malevolent.

In summary, the evidence is substantial and consistent in the finding that unemployment can have widespread and serious consequences for the meaning of working for individuals, for the social organization of primary groups and units, for institutions, and for society.

The decision to retire provides a second example of the integral relationship between work meanings and societal implications. Recent research with groups as diverse as civil workers and automobile workers indicates two major classes of variables that consistently predict the decision to retire are finance and work-related attitudes (Barfield, 1970; Barfield and Morgan, 1969; Schmitt and McCune, 1981). These studies have found that a lessened desire to work is one of the best predictors of future actual early retirement.

The significance of the meaning of working as a causal variable in social or institutional change

But these examples also indicate that philosophical and individual psychological significance of working are thoroughly intertwined with its societal significance. People not only develop work meanings as a result of their experiences with work and work conditions, but they use work meanings in changing organizations and social structures. Once certain patterns of work meanings have developed for individuals and groups of individuals, they will, in turn, affect organizations and society in areas such as mobility, conflict, productivity, or dropping out, thus modifying organizations and creating new ones. For if we know anything about the world of work, we know that it is man-made. It is man who is active; it is man who is the structurer of experience and meaning. This view of the *enacted environment* has been stressed by authors such as Udy (1970), Weick (1979), and Silverman (1970). It is this sense of causality that we are hypothesizing: that man is the definer of reality as well as being defined by it; that social interaction, as an example, "is a process whose course is predefined, yet one through which new definitions of reality emerge" (Silverman, 1970: 213).

The implications of these views and the associated frame of reference guide the present research on the meaning of working. To view man as totally determined by external forces is to accept only positivistic explanations of causality. To accept man as one causal agent is to reject strict positivism and to recognize that man interprets the world subjectively and transcends subjective experience (Polanyi, 1962). Therefore, it seems necessary to study the meaning attached to working behavior as a totality whether it is attached to behavior retrospectively, concurrently, or prospectively (Weick, 1979).

An additional implication of this view is that, while groups and organizations sustain meanings, the very fact that these collective structures develop in the first place, and endure, is likely the result of the overlaps in meaning structures of individuals that *precede* the collective structure (Allport, 1962).

> Having first converged on shared meanings of *how* a structure can form (i.e. nationalization, workers councils, or whatever), the persons then activate a repetitive cycle of interlocking behaviors—that is, they form an organization or a community. The range of their behavior narrows *before* the environment is formed, not after; the environment is made possible by this initial narrowing and convergence. (Weick, 1979: 90)

If we want to know what man's environment will look like tomorrow in the world of work, we should start with the meaning of working today. Work meanings do have consequences for organizations and society, and it is important to view the findings of studies of work meanings in both a present and a future sense.

The changing context of working: societal trends affecting the meaning of working

Even though it may be impossible to identify clear chains of cause and effect, it is possible to highlight changing environmental conditions and likely concomitant changes in the meaning of working.

"For Better or Worse" says a Club of Rome report, the future of mankind is linked to recent technological, microelectronic innovations that are likely to affect every second workplace within a fraction of a generation (Friedrichs and Schaff, 1980). While—due to these innovations—it would not seem to be a problem to increase productivity, a different problem potentially comes into focus: a double distribution problem: how to distribute work among willing workers and how to distribute the rewards created by those who have work with those who do not. Arendt's (1958) apprehensions of a workless work society have become present day concerns. The puzzlement and helplessness of politicians in many industrialized countries about current and most likely lasting, if not growing, structural unemployment give striking evidence to this distribution problem.

Another significant change in most Western industrialized nations that may have important repercussions on work-related values is the drastic increase in transfer payments. Transfer payments which redistribute income have at least doubled or even quadrupled in most countries during the 1970s. One fear among many politicians and economists is that transfer payments and social welfare systems might act as disincentives for people to take jobs that have few non-economic attractions and only marginal economic benefits (Reynolds, 1974).

Apart from growing structural unemployment is the dramatic labor market change since World War 2 in increased labor force participation of women. In the United States, the number of women working has more than doubled since 1950. Similar growth rates of female labor market participation prevail in the other countries taking part in this study. A corollary of this trend is the changing character of the family. The stereotypical view of the family with the husband as the only breadwinner and the wife at home as mother and caretaker is definitely becoming increasingly obsolete and a view of times past. Thus, the individual importance of working extends to an ever-increasing proportion of our active population, while at the same time, there seems to be, in some countries, a growing mismatch between labor supply and demand.

Increasingly, people feel they have a right to a job. This trend may signal an underlying change in the norms of distributive justice used to evaluate inputs relative to outcomes in the employment contract, and the more so for those out of work or denied the opportunity to work (IDE, 1981). The resistance of many older people to mandatory retirement indicates not only an interest in working but a sense that they are entitled to work if they want a job. It would seem that politicians are eager to interpret "flexibility of retirement age" to mean early retirement in order to create new job opportunities, while, for many of the older people, it means "flexibility up as well as down in retirement age," depending on personal circumstances and preferences. Hence, this rights-consciousness is manifested in a sense that one is entitled to a voice in decisions that affect one's job and working life. The right to a job is likely to be a mounting social and political issue. It bears a distinct relationship to the full employment concept first proposed by Beveridge (1945).

The issue is further aggravated by the trend towards higher life expectancies with its consequences for the age distribution in Western societies. It is estimated that, in Europe, the number of people above the age of 60 years will increase by 30.7% between the years 1970 and 2000, and those above 80 years of age by 63.4%. The term of the coming geriatric society is by no means utopian and two generations of retired people at a given moment may become common. The prospect of a retirement age of 55, as it is presently discussed in many European countries, would seem rather questionable when viewed in terms of these demographic trends and the social costs of having productive workers retire and draw ever-increasing public and private pensions for longer periods of time. Although the baby boom of the 1960s may mitigate some of the overall consequences, these trends will definitely affect the individual destiny of many of our older citizens. To put it into terms of classical political economy: What we are confronting is a mismatch of the state of productive means and productive relations. It is a mismatch along various dimensions. On the surface, it is a mismatch of shrinking labor demand and increased labor supply. At a deeper level, the mismatch may be between traditional work socialization and work (or competence and needs) with a corresponding gap between expectations and existing socioeconomic opportunities (Heller, 1982). It is a potentially disastrous mismatch between personal psychic structures and modern societal structures.

We are relatively safe and certain in describing the global and structural features of our labor market situations. But we know very little about the consequences of these conditions for our population's psychic structures of meanings attached to working. We know even less about what affects these structures: a generalized Zeitgeist? national character? a nation's historical experience? socialization through family, school, or work itself? As Mills wrote: "No adequate history of the meanings of work has been written" (1956: 215).

In summary, the significance of the present study of the meaning of working stems, in part, from historical–developmental–religious views of work still reflected in contemporary societies, and from trends and conditions presently affecting work and societies. These factors help to shape present meanings assigned to working by people, including instrumental and expressive meanings. But, the meaning of working is not solely a consequence of these historical and contemporary influences; it is a causal factor in the interpretation of these influences. In addition, the meaning of working is a potential causal influence on the form and direction of present and future changes in social and economic institutions. It is for these reasons that there is so much comparative research interest in the meaning of working.

The significance of the meaning of working as a topic in current comparative research

The major intellectual traditions in the study of working have been succinctly summarized by Dubin (1976) who also used the term *meaning of work* and the concept of *centrality of work* (elaborated in Chapter 2). It seems, therefore, appropriate to refer the interested reader to his summary of past research efforts and briefly direct the attention to the other relevant, ongoing, and partly complementary international research efforts.

The ongoing international debate on materialism versus post-materialism is closely linked to the work inspired by Inglehart (1977). Based on data from representative surveys in several Western countries and Japan, he concluded that, beginning in the late 1960s, a marked polarization can be noted in all investigated populations which resembles a shift from traditional values of industrialized society (materialist: economic and security concerns predominate) to post-materialist values (concern for quality of life and self-actualization); the former implies austerity and authoritarianism; the latter stresses hedonism and libertarianism (Inglehart, 1982). Age seems to play an important role in connection with these changes: younger generations tending to hold more post-materialist values then their seniors. Although, so far, only minorities are outspoken advocates of post-materialist attitudes, they begin to impact on larger publics due to the influence of elite groups and mass media.

A second international comparative research effort was stimulated by the U.S.-based Public Agenda Foundation with its "Jobs in the 80s Program." The research was conducted in six[1] countries. An attempt has been made to use more or less similar data collection techniques in the various countries (survey data mainly) in an attempt to shed light on the acceptability of various labor market policies and strategy options by the general public in these countries. Only preliminary findings have been published so far (Von Klipstein and Strümpel, 1984).

Another ongoing international comparative study is based on Super's (1970) work values inventory which has been expanded and validated in various languages. Its focus, so far, has mainly been on instrument development, and no detailed findings have been reported for this potentially very important research.

The focus of meaning of working (MOW)

What is the meaning of working life for human beings in modern society? That is the central question of this research. The answer is, as we have seen, by no means self-evident. The discussion of the significance of work implies that the meaning of working is closely related to the meaning of life in modern society. At a time when the post-industrialized society has been forged out of the remains of declining agricultural and industrial bases with the ingredients of new technologies and labor force structures, work-related values are bound to undergo important changes.

Triandis (1972: 35–36) has advanced four major reasons why cross-cultural research is of importance. They all, fully, or at least to some degree, provide the rationale for the study of the meaning of working in different national contexts with different cultural heritages and different labor trends or conditions.

The initial purpose of cross-national/cross-cultural research is to use different *cult units* (Naroll, 1968) as experimental treatment in order to investigate the consequences for some criteria variables. The different national and cultural backgrounds of different samples thus are considered to constitute a natural quasi-experiment. A second purpose is "to obtain information about the incidence of a particular phenomenon in different ecological environments." A third purpose is, "to study how cultures differ in their way of 'cutting the pie of experience'." Finally, there is the purpose to test general laws of behavioral science. Given that working is a universal *pan-cultural* phenomenon, it is of significance to see whether different cultural traditions and ecological settings impact on why people work and on how they experience working. Our justification in conducting international research is imbedded in the first three reasons mentioned. We are, however, somewhat more reluctant to claim testing of general social scientific laws. What may be achieved is to show that certain relationships, for instance, between characteristics of work and meanings people assign to work, are consistent, irrespective of their wider cultural environment.

But a fifth purpose may be added that bears on the practical side of our research. It relates to the aforementioned mismatch between values and expectations of the labor force on the one hand and the factual socio-economic and technological constraints and opportunities on the other. The mismatch cries out for action and policies. Whether they can be carried out through concerted international efforts or through nationally specific remedies alone is very much a question of the real nature of the mismatch. To answer that question, we urgently need to know what working means to people.

We have opted to study the meaning of working rather than the meaning of work in order to signal that what we are concerned with is not so much the philosophical significance of work, but rather the psychological meaning—the significance, beliefs, definitions and the value which individuals and groups attach to working as a major stream of human activity that occurs over much of their lives. It is this concept of working that we are seeking to develop conceptually, to identify empirically, and to understand in terms of its antecedents and consequences.

In essence we are asking people to step back from this stream of activity, this lifelong process, and provide us with the meaning they attach to it. Thus the choice of the verb "working" rather than the noun "work" seems to best capture the task we posed for people. While we do feel that "working" better captures our research purposes, we do use the verb and the noun interchangeably throughout the book. However, our focus is on the meaning of this stream of activity whether it is called working or work.

Within this basic focus, the goals of the research are as follows:

1. Identification of major patterns of meanings individuals and significant groups attach to working. The range of patterns identified obviously will be constrained by the possibilities inherent in our conceptualizations of work meanings, the instruments and methods of data collection, the range of countries involved, and the groups we select to study.

2. To understand how individuals and groups differ in their work meanings. This is a complex task that requires analysis of personal and family variables, work and career history variables, and macroeconomic environment variables as correlates of different work meanings.

3. To understand the consequences of meaning of working patterns for individuals, organizations, and societies. Concern for these consequences is built into the primary data collections procedures, but it is clearly recognized that alternative interpretations and professional debate of our findings are essential to this understanding.

4. To estimate the proportion of the labor force in each country which "holds" each major pattern of meaning of work. Such a goal requires that we obtain data from representative samples of the employed population in addition to a concentrated study of particular groups of prospective, present, and past workers.

5. To develop policy implications from our findings. Obviously, such implications must stem from the data and the country situations, but it seems reasonable to infer what the findings mean for public and private labor policy.

6. To compare work meanings, their developmental histories and their consequences across the countries involved in the study. This goal indicates that we are interested in both similarities (for generalization purposes) and differences (to capture group- and/or country-specific findings) concerning work meanings. We view this international comparative aspect of the research as a major requirement for a fuller understanding of the phenomenon of meaning of working. This goal necessitates that identical procedures and methods be employed by the various country teams. It requires a collective and communal spirit of an entire international team to succeed in this objective, a feature not frequently found in international research ventures and a feature in which we take considerable pride.

Notes

(1) United States, United Kingdom, Japan, West Germany, Sweden and Israel.

Chapter 2

Meaning of Working / Model and Concepts

The model

A well-articulated theory of the meaning of working (MOW) with transituational validity, including a multilevel perspective, and the capability of yielding clear-cut policy implications—desirable as it would be—is not available. Based on a conceptually sound understanding of the meaning of working itself, such a model would be able to specify the critical antecedents and consequences of the central variables. In the absence of any such generally accepted theory, it would seem unwise to allow any one theoretical position to specify all variables measured. Within these limits, our guiding model must be understood to be basically heuristic in nature. It is based on the conception that MOW is determined by the choices and experiences of the individual and by the organizational and environmental context in which they work and live.

The model which follows (Figure 2.1) shows the major variable sets and the most direct and straightforward relationships we initially considered to be of primary importance in the study of MOW. The arrows in the model simply indicate that we attempt to determine the extent to which variables of one set explain (in a statistical sense) variables of another set. A causal interpretation of such findings would, of course, have to take into account the probable developmental sequence of the studied variables in individuals' lives as well as the likely possibility that variable complexes may be interlinked in more than one manner. Our interpretative frame of reference may also have to be changed, depending on a particular group of respondents under consideration (e.g. national representative samples or specific subgroups).

Our heuristic model specifies those levels at which variables are being chosen and operationalized:

- Conditional variables (antecedents)
- Central variables (Meaning of Working)
- Consequences

In the following, we first focus attention on the conceptualization of the central variables then upon antecedent variables and briefly on consequences.

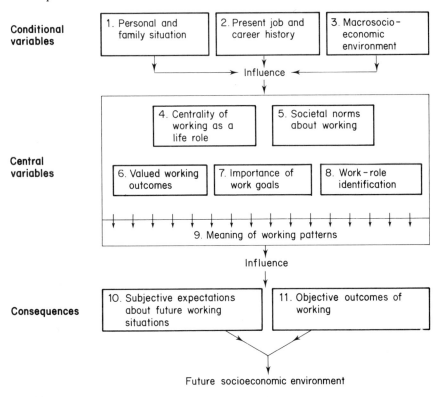

Figure 2.1. Heuristic research model.

The heuristic model presented in Figure 2.1 includes three major and distinct meaning constructs which relate individuals to the phenomenon of working. These three meanings are work centrality which consists of the identification with work and the strength of involvement with working; societal norms of a person's obligation to work and entitlements received from work; and valued working outcomes and work goals.[1] All three meaning constructs function theoretically to describe different bases for the attachment of individuals to the phenomenon of working. Initially, the present discussion examines the conceptual representation of each work meaning construct in terms of the properties of the construct. The relationship between construct definition and construct measurement, termed the *epistemic correlation* by Northrop (1959) or *operationism* by Bridgman (1927) is a critical connection for two reasons. First, there is, frequently, a tendency to assume isomorphism between a construct and measures of the construct when the two are less than isomorphic, due to deficiency (variability in the construct not captured by the measure) or contamination (variability in the measure not found in the construct). Second, theoretical predictions and explanations about a construct are derived from the conceptual representation, while testing of theoretical propositions about a construct come from measurement of the construct.

Our discussion also examines the conceptual relationship between each of the work-meaning constructs and other constructs of theoretical and practical importance. Included here are some expectations regarding relationships between measures of the particular work meaning and measures of the antecedent variables or consequences. Given the comparative nature of this investigation, we introduce relevant research findings from several of the countries included in this study that bear on our conceptualization of work meanings.

Work centrality

At the outset, it is important to remember that the referent in this study is working (paid employment) in general as opposed to working only on the present job. In addition, our concern is with the psychological meaning of working to individuals. Involvement with working is conceptually distinct from involvement with the present job (Kanungo, 1979, 1982). In this study, work centrality is defined as a *general belief about the value of working in one's life*. There are two major theoretical components of the work centrality construct, each with particular properties. The first component involves a value orientation toward working as a life role. The second component involves a decision orientation about preferred life spheres for one's behavior. The next two sections discuss each of these components and then provide a conceptual integration.

Belief/value component of work centrality

The two major properties of this component of work centrality are identification with work and involvement or commitment to working. Identification with work has been a major property in several previous discussions of work values (Lodahl and Kejner, 1965; Maurer, 1968; Lawler and Hall, 1970). Work identification is the outcome of a cognitive consistency process based on a comparison between work as an activity and perceptions of self. The outcome of this cognitive comparison is the development of a distinct type of identification with working central or peripheral to one's self-image—identification with working emerges from this process as a part of self-identification.

The second property of this component of work centrality is involvement or commitment. Work involvement is an affective response to working as a part of a person's life. Involvement with working also may include behavioral elements such as the amount of time spent participating in work activities. Commitment to work is partially free of short-run experiences. Thus the belief/value component of work centrality has a future intentional element as well as a present behavioral involvement element. In our view, work identification and involvement/commitment are mutually reinforcing.

The measurement issues are also clear, given this representation of work centrality. The person should use himself or herself as the referent. The task for the person is to make an evaluation involving both working and self as referents. Finally, the measurement procedure should capture the involvement/commitment property. The process examined by the general measurement task consists of the attachment of an affective element of involvement/commitment to a cognitive consistency comparison of working in relation to self-identification.

Decision orientation component of work centrality

The decision orientation view of work centrality parallels Dubin's (1956) central life interests, Barker's (1968) theory of behavioral settings, and Heider's (1958) theory of interpersonal relationships. This view begins with the premise that a person's experiences are segmented into different subspheres, and that people differ in their preferences for particular life spheres. A person will participate in less preferred life spheres because they provide rewards for calculative or instrumental behavior, but will attach greater significance to behaviors that take place in the life spheres which are more preferred.

There are two major elements in this representation of work centrality. First, there are the life sphere/behavior segments. The work segment can occupy a central or most preferred position among life spheres, share a position with other life spheres, or occupy a peripheral or less preferred position in one's life. This property implies a notion of identification based on a person's relative preferences for life spheres.

The second element in the decision orientation representation of work centrality is choice or the extent to which a person chooses a preferred life sphere and the behaviors associated with it. This choice of life sphere implies a notion of involvement and provides the conditions by which a person establishes affective and behavioural attachments to the environment. Since the person need not become equally involved or committed to all segments of their life (some behaviors may be prescribed rather than voluntarily chosen), commitment or involvement is a selective process. In summary, this second component of work centrality represents the process of identification as a consequence of interactions between persons and their segmented behavioral environments. Involvement or commitment depends on the choice of settings and the potential range of preferred behaviors available while in a particular setting.

The measurement issues posed by this second view of work centrality are clear. First, the measure must include major segments of the person's life—only one of which is work—as choice alternatives. Second, the person must be allowed to choose between the life spheres and order them to provide an indication of the degree of involvement or commitment.

By way of general summary, the value orientation and decision orientation representations of work centrality do have some conceptual similarities. Both include properties of involvement, both have relational properties, and both are concerned with a person's identification with working in general. However, there are differences in the content of the two representations. The relational component in the belief/value orientation view is work in relation to self, while in the decision orientation view, it is the work segment in relation to other life segments. Identification in the belief/value approach is a product of a cognitive consistency process between work as a life activity and the self as a referent. In the decision representation, identification is based on the preferences for working among multiple life spheres. Because of these differences in representation, measures of these two components of the work centrality construct are likely to be correlated only moderately. The combination of these two representations provides a more complete conceptualization of the work centrality construct as a general belief of the value of working in one's life. Work centrality is a measure based on cognitions and affects that reflect the degree of general importance that working has in the life of an individual at any given point in time.

Societal norms

One relatively unexamined aspect of the meaning of working concerns the standards people employ when making normative evaluations about work. There is potentially a large variety of norms or standards to draw upon, but we limit ourselves to two which capture much of the historical and contemporary discussion relevant to the meaning of working. In the ensuing discussion, we find it useful to begin with the developmental antecedents of the norms included in Figure 2.1. It is our view that a major antecedent of these norms is the development of normative reasoning in individuals. Therefore, we turn our attention, initially, to a discussion of the development of normative reasoning and link this discussion to its relevance for norms of social exchange and distributive justice in work. Then we present our conceptual representation of the two norms included in our study: obligation and entitlement orientation.

General considerations

Historically, political writers, legal scholars, social philosophers, and social scientists have relied on some form of social contract in examining the nature of a person's relationship to society. A major theme in developmental psychology, both in Europe and the United States, is the use of principles by adults in their normative reasoning (Kohlberg, 1963; Olafson, 1961; Piaget, 1965). From this perspective, a critical issue is the abstract principles of social justice and fairness that people use in the work situation for purposes of achieving cooperation or distributing the benefits of cooperation. However, we caution the reader that, in the discussion of norms and principles, we attempt to remain neutral and take no stance on the superiority of any normative orientation.

There are two contrasting reference points in much of the discussion of this view of normative principles based on a social contract. One reference point: Begin with the person and concentrate on social standards or norms concerned with an obligation to society. Within psychology, McClelland's (McClelland, Sturr, Knapp, and Wendt, 1958) idea of obligation to society includes such a notion. This notion is also prominent in Kohlberg's (1963) discussion of evaluative standards based on principles of social order and an obligation to duty; in Piaget's (1965) operational/concrete cognitive stage; in Durkheim's moral philosophy (1893), in Confucian values (*giri*) (Mae, 1981) and in the Protestant Ethic (Weber, 1964). Hence, in these sources, normative behavior consists of fulfilling one's duty or obligation to society, respect for delegated authority as a social obligation, and norms which support social order.

A second reference point also concentrates on the individual, but highlights the social standards or norms underlying the rights of the person and the obligation of society to the individual. As an example, within psychology, there are discussions of obligation to self (McClelland *et al.*,

1958). Such discussions are frequently linked to explicit or implicit assumptions about equitable exchange relationships between an individual's contributions and the social system's recompensation. The social theoretical concept of the social contract (Rousseau, 1916) might be considered as a guiding model of such approaches. In this context, it might be interesting to explore the conceptual similarities and differences of our own representation with those proposed in developmental psychology which often imply differential stages of development and maturation (Kohlberg, 1963, 1971; Piaget, 1965). Such an attempt would, however, surpass the immediate task and function of this chapter.

In summary, normative reasoning in this view consists of individual rights or entitlements that have been agreed upon as an obligation of society to its citizens. It is to these obligations to society and entitlements from society as major social norms in the meaning of working that we focus our attention.

The entitlement work norm as an evaluative standard

The entitlement norm as one component of the meaning of working has received extensive discussion by such diverse sources as public opinion pollsters (Yankelovich, 1979), organization behaviorists (Locke and Schweiger, 1979), and in institutional economic theories of unionization in the United States (Perlman, 1976). While the level of analysis differs between these sources, each tends to couch discussions of entitlement in terms of views of property rights and the psychological contract. As an example, "I would like to have a steady job," may be transformed into an imperative statement that, "We all have a right to a steady job." In theory, any motive or belief can be transformed into a right or entitlement through social or legal processes which establish its legitimacy. Aspects of this process in the development of normative reasoning have been discussed by Kohlberg (1971). The integral relationship between the social and legal processes as they affect *externally* established standards and principles governing work relationships and exchange has been discussed by Ledvinka (1982). The relationship between the social and quasilegal processes as they affect *internally* established standards and principles governing work relationships and exchange has been addressed in theories of internal labor markets (Doeringer and Piore, 1971).

Two special discussions of the entitlement views of work norms can be found in Perlman (1976) and Locke and Schweiger (1979). Perlman concludes that *social welfare* and *social institution* theories offer the best explanations of unionization in the United States. In social welfare theories, property claims or entitlements are restricted to economic issues. Social institution theories extend property claims or entitlements to include working conditions such as security and due process. Related to due process is decision participation as a form of property right. Locke and Schweiger (1979) examine decision participation as a worker right and compare the scope of claims, and the sociolegal vehicles for legitimizing the claims in the United States and Europe. One notion common to both these sources is that entitlement is concerned with rights or claims that regulate personal and collective action.

An example of an entitlement norm in this study is agreement with the statement, "Every person in our society should be entitled to interesting and meaningful work."

The obligation work norm as an evaluative standard

The question of the individual's obligation to his or her employer and to society through working has been of central concern in theories of organizational, political, and legal aspects of authority (Etzioni, 1961; Simon, 1947). Two aspects of this obligation are personal responsibility or internalized norms of duty, and social or institutional commitment. As used here, this orientation of the person follows the view of Parsons and Shils (1952) and has an "ought" element: The person *ought* to contribute to society through work or *ought* to save for their future security. In summary, the obligation norm represents the person's beliefs that all people have a duty or responsibility to social units through working. This form of reasoning is also conceptually similar to Kohlberg's (1963) Type 4 social order and obligation to duty orientation, and to Piaget's (1965) operational/concrete cognitive stage discussed earlier.

The relationship between levels of analysis of norms of entitlement and obligation

Throughout the discussion of societal norms, we have implicitly taken the view that there are two levels in the conceptualization of entitlement and obligation. One is the societal level; the other is the individual level. Therefore, it is appropriate to consider the relationship between these levels. In tracing this relationship and the implications for the meaning of working, we confess to engaging in a degree of speculation. We draw on the earlier discussion which sought to link the present conceptualization of these norms to different types of normative reasoning.

Social interaction can be conceptualized as an act of exchange in which each person invests certain inputs (time, effort, attention, and expertise) in exchange for outcomes (money, growth, and satisfaction). The relative proportion of a group's or society's total outcomes afforded a particular member by other members or institutions who control them can be seen, therefore, as a measure of the extent to which the distributor values another member's inputs to the group or to society. The modes of distribution reflect the distributor's attention to different kinds of inputs from members.

We are not certain as to the causal relationship between the norms and the distribution of socially mediated working outcomes. One explanation would suggest that the direction is from the individual level of a norm, entitlement as an example, to organizational or societally mediated outcomes. Individuals' entitlement claims may lead to actions aimed at legitimizing these claims. Another explanation suggests that the direction of causation is from working outcomes mediated by organizations or societies to the development of entitlement norms. That is, people who are dissatisfied with the distribution of working outcomes attempt to close the gap between themselves and others by adopting norms which espouse fair or equal treatment, irrespective of individual differences. Quite the opposite argument would be made for obligation norms.

While the organizational or societal implications of these norms are not entirely clear, we suggest some possible linkages to organizational and societal considerations. Social psychologists (Weick, 1979), sociologists (Coleman, 1966), and economists (Olson, 1965) all address the issue of the formation of groups (including unions, social movements, pressure groups, and special interest groups). Weick (1979), drawing from Allport (1962), argues that convergence of people with similar beliefs *precedes*, and is a necessary condition for, the emergence of groups.

> Thus an initial overlap among people in their beliefs—an overlap that looks like behavior controlled by norms—makes it possible for more enduring social relationships to emerge . . . Having *first* converged on shared ideas of how a structure can form (i.e., on means), the persons *then* activate a repetitive series of interlocking behaviors—that is, they form a collective structure. The range of their behavior narrows *before* a group forms, not after; the group is made possible by this narrowing and convergence. (Weick, 1979: 90)

Thus, to paraphrase Weick (1979), the causal impact would run from the individual level of social norms or claims, to a convergence of individuals with similar normative beliefs, then to social or political pressures which legitimize these normative beliefs regarding the appropriate modes of distributive justice.

Valued working outcomes and work goals

Any answer to the questions of the meaning of working would be insufficient if it did not include outcomes that people value from working and important work goals.[2] In discussing these two components of the meaning of working, we acknowledge the frequent criticism that the preferred outcomes included in research are usually selected without guidance from a theoretical framework that hypothesizes dimensions of working outcomes (Hulin and Triandis, 1981). However, our conclusion, based on a review of proposed taxonomies of working outcomes (i.e., Vroom, 1964; Dubin *et al.*, 1976; Hulin and Triandis, 1981), was that they are not particularly helpful. The classifications proposed do not yield mutually exclusive types of rewards or goals and often generate confusion rather than understanding. We only mention, based on these taxonomies, that the valued working outcomes and work goals included may or may not depend on considerations such as task performance and mediation by the person or external agents. These outcomes and goals can also have symbolic or concrete properties and may be particularistic (depending on the person receiving them) or universalistic. Little more than this can be said about the classification of outcomes, goals, and work identifications included in this study.

Importance evaluations of work outcomes and work goals

In this section, we address the question of what we mean by the term *value*. Here, value means importance evaluations which are defined to include what the person *knows* about each of the outcomes and the preference relationship among outcomes or goals. Thus, we assume that the person making the importance evaluation has sufficient knowledge or experience with each outcome so that they can link the outcomes to each other in an ordered manner.

Our conception of importance evaluations of work outcomes and work role functions has been influenced by Cragin's (1983) research. Specifically, we consider the importance or preference assigned to an outcome or goal to be a function of its cognitive centrality, the dependence of other outcomes on the outcome in question, the criticality of the outcome, and the salience of the outcome. By *cognitive centrality*, we mean the degree to which an outcome is in the forefront of a person's consciousness rather than remote, and the extent to which other outcomes organize around that outcome. By *dependence*, we mean the extent to which cognitions of an outcome influence the cognitions of other outcomes associated with it. By *criticality*, we mean the degree to which the person perceives readily available substitutes for the outcome in question. Finally, by salience, we mean the extent to which immediate socioeconomic and work conditions draw temporary, but forceful and explicit, attention to an outcome which would not otherwise be as dominant. In summary, the importance evaluations of the working outcomes and goals included in this study are a function of how central the outcome is in the person's cognitive structure, the dependence of other outcomes on it, the criticality of the outcome, and its temporal salience. Evaluations of importance or preference imply *choice*. Choice is the implementation of values for working outcomes and goals and for the specific type of identification with working.

Relationship between meaning of working concepts

The previous sections have treated the major meaning of working concepts separately for purposes of discussion. However, these concepts are related theoretically and empirically.

As an example, strong adherence to a norm of obligation also may be a statement of personal sense of obligation. To the extent that this reasoning is correct, the expectation would be that norms of obligation and work centrality beliefs will be positively related.

Also, working outcomes and goals can be inferred by examining what the worker is willing to give up in order to maintain employment. This idea is implicit in the choice representation of work centrality previously discussed. Other choice tasks in the present study also recognize and assess this view of outcomes.

A third example of conceptual and empirical relatedness is found in a study of Dubin, *et al.* (1976). They found that workers high in work centrality particularly valued outcomes such as the confidence their superior had in them, job responsibility, the usefulness of the organization's products or services, and the chances for advancement and promotion. In contrast, workers with low centrality scores particularly valued having time for personal needs, knowing tasks in advance, talking to others while working, the method of wage payment, and working in a modern plant.

There are some common and fundamental reasons for these conceptual and empirical relationships of the meaning of working concepts. The primary reason may lie in the structure of labor markets and occupations, and the influence of these on the salience and functional relationship of meaning of working concepts. Economists use the concept of dual labor markets to distinguish between segments in which workers would obtain high levels of several outcomes—included in this study—and have steady or steadier employment than segments with the opposite conditions (Reynolds, 1974). Often, this second group includes large proportions of women or minority groups in any society. Observations about occupations yield similar conclusions. As an example, the status-ordering of occupations would appear to be overdetermined since it depends on many, rather than any single underlying characteristic. Thus, high-status occupations tend to have better pay, more interesting content, better working conditions, greater responsibility for the welfare of others, greater autonomy in choosing tasks and methods of accomplishing them, and greater control over one's time (Vroom, 1964). These also are the occupations that Dubin et al. (1976) have found to contain relatively higher proportions of occupants with work reflecting a high central life interest.

Additionally, the salience and functional relationships between the meaning of working concepts may be a function of the uncertainty of attainment. If workers have high expectations for an outcome because of prior experience, family background, or reward history, then both frame-of-reference and cognitive consistency theories yield predictions of low salience (Hulin and Triandis, 1981). A similar level of salience might be expected when workers' expectations are very low. For many workers, their jobs do not provide for status or autonomy, but do provide income with moderate certainty during periods of employment.

Finally, in some parts of the world, working as an abstract concept is highly valued whereas, in other parts of the world, working is considered a necessary evil (Triandis, 1972). These differences may be due partially to an ideology of hard work (Weber, 1964). There are also differences between cultures in the degree to which they foster needs for achievement (McClelland, 1961). To the extent that working is perceived as a necessary evil, it is unlikely that work or the outcomes from working will be as highly valued as would be expected if working were viewed more favorably in the culture.

Thus, moderately difficult and demanding cultural contexts may influence the salience and functional form of several meaning of working concepts. Industrial societies may allocate rewards with differential probabilities to a greater extent than do more traditional societies (Soliman, 1970). Similarly, students from less demanding contexts—such as Northwestern Europe—hold a neutral or slightly negative view of working, while Oriental students from more demanding contexts hold a more positive view of working (Triandis, 1972). In conclusion, labor market characteristics, occupations, and cultural differences may be considered as existing major influences on the salience and functional relationships between the meaning of working concepts.

Antecedents of the meaning of work

In the prior discussion, we concentrated on the properties of several major meaning of working variables in the model shown in Figure 2.1. One purpose for this discussion was to distinguish between concept formation and the nomological network of the meaning of work constructs. We concur with Embretson (1983) that the distinction between construct representation and the nomological network of relationships is of crucial theoretical importance. In the ensuing discussion, we turn our attention to the second major task of this chapter: the nomological network of the meaning of working constructs. The discussion will follow the organization of the model presented in Figure 2.1.

Family situation

In this study, the present family situation primarily consists of the financial responsibility for the support of others. Financial responsibility for others may relate to measures of many of the meaning of working constructs. Heavier financial responsibilities may require a person to substitute (choose) work over family as a major life sphere and, therefore, correlate negatively with work centrality. Conversely, heavy financial responsibility may increase work identification and valuation in order to maintain perceptions of self as a worthy person and, therefore, correlate positively with work centrality and obligation norms. Financial responsibility also can relate to entitlement norms. These responsibilities are a type of need frequently used to justify and legitimize claims for modes of distributive justice on societies or organizations which provide financial support and employment security. These responsibilities also are one criterion commonly used to determine need for support. Finally, financial responsibilities are likely to relate to valued outcomes from working, particularly income.

Personal characteristics / age and birth cohort

The personal characteristics included as antecedents of the meaning of working constructs are age, sex, and education. In this study, age includes both individual life cyclical and birth cohort properties. Schaie's (1965) definition of birth cohort—members born within a particular time interval—is conceptually useful. Both chronological age and birth cohort suggest explanations for work meanings that complement each other.

Chronological age suggests person-related developmental processes that may account for relationships with meaning of working constructs. Birth-order cohorts recognize contextual or ecological events such as wars, major economic conditions, or major legal/social trends that differentially affect generations of people as influences on these constructs. These birth-order-cohort-related events can affect work socialization and learning, or influence societal dialectic, and thus, sociopolicy-affecting work.

Typically, both chronological age and birth-order-cohort-related influences are intermingled in explanations of age differences in the meaning of work. As an example (Hayashi, Nishira, Suzuki, Muzuno, and Sakamoto, 1977), maturational explanations are used to account for age differences in work centrality and societal norms of Japanese. But they also explain these differences by contrasting the meaning of working between people born prior to the Second World War, during the post-war reconstruction period, and subsequent to the economic boom of the early 1960s. Similarly, Trommsdorff (1983) uses both types of explanation in her comparison of value changes in Japan, the United States, and Europe. In the present research, we recognize that age-related processes and birth-order-cohort-related events which shape or modify socialization and dialectical processes may clarify observed relationship between age and meaning of working constructs.

Personal characteristics / sex

Societally-shaped socialization and dialectical processes (including those which differ for successive birth-order cohorts) operating prior to and during work experiences may help explain observed sex differences in the meaning of working. These processes include the general cultural values of a society (Psathas, 1968; Trommsdorff, 1983), the values of the family (Foreign Press Center Japan, 1977; Hall, 1976; Trommsdorff, 1981), feminine role perceptions (Crawford, 1978; Pharr, 1977) and lack of self-confidence among women (Maccoby and Jacklin, 1974). These processes and societal differences are reflected in the beliefs of adolescents that men should work while women should stay at home. In a recent survey, approximately one-third (31.7%) of the Japanese adolescents rejected this belief, while in West Germany and the United States, the respective figures of adolescents rejecting this belief were 58.7% and 71.4% (Youth Bureau, 1978: 9). Our expectation is for sex differences on measures of the meaning of working constructs, but these differences likely will vary in magnitude between countries, and vary in magnitude in different birth-order cohorts within countries.

Personal characteristics / education

Well-designed national surveys regularly find a relationship between education and values or beliefs of individuals in most countries even when other influences such as maturation, cohort, socioeconomic background, and work experience are statistically controlled (Hayashi, *et al.*, 1977; Kohn and Schooler, 1983; Youth Bureau, 1978). In our view, educational attainment, apart from providing high levels of technical competence, relates to the meaning of working because of the opportunity it provides for people to examine their beliefs and values more thoroughly and systematically. In addition, people are encouraged and reinforced for engaging in such a process of inquiry. Moreover, the process of learning which produces the greatest change would appear to be both dialectical and experiential where the person's cognitive development and experiences confront his or her values, beliefs, and norms (Murphy and Gilligan, 1980; Rest, 1979). Two consequences of this process of cognitive development are an increase in self-directed orientation and an increased valuation of self-direction for self (Kohn and Schooler, 1983). The self-directed orientation is a latent belief that one has the personal capacity to take responsibility for one's actions and that society is so constituted as to make self-direction possible.

The development of self-direction influenced by dialectic educational processes consists of a movement away from conformance to external authority and toward personal standards of responsibility, basic human rights as preconditions to social obligations, and social consensus as a major process for establishing social order. In summary, the opportunities for systematic reasoning provided by education may increase the capacity for self-direction and higher valuation of self-directed beliefs. These beliefs are, in turn, a major part of a person's cognitive restructuring, including formation of different evaluative norms of fairness and social order.

Similarly, the development of self-directed beliefs during education may be one reason education has been found to relate to preferences for task-dependent outcomes relative to environmentally dependent outcomes, and for internal rather than externally mediated standards in national labor force studies (Lacy, Bokemeier, and Shepard, 1983). Thus, we conclude that the educationally evoked development of self-direction changes valued working outcome preferences.

The general increase in self-direction resulting from education also may influence work centrality. Recall that the properties of work centrality include involvement, commitment, and choice. These properties are consistent with changes in individuals resulting from educational processes previously discussed. Dubin (1956), for example, views increases in work centrality as being closely related to changes in work values, particularly to the growth in personal responsibility as conceived by both sociologists and psychologists.

Job and working conditions / job characteristics

From Marx (1932) and Weber (Gerth and Mills, 1946) to the present day, sociologists and psychologists have developed theories and have sought to account for the influence of task characteristics and conditions on meaning of working. Kohn and Schooler's (1983) lengthy program of research on a national sample in the United States provides one demonstration of the relationship between properties of jobs or occupations and the meaning of working. A major concept in their research is occupational self-direction which occurs when people are relatively free from close supervision (have some autonomy and control over major task decisions), when they engage in complex work requiring higher-order mental and interpersonal processes, and when they work on non-repetitive tasks which form a complete, integrated unit.

The theoretical guidance we draw from Kohn and Schooler's (1983) study is based on the idea of reciprocal causation. Without occupational self-control (including autonomy and decision making, variety and some freedom from routine, and acquisition of new skills or knowledge), it may be increasingly difficult to develop higher levels of work identification and commitment which make working more central in one's life. Similarly, an increasing presence of occupational self-control is likely to increase valuation of expressive task or occupational characteristics and to decrease valuation (at least relatively) of pay and comfort. Finally, one would expect to find a relationship between increased personal control through occupational self-direction and norms of obligation and entitlement, although the magnitude of relationship between these job characteristics and obligation or entitlement norms may be culture-specific. It is possible that this relationship will vary, depending on whether individuals in a society view their inputs as placing a demand on the organization or society equally to provide opportunities for self-direction, or whether the individuals in a society view outcomes being distributed to everyone under a parity rule, regardless of input.

But in addition, individuals self-select themselves for jobs with particular levels of self-direction based partially on their values, beliefs, and norms. Similarly, Thompson (1968) suggests that organizations select individuals for jobs on a continuum of their capacity and motivation for self-direction. While unexamined in the present study, this causal explanation is both plausible and widely documented in research on work and organization socialization. Many of the findings of Kohn and Schooler (1983) regarding reciprocal relationships between job properties and psychological properties of people generalize to other countries including West Germany and Japan (Hoff and Grüneisen, 1978; Naoi and Schooler, 1981).

Work antecedents / work schedule

Between 20–30% of the work force in industrial societies work on shifts other than day shifts (Evans, 1975). People working other than day shifts tend to have certain common characteristics: They were employed primarily in blue-collar, lower white-collar, or service occupations; are younger, primarily male, and less educated (Hedges and Sekscenski, 1979). Ethnic minorities tend to be over-represented on the night shift (such as 11 P.M. to 7 A.M.). Research indicates that shift work can have widespread effects on the physical, psychological, and social well-being of individuals, but also indicates that the consequences may vary from community to community and from country to country. Large metropolitan areas in the United States often have a lower percentage of shift workers than many European countries (Dunham, 1977). The negative effects of shift work also, typically, are greater among urban workers in the United States than in Europe. However, national differences in relationships between work schedules and meaning of work do not appear to be as great in small towns, particularly where there is a higher percentage of shift workers.

In general, community characteristics and country differences in relationships between shift work and the meaning of working would seem to depend on two considerations. First, social sanctions (e.g., scheduling of work and non-work social activities) so that the various roles that individuals adopt are more in balance. Second, individuals' values, beliefs, and norms are, at least in part, socially determined. Community and country differences in these work meanings may reflect broader cultural values, beliefs, and norms concerning shift work.

The relationship between shift work and the meaning of working will vary when we use community or community size and country as the best approximations of these sociological explanations. Where these mediators are not supportive of shift work, the work centrality of second- and third-shift workers is likely to be lower than for first-shift workers because of the conflict created with other social roles and values. Obligation norms are likely to be lower and entitlement norms higher for these shift workers. Finally, comfort, social and extrinsic valued working outcomes are likely to be higher for these shift workers. Where community and countries are more supportive of shift work, we expect less relationship between this work condition and the meaning of working.

Aggravated work conditions

By aggravated work conditions, we mean the physical demands of the job or work situation. We include work load demands, unsafe conditions, and unhealthy conditions in this concept. The demands arising from the work load and threats to safety place the individual in a motivated or energized state of stress. When experienced over long periods of time, the person must constantly adapt and readjust to the work load demands and threats to personal well being. Selye (1974) terms this lengthy adaptation process to work load demands and unsafe or unhealthy conditions *distress*.

In our view, poor safety or health conditions existing for long time periods in work situations are likely to influence several meaning of working variables. The stress the person feels from these conditions may result in lower levels of work centrality and norms of obligation. Additionally, entitlement norm levels are likely to increase with increased stress conditions. Finally, stress conditions are likely to increase relative preferences for money and comfort as valued working outcomes.

Finally, work load demands of jobs (physical, mental, consequences of mistakes) must be considered in conjunction with job self-direction (autonomy, variety, decision making) to discern their influence on the meaning of working. Following Karasek (1979), an expectation would be that jobs that are matched at high levels on these aspects (high self-direction and demands) would be related positively to work centrality, a balance between obligation and entitlement norms and importance of intrinsic valued working outcomes. This expectation may be due to selection factors (self, organization) which place individuals in jobs based on their competence to exercise self-control over decisions, and to the rewards commensurate with these demands.

Career antecedents / unemployment and turbulent careers

Three career sources of influence on the meaning of working included in the present study are unemployment history, career turbulence, and career progress. By *turbulence* we mean a career characterized by a mixture of progress and decline, or progressive decline. We should mention, initially, that a significant history of unemployment and career turbulence are correlated notions (Parnes and King, 1977; Hepworth, 1980). Warr (1983) concludes that the career pattern for the unemployed person, therefore, may be one of further unemployment and movement down the occupational ladder. Wilensky (1961) suggests that careers characterized by unemployment and decline reflect a lack of functional relatedness between jobs or hierarchical status progression and terms these *disorderly* careers.

Careers characterized by unemployment and turbulence can have several influences on the meaning of working. The material and psychological outcomes valued by people and derived from working such as personal identity, money, variety, the use of skills, and social contacts are either removed (through unemployment) or obtained in diminished amounts (through career turbulence). Theories of motivation would suggest that economic factors such as pay would become more important, and that task variety, use of skills, and social contact less important with prolonged unemployment or career turbulence. Studies indicate decreased social contact by blue-collar workers who experience unemployment and turbulence (see Warr's 1983 review; Wilensky, 1961).

Prolonged unemployment can reduce feelings and beliefs concerned with personal control, a notion that underlies both obligation and entitlement norms. Some evidence indicates that the unemployed endorse norms of entitlement such as that the government should guarantee jobs for everybody (Rundquist and Sletto, 1936). This endorsement is likely to be more acute when the causal attributions for unemployment are economic conditions including levels of unemployment, inadequate management, or other environmental factors beyond the individual's control. The endorsement of norms of obligation to society are also likely to be lower among those who experience unemployment for any prolonged period or experience turbulent careers.

Work centrality would seem to act more as a mediator variable in relationship between unemployment or career turbulence and societal norms or valued working outcomes. Warr (1978) and Stafford, Jackson, and Banks (1980) both found that the negative psychological effects of unemployment are greater for people with high work involvement. Some evidence indicates that, for at least fairly prolonged periods of unemployment, work centrality does not decline (Warr and Jackson 1983). Studies also suggest that blue-collar workers (perhaps because of the greater financial strain), more so than white-collar workers, and older workers are likely to experience more frequent and prolonged periods of unemployment and turbulence. Thus, the levels of certain valued working outcomes, work goals, and societal norms for older or blue-collar workers with high work centrality, may be particularly affected by unemployment.

Career antecedents / career progress

Work careers characterized by progress are likely to be positively correlated with work centrality levels. Wilensky (1961) labels these as *orderly
careers* with the sequence of jobs being functionally related, thus allowing
for the acquisition of higher levels of skill knowledge and abilities, and
leading to increased status or prestige. Building on ideas like this, Hall
(1971) proposed a model of career subidentity development. In this model,
identity refers to an individual's perception of self in relation to the
environment, a view similar to properties of work centrality. Growth in
career subidentity occurs as a result of socialization processes and features
of tasks such as those included in Kohn and Schooler's (1983) concept of
self-direction (discussed earlier). Earlier jobs with these task properties are
related to later jobs with higher levels of these properties, and to work
values, beliefs, and norms. It is these features of careers that lead to an
increase in the centrality of working as a part of the total identity (Hall,
1971).

In summary, career theory suggests that there are important influences
on work centrality: the person's perceptions that his or her career has been
marked by progress, the absence of unemployment, and work tasks characterized by autonomy, variety, and a good match with skills. These career
features are likely to relate positively to a valuation of intrinsic outcomes
and negatively to a valuation of comfort. Finally, these career features are
likely to relate positively to an increased balance between the societal
norms.

Throughout this section, we have discussed several potential relationships between antecedent variables and the meaning of working variables.
Not all these relationships are examined in the present volume. To do so
would require a monograph devoted solely to that task. We view the
present volume as a first presentation of our findings and beg the reader's
patience while we investigate other questions in our ongoing research
effort.

Macrosocietal influences

At several points in the preceding discussion, the topic of societal
influences on the meaning of working was discussed. When age-cohort
explanations of differences in work meanings were examined, societal
events or conditions were a possible consideration. Societal differences in
whether a class of norms are viewed as entitlements or opportunities also
were discussed. Here the societal frame of reference may be a major

consideration in the assignment of meaning. Further, when considered in conjunction with norms of obligation and from the perspective of distributive justice, individuals may demand more from society than they contribute. Societies, as well, may demand more from individuals than they distribute in terms of entitlements, or the outcome of the exchange process between persons and institutions can be one of balance. Finally, the discussion of work schedules drew on differences in societal support as a mediator of the relationship between shift work and the meaning of work.

Conversely, the meaning of working can be a causal variable in relationships with societal characteristics. In the discussion of work centrality, it was mentioned that this construct may influence involvement in work as measured by labor force participation and hours of work. The discussion of societal norms emphasized the conceptual link to distributive justice and to strategic issues in social and labor law. From this perspective, distributive justice is part of an interpersonal process in which negotiation and conflict are major forces for deciding on allocations. Thus, Robinson and Bell (1978) found that in both the United States and the United Kingdom those who benefit from the present system of allocation favor norms conceptually similar to obligation, while those who do not benefit favor norms conceptually similar to entitlement. In summary, the norms included in this study would seem to have strategic societal and organizational implications. To paraphrase Williamson (1975), when markets fail, systems of exchange may be regulated by principles of justice and social norms as much as by centralized structures (or hierarchies) and power processes.

There are additional societal factors we have not mentioned which probably have a dramatic influence on the meaning of working. Yet it is difficult to measure the effect of these influences on the meaning of work with a cross-sectional design, or because sometimes there is little variation between our set of countries in the particular societal influences. Thus, unemployment levels in countries can have a substantial influence on a broad range of psychological and sociological properties (Dooley and Catalano, 1980). During the period in which the national and target group survey work was occurring, levels of unemployment were very high by historical standards in Belgium, the Netherlands, West Germany, the United Kingdom, Yugoslavia, and the United States. Unemployment rates were much lower in Japan and Israel, but Israel had a hyperinflated economy. As discussed earlier, prolonged unemployment can have widespread influence on the meaning of working variables. The national levels of work variables may reflect the influence of unemployment conditions but, due to the widespread nature of these labor economic conditions, it is difficult to discern their effect. It is difficult to state what effect events and conditions such as these have on the meaning of working.

Similarly, there are trends that may influence the meaning of working differently for members of different target groups. For example, international statistics trace the worsening trend in levels of production in the textile industries in all the countries in the present study except Yugoslavia and Israel. In these latter countries, levels of textile production were much higher in the late 1970s than in the late 1960s. Conversely, there has been a dramatic increase in labor demand for tool- and diemakers in the United States and Europe in recent years. These societal influences which differentially affect target groups may be reflected in differences in the meaning of working for members of these occupations. Similarly, part-time workers represent a growing segment of the labor force in industrial countries (U.S. Department of Labor, 1978). Part-time workers frequently represent a different segment of a country's population, face a different set of job characteristics, and represent a special case of work scheduling (Nollen, Eddy, and Martin, 1977; U.S. Department of Labor, 1978). Part-time employees may differ in work centrality from full-time workers. Research reviewed by Roberts and Glick (1980) suggests that part-time workers may value working outcomes such as interpersonal relations, comfort, and pay to a greater extent than full-time workers, and value intrinsic factors to a lesser extent. In summary, there are conditions and trends in most countries discussed in this study which can influence the meaning of working. However, the widespread nature of some of these trends and conditions and the cross-sectional design may mitigate against discerning their effects.

Consequences of the meaning of working

The consequences of the meaning of working have been embedded in much of the discussion to this point. A much fuller treatment of some of the theoretical issues related to the consequences and the present findings of relationships between meaning of work variables and selected consequences is given in Chapter 12. Therefore, we postpone lengthy discussion of these consequences until that chapter. In brief, the model in Figure 2.1 recognizes two major categories of consequences associated with the meaning of working: subjective expectations about future work situations and objective outcomes of working. Examples of the former category include the future importance of working, preferences for working fewer hours for less pay, and recommendation of their work to their children. Examples of the latter category include hours of work, behaviors such as training that the worker is engaging in to enhance present or future work opportunities, and choice tasks regarding work continuation or cessation, and types of jobs. Again, we direct the reader's attention to Chapter 12 for both the theoretical discussion and some selected findings.

General summary

In this chapter, we have had several major purposes. Our model, concepts, and research design develop a set of major meaning of working variables and patterns. Work centrality includes identification with work, involvement and commitment to work, and choice of working as a major mode of self-expression. The societal norms of entitlement and obligation were viewed as having their origins in the development of individuals. Each of these norms incorporates key notions of distributive justice: the right to rewards or opportunities, or duty and contribution to society. The valued working outcomes, work goals, and functional identifications include reward content and intensity as inducements to work and preferences for differential work situations.

In developing and measuring these major meaning of work variables in subsequent chapters, we treat each not only separately, but in combination. The idea of patterns of work meanings is an empirical extension of the ideas discussed in the earlier section on the relationship between meaning of work concepts. To examine individuals in terms of each of the separate meanings they assign to work is an important research task. But one weakness with this strategy is that it provides a segmented and disjointed view of individuals in their totality. The idea of patterns of work meanings provides a more idiographic and holistic view of individuals in terms of the interrelated meanings they assign to work that we, and hopefully the reader, will find useful.

The scope of our research is international. We have measured the work meaning variables and patterns at the level of the individual in national labor force samples and in target groups. We have sought to review the literature from several countries to ensure that our concepts are decentered from strictly ethnocentric biases. By using concepts and measures that have general relevance to several countries, and by using specified target groups and representative national labor force samples, we can better test hypotheses, make generalizations, or make distinctions based on the findings. In the initial chapters on the findings, the similarity of the work concepts and meanings for each country is a paramount issue. Without reasonably similar structures of work meanings, the cross-national comparisons of specific meanings would be an inappropriate research task.

Our intention is to relate the measures of the meaning of working concepts to antecedents and consequences at the level of individuals, occupations, and societies with full recognition of the possibility for reciprocal causation between the concepts included in the model. Common to all three of the major categories of antecedents in Figure 2.1 is the view that identification with and valuation of working in one's life is a function of past cultural conditioning, personal development, and socialization. Additionally, socioeconomic conditions influence meanings assigned to working. We view the consequences of work meanings to include some of the major choices individuals make in their lives. These choices include decisions to work or not to work, how much to work, and the choice of type of work or job. In subsequent chapters, antecedents and consequences are considered in combinations or patterns as they relate to the meaning of work, not only separately.

Finally, reciprocal causation is a major issue in our research. We recognize that work meanings are both affected by and affect social, work, and societal factors. Cultural conditioning, learning, development, and socialization are important processes which influence the meaning of working. Self-selection, the formation of groups, and organization or societal change are processes affected by meanings assigned to working. Without the recognition of the importance of work meanings as a causal variable, as well as an outcome variable, the implications of our research for organization and public policy would be lost.

Notes

(1) This chapter does not include a discussion of work-role identification. There is some discussion of this concept and findings in Chapter 4.

(2) A special measurement procedure was developed in this study for the preferences. A detailed discussion of the procedure and the findings is undertaken in Chapter 8. Conceptually, this procedure and the findings revealed by the use of the procedure are a special example of important work goals.

Chapter 3

Meaning of Working / Design and Methods

Introduction

This chapter attempts to provide an overview of procedures, methods, and decisions which relate to data collection and data analyses of the MOW study. In providing this overview, we try to strike a balance between the extremes of a superficial bird's-eye view and a minute account of every technical detail. The reader who is interested in the basic methodological aspects of our study will be sufficiently informed by this chapter. The more technically interested colleague is advised to consult the Appendixes to this chapter. Both must be seen as complementary in telling the whole study on methods and procedures as much as is feasible in this volume.

Large-scale multinational comparative and interdisciplinary studies are time-consuming. Especially so when the research is conducted in a collective spirit which often requires lengthy processes of consensus finding on all critical aspects of the research such as definition of objectives, basic analytical framework, concept operationalization, and data analysis strategies. Hence, the timetable of the MOW study looks roughly like this:

1978: Development of the idea and objectives of the study and the formulation of possible research procedures
Review of the relevant literature in various countries

1979: Pre-pilot study; the development and first tryout of potentially useful questions, scales, and interview schedules

1979–1980: Pilot study; a systematic pretest of the selected questions and scales. Specification and definition of the research samples to be utilized

1980–1982: Data collection in each of the eight participating countries

1981–1983: Data analysis and interpretation, both at a national and international level

1983–1984: Preparation of national level reports and completion of the international MOW publication.

A critical choice was made for a decentralized, collective research process, as indicated in Chapter 1. This implied that deliberate attempts had to be made to involve each member of the MOW team as much as possible in the decisions in various research phases. At the same time, the complex research tasks required division of labor such as the formation of committees for analysis or report drafting, and the establishment of central computing and analysis units. However, major decisions were considered the exclusive prerogative of the MOW team plenary which kept the group as a whole both informed and responsible. At the same time, use could be made of specific expertise needed and available in the group.

Considerations in cross-national or cross-cultural research

Research of the kind reported here is sometimes described as *cross-national* or *cross-cultural*, as if these terms were interchangeable. There is a difference, however. Before one can legitimately use the term *cross-cultural* one has to show that culture is the explanatory factor when differences are found and this requires an operational definition of the term *culture*. In anthropology, two approaches have emerged; one comes from Kroeber and Boas and sees culture in terms of traditional (that is, historically derived and selected) ideas and, in particular, their attached values. The other tradition descends from Radcliffe-Brown and describes culture as a network of social relations including persistent social groups and social classes.

In order to do justice to either line of definitions or derivations from them, one has to design the research from the beginning to measure variables that clearly differentiate between factors to which cultural significance is attached. In work psychology research, this is rarely done. Instead, culture is often used as a post facto explanation of residual differences between countries. This trend has been severely criticized (Roberts, 1970). In general, where research selects its samples from different countries without special attention to cultural variables, it is more appropriate to end up with country differences; this is the preferred strategy of the MOW project.

However, we realize that many readers of cross-national studies will attempt to extract "cultural" explanations. This is particularly relevant when one or more samples come from a country which has a very long and fairly homogeneous tradition of ideas and values such as Japan. We, therefore, follow Curle (1947), who defines culture as consisting "of a cluster of socially determined attitudes and behaviour patterns grouped and elaborated around structurally defined roles and relationships." In several analyses, as is seen later in this and subsequent chapters, we use statistically derived patterns or clusters to reflect value preferences. In cases when other explanations of country differences are not appropriate, Curle's (1947) approach to culture may be helpful.

Cross-national research has to be well planned and organized to achieve acceptable quality levels. A number of distinct organizational arrangements exist—some are easier and cheaper to carry out than others and often are chosen for those reasons but may yield less valuable results. Three basic organizational forms have been distinguished (Drenth and Wilpert, 1980):

1. *"Safari" or replication research.* This is a type of research project which is conceived, developed, implemented and controlled by one scholar or a group of researchers in one country. The same research is repeated in other countries by the same scholars or by "native" collaborators. Data analysis and ownership are centrally organized. A clear advantage of this type is the central control, but the possible disadvantages are the lack of enculturation of methods and intracultural data interpretation.

2. *Adaptation research.* Such projects are usually conceived and developed by one researcher or research team, but colleagues from other countries then are persuaded to adopt the study and to take responsibility for their own national substudy. Findings and data ownerships often are decentralized or mixed. This leads to a higher responsibility and identification of the national team and, correspondingly, a different distribution of influence on the outcomes of the research.

3. *Decentralized collective research.* In this type of cross-national research, collaborators from various countries jointly participate in the design, development, implementation, and analysis of the project. The MOW study was organized in this way. The success of such an organizational structure depends on the degree of consensus reached in the international team, flexibility and willingness to compromise, and, at the same time, determination and goal orientation for the team to stick together, often for extended periods of time. Difficulties may arise on issues such as the ownership of the instruments and data, proper acknowledgments of sponsorship, senior and junior co-workers. In the MOW study, these problems were guarded against by drawing up a written "social contract" that regulated all the mentioned and related issues. Among the

advantages of this approach three stand out (Heller, 1982): The scientific value is enhanced by (a) enabling each country to assess cross-national or cross-cultural differences from the perspective of its own experience; (b) cross-national teams often include people who were trained in different disciplines, and this adds richness to design and interpretation; (c) cross-national teams usually include people who have a diversity of values. No social research is value-free, but plurality allows for a more objective assessment of evidence.

In addition, it was acknowledged that cross-national studies often suffer from a number of scientific and methodological drawbacks and difficulties (Drenth and Groenendijk, 1984). Quite some effort was taken to eliminate or reduce the distorting conditions or to cope with the methodological difficulties.

Problems of translations always exist in cross-national research, and perfection is virtually impossible. We have used *back translation* which involves the independent translation from each language back into the original language (English, in this case). The back translation and the original are compared and, if necessary, the translated version is adjusted.

To achieve conceptual equivalence between countries on concepts like "work," we have allowed differences in definition to emerge from idiosyncratic use in each country and based further analysis of data on the definition of working of each respondent.

Social desirability and response-set problems are difficult to overcome in single as well as multicountry studies. In our research, we sought to minimize problems by using behaviorally anchored scales, concrete or objective questions, multimethod approach for cross-checking, and forced distribution (for instance, ranking or distributing answers over 100 points).

We believe that in spite of difficulties and cost, cross-national research yields scientific results which contribute significantly to the general validity of theories and to the identification of contextual (for instance, cultural) variables that moderate hypothesized relationships. In the complex world of work and international business, cross-national research should also play a useful role in policy making at the level of organizations and, possibly, at the national level as well.

Nature of the study

The study can be characterized as empirical/survey research. Although other general approaches (e.g., field experiment, simulation study, participative observation, in-depth analysis of cases) would not have been inappropriate or impossible, the advantages of a survey-type study pre-dominated. Particularly in view of the international comparative character of the study, optimal standardization of instruments and comparability of samples was felt to be mandatory. The possible limitation of survey-type research into sensitive, and often personal, themes (unemployment, the role of money, future plans) could not be neglected. Attempts were made to deal with these difficulties in the choice of the questions to be asked and the nature of the interviewing setting during which the data were collected. This issue is discussed in more detail in the following section.

Furthermore, a choice was made for a *cross-sectional*, rather than a longitudinal study. Although developmental aspects and reference to future development were considered highly central to the topic of research, the decision was made to try to deal with these aspects cross-sectionally, in view of practical and financial problems associated with a diachronic study of this size. This decision made it necessary for particular questions to be asked and particular samples to be selected. At the same time, the MOW research team realized that conclusions, especially pertaining to causal relationships, would be more tentative.

Attention was devoted to the issue of the process nature of the phenomena under study in various ways: the development of values and attitudes, the relationship with aspects of individual career development, and reference to future developments and expectations with respect to the meaning of working:

1. Questions were formulated to explore specific perceptions of these developmental aspects and subjective expectations with respect to future developments. Reference to the past and the future, therefore, was made through the eye of the respondents. Such an approach was recognized to have limitations, but certainly not without value as one source of information.

2. A number of questions were incorporated in the study which have been used in previous studies under different economic and political circumstances (lottery question, future expectations, work centrality: See the questionnaire in Appendix 3.1).[1] The comparison of answer distri-butions between the present and previous studies may generate additional insight to the changes taking place over time.

3. A deliberate selection of particular samples of respondents was made to assist in dealing with this issue. A number of target groups were selected to reflect different and crucial stages in the adult career (beginning, mid-career, final stage, and retirement), thus to provide useful information for developmental interpretation.

This same purpose also was served by selecting groups of respondents who are critically important to societal development and future policy concerns, e.g., part-time workers, long-time unemployment, and workers in a declining industry, since these types of working situations may increasingly call for policy decisions.

The foregoing consideration suggested development of instruments with the following characteristics:

- Width of applicability, i.e., covering as many aspects in the field of meaning of working as possible. The exclusive concentration on only one of the dimensions discussed in the literature was considered to be too limited for such a complex and multifacet phenomenon. The total map of "Meaning of Working" should be covered.

- Inclusion of both open-ended and closed questions; the latter in view of comparability and standardization; the former in view of the personal, often "rich," information they provide. Information from open questions can be used for illustrative and interpretative purposes as well as for hypothesis generation.

- Multimethod measurement of the various concepts, wherever possible, to permit greater confidence in the utilized information than that provided by any single method and in order to enhance the information which would be limited if measured by a single question or scale.

- Relevance to a wide range of diverse groups of respondents. The questionnaires were to be used with respondents differing considerably in professional and occupational level, educational background, and age; and residing and working in different geographical sections of each country. This called for careful wording and phrasing to generate comparable responses.

- Maximal comprehensibility and usefulness. The latter criterion refers also to the requirement to produce usable variance. In this connection, attention was paid to past experience where Likert-type scales—attempting to assess sensitive issues—run a serious risk of producing highly socially desirable responses with hardly any variance.

In view of this danger, a ranking or forced distribution procedure was selected instead of, or in addition to, Likert-type items.

- Interest and motivation generating. Careful attention was devoted to the sequence of the questions, the type of questions and the total length of the questionnaire.

- International comparability. Early on in this project, attention was focussed on this important issue. Various methods for controlling and improving the equivalence of scales were discussed which served as guidelines for the construction of comparable scales and question-naires in the present study.

Before providing a more detailed overview of the selected questions and scales, we address the issues of sampling of the respondents and the interview procedures.

Samples

In a study of national similarities and differences regarding the place which working occupies in the total set of values, selection of national representa-tive samples seems most appropriate for comparison at the national level. However, this procedure also raises a number of problems, the most important of which is that national representative samples of the work force inevitably show differences in many respects such as types of occu-pation, age distribution, sex distribution, and educational background. Many of these factors may be partially responsible for observed differences in the variable under consideration. In other words, *national* is a higher-level aggregation variable which covers a variety of possible confounding factors for explanation purposes. In such a case, it virtually may be impossible to identify *true* determinants. In view of the potential lack of explanatory power from this approach, it was felt inappropriate to consider this as the only way of sampling. We decided to pursue the research with reference to the separate samples in each participating country: a *target group* sample and a *representative* sample.

Target group samples

A set of 10 target groups was to be studied in each country. The selection of these groups was guided by the following principles:

- Each target group should be homogeneous with respect to a number of characteristics considered of particular relevance (age, sex, and education).
- Some of the groups selected should be critically important to policy making within the participating countries (e.g., due to their growing importance in the labor force, such as women and part-time workers; current and potential problem groups, such as unemployed and workers in declining industries).
- The target groups taken together should reflect different degrees of integration into the work force (e.g., fully employed, unemployed,

temporarily or partially employed, people just before employment), different work settings and work histories (e.g., occupational level, degrees of professionalization), and major differences in personal and social background.

- It should be possible to identify similar groups in each participating country.

The actual choice of target group respondents was further guided by the stipulations that:

- Respondents in each target group of each country should be selected from at least two major industrial centers (i.e., a mix within target groups from the chosen regions was recommended).
- The optimal size of target groups was considered approximately 90.

In addition to the mandatory set of 10 target groups, individual countries have added a few other groups, which were particularly relevant to them. The instructions for the identification of the mandatory target groups were as follows:

- *Unemployed*: ($N = 90$) 50% male, 50% female. Medium- to low-skill levels, all having been unemployed for at least the past 6 months. Do not include physically handicapped individuals or seasonal workers (construction and building, dock workers, and hotel workers).
- *Retired*: ($N = 90$) 50% male, 50% female. Not presently working and of normal retirement age. If possible, select from among teachers, low-skilled white-collar workers, and chemical engineers.
- *Chemical Engineers*: ($N = 90$) All males. Graduates of university-level training and currently doing professional chemical work (not managers) in companies of more than 200 employees. Do not select from food companies or pharmaceutical companies.
- *Teachers*: ($N = 90$) All females. Teaching 9–10-year-old students and in situations where they have the main teaching assignment for a whole class as opposed to teaching only one subject to many classes. Where appropriate, select teachers from both private and public schools in approximate proportion to their relative proportion in the industrial area (city) from which data are being collected.
- *Self-employed businessmen*: ($N = 90$) All male. Select only those with less than eight employees. Select from among commercial, service, and crafts-type businesses. Do not use professional such as lawyers, physicians, or dentists. The intent is to select "small shopkeepers."
- *Tool- and diemakers*: ($N = 90$) All male. This is a high-skill-level group which should be selected from the automobile industry or related industries.

- *White-collar employees*: 50% male, 50% female. The intent is to select low- to semi-skilled, or lower-service-function employees whose occupations are being influenced by automation and technology. Select from the banking and insurance industry.
- *Textile workers*: ($N = 90$) 60% males, 30% females. Low- or semi-skilled job level such as "weaver."
- *Temporary workers*: ($N = 90$) All female. Doing clerical work, non-skilled to low-skill levels. They work for, and are assigned to, temporary work somewhere by either private or governmental employment agencies. We do not want students but rather people whose present occupation is temporary clerical work through an agency.
- *Students*: ($N = 90$) 50% male, studying mechanical or machine trades or equivalents in vocational–technical schools; 50% female, studying for clerical–secretarial occupations in full-time schools. These individuals may be employed part time, but we are seeking individuals who are primarily students supposed to go directly into employment after their vocational–technical training. Do not include those who go directly on to university-level education.

National representative samples

The rationale for including a national sample in each country was threefold:

1. It provides a national picture of work-meaning patterns for policy evaluation, for comparison with past studies and as a reference point for future studies.
2. It serves as a national reference group for evaluating and understanding critical target group data.
3. It forms the basis for cross-national comparisons and hypothesis testing concerning the impact of specified national dimensions upon meaning of work patterns.

The plan was that the representative samples of the labor force would consist of about 1000 individuals in each country. As indicated in the following, not every country was able to incorporate the full-size national sample in its study. In some countries, only a smaller and/or less representative sample could be interviewed. Moreover, the length of the questionnaire, which was used for the national sample study, varied considerably over the countries. In a number of countries, only a minimum crucial set of questions was asked; in other countries, the total questionnaire was administered.

In view of this lack of completeness and/or representativeness, the following data chapters present data both for the total set of target groups and the national samples whenever appropriate for the analyses utilized. Tables 3.1, 3.2, and 3.3 present information concerning actual sample sizes and sample characteristics (sex, age, and education) for the target groups and the national samples. The national survey shows a usually high, but in some cases, varying degree of representativeness as judged against national census data. Moreover, the total set of target groups certainly deviate from the national distribution in a number of ways. This was to be expected as the target groups were not selected in order to provide a national representative picture.

Further comparison of the data on the target groups with their own specific occupational national data shows that representativeness cannot be claimed for a number of these groups. Again, this was never intended. The data do show, however, for which specific groups a certain representative character can and cannot be assumed.

Table 3.1. Summary of target groups,* national sample,* and general work force by sex.

		Male %	Female %	Total N
Belgium	Σ Target groups	56.6	43.4	896
	National sample	68	32	450
	Census	68	32	—
Britain	Σ Target groups	—	—	—
	National sample	47.8	52.2	840
	Census	60.9	39.1	—
Germany	Σ Target groups	53.7	46.3	694
	National sample	64.9	35.1	1278
	Census	61.8	38.2	—
Israel	Σ Target groups	55.4	44.6	874
	National sample	57.4	42.6	961
	Census	63.8	36.1	—
Japan	Σ Target groups	55.3	44.7	1127
	National sample	66.6	33.4	3224
	Census	62.3	37.7	—
Netherlands	Σ Target groups	58.3	41.7	907
	National sample	73.3	26.7	996
	Census	70.5	29.5	—
United States	Σ Target groups	53.6	46.4	856
	National sample	53.4	46.6	1000
	Census	57.2	42.8	—
Yugoslavia	Σ Target groups	49.9	50.1	541
	National sample	—	—	—
	Census	55.4	44.6	—

Σ Target groups (TG) = 5895   Σ Representative sample (RS) = 8749.

* In the subsequent chapters throughout this book, for brevity's sake, we frequently speak of results from a "country" by which we always mean results from the respective sample of a given country. Sample sizes reported in various chapters vary somewhat due to missing data in one or more of the variables under consideration.

Table 3.2. Summary of target groups, national sample, and general work force by age.

		Percentage < 30 years	Percentage 30–50 years	Percentage > 50 years	Total N
Belgium	Σ Target groups	38.4	42.7	18.9	896
	National sample	39.1	45.3	15.6	450
	Census	34	47	19	—
Britain	Σ Target groups	—	—	—	—
	National sample	29.8	46.9	23.2	831
	Census	31.4	45.5	23.1	—
Germany	Σ Target groups	38.8	41.5	19.7	689
	National sample	28.6	48.2	23.2	1278
	Census	31.6	46.9	21.3	—
Israel	Σ Target groups	44.3	34.4	21.3	889
	National sample	26.2	51.4	22.4	958
	Census	30.4	40.9	28.8	—
Japan	Σ Target groups	45.3	35.0	19.7	1122
	National sample	20.1	58.0	21.9	3221
	Census	24.4	49.1	26.5	—
Netherlands	Σ Target groups	45.2	37.5	17.3	907
	National sample	31.0	53.8	15.2	996
	Census	30.9	52.2	16.9	—
United States	Σ Target groups	34.2	39.6	26.7	854
	National sample	33.6	50.5	15.9	1000
	Census	35.3	43.2	21.3	—
Yugoslavia	Σ Target groups	28.1	61.6	10.4	541
	National sample	—	—	—	—
	Census*			18.6	—

Σ (TG) = 5898   Σ (RS) = 8734

* < 25: 21.0; 25–50: 60.4

Development of instruments

Pilot studies

Extensive pilot studies were carried out in all countries but Britain. In the pilot studies, the selected questionnaires and scales were evaluated with respect to their applicability for the populations in question, their reliability, and other required or desired properties. Moreover, on the basis of the pilot information, changes and adaptations were made.

It was not possible, in the pilot studies, to cover each target group in each country separately, but some representation of all target groups in the total pilot sample over countries was pursued. In fact, this was accomplished quite well. All target groups were covered in the combined pilot studies, although some more extensively than others. The size of the pilot

Table 3.3. Summary of target groups, national sample, and general work force by education.

		Primary school percentage	Secondary school percentage	Some college percentage	University degree percentage	Total N
Belgium	Σ Target groups	25.2	35.5	34.2	5.1	896
	National sample	16.0	47.6	24.4	12.0	450
	Census	43.0	44.0	7.0	6.0	—
Britain	Σ Target groups	—	—	—	—	—
	National sample*	—	—	—	—	—
	Census					
Germany	Σ Target groups	18.0	49.6	12.5	19.9	688
	National sample	17.4	65.5	6.7	10.3	1273
	Census**	—				—
Israel	Σ Target groups	22.5	41.7	20.2	15.6	892
	National sample	19.1	46.0	18.5	16.3	962
	Census	19.0	45.5	18.3	16.1	—
Japan	Σ Target groups	2.8	51.3	15.0	30.9	1069
	National sample	1.7	57.8	13.7	26.8	3200
	Census**	—				—
Netherlands	Σ Target groups	11.4	49.4	27.5	11.7	905
	National sample	13.1	60.5	22.5	4.4	993
	Census	30.5	38.9	26.1	2.6	—
United States	Σ Target groups	5.4	30.4	27.1	37.1	856
	National sample	5.4	34.9	29.9	29.9	998
	Census	20.0	39.9	17.7	22.6	—
Yugoslavia	Σ Target groups	16.8	57.9	8.3	17.0	541
	National sample	—				—
	Census**	—				—

* Educational level in Britain was indicated by a different method so is not reported here.
** Not available due to different breakdown of census statistics.

samples in countries ranged from 79 to 104 cases with a combined total of 669 cases.

Questionnaires

The following decisions and suggestions were based upon the pilot study experiences and were implemented in the final set of questionnaires and interview procedures:

- The total length of the interviews were not to exceed 1 hour in order to maintain interest and motivation of respondents.
- The number of open questions, although providing interesting information with a "personal touch," were kept to a minimum.
- Certain types of questions were deleted in the final questionnaire because of their difficult or time-consuming character (e.g., Osgood's semantic differential and a sentence-completion list).
- A number of questions were deleted on grounds of lack of variance, too much time required for explaining or answering them, or a too-obvious influence of social desirability factors.
- Many questions were changed and improved on the basis of the reactions of the respondents, the distribution of the answers and/or the post-questionnaire interviews which were held with a large number of respondents.
- The results of a number of factor analyses, item analyses, and inter-rater reliabilities were further used to select questions or scales from duplicating or parallel sets of questions/scales which had been incorporated for comparative purposes.
- Standardizing decisions were made as to the final formulation of the instructions (general and per question), the choice of the sequence of questions, interviewing modes and procedural aspects—such as the introductory letter—anonymity, and feedback procedures.

Three versions of the final questionnaire had to be developed, since not every question applies equally well to each target group. The questions in each questionnaire are similar but, whenever necessary, were adapted for application to a particular category of respondents.

1. Form A, for use with employed samples, including target groups of chemical engineers, teachers, self-employed, tool- and diemakers, white-collar employees, textile workers, and temporary workers (see Appendix 3.1. where this questionnaire has been reproduced).
2. Form B, for unemployed and retired.
3. Form C, for students.

Table 3.4. Guidelines for sampling and interviewing procedures in countries involved in pilot study.

Belgium

National sample
Interviewers: Advanced doctoral students, trained and experienced in interviewing techniques.
Mode of interviewing: Individual.
Selection of respondents: By interviewers using strictly controlled rules regarding choice criteria (municipality, occupation, sex, and age). All respondents from Dutch-speaking part of Belgium.
Time of interviews: January–May 1982.

Target group sample
Interviewers: Advanced psychology students for unemployment and retired target/groups, professional interviewers for all other target groups.
Mode of interviewing: Mostly individual; few interviews in group setting among chemical engineers, tool- and diemakers, white-collar workers; interviews of students all in group setting.
Selection of respondents: Unemployed, retired, teachers and self-employed by interviewers; chemical engineers, white-collar workers, tool- and diemakers, textile workers, and students approached through their work organization/schools; for selection of temporary workers both methods were used. All respondents from Dutch-speaking Belgium.
Time of interviews: January–October 1981.

Britain

National sample
Mode of interviewing: As part of a wider survey subcontracted by MOW. After explaining the survey to each subject, the questionnaire was left to be filled in and returned in a stamped envelope (return rate 90%).
Time of interviews: Spring 1983.

Targe group sample
Not available.

Federal Republic of Germany

National sample
Interviewers: Trained interviewers hired by professional opinion-survey agency.
Mode of interviewing: Individual.
Selection of respondents: Random quota sampling of German work force.
Time of interviews: November–December 1983.

Target group sample
Interviewers: Advanced students in psychology trained in interviewing techniques.
Mode of interviewing: Individual except for student target group which was in group setting.

Table 3.4. (continued)

Selection of respondents: Chosen by interviewers using — as much as possible —
    quotes for the final composition of target groups according to sex, age,
    and education. Respondents from Berlin (West) and Federal Republic
    of Germany. Target group of chemical engineers not available.
Time of interviewing: October–February 1982.

Israel

National sample
Interviewers: Professional interviewers hired by national opinion-survey agency.
Mode of interviewing: Individual.
Selection of respondents: Stepwise random selection of respondents ($\geq$ 18 years)
    according to (a) random household identification and (b) random choice
    of the respondent from those who fell within the prescribed categories
    of respondents.
Time of interviewing: September 1981.

Target group sample
Interviewers: Professional interviewers as with national sample.
Mode of interviewing: At work, schools or home (unemployed, retired).
Selection of respondents: Intended intratarget group representativeness was
    achieved for tool- and diemakers, retired, unemployed, temporary
    workers, chemical engineers; approximation for other groups.
Time of interviewing: May 1981.

Japan

National sample
Interviewers: Trained interviewers.
Mode of interviewing:
Selection of respondents: Random sample of national work force after exclusion of
    people employed less than 16 hours per week.
Time of interviewing: July–August 1982.

Target group sample
Interviewers: Trained interviewers.
Mode of interviewing: Individual, mostly at workplace; minority at home.
Selection of respondents: From Osaka and Fukuoka metropolitan areas.
Time of interviewing: July–August 1982.

Netherlands

National sample
Interviewers: Employees from professional survey agency.
Mode of interviewing: Individual.
Selection of respondents: Stepwise as in Israel.
Time of interviewing: February 16–March 13, 1981.

Table 3.4. (continued)

Target group sample
Interviewers: Part-time employed psychology students experienced with interviewing techniques.
Mode of interviewing: Individual.
Selection of respondents: Mostly by national research team through personnel departments of organizations; self-employed, teachers, and additional group of housewives chosen by interviewers themselves according to specific MOW rules. Lack of sufficiently large number of production workers in textile industry forced addition of other production workers (from harbor workers and food industry). Respondents and participating organizations received summaries of answers of their target groups.
Time of interviewing: December 1980–July 1981.

United States

National sample
Interviewers: Professional interviewers.
Mode of interviewing: Telephone interview of national labor force sample.
Selection of respondents: Initially, the chosen procedure established the sample to be drawn from each state, and within each state, from each telephone area by using data on the state's labor force in current reports from the Bureau of Labor Statistics.
A computer program for the random generation of telephone numbers in each area was applied and rules for "no answer," "busy signal," or "none at home" were developed.
The selection of a respondent from among household members was accomplished through a random process (Troldahl and Carter, 1964).
Time of interviewing: Spring 1982.

Target group sample
Interviewers: Professional interviewers.
Mode of interviewing: individual.
Selection of respondents: by director of interviewing, approximately half of each target group from Oklahoma City, Oklahoma and the other half from Minneapolis, St. Paul, Minnesota regions. The employed target groups came from no less than five different organizations while the non-employed target groups were obtained from as wide a range of sources as possible.
Time of interviewing: 1981.

Yugoslavia

National sample: Not available.
Target group sample
Interviewers: Professional interviewers.
Mode of interviewing:
Selection of respondents: Only respondents from the state of Slovenia. Unemployed, retired, temporary workers, and students not included.
Time of interviewing: End 1981–beginning 1982.

The answer alternatives for the closed questions were directly transformed into a code. For a number of answers some form of more complex categorization had to be selected, as f.i. for open questions which was collectively developed on the basis of pilot studies in Belgium, Japan, the Netherlands, and United States.

Interview procedures

The procedures followed in administrating the target group surveys and the national surveys are described generally in this section. The general introductory statement at the beginning of each interview was as follows:

> This interview is about *working*. About what working means to you in general, about your specific working situation and about how you view working in the future.
>
> The interview is anonymous. That is to say, no one will see or hear your answers except for the researchers who are conducting the study. Many different types of people will be interviewed. Therefore it is possible that some questions do not apply exactly to your situation. If a question is not clear to you, or if you have any comment, please feel free to ask or tell the interviewer.
>
> Many different types of questions are covered in this study. There are no "right" or "wrong" answers but it is important that you give us your opinion. You will answer some questions directly on the forms provided and the interviewer will record your answers on other questions. These questions are being asked of about 2000 individuals in each of ten countries[2] throughout the world to find out what *working* really means to people. The . . . portion of the study is being conducted by a research team from the University . . . Your answers are important and we thank you in advance for helping us in this important study.

Although general guidelines for sampling and interviewing were accepted, each country had to adapt the procedures to its own requirements and conditions, including restrictions in time, money, and respondent accessibility. The specifics in each country are mentioned in Table 3.4.

Summary of items and scales

The underlying model in the present study is based on the conception that the Meaning of Working is determined by the choices and experiences of the individual and by the organizational and environmental contexts in which he or she works and lives. For an illustration of this conceptual model see Figure 2.1. presented and discussed in Chapter 2. This model represents the major variable sets and the most direct and straightforward relationships that can be studied.

As indicated in the model, the variables have been chosen and operationalized at three different levels.

1. *Conditional variables*: This level includes:
    A. *Personal and family circumstances*: Such as age, sex, family status, spouse's work situation, education, religious orientation, urban–rural upbringing, parents' education, similarity/difference parents "to respondents" education, individual and family income (see questions 69–77 in the Questionnaire, reproduced in Appendix A3.1).
    B. *Variables concerning present job and career history*: Such as present job situation, job level, frequency and direction of career changes, unemployment (frequency and duration), factors which prompted job changes (see questions 1–27 in the Questionnaire).
    C. *Variables concerning the social and economic environment*: Such as laws, industrial relations systems, labor force participation rates, educational system and levels, levels of "unemployment," and level of affluence in the society. These data were to be collected at the national level and used primarily to dimensionalize the variable "country" in seeking to understand country differences in MOW data and patterns. In actuality, we were not successful in meaningfully relating this broad class of variables within our comparative international analyses. They were utilized, however, in individual studies.
2. *Central variables*: In this category, the core variables in the MOW study are operationalized. The meaning attributes refer not just to the present job or work, but rather the interest in the importance, the value, the significance, and the meaning of having work and performing work per se. Meaning of work was defined conceptually in terms of the following five major domains:
    A. *Centrality of working*: As a life role (Questions 29, 30). The major issue is: How central is the role of working in one's life in absolute terms and as compared to other life roles?
    B. *Societal norms*: About working (Question 47): This scale contains a set of questions about work and working in terms of what should be expected from working (entitlements) and what the society should expect from all individuals in terms of working (obligations).
    C. *Valued working outcomes* (Question 28): In this question, the respondent is asked to indicate what outcomes he or she is seeking

from working and what are their relative importances. The major expressive and instrumental meanings identified in the literature are incorporated.

D. *Importance of work goals* (Question 32): Respondents are asked what is the relative importance of various aspects of working, such as variety, autonomy, skill utilization, pay, security, promotional opportunities, and physical working conditions. In addition, a great number of hypothetical choices are presented to the respondent. A pattern of responses indicates a particular priority of work-aspect preferences (Questions 33–46).

E. *Work role identification* (Question 31): The question concerns the extent to which one personally defines and identifies working in terms of various roles such as task role, organizational role, product or service role, and occupational/professional role.

3. *Consequences*: A third set of variables deals with expectations, plans, aspirations, and intentions for the future about working (Questions 56–68). Questions refer to expected future mobility, expected types of work, and changes in work. Most of them have a *subjective* character. Some questions, however, are more *objective* or behavioral in nature, such as those referring to concrete steps currently being taken to achieve expected or aspired-to work situations in the future.

Finally, some *additional* questions were incorporated in the questionnaire to provide information on a number of other aspects of the work situation or work attitudes, which were felt to be relevant for the present research question:

1. The well-known *lottery question* (Question 48), which has been used in a number of previous studies, and which would make it possible to make relevant comparisons across time and national borders (Jakubowski, 1968; Kaplan and Tausky, 1974; Morse and Weiss, 1955; Parker, 1965; Parker and Smith, 1976; Tausky, 1969; Warr, 1983).

2. A question which tries to identify the aspects that are considered essential in the definition of working, providing a basis for a possible international semantic analysis (Question 49).

3. A question on job or occupational satisfaction (Question 59), a question on expected attitudinal change towards working (Question 51), a question on organizational commitment (Question 52), and three questions on the relationship between work and leisure time (Questions 53–55; see also Jakubowski, 1968; Kaplan and Tausky, 1974; Morse and Weiss, 1955; Parker, 1965; Parker and Smith, 1976; Tausky, 1969; Warr, 1984) were included.

In view of the large number of questions included in the study, it should be made clear that not all of these could be analyzed with the same degree of extensiveness in this volume.

Indices

The questionnaire provides information at a very specific level. For information purposes at a detailed level, straight frequency distributions were used. In more complex interrelation analyses, however, some aggregation of the information was considered necessary. Interaction or regression studies at the level of questions themselves would lead to highly complex and uninterpretable patterns so that one could not see the forest for the trees. Therefore, *indices* were constructed, using a number of questions or answer alternatives aggregated into combined measures. In the following, we provide brief descriptions of the indices constructed. They fall into two main categories: (1) Non-central MOW indices (i.e., indices derived from antecedent or consequence variables), and (2) central MOW indices. The reader whose interest goes beyond the basic description of indices to details of items, their scoring for construction of the indices, and the intercorrelation of MOW indices is referred to Appendix 3.2. The sequence of the indices follows the sequence of the subsequent presentation in this chapter.

1. *Non-central MOW indices* For the non-central MOW indices, the aggregation was based upon logical analysis of the answers, answer distributions, and information provided by factor and item analysis carried out on the pilot study responses.
   The following non-central MOW indices were developed:
   A. *Aggravating work conditions* (AGGCON): The extent to which people have to work under unhealthy and/or dangerous conditions. It includes three items: dangerous job (Question 14), unhealthy job (Question 15), physically taxing (Question 16).
   B. *Quality of work* (QOFWORK): An index for the quality of present work measured by combining work-related items variety (Question 8), learning (Question 11), skill utilization (Question 18).
   C. *Work schedule* (SCHED): Indicating to what extent people work in irregular work schedules measured by two items: work schedule (Question 6A) and weekend work (Question 6C).
   D. *Occupational satisfaction* (OCCSAT): Includes two items to measure satisfaction with one's occupation: Choose same occu-

pation again (Question 50A) and recommend occupation to own children (Question 50B).

E. *Mobility in work history* (MWH): Indicates the extent to which the respondent has changed jobs or positions in his work history by using items on first (Question 21A) and a number of subsequent jobs (Questions 22A1–F1), one item on the number of years worked in the first (Question 21D), and several subsequent (Questions 22A2–F2).

2. *Central MOW indices*: For the central MOW indices, a different procedure was followed. These indices were developed after the data had been collected and were based upon the results of factor analysis on the international data. Factor analysis was carried out on all central MOW variables (see Chapter 4). The total sample over target groups over countries ($N = 5895$) was used. For an in-depth discussion of the procedures, and theoretical and methodological problems of the central MOW indices, we once again refer the interested reader to Appendix 3.2. A short description of the indices we constructed follows. They prove to be homogeneous and internally consistent (see Appendix 2, Table A2):

- *Contact* index. Based upon the indication of contact as valued working outcome (Q28A4), the important work aspects *people* (Q31D), and *interpersonal relations* (Q32B).
- *Economic* index. Based upon the following aspects: *income* as valued working outcome (Q28A2), *money* as work role definition (Q31F), and the job importance aspect, *pay* (Q32I). The economic index consists of pay aspects.
- *IR* index. IR stands for intrinsic working outcomes. This index seems to indicate explicitly the intrinsic work value and intrinsic satisfaction orientation. It is based upon the intrinsic valued working outcome (Q28A6), and the job importance aspects *variety* (Q32E), *interesting work* (Q32F), *match between capacities and task* (Q32H) and *autonomy* (Q32K).
- *OBL* index. OBL stands for obligation norm. This index is based upon the obligation items in the obligation-entitlement question (Q47B, D, and J).
- *ENT* index. ENT stands for entitlement norm. This index is based upon the entitlement items from this same question (Q47A, Q47E, Q47G, and Q47I).
- *CW* index. CW stands for work centrality. The centrality of working index is based on both results of factor analysis and logical reasoning. The direct question, importance of working (Q29), as well as the

question on importance of life areas (Q30), which requires the respondent to distribute 100 points over various life roles including work, attempts to measure the centrality of working.

Two additional central MOW indices were created from the items relating to the preference of different job images (Q33–Q46). Although these indices were also based on principal component analysis, their construction was different from the previously discussed central MOW indices. More details are presented in Appendix 3.2. and Chapter 8. The two additional central MOW indices were:

- *Preference for Intrinsic Work Situations* (PIW). Providing a score on the intrinsic versus extrinsic rating of work (Q33–40).
- *Preferability for Leisure Time* (PL). Providing a score on a person's preferences of increased leisure over skill use and attractiveness of a job (Q41–46).

MOW patterns

A further insight into the meaning of working was achieved through the identification of patterns of MOW conceptions and values, and an attempt to classify the respondents into categories according to their most salient work orientations.

Several ways to construct such patterns of profiles are available.

First, there is *a priori* profile construction. On the basis of a priori theoretical considerations, a selection can be made of the required combined scores of the various indices. For example, one might postulate the profile of a typical representative of a workaholic prototype: to be made up of a relative high score in the work centrality, a significant higher score for obligation than for entitlement orientation, relative preference for intrinsic over extrinsic work goals, and the strongest identification with the product or service to be provided. Likewise, a strongly motivated careerist and social climber might be typified by high centrality, high scores on status, prestige, and contacts, and a strong identification with the organization.

The MOW team, however, selected an *empirical* method for pattern identification. The simplest form is a classification of the individuals based on the levels high, medium, and low on the major MOW dimensions. A more sophisticated method is the use of cluster analysis or Q-type factor analysis. After some experimental tryouts on a national sample, we decided to use a *cluster analysis* method with six central MOW indices (CW, CONTACT, IR, PAY, OBL and OPP) as variables and the total target group sample as individuals.

The objective was to identify a (restricted) number of interpretable clusters of individuals. The individuals within one cluster should be as similar as possible to each other and as dissimilar as possible to the members of other clusters.

Ward's hierarchical clustering method was chosen which, according to Wishart (1978: 33), is possibly the best of the hierarchy options. Ward's method results in tight, spherical clusters of approximately similar size which are mutually exclusive.

The total sample of target group respondents was 5933. However, the available statistical package only allows a maximum of 999 respondents. Therefore, a selection of the total sample was used to construct the clusters ($N = 901$). The target groups as well as the countries were represented as equally as possible.

Following this procedure, a number of insightful MOW patterns have been identified within the selected sample. (The discussion and interpretation of these patterns are presented in Chapter 10.) Of course, the remaining 5032 cases from the total target group still had to be classified within one of the clusters. For this purpose, use was made of *multiple discrimination analysis*. This method assigns each individual to a certain category (work meaning pattern), based on the score of a number of discriminating variables (central MOW indices). The optimal linear combinations of the MOW indices form so-called discriminant functions. These functions discriminate the patterns as much as possible. For the actual discriminant analysis, use has been made of the SPSS subprogram *discriminant* (Nie and Hull, 1975: 457).

Further MOW analyses

A second cluster analysis procedure was used to construct another categorical variable, using the reaction on Q49: the subjective definition of working. The objective here was to identify subpopulations who define work similarity. Work definition patterns were defined by a procedure analogous to that used for MOW patterns previously described. The discussion of these patterns of work definitions is presented in Chapter 9.

A number of chapters make extensive use of *multiple regression analysis* techniques. These analyses pertained to:

- The regression of MOW profiles on the personal antecedent variables (personal and family situation, work history).
- The regression of future expectations and behavioral consequences on the personal antecedent variables and the MOW profiles.

  These analyses have been done per target group per country, per country over target groups (to identify the effect of the variable "country"), and per target group over countries (to identify the effect of the variable *target group*).

- Chapter 13 utilizes a special form of multivariate classification which has been developed by Hayashi *et al.* (1977). The procedure termed *quantification on response pattern* was developed for analysis of inter-relationships in categorical data and form the basis for the analysis in Chapter 13.

This chapter presents an overview of the different instruments, questions, and indices which have been used in this study, and of the various procedures which have been followed in the analysis and interpretation of the data.

The overview has not been more detailed than was considered necessary to understand how the data have been collected, analyzed, and interpreted. For a full description of the analysis procedures and the development of the scales, indices, and patterns, a report by one of the authors is available (Holvoet, 1984). Further insight is obtained in reading the following chapters where the results from these analyses will be discussed in detail.

Notes

(1) Appendixes to Chapter 3, 8, 9 and 13 follow Chapter 14.
(2) Actually, only eight countries finally participated in MOW.

Chapter 4

The Structure of Meaning of Working

Introduction

Few people will argue about the importance of working as a life role, but variations about commitment to that role exist. While working has many functions (as discussed in chapters 1 and 2), a crucial one for most people would seem to be its role as a means of providing food, shelter, and a variety of luxuries or nonessentials which people desire with different degrees of intensity. Furthermore, working has social and psychological significance for individuals, and broader economic and social meaning for organizations and society as a whole. Consequently, the meaning of working is one of the most relevant sets of issues today and will remain so for a long time to come.

Accepting this view of working as being fundamentally important to individuals, to organizations, and to societies highlights the conceptual value of identifying and understanding the variety of common meanings attached to working by individuals. While it is possible to approach this task from various levels of analysis (individual, organizational, and societal), this chapter starts at the level of the individual. Here, we are concerned primarily with identifying and understanding a common structure of what working means to individuals. Subsequent chapters will explore, develop, and modify these common work meanings at different levels of aggregation and for different purposes. At present, however, we attempt to answer two broad questions about individual work meanings:

1. What empirical structuring of work meanings is revealed when we view the meaning of working data in totality across all participating countries?
2. How consistently is this same general structure of work meanings found when we view the meaning of working data in each country separately?

First, we must specify the methods used to answer these basic questions. Measurement of meaning of working.

Measurement of meaning of working.

The basic data utilized in this chapter for identifying the empirical structure of work meanings come from the five major item or measurement domains shown in the heuristic research model (Figure 2.1) in Chapter 2. It again should be noted that it is not meaning attributes related only to the present work performed or the present job that are of interest; rather, the concern is with the importance, the value, the significance, and the meaning of working in general.

While the primary theoretical development of the MOW domains has been addressed in Chapter 2 and will be the subject of more detailed analysis and discussion in following chapters, it is useful to highlight the core notion being addressed in each central MOW item domain and the related measurement scales. (Item numbers are retained for reference to the data collection instrument and to Table 4.1.)

1. *Centrality of working as a life role*: How central or important is the role of working in one's life as compared to other life roles *and* in absolute terms? The series of *central life interest* studies by Dubin and colleagues were most helpful in developing items in this domain (see Dubin, 1956; Dubin, Champoux, and Porter, 1975; Dubin, Hedley, and Taveggia, 1976). The relative measure of work centrality as compared to other life roles was obtained from the number of points (out of 100) assigned to "My work" (Item 30C). The scaled measure of work centrality (Item 29) was a 7-point scale of work importance from "one of the least important things in my life" to "one of the most important things in my life."

2. *Societal norms about working*: This is a set of normative statements about work and working in terms of what should be expected from working (entitlements), and what should be expected from one in working (obligations). The intention has been to utilize the evaluative rather than the descriptive meaning of norms; norms tell us what should be, not what is. The definitional form utilized in developing the societal norm statements came from the work of Triandis on subjective culture: "Norms involve relationships between a person category and a behavioral category and they usually specify whether the behavior is appropriate" (Triandis, 1972). An example of such a norm dealing with obligations in work is: "It is the duty of every able-bodied citizen to contribute to society by working." "Every able-bodied citizen" is the person category, "contribute to society

by working" is the behavioral category, and "It is the duty" specifies the appropriateness of the behavior. An original set of 42 societal norm statements about working was reduced through international pilot testing to the present 10 statements (Item 47A–47J). Statements 47A, 47C, 47E, 47G, and 47I represent entitlement norms while statements 47B, 47D, 47F, 47H, and 47J represent obligation norms.[1]

3. *Valued working outcomes*: What are the general outcomes and/or opportunities one is seeking from working and what are their relative importances? The valued outcome measure of working (Item 28A1–28A6) utilizes six general functions of working as developed by Kaplan and Tausky (1974) from review of research on the functions and meanings of working: status and prestige providing function of working, income-producing function of working, time-occupying function of working, interpersonal contact function of working, societal service function of working, and the intrinsic function of working (working being basically interesting and satisfying to the individual).

4. *Importance of work goals*: What is the relative importance to the individual of various work goals or aspects of working? The relevant literature for making work goals operational is voluminous and covers the job satisfaction, work values, and work needs literature. The Minnesota Importance Questionnaire development and validation (Weiss, Dawis, England, and Lofquist, 1964, 1968) and the more recent review of job satisfaction by Locke (1976) were extensively utilized. It should be noted that a combined ranking/rating method of work goal importance appraisal was used. This procedure roughly attempts to standardize the *degree* or *level* of the goal being evaluated by the subject and was adopted after pilot experimentation with several formats. Item 32A–K includes the following work goals:

- A lot of opportunity to *learn* new things
- Good *interpersonal* relations (supervisors, co-workers)
- Good opportunity for upgrading or *promotion*
- *Convenient* work hours
- A lot of *variety*
- *Interesting* work (work that you really like)
- Good job *security*
- A good *match* between your job requirements and your abilities and experience
- Good *pay*
- Good physical working *conditions* (such as light, temperature, cleanliness, low noise level)
- A lot of *autonomy* (you decide how to do your work)

5. *Work role identification*: What role identifications (e.g., task roles, company or organizational roles, product or service roles, occupational, or professional roles) are viewed as important by the individual?

The sample utilized

The present analyses utilize the target group samples as the source of data for the following reasons:

1. The target group samples are occupationally diverse within countries but occupationally similar across countries; thus, one is establishing meaning of working structures on diverse occupational groups but will be comparing meaning of working structures across countries on similarly composed occupational samples.
2. Target group sample data collection utilized the ranking/rating method of obtaining information about work goals while a simpler ranking method was utilized in the national sample data collection. The problem of ipsativity between work goals is thus not present when utilizing target group samples.

The first structure analysis combined all target groups in all countries into one total international target group sample of 5933 individuals. This analysis is viewed as presenting a general, but systematic, view of common meaning of working structures across occupational groups and across countries. The second set of analyses combines all the target groups within a given country and uses this sample for the representation of meaning of working structures within that country.

Analytic method

The method of analysis for identifying and interpreting meaning of working structures consisted of principal component analysis of the 37 scores available from the five major MOW domains previously described. Prior communality estimates were set at 1.0 and no iterations were made. Factors with eigenvalues exceeding 1.0 were rotated to simple structure by the varimax procedure. Factor loadings with an absolute value greater than or equal to .40 were used in defining and interpreting the factors. Relevant information from the initial item intercorrelation matrix was used to verify and clarify some interpretation decisions.

Empirical structure of meaning of working

Table 4.1 displays a factor matrix arranged by content dimensions of work meanings for the international target group sample (all target groups in all countries). Item loadings with an absolute value of less than .40 are omitted from Table 4.1 and all loadings are reported to two places after the decimal point to simplify presentation. Thirteen factors with eigenvalues greater than 1.0 emerged and accounted for 58% of the common variance among the 37 MOW scores.

Factor analysis interpretation

Factors are discussed in a logical content order following Figure 2.1 in Chapter 2 rather than in order of factor extraction. Factor 3 shows significant loadings with the relative importance of working to the individual when compared to other life roles (Item 30C); secondly, with the scaled measure of work centrality (Item 29). These measures of work centrality differ chiefly in that the former specifies the comparative standards against which working is evaluated (other specified life roles) and it involves a cognitive and decision-making framework for responding. The comparison standards and framework for responding are not specified in the latter measure and thus, are apt to be more idiosyncratically interpreted by individuals. The high negative loading of this factor—together with Item 30A (the importance of leisure)—suggests a polarity between work and leisure. On balance, it seems that the work centrality dimension represents a generalized, but personal, importance attached to working as a life role. The essence of high scores on this dimension is the evaluation that "working is important and central to your life." We would expect individual work centrality levels to be positively related to time spent in working without implying causality in either direction. Clearly, work centrality should be viewed as a fundamental and general aspect of the meaning of working for individuals. While there is, as yet, no clear and consistent theoretical rationale for specifying expected country differences in levels of work centrality, there are cogent arguments and related data which suggest that certain country differences in work centrality are likely to occur. The empirical results and their interpretation are addressed in later chapters.

Factor 4 shows significant loadings from each of the four entitlement statements in the societal norms about working. These items involve entitlements that *all* should expect from working. Entitlement flowing to individuals because of the responsibilities of organizations or society toward working are paramount in these items. The essence of high scores

Table 4.1. Significant Factor Loadings of MOW Items for the International Target Group Sample (N=5933)

Factors	Work Centrality	Entitlement	Obligation	Income	Self-Expressive	Interpersonal Contact	Comfort	Learning and Improvement Opportunity	Religious and Societal Service	Product Role	Task Role	Organization Role	Family versus Leisure
MOW Items Item description*	F3	F4	F10	F1	F2	F5	F6	F7	F9	F11	F12	F13	F8
28A1 Status/prestige								.51					
28A2 Income				.80									
28A3 Time absorbing							.46						
28A4 Interpersonal contact						.65							
28A5 Serve society									.57				
28A6 Intrinsically interesting				−.49									
29 Work importance	.65												
30A Leisure role importance	−.58												−.56
30B Community role importance									.64				
30C Work role importance	.77												
30D Religious role importance									.62				
30E Family role importance													.92
31A Task Identification											.89		
31B Organizational Identification												.90	
31C Product Identification										−.87			
31D Interpersonal Identification						.75							
31E Occupational Identification										.50	−.54	−.47	
31F Income Identification				.72									

Factors	Work Centrality	Entitlement	Obligation	Income	Self-Expressive	Interpersonal Contact	Comfort	Learning and Improvement Opportunity	Religious and Societal Service	Product Role	Task Role	Organization Role	Family versus Leisure
32A Learning Opportunity								.55					
32B Interpersonal Contact						.49							
32C Promotion Opportunity								.68					
32D Convenient hours							.66						
32E Variety					.63								
32F Interesting work					.66								
32G Job security							.41						
32H Ability/job match					.64								
32I Good pay				.68									
32J Good Working Conditions							.70						
32K Autonomy					.63								
47A Retraining responsibility		.57											
47B Duty to work			.48										
47D Saving responsibility			.40										
47E Employee participation		.63											
47G Meaningful work entitlement		.64											
47H Monotony/pay acceptance			.65										
47I Job providing responsibility		.62											
47J Response to value work			.64										

* The short item description provides a partial view of the item content but should be accompanied by a thorough reading of the questionnaire as shown in Appendix A3.1.

on this dimension is the normative belief that "working should provide a high level of entitlement to everyone." While there is clearly an egalitarian element to high scores on this dimension, attribution theory reminds us that some individuals who espouse entitlements as being due to all may be doing so primarily as a way of indicating a strong belief that the entitlements are due them as individuals. Thus, it is useful to retain this potential duality of meaning from high entitlement scores in interpreting later results. To the extent that we have been successful in generating items that do indeed tap societal beliefs about entitlements, we would expect national differences to be more likely than occupational differences. Age and sex differences in entitlement norms within a country also are a reasonable possibility, but again, it seems best to await the empirical evidence in Chapter 6.

Factor 10 shows significant loadings from each of the four obligation statements in the societal norms about working. These items involve obligations that all individuals have toward working as a life activity. Obligations flowing from individuals to work organizations and society are paramount in these items. The essence of high scores on this dimension is the normative belief that "all individuals should contribute to society by working and valuing their work." Again, we should be reminded that some individuals who espouse generalized obligation beliefs may be making statements about their own personal sense of obligation toward working. To the extent that this latter observation is correct, one might expect some degree of positive relationship between work centrality and obligation beliefs. As was the case for entitlement beliefs, we would expect obligation beliefs to differ more substantially between countries than between occupations. Age and sex differences also are a possibility.

Factor 1 shows significant loadings on all items where income (Item 28A2), money (Item 31F), and pay (Item 32I) are being evaluated.[2] The negative loading of Item 28A6 (working is basically interesting and satisfying) suggests some polarity between intrinsic and income-producing meanings of work. Factor 1 clearly represents a valued working outcome preference for income or opportunity for income. It should be noted, however, that part of the reason this factor emerges as the first factor and so clearly as an income factor may be attributed to the fact that we had items dealing directly with income or money in three of the MOW item domains. In Chapter 7, where work goals are separately analyzed and where good pay is only one of 11 work goals, a broader factor of economic work goals emerges. At present, high scores on Factor 1 clearly indicate a preference for income from working—with the caveat that this factor also can be viewed as part of a broader dimension of economic opportunity or economic return from work.

Factor 2 shows significant loadings on the importance of your work life containing: "a lot of variety" (Item 32E), "interesting work (work you really like)" (Item 32F), "a good job match between your job requirements and your abilities and experience" (Item 32H), and "a lot of autonomy" (Item 32K). It should be noted that Item 28A6, "working itself is basically interesting and satisfying," has a .37 loading from this factor. The core element of high scores on Factor 3 is valuing a work setting which is conducive to investment of self or expression of self in working. The somewhat overused term *self-expressive* is the label chosen for this function of working.

Factor 5 receives significant loadings on "working permits you to have interesting contacts with other people" (Item 28A4), on "the type of people with whom I work" (Item 31D), and on (Item 32B), "importance of good interpersonal relations." This factor also draws items from three domains and reflects a dimension centering on the *interpersonal contact* function of working and is so named.

Factor 6 receives the highest loadings on Items 32D, "the importance of convenient work hours," and Item 32J, "the importance of good physical working conditions." Item 32G, "the importance of good job security," and Item 28A3, "working keeps you occupied," load at a lower level on this factor. This factor reflects a dimension centering on the *comfort* function of working and is so named. Previous research on work context dimensions such as this would lead us to expect national, occupational, sex, and age differences on the comfort function of working.

Factor 7 receives high loadings on Items 32C, "good opportunity for upgrading or promotion"; Item 32A, "a lot of opportunity to learn new things"; and Item 28A1, "working gives you status and prestige." This factor reflects a dimension which centers on *learning and improvement opportunity* in one's work life and the accompanying status and prestige which go with these improvement opportunities.

Factor 9 shows significant loadings on "working is a useful way for you to serve society" (Item 28A5), on the importance of "community" (Item 30B), and "religion" (Item 30D) as major life roles. Factor 9 is a dimension of work meaning which reflects the religious and societal service function of working. The religious and societal service function of working is one of the generalized work meanings which logically would be expected to differ between countries because of historical differences in the way work is viewed and between generations over time.

The next three factors are based totally on the work role identification domain of MOW. Factor 11 represents a work role identification with the *product or service* produced; Factor 12 represents a work role identification with the *tasks* one performs in working, and Factor 13 represents a work role identification with the *company or organization* in which one works. It is interesting to note that all three of these work role identification factors are bipolar in nature and that the other pole in all cases is Item 31E, "the type of *occupation or profession* I am in." This suggests that there is a generalized work role identification with one's occupation or profession. While it does not emerge as a separate factor, it is identified consistently and should be recognized. In this sense, we can say that four major work role identifications have been observed in the data.

Factor 8 is a bipolar factor which reflects a dimension in which the "importance of family" (Item 30E) is contrasted with the "importance of leisure" (Item 30A). It is interesting to note that it is leisure and not work that is in opposition to family. While this dimension has obvious importance in other contexts, it is seen only as an indirect element of the meaning of working and is not dealt with as a work meaning.

These 13 empirically identified dimensions of common work meanings can be organized into four major content subsets as shown in Figure 4.1. Thus, we have identified 13 separate common dimensions of work meanings among all the target group respondents in the seven countries and have organized them into four content sets. The four major content sets of work meanings are: (1) work centrality or the importance of working; (2) societal norms about working; (3) valued working outcomes and work goal preferences; and (4) work role identifications in working. The first two sets of work meanings deal with the importance of working as a life role and normative expectations connected to that role. On theoretical grounds, we expect these sets of work meanings to differentiate between countries and to be related to measures of general work involvement such as time and effort spent in working.

The set of valued working outcome and work-goal preference meanings deal with important and/or preferred outcomes and work goals in one's working life. Alternatively, they may be viewed as important functions performed for individuals through the role of working. At a broad level, the functions performed for individuals by the role of working include: (1) a function of providing economic well-being and/or economic opportunity; (2) a function of allowing one the opportunity for investment of self or self-expression; (3) a function of interpersonal contacts and relationships with others; (4) a function of providing opportunity for progress in working and the accompanying status and prestige; (5) a comfort function; and (6) a function of serving societal and/or religious convictions through the process of working.

This wide spectrum of valued working outcomes or functions performed by the working role is likely to be responsible in part for the relatively high degree of overall attachment individuals have to working as a life role (as will be shown in later chapters). Additionally, we would expect to see valued working outcome preferences associated with behavioral intentions and actual behavior which are logically consistent with the preference. For example, individuals who highly value the economic outcome of working would be expected to make job choices which would appear to them to further this preferred outcome.

The major work role identifications which we have identified include: (1) an identification with the tasks one performs in working; (2) an identification with the products or services one provides; (3) an identification with

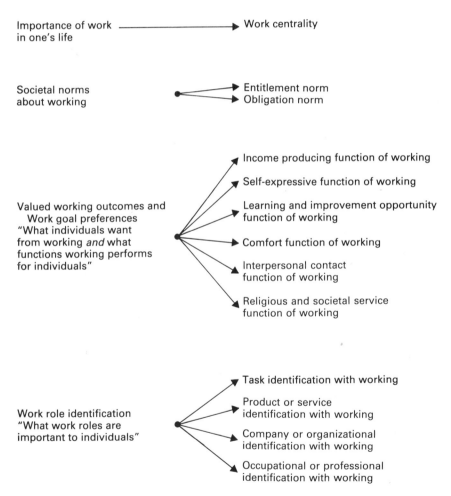

Figure 4.1. Major content sets of work meanings.

the occupation or profession of which one is a member; and (4) an identification with the company or organization for which one works.

Although extensive analysis was done with the work role identification data, our a priori estimate of its useful information yield as a domain was highly inflated. We are unsure exactly why this is so but suspect that it concerns the fact that the two most selected role identifications were incorporated into the valued working outcome/work goal variables; and secondly, because of the single-item measurement of each work role identification. In any event, little will be reported about the work role identification data in later chapters because we found little substantial information from these analyses.

Work centrality, societal norms about working, and valued working outcomes/work goal preferences are three major content (empirically derived) variable complexes underlying the meaning one attaches to work and working and should prove useful in studying both similarities and differences across subgroups of workers at the levels of occupations, age groups, sex groups, organizations, industries, and nations.

Again, it should be emphasized that these are common work meanings which are relevant in a structural sense to individuals and not necessarily to aggregations of individuals such as occupations or nations. They certainly *may* be relevant at other levels of analysis, but one should not prejudge the issue (see, for example, Hofstede, 1980). To shed some light on one aspect of this latter issue, we address the question, How consistently is this same general structure of common work meanings found when we analyze meaning of working data in each country separately?

Qualitative similarity of meaning of working structures found in each country

While there are a variety of ways in which one could assess work-meaning structure similarity across a set of seven countries, it seems most helpful to compare the dimensions found in each country with the dimensions found in the total international sample. The same factor analytic procedure was used to derive factors in each country and in the international sample, but the determination of whether two factors are similar here was arrived at by way of a qualitative judgment. We restricted the number of factors to be extracted in each country to 13 (the number found in the international sample) as a means for making more meaningful comparisons. The 13 factors extracted in each country accounted for 58–60% of the common variance among the 37 MOW scores. As shown in Table 4.2, there is a reasonably high degree of structural work-meaning similarity across the

seven countries.[3] Depending on how strict one is in assessing factor similarity, qualitatively similar work-meaning structures are found across
countries in 75–90% of the possible instances. Factors found in individual
countries which are not found in the total sample (bottom two lines of
Table 4.2) are work as a time-absorbing activity factor found in Belgium,
Germany, Japan, and Yugoslavia, and work as a status-producing activity
found in Japan, Netherlands, and Yugoslavia. Major omissions are: (1) no
separate opportunity for progress dimension is found in Germany, Israel,
Japan, and the Netherlands; (2) no religious and societal service function
of work dimension is found in Yugoslavia; (3) no product or company
work-role identification factors are found in Yugoslavia; and (4) no task
work-role identification factor is found in Germany.

It should be noted that several meaning of working dimensions found in
the total sample are represented by two separate factors in several of the
countries. An example of this would be the interpersonal function of
working in Yugoslavia. Here, Factor 9 receives a high loading on Item
31D, "the type of people with whom I work," and Factor 10 has its highest
loading on Item 28A4, "working permits you to have interesting contacts
with other people." In the total international sample, these two items
loaded on the same factor which identified the interpersonal contact work
meaning. Similar factor separation occurred in the seven instances in Table
4.2 where two factor numbers are found in a single cell. This factor
separation occurs most often with the self-expressive function of working.

Factor numbers which are listed in parentheses in Table 4.2 are one end
of a bipolar factor. For example, in Belgium, Factor 1 is a bipolar factor
where the economic items have significant negative loadings and the
religious and societal service function items have significant positive loadings. Thus, the bipolar Factor 1 in Belgium encompasses both the economic function *and* the religious and societal service function of working. As
would be expected, bipolar factors occurred most often in the work-role
identification domain where scoring is ipsative in nature.

Complex factor composition most often is found in Japan. In Japan,
Factor 3 encompasses the items found internationally in the comfort
function *and* in the opportunity for progress function of working. Also, in
Japan, Factor 7, which is a bipolar factor, shows the product role and the
task role combined as one pole and the occupational role at the other pole.

Summary

The results presented clearly show both similarities and differences in
work-meaning structures between countries when measured and treated at

Table 4.2 Qualitative comparison of meaning of working factor structure found in all countries with the structure found in each country****

Work meaning structure dimensions (combined target group sample)	Belgium	United States	Netherlands	Germany	Yugoslavia	Israel	Japan
Work centrality	F9	F7	F8	F3	F3	F7	F8
Entitlement	F4	F2	F6	F7	F2	F4	F5
Obligation	F10	F13	F4	F2	F10	F11	F12
Income function	(F1)*	F1	F1	F1	F1	F1	F1
Self-expressive function	F3 + F5**	F3	F2	F9 + F11	F4	F2 + F5	F2 + F10
Interpersonal function	F2	F8	F3	F4	F9 + F12	F9	F4
Comfort function	F7	F9	F5	F5	F5	F3 }	***
Opportunity for progress function	(F6)	F6	—	—	F6	—	F3
Religious and societal service function	(F1)	F5	F9	F13	—	F8	F6
Product role	(F6)	F12	(F11) + (F13)	(F8)	—	(F12)	(F7)
Task role	F12	F11	(F13)	—	(F8)	(F13)	F11
Company role	(F8)	(F10)	F12	F10	—	(F10)	(F7)
Occupational role	(F8)	(F10)	(F11)	(F8)	(F8)	(F10) + (F12) + (F13)	(F11)
Time absorbing function	F13	—	—	F12	F13	—	F13
Status function	—	—	F10	—	F11	—	F9

* Factor numbers in parentheses indicate that the dimension is one end of a bipolar factor.
** Where two factors are listed in a cell, the original factor is separated into two parts.
*** Complex factors that merge two dimensions.
**** The nontabled factor (family versus leisure) was, respectively (F11, F4, F7, F6, F7, F6, none found), in the seven countries.

the level of the individual. On balance, there is a qualitative similarity of 75–90% across the seven countries in the structure of individual work meanings. This degree of structural similarity certainly does not preclude level differences among countries on the various work meanings, but it does suggest that there is sufficient structural similarity to make level comparisons of scores across countries meaningful. Later chapters will focus on these level comparisons.

The three broad content sets of work meanings which have been identified and prove useful in later analyses are, work centrality, societal norms about working and a set of valued working outcomes and work goal preferences. These are the major building blocks for studying the meaning of working.

Notes

(1) Items 47C and 47F were not consistently related to the appropriate societal norm dimension in several countries, and so were excluded from the structure analyses performed within this chapter.

(2) The reader will note that Factor 1 combines items drawn from three item domains identified in the heuristic model (Figure 2.1) in Chapter 2. The three item domains are valued working outcomes, importance of work goals, and work role identifications. The content similarity of the items (income, pay, and money) was sufficiently strong to overcome the fact that the items were located in three different item complexes, each of which utilized a different scaling procedure. The same tendency is found with several other factors which cross item domains and empirically "correct" some of the *a priori* item classifications into domains of the heuristic model.

(3) Factor analyses tables by country are available but not shown, due to space limitations.

Chapter 5

Work Centrality

Introduction

There is widespread recognition that the activity of working and the outcomes flowing from working are of fundamental significance to most individuals. In most industrialized societies, the average working person spends about one-third of his/her waking hours at work activities. Additionally, the time one spends in training and preparation for work and the time one spends worrying about being out of work or planning for a better work situation suggest that work-related activities make up a substantial part of the adult's life. A majority of individuals in most societies derive the major part of their economic well-being from income generated by their work activities. It is evident that working activities also fulfill non-economic needs of individuals. Were this not the case, it would be difficult to explain why 65–95% of individuals in national labor force samples in a variety of countries state they would continue to work even if "they had enough money to live comfortably for the rest of their life without working." While the percentages so responding vary by the country and the decade during which the study was done, a clear majority always state that they would continue to work (see Vecchio, 1980; Warr, 1982; and this study). Many workers also indicate that "working gives them a feeling of being tied into the larger society, of having something to do, and of having a purpose in life" (Morse and Weiss, 1955). The significance of working to individuals also is indicated by the impact of unemployment and retirement on people who have been productive and active all their lives (Friedman and Havighurst, 1954). If the non-working person cannot find some other kind of activity, work, or a hobby, the effects of inactivity and idleness can be very demoralizing. Working, and the activity it implies would seem to be of significance to the individual in both an economic sense and in a sociopsychological sense. The rather dramatic changes during the past 30 years in the legal and societal conceptions about "working rights" in general, and for various subgroups such as women, racial minority groups, protected age categories, and a variety of disadvantaged groups, have certainly altered employment policies and practices substantially. It seems highly likely that these legislated changes and the accompanying costs and benefits would impact over time on the significance attached to working by the working population and by various segments of that population. The increasing levels of education in most industrialized countries and the sweeping developments that occur in the process of industrial development with reference to the possibilities of performing work in general and certain types of work in particular most certainly impact on the significance that is attached to working.

Given this recognition about the general importance of working in the lives of most individuals, it is not surprising that scholars and researchers have focused attention on a variety of concepts and measurement procedures to assess and study the importance of working. Morrow (1983), for example, reviewed research in the area of work commitment and classified five major approaches to studying work commitment which, respectively, focus attention on values, careers, jobs, employing organizations, and unions. While the degree of redundancy among these forms of work commitment is correctly viewed as a methodological problem by Morrow, we argue that a more serious conceptual problem would be identified if different approaches to work commitment did not show some reasonable amount of overlap. This reasoning, however, assumes that researchers in the area all are attempting to study a general, overarching, genotypical view of work importance and that the different focuses primarily reflect different approaches to this task. Obviously, such an assumption is problematical.

The concept of work centrality

In the MOW project, we have attempted to develop a scientifically useful concept which focuses on the generalized importance of working. The concept is named *work centrality*. It is a concept which deals with the life of an individual as being the focal unit for study and the *relative importance of working in one's life* at a given point in time as the content of concern. We do not single out any a priori reason why working should be important in one's life or in what way it is important in one's life and attempt to have work centrality represent that particular rationale for work importance; rather, we purposely choose to be neutral toward different rationales for work importance. Working may be important to one individual primarily because of what is received from working; to another, primarily because of what he or she invests in the process of working, or because of some combination of these rationales. Our general concept of work centrality, therefore, remains neutral to these differing rationales for work importance as must our measurement procedures. We are in agreement with the conceptual distinction that Kanungo (1982) makes between work involvement and job involvement and with his argument to separate measurement of the state of involvement (centrality, in our terms) from its antecedents or from its consequences. In short, work centrality is defined as *the degree of general importance that working has in the life of an individual at any given point in time*. See Dubin (1956), Dubin *et al.* (1975) and Dubin *et al.* (1976) for a similar concept.

The measurement of work centrality

While there are a variety of measurement procedures which could be used to assess the general importance of working in one's life (see Kanungo, 1982, for three related measurement devices), we chose to use two measurement procedures. In the first procedure, the importance of working is directly compared with the importance of other major life areas. The evaluative frame of reference for this procedure is a complex but structured frame of reference involving self, working versus self, and other major life areas. The primary intended characteristics of this measurement procedure are comparative in nature and involve cognitive and decision-making elements. Figure 5.1 shows the comparative item that was used to assess work centrality (Question 30).

From Item 30 shown in Figure 5.1, it is possible to derive the ordinal position of work for a given individual among the five life areas that are evaluated in relative importance. For any individual, work may be the most important life area (that is, more points are assigned to it than to any other life area), second most important life area, third, fourth, or least important life area. Certain standard decision rules can be (and have been) adopted to handle situations where there are ties in the number of points assigned to two or more life areas and the result is the ordinal importance position of work among the five life areas for any given individual.[1]

The measurement procedure just described, whereby work centrality is assessed in terms of the ordinal position of work among a set of *important* life areas, reflects our defined conceptual meaning of work centrality, it relies upon a relatively stable measurement process, and it is interpretable at the level of the individual and/or at the group level. When dealing with aggregations of individuals, the focus is on the relative incidence of defined ordinal levels of work centrality in the group.

The second measurement procedure used as an indicator of work centrality consists of a seven-point scaled response to the question, "How important and significant is working in your *total* life?" The anchor statement at the low end of the scale was "one of the least important things in my life," while the anchor statement at the high end of the scale was "one of the most important things in my life" (Question 29). Here the frame of reference is self in working and no comparative standards are specified as was the case in Question 30.

Assign a total of 100 points to indicate how important the following areas are in your life at the present time.

—— A. my Leisure (like hobbies, sports, recreation and contacts with friends)

—— B. my Community (like voluntary organizations, union and political organizations)

—— C. my Work

—— D. my Religion (like religious activities and beliefs)

—— E. my Family

(100 Total)

Figure 5.1. Work centrality measure.

The two indicators of work centrality are moderately related (r = .29 over all individuals in the combined national samples from the eight countries).[2] Although the two indicators are not highly correlated, they are combined to provide a general measure of work centrality at the level of the individual.

The method chosen for combining the two indicators for each individual was a simple addition after each indicator was transformed to the ordinal position of work on a scale of 1–5.[3] Thus, the possible range of the combined work centrality measure is from 2 to 10. The minimum score of 2 is obtained by an individual if his/her response to Question 29 is 1, 2, or 3 *and* working is the *least* important of the five life areas. Conversely, the maximum score of 10 would result from a 7 on Question 29 *and* evaluating working as the *most* important life area on Question 30. The work centrality measure mean is 6.98 with a standard deviation of 1.83 for the combined national samples from all countries ($N = 8661$). The data from each country are weighted equally, regardless of sample size in obtaining the given parameter estimates.

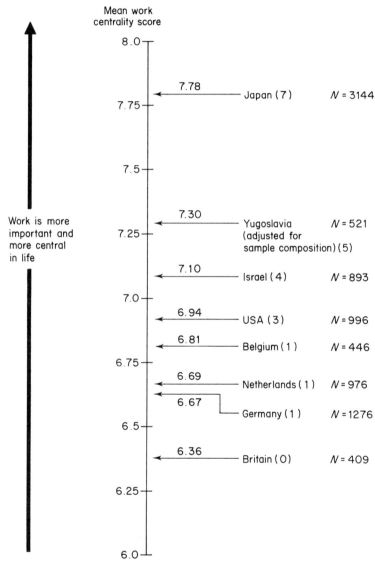

Figure 5.2. Work centrality score (mean score) for each country.

Work centrality scores for countries

Figure 5.2 shows the mean work centrality score for each country.

The levels of measured work centrality among the countries in the MOW project are clearly not the same. Japan has the highest work centrality and Britain has the lowest work centrality. While the statistically significant differences between countries are indicated in Figure 5.2, the pattern of *relative* work centrality levels among the eight countries seems best indicated by the groupings in Figure 5.3.

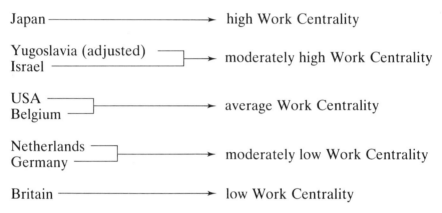

Japan ⟶ high Work Centrality

Yugoslavia (adjusted)
Israel ⟶ moderately high Work Centrality

USA
Belgium ⟶ average Work Centrality

Netherlands
Germany ⟶ moderately low Work Centrality

Britain ⟶ low Work Centrality

Figure 5.3. Groupings by country of relative work centrality levels.

While there is considerable overlap between the country distributions of work centrality, it is instructive to note that the Japanese mean is over three-fourths of a standard deviation higher than the British mean. Thus, we are dealing with not only statistically significant differences but with differences that would be expected to impact on practical consequences as well. The potential for these practical consequences can be observed more clearly from Table 5.1 which shows the frequency of different work centrality levels obtained by individuals among the national samples.

From Table 5.1, we see that there are about 12 times as many high scorers as low scorers in Japan. The same proportion is about 4:1 in the United States, and drops to approximately 2:1 in Britain. These are differences that should clearly make a difference in outcomes.

Work centrality levels for target groups (target group samples)

Figure 5.4 shows the mean work centrality score for each target group combined across all countries. Again, we see that there are significant

Table 5.1. Percentage distribution of work centrality scores by country

Country	High centrality Scores 8, 9, or 10	Moderate centrality 5, 6, or 7	Low centrality 2, 3, or 4
Japan (N = 3144)	59	36	5
Yugoslavia (N = 521)	54	40	6
Israel (N = 893)	43	48	8
United States (N = 996)	41	49	10
Belgium (N = 446)	39	50	10
Netherlands (N = 976)	35	55	10
Germany (N = 1276)	35	51	14
Britain (N = 409)	26	61	13
All countries combined (N = 8661)	41	49	10

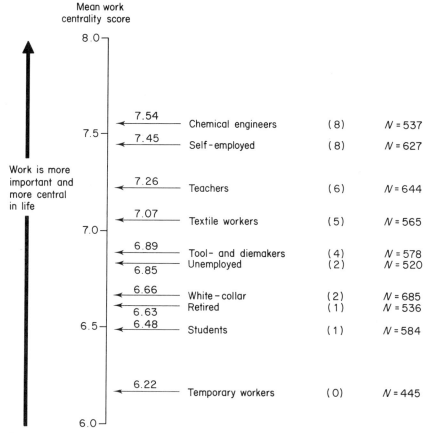

Figure 5.4. Work centrality score (mean score) for each occupational group (target group samples).

occupational (target group) differences in work centrality scores. Chemical engineers and self-employed owners of small businesses have the highest work centrality, while temporary workers have the lowest scores.

More clarity about the magnitude of these target group differences can be observed in Table 5.2 which presents the percentage distribution of various work centrality score levels for the 10 target groups.

Table 5.2. Percentage distribution of work centrality scores by target group

Target group	High centrality Scores 8, 9, or 10	Moderate centrality 5, 6, or 7	Low centrality 2, 3, or 4
Chemical engineers ($N = 537$)	56	39	5
Self-employed ($N = 627$)	56	35	9
Teachers ($N = 644$)	46	50	4
Textile workers ($N = 565$)	46	44	10
Tool- Diemakers ($N = 578$)	38	51	11
Unemployed ($N = 520$)	42	44	14
White-collar ($N = 685$)	36	52	12
Retired ($N = 536$)	32	53	15
Students ($N = 584$)	30	57	13
Temporary workers ($N = 445$)	27	55	18
Total sample ($N = 5721$)	41	48	11

As shown in Tables 5.1 and 5.2, country differences in measured work centrality are somewhat greater than target group differences. A multiple classification analyses of work centrality scores by country and target group shows that country explains about $1\frac{1}{2}$ times as much of the total work centrality variance as does target group. Thus, variation in work centrality level seems more a function of aspects of one's nation than of one's occupation.

Work centrality levels for age groups

Table 5.3 shows work centrality scores (means and standard deviations) and score distributions for three age groups (combined national sample data).

Each successive age group is significantly higher in work centrality than younger age groups ($P < .05$). As seen in the distribution data, the ratio of high scores to low scorers for the under-30-years-of-age group is about 3:1 while the same proportion for those 50 years and older is about 7:1. Age, then, is moderately but consistently related to work centrality in a positive

Table 5.3. Work centrality scores and distributions for age groups
(combined national sample data)

Age category	N	Mean*	Standard deviation	High centrality 8, 9, or 10	Moderate centrality 5, 6, or 7	Low centrality 2, 3, or 4
Under 30	2570	6.66	1.78	34%	55%	11%
30–49	4388	7.07	1.83	44	47	9
50 and +	1680	7.37	1.82	51	42	7

* Countries are equally weighted, regardless of sample size in determining all parameters in this table.

manner. Whether this difference represents true intergenerational effects or maturity and learning effects is an important topic but beyond the scope of the present analysis.

Work centrality levels for males and females

Table 5.4 shows the work centrality scores (means and standard deviations) and score distributions for males and for females in the combined national sample data.

Table 5.4. Work centrality scores and distributions for sex groups
(combined national sample data)*

Sex	N	Mean	Standard deviation	High centrality 8, 9, or 10	Moderate centrality 5, 6, or 7	Low centrality 2, 3, or 4
Male	5437	7.11	1.84	45%	46%	9%
Female	3206	6.77	1.79	37	53	10

* Countries are equally weighted regardless of sample size in determining all parameters in this table.

While males have significantly higher work centrality than females at the .05 level of significance, the distribution data shown in Table 5.4 indicate that the differences are concentrated mainly in the high and moderate centrality categories. It should be noted that in Japan, males score considerably higher than females on work centrality (males = 8.09, females = 7.15)—a difference that is significant statistically and probably important in a practical sense as well.

Figure 5.5 allows one to visualize the relative size of country differences, age differences, and sex differences in work centrality when all are placed on a common scale. The sample being considered is the same in all three

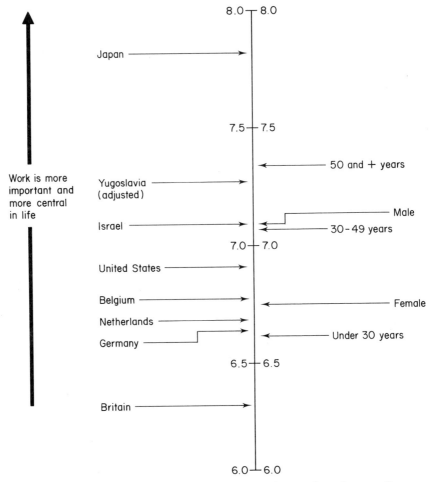

Figure 5.5. Country, age and sex group comparisons of work centrality.

cases (combined national samples), but it is separately distributed by nation; then by age of the individuals; and finally, by the sex of the individuals. As can be seen in the figure, country mean scores cover about twice the scale distance (from high to low) as do age group mean scores, and age group mean scores cover about twice the score range compared to sex group mean scores. This is one rough indication of work centrality variability that is associated with each of the three variables (nation, age, and sex).[4]

Work centrality and involvement with working and commitment to working

A major theoretical proposition about work centrality that has been advanced in chapters 2, 4, and the present chapter is that work centrality over the working life span of an individual is positively related to involvement with working and commitment to working. It is obvious that no single cross-sectional study adequately can test this proposition in a rigorous scientific fashion. We clearly recognize this fact and must offer our evidence in this spirit.

In the MOW project, one measure which represents involvement with working is the average number of hours worked per week (including overtime). In the combined national sample of the eight countries, the mean number of hours worked per week was 44.5 hours with a standard deviation of 12.8 hours. This suggests a great deal of variation among the 8297 individuals for whom data were available in the eight countries. Roughly, about one-sixth of this total sample works less than 38 hours per week, about two-thirds works from 38 to 54 hours per week, and one-sixth works over 54 hours per week. While a great deal of this variation in the number of hours worked per week is accounted for by employer policies and employer scheduling practices, it is the case that individuals also influence this variability in hours worked per week to some extent in terms of their acceptance or non-acceptance of particular amounts of scheduled work hours per week (both below and above some accepted or contractually set norm). This point is particularly relevant for the 30–60% of our country samples who are managerial, professional, self-employed, or part-time members of their respective labor forces who can, and do, influence the amount of time they work. The mean number of hours worked per week in national samples varied from a low of 39.9 hours per week in Germany to 48.9 hours per week in Japan. The standard deviations in the national samples varied from 7.4 hours to 14.6 hours. Thus, there is considerable variability within each country and across countries in the amount of time individuals work per week, and it can be reasonably argued that a part of this variability can be influenced by individuals. While recognizing its limitations, we have chosen this time measure (hours worked per week by an individual) as the best available direct measure of involvement with working.

In a similar fashion, we have chosen the lottery question (Question 48A) as the best available measure of an individual's non-financial commitment to working. The lottery question is future-oriented and asks an individual whether or not he/she would continue working (not necessarily in the same job and/or in the same work situation) if "you won a lottery or inherited a large sum of money and could live comfortably for the rest of your life without working?" Thus, the attempt is to remove the underlying financial rationale or the financial necessity behind working and evaluate commitment to work in non-financial terms, which are essentially psychological or sociological in nature. In the combined national sample of the eight countries, 86.1% of all individuals said they would continue to work even if all financial need were eliminated. The percentage of individuals who would continue to work[5] in individual countries varied from a low of 68.9% in Britain to a high of 96.3% in Yugoslavia. Thus, there is sufficient individual variability in response to the lottery question within the com-

Table 5.5. Correlations between work centrality and measures of involvement with working and commitment to working

	Work Centrality Index Correlated with:	
Country	Q4 — Hours Worked	Q48A — Work Continuation
Belgium	.19***	.14**
Britain	NA	.17**
Germany	.21***	.22***
Israel	.16***	.20***
Japan	.21***	.12***
Netherlands	.17***	.15***
USA	.15***	.20***
Yugoslavia	.19***	.08
Age Groups		
Under 30	.19***	.20***
30–49 years	.26***	.19***
50 and + years	.25***	.24***
Sex Groups		
Male	.21***	.19***
Female	.22***	.21***
Target Groups		
Unemployed	.09*	.26***
Retired	.15***	.19***
Chem. Engineers	.14***	.19***
Teachers	.13***	.16**
Self-Employed	.15***	.10*
Tool- Diemakers	.22***	.26***
White Collar	.31***	.30***
Textile Workers	.24***	.23***
Temporary Workers	.18***	.24***
Students	NA	.22***

* = .05, ** = .01, *** = .001 levels of significance
NA = Not Applicable or Not Available

bined national sample and within each country to utilize it as a measure of non-financial commitment to working.

Following the previous rationale, Table 5.5 presents the relationships between work centrality scores *and* hours worked per week and stated work-continuation intentions. These two relationships are presented for the combined national sample classified by: (1) country, (2) age category, and (3) sex category. Finally, the table presents (for a different sample, the target group samples) the two relationships for each target group combined across countries.

As shown in Table 5.5, the relationships between work centrality and the involvement and commitment measures are uniformly positive and significantly different from 0 in 43 of 44 instances. Thus, clearly, there is a positive low to moderate relationship between work centrality *and* involvement with working and commitment to working whether we look within nations, within age categories, within sex groups, or within occupational groups (target groups).

The consistency of this relationship provides uniform but moderate support for the theoretical proposition previously stated and reinforces our view that work centrality is one important work meaning which probably has significant impact on individuals, organizations, and societies. We would argue that work centrality for the individual human organism is a fundamental concept which is nearly universal within industrial societies. Work centrality is a useful scientific concept which probably has important practical and policy-relevant implications for those concerned with the present and the future of work, working, and working lives.

Notes

(1) The decision rules were based on the number of life areas the respondent gave (a) fewer points than working, (b) points equal to working, and (c) more points than working. Since there are five life areas (including work), there are 15 possible scoring combinations. The decision rule adopted (and confirmed by a biplot of the 15 v 3 matrix which has a row for each possible score and columns as noted in *a*, *b*, *c* above) is as follows: If working ranked first (all other life areas were given fewer points than work), the response is *scored* as 5; a rank of second (one life area given more points than work and the rest fewer, or no life areas given more points than work but one or two areas equal to work) *scored* 4; third (two life areas greater than work, or one greater and one or two equal, or none greater but three or all four others equal) was *scored 3*; fourth (three greater, or two greater, and one or two equal, or one greater and two or three equal) *scored* as 2; and fifth (four greater than work, or three greater and one equal) *scored 1*.

(2) It should be noted that the "combined national samples from the eight countries" in the present chapter includes actual national samples from seven countries and our best representation of a national sample from Yugoslavia which is defined as the combined target group samples from Yugoslavia.

(3) Since low scores of 1, 2, or 3 on Question 29 were quite rare (ranging from 2% in Japan to 11% in Germany), they were transformed to a value of 1, while scores of 4 were transformed to a value of 2, scores of 5 to a value of 3, scores of 6 to a value of 4, and scores of 7 to a value of 5. Scores on Item 30c were transformed to represent the importance rank of working compared to the importance of other life areas as previously specified.

(4) A similar conclusion is reached if one contrasts average differences in work centrality scores between all country pairs: *with* average differences between all age pairs, *with* male versus female difference. Average differences between nations and between age groups are greater than sex differences.

(5) The issue of whether there are important distinctions between those who would continue in the same job and those who would want a different work situation can be considered by reviewing relevant data from chapters 8, 12 and 13.

Chapter 6

Societal Norms about Working

Introduction

The normative views about working which are held by a society or by particular groups within a society have been a topic of interest for scholars periodically throughout the ages (as indicated in chapters 1 and 2). Currently, the interest in normative views about working is again keen. This current interest seems propelled by actual and anticipated changes in many facets of work and working. Technological change, organizational restructuring, an increasing number of women in the labor force, increased educational levels in labor forces, shifts of employment toward Third World countries, and growth in the service sector in many countries—all seem likely to influence the types and amounts of work to be done in industrialized nations and the normative views toward working.

One question which emerges from consideration of these important trends is: To what extent are these changes in work and working situations accompanied by changes in the meaning of working in the lives of individuals and, consequently, by changes in the standards people utilize as a basis for reasoning about work? A number of authors suggest that the so-called *traditional work ethic* view—that work is good and non-work is bad—has strong survival power (Kahn and Weiner, 1973; Sessions, 1978). It is apparent that this traditional work ethic which sees work as a duty or moral obligation traces its recent heritage to the Protestant Work Ethic as developed by Weber (1922) and later articulated by others such as Blood (1969). However, there is a counterview on this issue (Macarov, 1980; Rosow, 1981; Schmidt, 1974), which suggests that the traditional work ethic is being replaced through the development of standards about working which are more heavily based (than in the past) on values such as leisure, family life, educational pursuits, and the dominance of work rights over work duties.

This chapter reports on the investigation of two societal norms about working which focus on *rights* and *duties* connected to working and, thus, are viewed as important to contemporary discussion about the future of working (see also the relevant discussion on this topic in chapters 1, 2, and 4). Our analyses focus on the work norms of major groups of people (national labor force samples; target groups samples; and groupings by age, sex, and educational level), which is in keeping with our notion that we are dealing with *societal level* norms and not simply an aggregation of individual views.

Entitlement and obligation norms toward working

The *entitlement* norm as developed and used in this chapter represents the underlying work rights of individuals and the work-related responsibility of organizations and society toward all individuals. This norm includes the notions that all members of society are entitled to meaningful and interesting work, proper training to obtain and continue in such work, and the right to participate in work/method decisions.

The *obligation* norm developed and used here represents the underlying duties of all individuals to society with respect to working. This norm includes the notions that everyone has a duty to contribute to society by working, a duty to save for their own future, and the duty to value one's work, whatever its nature.

The measurement of these two societal norms comes from the extent of agreement with the 10 normative statements about working entitlements and obligations in Q47 (Appendix 3.1). It should be noted again that we have utilized the evaluative rather than the descriptive meaning of norms, that is, norms tell us what should be, not what is. The 10 statements involve general expectations about appropriate behavior concerning working.

Two indices (entitlement index and obligation index) have been derived from subsets of the 10 statements as described in Chapter 3. After a number of principal components analyses, it was found that statements in items 47A, 47E, 47G, and 47I (entitlement items), and 47B, 47D, and 47J (obligation items)—per country—generally form the appropriate dimension. Only in Yugoslavia does one complex factor appear that merges the two dimensions (see Table 6.1).

Location of countries in the work norm space

Since we consider these two work norms as primarily societal or group representations as opposed to individual representations, it is most appropriate to focus on group comparisons (e.g., nations). It also seems appropriate to explore the extent to which the two norms might be considered balanced within a country in terms of relative agreement with the items defining entitlement and obligation. Since we lack an adequate standard for translation of levels of agreement with statements comprising each norm into *balance* terms for each country (i.e., meaning equivalence on the two norm indices), we have chosen to report a crude measure of balance obtained from the total societal norm space as defined by the two norms in all countries. It will be recognized that this crude indicator of balance between the norms in a given country is relative in nature to within country differences in norm agreement levels as referenced against such differences in all countries. For some purposes, such a procedure would be inappropriate; we attempt, however, not to make interpretations that are produced primarily by the method of analysis chosen. Also, the potential sample-specific bias that might be introduced by such a relative procedure probably is minimized where we have national samples to represent the norms for a country.

Table 6.1. Factor structure of societal norms per country (national samples); (Q47, 47A, 47E, 47G, 47I, 47B, 47D, 47J)

Country	N	Items loading with ≥.35*	Label
Belgium	449	B D J	Obligation
		A E G I	Entitlement
Germany	1267	G I E A	Entitlement
		J B D	Obligation
Britain	798	G I E A	Entitlement
		J B D	Obligation
Israel	937	A G I (E.31)	Entitlement
		B D (J.29)	Obligation
Japan	3085	A E G I	Entitlement
		(B.34) D J	Obligation
Netherlands	975	(A.31) E G I	Entitlement
		B D J	Obligation
United States	992	(A.33) (E.28) G I	Entitlement
		(B.31) (D.32)	Obligation without J
Yugoslavia**	536	B (D.34) E G I J	Entitlement Obligation
		A	Right to retraining and reemployment

* In parentheses are loadings smaller than .35 but still defining the dimension.
** Target group data.

NOTE: The seven items from Q47 which are used here to create the entitlement and obligation indices are included in the eight items which defined the same dimensions in the analysis reported in Chapter 4. The fact that one item is excluded here seems to be a function of national representative samples being separately considered here while Chapter 4 utilized a combined sample of all target groups in all countries. The similarity, however, in two distinct sets of samples at different aggregation levels increases confidence in the core meanings of the two dimensions.

Figure 6.1 presents the location of countries in the societal norm space as defined by the entitlement and obligation indices. T scores with a mean of 50 and a standard deviation (SD) of 10 are presented as explained in Chapter 3. The orthogonal characterization of the two indices in Figure 6.1 is based on the orthogonality of the entitlement and obligation factors as reported in Chapter 4.

Figure 6.1 portrays two major features of the societal norm space: (1) relative levels of agreement with *each* norm among the eight countries, and (2) relative levels of balance between the two norms in *each* country. It can be observed that Yugoslavia, Israel, and the United States show the highest agreement with the obligation norm; Japan, Germany, Britain, and Belgium are in a middle category in this respect; the Netherlands shows least agreement with the obligation norm. Concerning the entitlement norm: Yugoslavia, Netherlands, Germany, Belgium, and Israel show the most agreement; Japan and Britain are in a middle category in this respect; the United States clearly shows the lowest agreement with the entitlement norm.

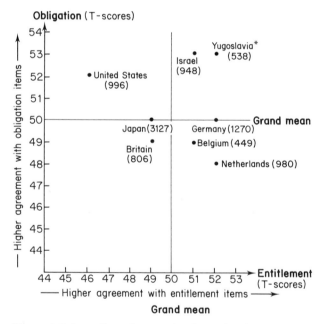

Figure 6.1. Location of countries in societal norms space.

* Target group data. NOTE: Country results on the two indices are weighted equally regardless of sample size. Country numbers are shown in parentheses. Differences of 1–2 T-scores points between samples compared here can be considered significantly different in a statistical sense which, of course, does not necessarily imply a meaningful difference in practical terms.

In terms of the relative balance between the two norms in each country, the following categorization is portrayed in the data:

1. Israel and Yugoslavia show balanced levels of agreement with the two norms and are balanced at a rather high level of agreement with the norms. One could speculate that this observation might be due, in part, to an "agreement" response-set bias operating in these two countries, but we have no external evidence supporting this possibility. It should be remembered, however, that the factor structure of the two norms was distinctly different in Yugoslavia than was the case in the other countries. Generally, it seems most reasonable tentatively to accept the balance designation at a high level of agreement for these two countries, but to be cautious about interpretations.

2. Japan and Britain show balanced levels of agreement with the two norms and are balanced at a more average level of agreement with the norms.

3. Belgium and Germany show a moderate degree of imbalance in levels of agreement with the two norms. Entitlement agreement is somewhat greater than obligation agreement in both countries.

4. The United States and the Netherlands show a relatively high level of imbalance in levels of agreement with the two norms. The imbalance in these two countries, however, is in opposite directions. For the Netherlands, agreement is relatively much greater for the entitlement norm and much lower for the obligation norm. In the United States, agreement is relatively much lower for the entitlement norm than for the obligation norm.

The implications of these country-level differences in each of the two norms and of different balance configurations within groups of countries is far from clear at the present time. Intuitively, it would seem desirable in many respects if there were a reasonable balance between the duty and rights orientation toward work and working in a society at any given point in time. If this intuition is basically correct, then, the United States and the Netherlands would be in the most questionable position. Perhaps, the Netherlands is *too* entitlement oriented (given its obligation level) and the United States is not sufficiently entitlement oriented (given its obligation level), or perhaps, the focus should be upon the obligation levels given each country's entitlement level. In terms of contemporary discussion about the traditional work ethic, the Netherlands position might be interpreted as a move *away* from the traditional work ethic and the United States position as an instance of support for *continuation* of the traditional work ethic. Evaluation of the desirability of either position is certainly value-laden, and cogent arguments can be made in either direction. It would seem most useful to recognize these normative differences in rights and duty expressions as important statements made by each labor force which should be evaluated within the context of each nation's situation and aspirations concerning the role of working in life. Clearly, we observe country differences in the levels of the two norms across countries and in the degree of balance between the two norms in different countries. Also, there is similarity of norm and balance levels among countries. What we understand about the societal norms toward working in our eight countries—at the present time—is much more appropriate to reasonable hypothesis generation than to hypothesis testing. The data reported in chapters 10 and 12, where these work norms are related to various work outcomes and MOW cluster compositions, provide specifics for several hypotheses.

Location of target groups in work norm space

Figure 6.2 shows the location of each target group (combined across all countries) in the societal norm space in a similar manner to that done for countries.

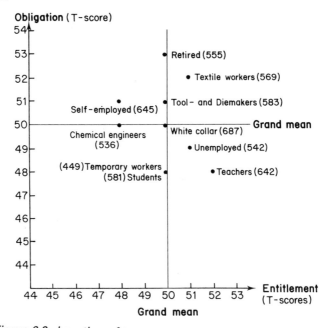

Figure 6.2. Location of target groups in societal norms space.

NOTE: Due to sample design, target groups have approximately the same size in each country. Target group numbers are shown in parentheses.

As shown in Figure 6.2, target groups (combined across countries) vary more on the obligation than on the entitlement norm. It seems plausible that target-group variation on the obligation norm might be more a function of age, gender, and educational differences (since we observe target group differences on obligation scores and there are clear differences in these classifying characteristics across the target groups). Variation in entitlement, however, may be more a function of aspects of nation or culture.

In terms of the previously introduced concept of balance between the two norms, textile workers, tool- and diemakers, white-collar employees, chemical engineers, temporary workers, students, and the unemployed show a rough balance between the obligation and entitlement norms. The other three target groups show less balance between the two norms. The self-employed target group is imbalanced in a direction away from entitlement orientation; the retired target group is imbalanced toward higher-obligation orientation; and the teacher target group is imbalanced toward entitlement orientation.

It seems of interest that generally across countries, students and unemployed target groups do not deviate greatly from the employed groups either in level on the two norms or on balance between the two norms. Certainly, no general, or large, shift away from the traditional work ethic is indicated by this aspect of our data from the eight countries.

Since it was observed that countries differ considerably in their location within the overall societal norm space, it seems appropriate to look at target-group location in the societal norm space in a way that gives consideration to a country's location. Thus, Figures 6.3–6.7 show the location of target groups per country where target group location is determined by the target group's mean score on the entitlement index and the obligation index as compared to the norm space created on combined national samples (i.e., Figure 6.1).

In looking at Figures 6.3–6.7, it is at once apparent that the location of a country in the overall societal norm space has a substantial impact on the relative location of most of its target groups. In 53 out of a possible 65 instances in Figures 6.3–6.7, target-group samples for a country are located in the similar quadrant of the societal norm space as was indicated by country location. This 80% location similarity also is approached quite closely whether the focus is on target-group distribution over each country or country distribution over each target group and again shows the powerful effect of aspects of country upon target-group location. Yet, as we observed in Figure 6.2, there are overall target-group (or occupational) differences in degrees of entitlement and obligation orientation. These findings reaffirm the suggestion of Hofstede (1980, 1982) to take both

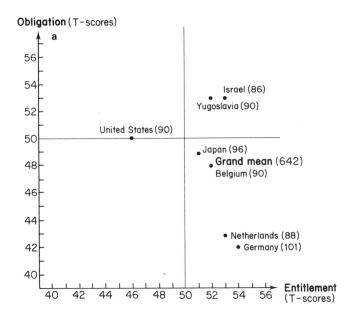

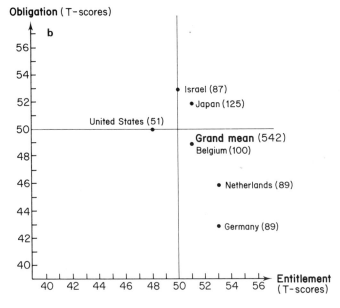

Figure 6.3. Location of teachers (a) and unemployed (b) in societal norm space per country.

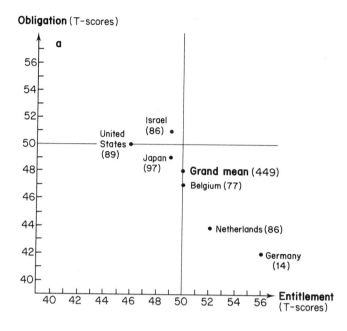

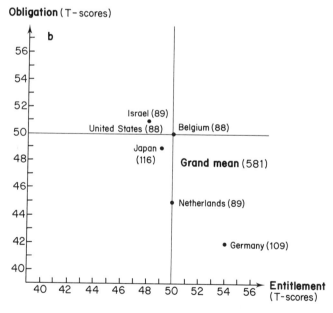

Figure 6.4. Location of temporary workers (a), students (b),

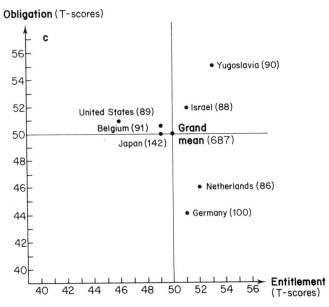

Figure 6.4. (continued). white-collar employees (c) in societal norm space per country.

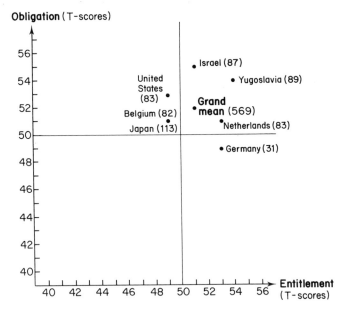

Figure 6.5. Location of textile workers in societal norm space per country.

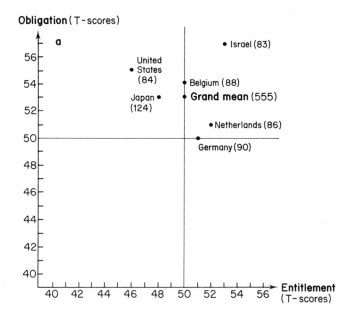

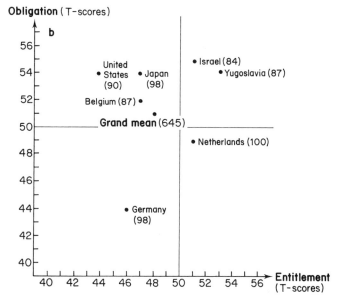

Figure 6.6. Location of retired (a), self-employed (b),

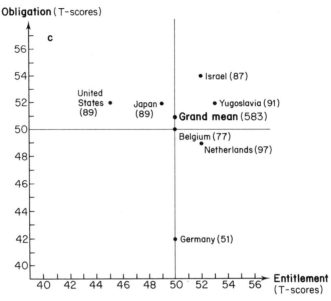

Figure 6.6 (continued). tool- and diemakers (c) in societal norm space per country.

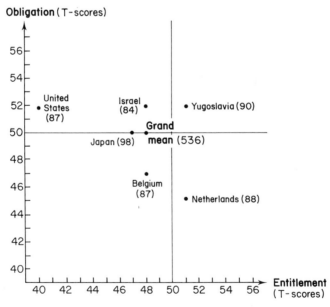

Figure 6.7. Location of chemical engineers in societal norm space per country.

nationality and occupational level into account when studying work-related values.

Focusing on the relative position of target groups of different countries (as shown in Figures 6.3–6.7), the following observations seem warranted:

1. German and Dutch teachers and the unemployed deviate most from the general position of those two target groups. The deviation is toward a higher entitlement orientation (see Figure 6.3).

2. German and Dutch temporary workers, white-collar employees, and students again deviate most from the generally balanced position of these three target groups. The deviation is again toward a higher entitlement orientation. Yugoslavian white-collar employees are both more entitlement-oriented and more obligation-oriented than the target group in general (see Figure 6.4).

3. American textile workers deviate most from the general pattern of balance at a relatively high level of agreement with both the obligation and the entitlement norms. This deviation is away from an entitlement orientation (see Figure 6.5).

4. Israeli, American, Dutch, and German members of the retired and tool- and diemaker target groups deviate from the general pattern in the expected direction, given their country position in the overall societal norm space. Germany and Japan deviate from the expected pattern (given their overall position) for the retired target group, while the position of the target groups in the other countries is as would be expected by their overall national location (see Figure 6.6).

5. Each nation's chemical-engineer target group occupies the societal norm space that would be expected from the respective country location. The target group, in general, is balanced but shows somewhat low entitlement scores (see Figure 6.7).

The influence of sex, age, and educational level on the societal norms about working

Important influences in labor-market development in the future would seem to be gender (more women will be involved in working); age (youth unemployment problems and increasing number of retired due to decreasing retirement ages); and educational level (likely will increase, due to the effect of individual growth as a central life value and as a possible solution for youth unemployment). In the relevant literature, these same three variables are identified as important because they represent differentiating standards toward working (Buchholz, 1978; Iso-Ahola and Buttimer,

1981). Thus, even though our conceptualization of societal norms about working is focused at the country level, it seems useful to explore the observed influence of age, gender, and education ·on societal norm data.

In four countries with quite different locations in the societal norm space (Belgium, the Netherlands, United States, and Yugoslavia), female respondents show slightly higher entitlement orientation than do male respondents. In the other four countries, there are no gender differences in terms of agreement with entitlement items as reflected in the entitlement index (see Table 6.2). In all countries but Britain and Yugoslavia (where gender shows no relationship to obligation orientation), male respondents are more obligation-oriented than are females. The greatest difference in this respect occurs in Belgium (see Table 6.2). The influence of gender is clearly larger and more general over countries on obligation orientation than on entitlement orientation. The finding that males have higher obligation scores than females in six of eight countries may be due to the long socialization histories males have had as the working sex (in paid employment terms). We would speculate that this difference has changed and will continue to change as women have longer tenure and more equal opportunity in employment. The rate of such change might well be different in different countries.

Table 6.2. Entitlement and obligation scores (mean T-scores) per category per country (national sample data)

Country	N	Entitlement scores		Obligation scores	
		Males	Females	Males	Females
Belgium	(448)	51	52	50	46
Germany	(1270)	52	52	51	49
Britain	(773)	49	49	49	49
Israel	(906)	52	52	54	52
Japan	(3059)	50	50	50	49
Netherlands	(974)	53	54	48	46
United States	(990)	46	47	52	51
Yugoslavia*	(537)	52	53	53	53

* Target group data.

The relationship between age and entitlement-orientation levels is not substantial in most countries, and the direction of the relationship is highly inconsistent. Certainly, there is no *general* support in these data for the frequently expressed notion that the younger worker is more entitlement orientated than his/her older colleagues. Indeed, the support for that proposition in our data is almost nil, except in the case of the United States, where such an argument could be made and slightly supported in these data (see Table 6.3). However, agreement with the obligation norm clearly increases with age in all countries.

Table 6.3. Entitlement and obligation scores (mean T-scores) per age category per country (national sample data)

Country	N	Entitlement scores			Obligation scores		
		Young (under 30)	Middle (30–50)	Old (over 50)	Young (under 30)	Middle (30–50)	Old (over 50)
Belgium	(448)	52	51	52	45	50	53
Germany	(1270)	53	52	52	47	50	53
Britain	(773)	49	49	51	47	49	53
Israel	(906)	51	52	52	52	53	55
Japan	(3059)	50	50	49	48	50	51
Netherlands	(974)	53	53	53	46	48	51
United States	(990)	48	46	45	51	52	52
Yugoslavia*	(537)	53	52	53	52	53	55

* Target group data.

Education has no consistent or substantial relationship with level of entitlement orientation over countries. However, educational level is clearly related to obligation orientation: the higher the educational level, the lower the agreement with the obligation norm in all countries. Two minor exceptions are Japanese respondents with university-level education and British respondents who have completed their full-time education at 21 years or over. While the magnitude of the relationship varies by country, it is most pronounced in the Netherlands and Belgium.

Summary of societal norms results

To the extent that we have been successful in identifying and developing two societal norm indices that truly tap a significant portion of the normative rights expectations about working and the normative duty obligations to organizations and society through working, our findings undoubtedly have value.

First, it seems clear that there are country differences in the measured levels of work entitlement and work obligation and in the degree of balance between these two norms within countries. Israeli and Yugoslavian work forces appear to be in a state of general balance in terms of relative agreement with the entitlement norm and the obligation norm. This balance occurs at a high level of agreement with both norms, but we are

Table 6.4. Entitlement and Obligation Scores (Mean T-scores) per Educational Level Category per Country (National Sample Data)

Country	N	Entitlement scores					Obligation scores				
		Primary	Secondary	Some college	University level		Primary	Secondary	Some college	University level	
Belgium	(448)	51	52	52	50		53	49	46	45	
Germany	(1265)	52	53	50	52		49	51	51	48	
Britain**	(773)	51	49	49	48	49	52	50	48	47	49
Israel	(906)	52	52	53	51		55	53	53	51	
Japan	(3059)	49	50	50	49		52	50	48	50	
Netherlands	(974)	53	53	54	53		52	48	45	42	
United States	(990)	47	47	47	45		52	52	51	51	
Yugoslavia*	(537)	54	53	53	50		54	54	53	52	

* Target group data.
** Levels of educational level in Britain: age of completion of full-time education: < 14 y, 15 y, 16–18 y, 19–20 y, < 21 y.

unsure of the correct interpretation to place upon the level of agreement at which balance takes place. Japan and Britain also show a balanced position concerning the two norms, and the balance takes place at more modest or average level of norm agreement. As suggested earlier, a reasonable level of balance between rights expectations and duty obligations in the working role seems intuitively desirable. Perhaps, one needs to know more, however, than we currently do to assess the meaning of balanced societal norms toward working. It might be informative to know what proportion of the labor force in a country is in reasonable balance between work rights and duties rather than only whether there is an overall match in the two norms at the country level. It also might be informative to know the characteristics of the balanced and less balanced groups in a given work force.

Belgium and Germany show somewhat of an imbalance between the two norms in the direction of entitlement orientation. The Netherlands is highly imbalanced toward entitlement and away from obligation, while the United States is highly imbalanced in the exact opposite direction. In toto, the country results on the entitlement and obligation norms toward working offer little general support for the position that the work ethic is in severe danger; it does not seem to be. One can note, however, that the meaning of working might be changing in countries such as Germany and the Netherlands where the societal norm imbalance is toward entitlement and where Work Centrality is relatively low.

Secondly, we observe that target-group results in a country are strongly influenced by the position of that country in the overall societal norm space. Perhaps, the major observation about target-group results which bears repeating is that non-employed groups such as students and the unemployed have a work/norm pattern that is similar to many of the employed groups. In terms of work rights and duties, our samples of those about to come into the labor force and those who have been unable to continue in the labor force for 6 months or longer are nearly indistinguishable from their employed counterparts.

The major finding concerning age, gender, and educational relationships to the entitlement and obligation norms is that they very slightly are related to entitlement but rather consistently and strongly related to the obligation norm. The pattern is to find higher-obligation orientation among males, among older members of the work force, and among the less educated members of the labor force. It is this particular subset of the labor force, however, that may well decrease in proportion during the last part of the twentieth century. Will this potential loss of duty orientation to work occur and, if so, will it be generally beneficial or harmful? This is a question that poses weighty challenges to both social science research and policy making.

The two societal norms about working, entitlement, and obligation do seem to provide relevant information and generate a range of hypotheses which will be tested in greater detail in future studies.

Chapter 7

Valued Working Outcomes and Work Goals

Introduction

Systematic information about what outcomes individuals seek from working and what functions are served for the individual through the process of
working are clearly part of the general picture of the meaning of working
(as shown in chapters 2 and 4). Such information sheds light on the basic
question of why people work (and to some extent, on why they exert more
or less effort at work or why they may be more or less effective workers).
Additionally, such information is widely used to explain why individuals
may be satisfied with some jobs or occupations and not with others and
why some work situations are attractive to individuals while other work
situations are unattractive. Finally, such information provides a rationale
for making plausible suggestions concerning ways of designing work organizations which might be optimal for individual, organizational, and societal
purposes at the present time and in the future.

The present chapter is written in the context of the expectations about
the potential importance of valued working outcome data.

A broad assessment of the functions of working

The most useful data in the present study for assessing the relative importance of the broad functions performed for individuals through the process
of working come from the domain entitled "Valued Working Outcomes"
(Question 28). As shown earlier, this domain is based on a typology of
various meanings of work, including a range of both expressive and
instrumental meanings attached to working (see Kaplan and Tausky, 1974;
Tausky and Piedmont, 1967). Question 28 asks each individual to assign a

total of 100 points to six broad functions or outcomes of working to indicate their relative importance in explaining what working means to the individual. The six functions were:

- the status and prestige-producing function of working
- the income-producing function of working
- the time-occupying function of working
- the interpersonal contact function of working
- the societal-service function of working
- the intrinsic or self-expressive function of working.

Table 7.1 shows the mean number of points assigned to each of these functions of working for the country samples. National sample data are presented for the seven countries having national samples and combined target group sample data are presented for Yugoslavia. National samples certainly provide the best representation of the relative importance of the various functions *for a country* but the combined target group samples probably provide a reasonable representation of the importance of the functions for Yugoslavia.

Table 7.1 shows that the *income-producing function* of working is perceived as the most important function by the labor force in every country. On the average, slightly more than one-third of the possible points are assigned to the income-producing function of working. The Japanese and German samples evaluate the income-producing function of working as significantly more important than do their counterparts in other countries, while the sample from the Netherlands evaluates the income-producing function as significantly less important. The other five countries attach about equal importance to the income-producing function of working.

We obtain additional insight into the importance of the income-producing function of working when we observe—for the 8792 individuals in the total of all samples shown in Table 7.1—that:

- Sixty percent of all individuals assign more points to the income-producing function than to any of the other five functions.
- only 3% of all individuals assign the least number of points to the income-producing function as compared to the other five functions.

While there are large differences in the perceived importance of this function among individuals and significant country differences, it does seem clear that a key underlying rationale for working for a majority of individuals is that it provides an income which is needed in one's life.

The *intrinsic function of working* (working being basically interesting and satisfying to the individual) is second in importance in all countries except in Japan where it is third in importance. Israel, the Netherlands,

Table 7.1. Mean number of points out of 100 assigned to working functions (Q.28) by country samples

Country	N	Working provides you with an income that is needed	Working is basically interesting and satisfying to you	Working permits you to have interesting contacts with other people	Working is a useful way for you to serve society	Working keeps you occupied	Working gives you status and prestige
Japan	3180	45.4	13.4	14.7	9.3	11.5*	5.6***
Germany	1264	40.5	16.7	13.1	7.4	11.8	10.1
Belgium	447	35.5	21.3	17.3	10.2	8.7	6.9
Britain	471	34.4	17.9	15.3	10.5	11.0	10.9
Yugoslavia	522	34.1	19.8	9.8	15.1	11.7	9.3
United States	989	33.1	16.8	15.3	11.5	11.3	11.9
Israel	940	31.1	26.2	11.1	13.6	9.4	8.5
Netherlands	979	26.2	23.5	17.9	16.7	10.6	4.9
All countries combined	8792	35.0**	19.5	14.3	11.8	10.8	8.5

* Working keeps you occupied was translated in Japan in such a manner that there is real question about how similar its meaning was to that intended.
** The combined totals weight each country equally regardless of sample size.
*** The mean points assigned by a country to the six functions add to approximately 100 points.

and Belgium show significantly higher scores on the intrinsic function while the other countries are approximately equal. Seventeen percent of the individuals from the total sample assign more points to the intrinsic function than to any other function while 11% assign it the fewest points. Again, we observe significant differences among individuals and between countries in the perceived importance of this function of working. Doing work that is perceived by the individual to be intrinsically interesting and satisfying is an important function of work for many individuals. This does not imply, however, that there is a uniform evaluative framework among individuals as to *what* makes work intrinsically interesting and satisfying; only that being able to perceive your working situation as intrinsically interesting and satisfying is a valued outcome or function of working.

The *interpersonal function* of working (permitting you to have interesting contacts with other people) generally is evaluated as being third in importance. Yugoslavia and Israel are the exceptions to this pattern. Workers from these two countries assign significantly fewer points to this function of working than do their counterparts in the other countries. Eight percent of the individuals in the total sample assign more points to the interpersonal function than to any other function, while 12% assign it the fewest points. On balance, the opportunity to interact with others in the work situation is a moderately important function which working fulfills. Again, we observe large differences among individuals as to the importance of the interpersonal function and two significant country difference from the general pattern.

Working *as a useful way to serve society* generally is viewed as the fourth most important function of working. The Netherlands, Yugoslavia, and Israel assign significantly more points to this function than do the other countries. In the total sample, 6% of the individuals assign more points to working as a useful way to serve society than to any other function, while 21% assign the fewest points to the function. Relatively, the societal-service function of working is of minor importance but to a few (6%) it is most important.

The *time-occupying function* of working generally is allocated about 10% of the total points. There are no large country differences on this function of working and, in a relative sense, it is of minor importance. However, the fact that about 5% of the total sample allocates more points to the time-occupying function than to any other function indicates its importance to some individuals. Twenty percent of the total sample assign the fewest points to this function.

In order of general importance, the *status and prestige-producing function* of working is last. In the total sample, only 4% of the individuals assign more points to the status and prestige-producing function than to any other function, while 33% assign it the fewest points. Workers in the

United States, Britain, and Germany assign this function the most points, while workers in the other countries assign fewer points to the status and prestige-producing function. Clearly, for one-third of our sample, this function is perceived as the least important among those studied.

Further support for the reality and meaning of the importance of these functions of working comes from the responses to Question 28B, "I would like you to tell me, in your own words, what is most important to you about working." Content analysis of these open-end responses from the combined target group samples in all countries shows the pattern[1] of Table 7.2.

Table 7.2. Support for functions of working in order of importance in all countries.

Response category	Percentage of individuals who identify each category
Family support or income	35
Like my work or like working	20
People contact or belonging	18
Accomplishment or creativeness	13
Service to others or contribute to society	9
Gives meaning or goals to my life	8
Self-realization or growth	7
Keeps me occupied or busy	5

[1] See Holvoet, M. (1984) for the content analysis methodology. This open-ended question was used only in target group samples.
[2] Yugoslavia and Britain did not obtain data on this item so response data are based on the other six countries.

While a wide range of other responses occurred, none of them were mentioned by 5% or more of the combined target group samples.[2] The ranking of the first three reasons neatly replicates findings from national samples as shown in Table 7.1.

Work goals

A second way of understanding what is important to individuals in their working life is to focus on a uniform set of work goals or facets of working and to ascertain how important each is to individuals in an absolute sense and in a relative sense. (This is the measurement domain identified as "Importance of work goals" in Figure 2.1 in Chapter 2.) The relevant literature for making work goals or work aspects operational is voluminous and covers job satisfaction, work values, work needs, and incentive preference literature.

Herzberg, Mausner, Peterson, and Capwell (1957) reviewed 16 studies in which employees had been presented with job facets to be rated in terms of their importance. The samples varied markedly with some dissimilarity as well in terms of the sets of job facets investigated and the particular types of ratings or rankings that were employed. On the basis of the results of these studies, Herzberg *et al.* (1957) constructed a detailed composite of the importance ranking of 14 job facets, provided by 11,000 workers that were heterogeneous with regard to education, sex, occupation, and skill level. These facets were: security, interest, opportunity for advancement, appreciation (from supervision), company and management, intrinsic aspects of the job, wages, supervision, social aspects of the job, working conditions, communication, hours, ease, and benefits.

A few years later, Weiss *et al.* (1964) constructed the Minnesota Importance Questionnaire (MIQ), which was designed to measure 20 vocationally relevant need dimensions (to accompany the Minnesota Satisfaction Questionnaire). These need dimensions refer to specific reinforcing conditions which have been found to be important to job satisfaction. The needs were: ability utilization, achievement, activity, advancement, authority, company policies and practices, compensation, co-workers, creativity, independence, moral values, recognition, responsibility, security, social service, social status, supervision/human relations, supervision/technical, variety, and working conditions.

Quinn (1971) reported on the importance ratings of 23 job facets from a national probability sample of 1533 American workers and found that no single job facet was preeminently important. According to workers' mean scores on five summary indices, the most important general aspect of workers' jobs was having sufficient resources to perform adequately. This was followed by, in order of decreasing importance; receiving adequate financial rewards; doing challenging, self-enriching work; having pleasant co-workers; and having a job that was "soft" and undemanding. Quinn's (1971) study had comparable facets for 12 of the 14 facets ranked by Herzberg and others (1957).

Most studies comparing occupational groups have shown systematic occupational differences in the importance rating of various job facets (Friedlander, 1965; Hinrichs, 1968; Hofstede, 1972), although others have shown substantial agreement among diverse employee groups (Ronen, 1970; Starcevich, 1972). Kraut and Ronen (1975) found occupation to be an important predictor of an employee's intent to stay with the organization.

In line with the findings of two cross-national comparisons that emphasized the similarity in importance of job facets among different nationalities (Haire, Ghiselli, and Porter, 1966; Sirota and Greenwood, 1971), Kraut and Ronen (1975) found relatively little difference in the importance of various job facets from country to country.

Table 7.3. Factor loadings on work goals for the total sample (all target groups in all countries) and for combined target groups in each country

Samples	Expressive						Economic							Comfort				Learning			Expressive II			
	E	F	H	K	(A)	(B)	C	G	I	(A)	(B)	(J)	(K)	D	J	(G)	(A)	A	C	(B)	F	H	K	G
All countries combined* (N=5259)	.52	.59	.53	.48			.48	.37	.71					.48	.51			.55	.45					
United States (N=767)	.88	.36			(.34)	.35	.51	.52	.57					.68	.43									
Belgium (N=774)	.66	(.33)				(.34)		(.32)	.66	−.42	−.38			.49	.56			.35	.68					
Germany (N=582)	.60	(.32)			(.34)	.39	.80	.50	.42					.67	.38						.35	.74		
Netherlands (N=882)	.35	.49	.39	.49			.87	(.26)	.46					.48	.59	.43	.43	.42						
Japan (N=1071)		.56	.62		.53		.48	.41	.81					.39	.55		.44							.71
Yugoslavia (N=512)	.69	.48	(.24)	(.27)					.53		−.39	.53	.35	.56		.53		.39	.59					
Israel (N=671)	.55	.55	(.26)	.41	.52		(.21)	(.31)	.60				.54				.68	(.26)	.68		.44			.48

NOTE: All loadings with an absolute value of .35 or greater are shown. Loadings which would be expected to appear for each country sample but did not are shown in parentheses if they were .20 or higher in absolute value.

NOTE: Letters in the table heading identify specific work goals. For example, E identifies Q 32E, "A lot of variety." Letters in parentheses identify specific work goals which were a part of the designated dimension for one or more countries but were not a part of the dimension for the combined sample.

* Britain did not have target group samples so was not included in this analysis.

Previous results generally support the view that women are more oriented than men to the interpersonal facets of their jobs (Centers and Bugental, 1966; Hardin, Reif, and Heneman, 1951; Herzberg *et al.*, 1957; Jurgenson, 1947; Kilpatrick, Cummings, and Jennings, 1964).

In the MOW study, a combined ranking/rating method of facet appraisal was utilized with the target group samples. This procedure roughly attempted to standardize the degree or level of the facet being evaluated by the respondent and was adopted after pilot experimentation with several formats. The Minnesota Importance Questionnaire on development and validation (Weiss *et al.*, 1964) and the more recent review of job satisfaction by Locke (1976) were heavily utilized. Respondents in the present study evaluated 11 facets of work or work goals in terms of their importance (Question 32). All of the 11 facets, with the exception of variety are similar to facets utilized by Quinn (1971) and Quinn and Cobb (1971), and most of them (interesting work, good pay, good job security, convenient work hours, good physical working conditions, good interpersonal relations, good opportunity for promotion) are similar to the facets reported by Herzberg and others (1957).

It was necessary first to inquire about the underlying structure of work goals, much as we did about the general "meaning of working" structure in Chapter 4. Table 7.3 identifies factors and presents factor loadings for the 11 work goals in the international target group sample and for the combined target group in each country. The factor analysis procedures used consisted of principal factor analysis of the 11 work goal importance scores. After iteration, factors with eigenvalues exceeding 1.0 were rotated to simple structure by the varimax procedure. Factor loadings with an absolute value greater than or equal to 0.35 were used in defining factors.

In the international target group sample, four factors explained 56% of the common variance in the 11 work goal items. For comparative purposes, four factors also were extracted from each country's data. The dimension identified in the international target group sample by each factor and the items comprising the dimensions are as follows (see Table 7.3):

Expressive dimension

- Interesting work (work that you really like) (Q32F).
- A good match between your job requirements, your abilities, and your experience (Q32H).
- A lot of variety (Q32E).
- A lot of autonomy (you decide how to do your work) (Q32K).

Economic dimension

- Good pay (Q32I).

- Good opportunity for upgrading or promotion (Q32C).
- Good job security (Q32G).

Comfort dimension

- Good physical working conditions (such as light, temperature, cleanliness, low noise level) (Q32J).
- Convenient work hours (Q32D).

Learning/improvement opportunity dimension

- Opportunity to learn new things (Q32A).
- Good opportunity for upgrading and promotion (Q32C).

As shown in Table 7.3, each country has an *expressive dimension* of work goals which is reasonably similar—but certainly not identical. Differences in the structure of the expressive dimension between countries which should be noted include the following:

- United States, Germany, and Israel show Item 32A, "learning opportunity" to be part of the dimension
- Japan includes Item 32B, "good interpersonal relations" as part of the expressive dimension
- Germany, Japan, and Israel have an additional expressive dimension (identified as Expressive II).

On balance, there is about a 70% equivalence (in qualitative terms) in the structure of the expressive dimension among the seven countries.

The *economic dimension* is structured similarly in all countries except Yugoslavia. Yugoslavia has the most different economic dimension where good pay, good physical working conditions, and a lot of autonomy have positive loadings and good interpersonal relations has a negative loading. In Israel, good physical working conditions is also part of the economic dimension. There is about a 75% qualitative equivalence in the economic dimension across the seven countries.

The *comfort dimension* is reasonably similar across the countries with the exception of Israel where no such dimension can be identified. In Yugoslavia and the Netherlands, the comfort dimension is merged with job security from the economic dimension. In Japan, the comfort dimension includes opportunity for learning. There is a qualitative equivalence of about 80% in the comfort dimension across the seven countries.

A separate *learning/improvement opportunity dimension* is not found in the United States, Germany, or Japan. The Netherlands combines Item 32A, learning opportunity, with Item 32B, good interpersonal relations. Israel, Yugoslavia, and Belgium approximate fairly closely the learning/

improvement dimension found in the international sample. There is an approximate 45% level of qualitative equivalence in this dimension among the seven countries.

In general, there is sufficient common structure in the work goal dimensions within the seven countries (particularly among the first three dimensions) to allow meaningful country comparisons in the relative level of importance of the identified dimensions. As noted previously, similar factor structure across a number of countries does not preclude meaningful level differences among countries.

The relative importance of work goal dimensions among countries

National sample data (and its best approximation in Yugoslavia) certainly provide the best representation for determination of the relative importance of the four general work goal dimensions in each country. It also should be noted that the 11 work goals were ranked from most important to least important by individuals in the national sample data collection

Table 7.4. Relative importance of work goal dimensions (mean ranks) (national sample data)*

Country	N	Expressive dimension		Economic dimension		Comfort dimension		Learning and improvement opportunity dimension	
Netherlands	967	7.06	H	5.08	L	5.31	M	4.34	L
Japan	2897	6.79	H	5.53	M	4.82	L	4.80	L
Belgium	446	6.64	H	6.14	H	4.45	L	5.15	L
United States	988	6.37	H	6.07	H	5.05	L	5.62	M
Yugoslavia	512	6.25	H	5.31	M	5.48	M	5.30	M
Germany	1248	6.18	H	6.59	H	5.05	L	4.72	L
Britain	742	5.99	M	6.40	H	5.49	M	4.91	L
Israel	772	5.81	M	5.71	M	5.40	M	5.56	M
Mean dimension scores across all countries where each country sample is given equal weight regardless of sample size (N=8572)		6.39		5.85		5.13		5.05	

* Target group data was used as the best available estimate of a national sample for Yugoslavia.

NOTE: High values represent more important dimensions.

The dimensions and their item composition utilized in this analysis are those previously found for the combined samples. Thus, each dimension is composed of the same work goal items in each country.

procedure. This is a simpler procedure than was used with the target group samples and was utilized to minimize interviewing time.[3]

Table 7.4 shows the mean rank for each dimension (mean rank of the items in the dimension for each individual summed and divided by the number of individuals) for each country. Thus, the ranks in Table 7.4 portray the relative importance of the work goal dimensions within each country and across countries. To aid in interpretation, the dimension scores have been divided into approximate thirds and designated:

H = High importance (highest 10 scores)
M = Middle importance (middle 12 scores)
L = Low importance (lowest 10 scores)

Table 7.4 permits one to focus on results for a given country across the four work goal dimensions or, alternatively, to focus on results for a given dimension across countries. The general pattern is for the expressive dimension to be most important, the economic dimension to be second in importance, the comfort dimension to be third in importance, and the learning and improvement opportunity dimension[4] to be last in importance. Some deviation from this general pattern is found in the data for all countries but Japan.

Differences and similarities between country pairs in the relative importance of the dimensions can be seen from the data in Table 7.4. The clearest example of country differences is observed in comparing the Netherlands and the United States. In the Netherlands, the expressive dimension is evaluated as being high in importance, the comfort dimension as moderate in importance, and the economic and learning/improvement dimensions are evaluated as being of low importance. In the United States, the expressive and economic dimensions are evaluated high in importance, the learning/improvement dimension is moderate, and comfort is low in importance. The clearest example of country similarities involves Germany and Britain where the ordering of the four dimensions is identical, and the magnitude of the country ranks on the respective dimensions is also relatively similar. It also is apparent that dimension ranks differ much more from high to low in some countries (the Netherlands, for example) while other countries (i.e., Israel) have relatively similar ranks on each of the four dimensions.

The relative importance of individual work goals

It is useful to consider each work goal separately and inquire about the relative importance of these individual work goals. The basic data for this

Table 7.5. Mean ranks and intracountry importance ranks of work goals (national samples)

Work goals	Belgium (N = 446)		Germany (N = 1248)		Israel (N = 772)		Japan (N = 2897)		Netherlands (N = 967)		USA (N = 988)		Yugoslavia (N = 512)*		Britain (N = 742)	
Interesting work	8.25	1	7.26	3	6.75	1	7.38	2	7.59	2	7.41	1	7.47	2	8.02	1
Good pay	7.13	2	7.73	1	6.60	3	6.56	5	6.27	5	6.82	2	6.73	3	7.80	2
Good interpersonal relations	6.34	5	6.43	4	6.67	2	6.39	6	7.19	3	6.08	7	7.52	1	6.33	4
Good job security	6.80	3	7.57	2	5.22	10	6.71	4	5.68	7	6.30	3	5.21	9	7.12	3
A good match between you and your job	5.77	8	6.09	5	5.61	6	7.83	1	6.17	6	6.19	4	6.49	5	5.63	6
A lot of autonomy	6.56	4	5.66	8	6.00	4	6.89	3	7.61	1	5.79	8	5.42	8	4.69	10
Opportunity to learn	5.80	7	4.97	9	5.83	5	6.26	7	5.38	9	6.16	5	6.61	4	5.55	8
A lot of variety	5.96	6	5.71	6	4.89	11	5.05	9	6.86	4	6.10	6	5.62	7	5.62	7
Convenient work hours	4.71	9	5.71	6	5.53	7	5.46	8	5.59	8	5.25	9	5.01	10	6.11	5
Good physical working conditions	4.19	11	4.39	11	5.28	9	4.18	10	5.03	10	4.84	11	5.94	6	4.87	9
Good opportunity for upgrading or promotion	4.49	10	4.48	10	5.29	8	3.33	11	3.31	11	5.08	10	4.00	11	4.27	11

Countries

NOTE
Mean ranks.
Right: The rank of each work goal within a given country. Rank 1 is the *most* important work goal for a country while rank 11 is the *least* important work goal for a country.
* Combined target group data were used for Yugoslavia.

analysis are the mean rank of each of the 11 work goals for each country (national sample data). Table 7.5 presents these data in terms of mean ranks (and in terms of ranking of the 11 mean ranks within each country for ease in visualization).

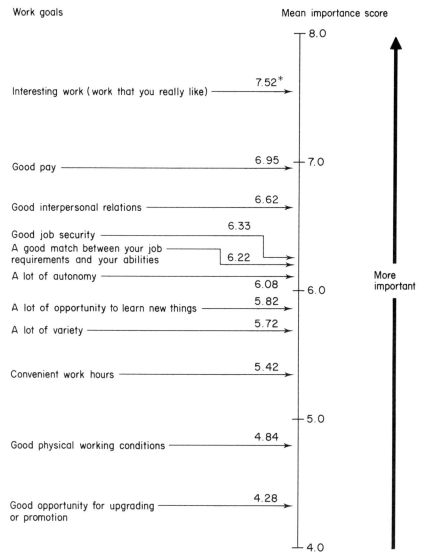

Figure 7.1. Relative importance of work goals for combined national samples (N 8572).

NOTE: Mean rank of work goals for combined national samples where each country is weighted equally regardless of sample size.

Figure 7.1 displays the relative importance of the 11 work goals for the composite national samples where each country sample is given equal weight regardless of sample size.

As shown in Figure 7.1, the most important work goal by a wide margin is to have interesting work. Four countries ranked this goal as the most important aspect of their work life, while four countries ranked it second or third (Japan, Netherlands, Yugoslavia, and Germany). The degree of difference between country importance scores on this aspect of working can be seen in Table 7.5 (as well as the country differences on any work goal). It should be remembered that interesting work was one of the core elements in the expressive dimension of work goals previously discussed.

In terms of importance, the work goals good pay, and good interpersonal relations, are, respectively, next in order. As shown in Table 7.5, the mean ranks on good pay ranged from a high of 7.80 for Britain to a low of 6.27 for the Netherlands. Good interpersonal relations ranged from a high of 7.52 in Yugoslavia to a low of 6.08 in the United States. Again, it should be remembered that good pay was a core element in the economic dimension.

Next in order of respective importance are three work goals: good job security, a good match between you and your job, and a lot of autonomy. Good job security was an element of the economic dimension, while the other two work goals were part of the expressive dimension. As shown in Table 7.5, there are large country differences in the rated importance of each of these work goals, covering a range of mean ranks from 4.69 to 7.83.

A lot of opportunity to learn new things and a lot of variety are next in importance, and they vary in importance to a considerable degree among the eight countries as shown in Table 7.5.

Convenient work hours and good physical working conditions combine to form the comfort dimension, and they are evaluated as next in importance. Again, there are substantial country differences on these two work goals (the major differences being that British workers rate convenient work hours and Yugoslavian workers rate good physical working conditions as considerably more important than do workers in the other countries).

Opportunity for upgrading or promotion is the least important among this set of work goals by a wide margin. It is consistently ranked tenth or eleventh in all countries except Israel where it ranks eighth.

We should note that the preceding discussion focuses on the *relative importance* of the eleven work goals studied. If we refer back to the target group data collection (see Appendix A3.1., Q32) and look at the absolute scale of importance which individuals used to evaluate the work goals, we see an importance range varying from 15 (extremely important) to 1 (of little importance). The lowest mean score on this 15-point scale by any country on any work goal was 5.7, while the highest was 12.4. Thus, all of the group means range from *of some importance* to *very important*. It should be noted that we are not dealing with unimportant work goals for groups but with work goals which range from a modest level of importance (of some importance) to a high level of importance (very important).

Age, sex, and occupational differences in the importance of work goals

Table 7.6 presents the ranking of work goals (national samples for all countries combined) by each of three age groups and for males and females.

As shown in Table 7.6, there is both similarity among the work goal rankings by the three age groups and systematic age effects. Interesting work is ranked as most important and good pay is ranked as second in importance by each age group. Opportunity to learn is consistently less important as age increases. A good match between your job requirements and your abilities and experience was rated seventh in importance for the younger age group and fifth for the other age groups. A likely reason for this finding is that the young workers may be more eager to experiment with different work settings and roles and have not crystallized their work personalities to the extent that longer-term workers have. The more important rankings given to variety and learning opportunity by younger workers would lend some support to this possible explanation. In many industrialized countries, the higher ranking of job security by the older age group may signify the greater impact of actual and potential unemployment for this age group in recent years. The importance of a lot of autonomy at work increases with increasing age; good interpersonal relations are less important for the older age group.

On balance, age differences in the relative importance of work goals are moderate in magnitude in general when one looks at workers from all the eight countries together, although specific work goals do seem to be related to age.

The work goal rankings for males and females also show both similarities and differences. Both groups rank "interesting work" and "good pay" as important work goals while "good physical working conditions" and "good opportunity for upgrading and promotion" are the least important work goals. The major differences in importance ranks between males and females occur on the goals "good interpersonal relations," "convenient work hours," "good job security," and "a lot of autonomy." The first two goals are substantially more important to females than to males, while the

Table 7.6. Work goal ranking by age and by sex (national samples)*

Work goal	Age category			Sex	
	30 and under years	31–50 years	Over 50 years	Male	Female
	N = 2542	N = 4353	N = 1650	N = 5338	N = 3215
Interesting work	1	1	1	1	1
Good pay	2	2	2	2	3
Good interpersonal relations	3	3	6	5	2
Good job security	5	4	3	3	6
Good match between requirements and abilities	7	5	5	6	4
A lot of autonomy	8	6	4	4	9
A lot of opportunity to learn	4	7	10	8	7
A lot of variety	6	8	7	7	8
Convenient work hours	9	9	8	9	5
Good physical conditions	11	10	9	10	10
Good opportunity for promotion	10	11	11	11	11

* Each country was weighted equally in arriving at the rankings regardless of the sample size in the country.

NOTE: Rank 1 is the *most* important work goal, while Rank 11 is the *least* important work goal.

Table 7.7. *Work goal ranking by target groups (target group samples)*

				Target group						
Work goal	Retired $N = 573$	Unemployed $N = 556$	Students $N = 592$	Chemical engineers $N = 549$	Teachers $N = 652$	Self-employed $N = 665$	Tool- and Diemakers $N = 598$	Textile workers $N = 588$	White-collar $N = 695$	Temporary workers $N = 465$
Interesting work	1	1	1	1	1	1	2	6	1	1
Good pay	3	2	2	4	9	3	1	1	2	4
Good interpersonal relations	2	4	4	3	2	6	3	3	3	2
Opportunity to learn	5	3	3	2	3	4	4	7	4	3
Good job security	4	5	6	9	8	9	5	2	5	10
Match between requirements and abilities	6	8	10	5	4	5	9	9	9	7
A lot of autonomy	7	9	11	7	5	2	11	10	11	6
A lot of variety	9	10	7	6	6	7	8	11	8	8
Good physical working conditions	8	7	8	10	10	8	6	5	10	9
Convenient hours of work	10	6	9	11	7	10	10	4	7	5
Good opportunity for promotion	11	11	5	8	11	11	7	8	6	11

NOTE: Rank 1 is the *most* important work goal while rank 11 is the *least* important work goal.

reverse is true for the latter two work goals. These general patterns are similar to those reported in the literature but one should be aware that age, sex, and occupational differences undoubtedly are somewhat confounded in this presentation as well as in reports of many other studies. Chapters 8 and 10 examine these interactive effects in more detail.

The importance rankings of work goals by each target group (combined across all countries) are shown in Table 7.7. As has been reported in other literature, there are some substantial differences in the rated importance of work goals by the target groups in our sample. On the first four work goals listed in Table 7.7, there is considerable similarity in importance ranking across the target groups with the exception of one target group on each work goal. Textile workers, for example, assign less importance than do other target groups to interesting work and opportunity to learn. Teachers assign much less importance to good pay and self-employed to good interpersonal relations than do their counterparts. The importance ranks across target groups differ most on the importance of good job security and a lot of autonomy. Job security is relatively less important to professional groups and temporary workers (groups that may have to worry less about unemployment) and more important to the other target groups, particularly for textile workers (who have experienced considerable job loss in most industrialized countries). Having a lot of autonomy is highly important to the self-employed, moderately important to four groups (teachers, temporary workers, chemical engineers, and retired) and low in importance to the remaining five target groups. The comfort goals are most important to textile workers and least important for chemical engineers. Students value promotion opportunity most highly while the other target groups vary in importance ranking from sixth to eleventh. For a consideration of the relationship between organizational level and work goal preferences, see Chapter 11.

On balance, our data reveal a general similarity among target groups in the importance rankings of work goals as well as some target group specific differences. The extent to which these effects are functions of occupational role expectations, actual work experiences, and target group similarities because of selection criteria utilized or because of attractiveness of target groups to similar kinds of individuals is difficult to specify and the reader is referred to chapters 8 and 10 for further exploration.

Summary of valued working outcomes

It seems clear that most individuals among the eight countries express the view that providing an income for themselves and their families is the dominant underlying reason or rationale for working. It is in this sense that one could correctly say that the major reason *why* people work is to secure an income (to purchase those items needed or desired at the present time or in the future). It is also true, however, that there are other important reasons why people work and that there are non-financial outcomes from working that are highly valued. If this latter were not true in a very powerful way, why, for example, do over two-thirds of the individuals in each country say that they would continue to work even if they had enough money to live comfortably for the rest of their lives without working (see Chapter 5)? Or why, for example, does the work goal, "interesting work," have an importance rank that is considerably higher than that for the work goal, "good pay"? Or why is the Expressive II dimension of work goals evaluated as more important than the economic dimension in six of our eight countries? Clearly, the reasons and rationales for working and the valued working outcomes that are being sought from working are multi-dimensional and interactive and must be viewed in this way. The economic underpinning of work and working is powerful but not all-powerful.

Figure 7.2 portrays one view of our data concerning the multifaceted area of valued working outcomes and work goals.

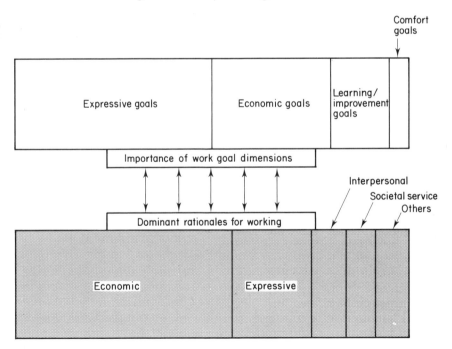

Figure 7.2. Summary diagram of valued working outcomes and work goals.

As shown in Figure 7.2, our results are best understood if we clearly show that valued working outcomes should be considered at two levels of abstraction.

1. There is a general level which really identifies a *dominant rationale for working* or the *basic reasons why individuals are working*. Here, the economic rationale is predominant for about 55% of individuals, the expressive rationale is predominant for about 20% of individuals, the interpersonal rationale is predominant for about 9% of individuals, the societal service rationale is predominant for about 7% of individuals, and other rationales are predominant for about 9% of individuals. These basic rationales, however, may have limited utility for understanding individual behavior that takes place within the work place if viewed in isolation.

2. We have a less general level of valued working outcomes which identify the *important work goal dimensions which people prefer to find or obtain in their work*. This level seems closer to the day-to-day reality of working lives. Here, we find that the expressive dimension of work goals is most important for about 50% of individuals, the economic dimension is most important for about 30%, the learning and improvement dimension is most important for about 15%, and the comfort dimension is most important for about 5%. We would suggest that these work goal preferences are not in opposition to or do not contradict the basic rationales for working. Rather, our understanding of each in a complementary sense should enhance our knowledge. Thus, it may not be contradictory to observe that the economic rationale for working is dominant for a majority of working people and, at the same time, expect that choices made by the same people between two hypothetical jobs could be influenced more by expressive concerns than by economic concerns. *Why one works and what one wants from working* are related but not identical concepts.

Indeed, in a general sense, all of the major meaning of work variables need to be considered as interacting in their influence on the broad area of work behavior. We isolate them only to gain better understanding and to describe them more easily, but attempt to put them back together in several concluding chapters.

Notes

(1) See Holvoet (1984) for the content analysis methodology. This open-ended question was used only in target group samples.

(2) Yugoslavia and Britain did not obtain data on this item so response data are based on the other six countries.

(3) Work goal data for Yugoslavia and Israel were collected using a ranking/rating method of response. These data were converted to ranks 1–11 for each individual to give them an identical scale as was the case for the other countries.

(4) Again, it should be noted that this dimension was least similar in structure among the countries.

(5) Different target groups were initially considered as representing occupational and thus to some extent organizational level. Further analysis is required to test this presumption.

Chapter 8

The Meaning of Working in Terms of Preferences

Introduction

In this chapter, our aim is to present one possible way of thinking about the value dimensions of the meaning of working as they relate to preferences for jobs and leisure. A job can be described in terms of a set of relevant characteristics such as the tasks it contains, products or services produced, degree of autonomy, and so on. Each job characteristic can be viewed as a set of states. When describing a job, we specify which state the job possesses. By considering several job characteristics and specifying a state for each of them, we obtain a pattern of states which we call a "job image." A pattern of states, such as a lot of autonomy, a lot of variety, and average pay is an example of a three-component job image. If S1, states of autonomy; S2, states of variety; and S3, states of pay are distinguished, then S1 × S2 × S3 different three-component job images can be defined in terms of autonomy, variety, and pay.

In general, if m job characteristics *C1, C2,* . . . *Cm* are considered, and if there are sets of *S1, S2,* . . . *Sm* distinguishable states, then choosing a state from each of them yields an m-component job image, and product S1 * S2 * . . . * Sm gives the number of different m-component job images which can be defined in terms of characteristics C1, C2, . . . Cm. An m-component job image can be defined rigorously (see Antoncic, 1984) as an ordered m-tuple, i.e., as an element of the Cartesian product C1 × C2 × . . . × Cm. The number of different m-component job images which can be defined in terms of characteristics C1, C2, . . ., Cm is the number of elements of the Cartesian product C1 × C2 × . . . × Cm.

Two job images are said to be *conforming* if they have the same number of components and if their components refer to the same job characteristics. Thus, for the job images:

A = a lot of autonomy, a lot of variety, average pay
B = a lot of autonomy, a lot of variety
C = a lot of autonomy, a lot of variety, no chance for upgrading
D = hardly any autonomy, no variety, pay 20% above average

we see that A and D are the only conforming images.

Suppose a job has been described in terms of three relevant characteristics. This means a three-component job image has been determined. If another two job characteristics are taken into consideration, these characterizations extend the former three-component job image into a five-component job image. Any $m + k$-component job image, where $K > 1$, is an *extension* of an m-component job image, if each job characteristic which is considered in the m-component job image is included in the extension, and if the corresponding components of the two job images are equal.

People prefer some jobs over others. We assume that each person can express, at least, a weak preference for every pair of jobs. Following Suppes (1957), we can take weak preference as a primitive notion to define strict preference or indifference. Between two jobs, exactly one of the following conditions holds: a person (1) strictly prefers Job A to Job B, (2) strictly prefers Job B to Job A, and (3) is indifferent to jobs A and B. In the theory of preferences, this is known as the *trichotomy* condition (see, for example, Fararo, 1973; 91).

We now raise the question of whether a common attribute may be underlying the preferences of individuals among the alternative jobs. It is reasonable to expect that preferences for jobs are associated with job characteristics. If two jobs are available to a person, they are expected to choose the job which is seen as being in better agreement with their preferences. This leads to the assumption that job images represent the multidimensional attribute which accounts for the preferences referring to jobs. We postulate:

1. Job A is strictly preferred to Job B if, and only if, there is an m-component image of Job A which is strictly preferred to the conforming image of Job B and each extension of that m-component image of Job A is also strictly preferred to the conforming image of Job B.
2. The indifference between jobs A and B occurs if, and only if, there is an m-component image of Job A and the conforming image of Job B such that none of them is strictly preferred to the other one and the same is true for each pair of their conforming extensions.

This amounts to reducing the preferences for jobs to the preferences for job images.

Preferences imply choice. Choice is the implementation of values. Consequently, we may say that preferences for some jobs over the others display work values. An example might clarify this statement. Imagine two jobs which differ in the state of only one characteristic. Their three-component images could be:

A = a lot of autonomy, a lot of variety, average pay
B = a lot of autonomy, little variety, average pay

Observe that these two images differ only in the amount of variety. Accordingly, if A is strictly preferred to B, we may conclude that it is so owing to the difference in variety: Clearly, the state, "a lot of variety" is strictly preferred to the state, "little variety." If, when variety is concerned, a person strictly prefers more to less, we say that variety is a *valued* job characteristic for that person.

Let m-valued job characteristics be partitioned into two classes. We can call them simply "first" and "second" class. Suppose that two m-component job images, say A and B, satisfy the condition of *opposite compositions*, i.e., the first-class component of A is strictly preferred to the corresponding component of B and each second-class component of B is strictly preferred to the corresponding component of A. Note that we have stated a condition which deals with preferences for the individual components appearing in job images A and B. Nothing has been said as to a preference for one total job image over the other total job image. If, under the condition of opposite compositions, job image A is strictly preferred to job image B, this strict preference can be viewed as showing the relative importance of job characteristics. In other words, if, under the condition of opposite compositions, a person strictly prefers Job A to Job B, that which is offered in Job A and is missing in Job B is, to this person, more important than that which is offered in Job B and is missing in Job A. In the two classes of job characteristics, we may have only one characteristic, for example, pay or autonomy. In such a case, the strict preference for one of the two jobs can be considered to show how important that single job characteristic is when compared to the importance of other job characteristics. Thus, the notion of importance is given an empirically meaningful interpretation. Concepts without empirical meaning serve no theoretical function in an empirical science (DiRenzo, 1967). Or as stated: "If science is to tell us anything about the world, if it is to be of any use in our dealings with the world, it must somewhere contain empirical elements" Kaplan (1964: 34).

Preferability of intrinsic work

Let us introduce a two-class partition of job characteristics which is of paramount theoretical significance and highly relevant for employment

policy. Namely, we can distinguish between job characteristics corresponding to one's instrumental values and noninstrumental values associated
with working. A noninstrumental characteristic may be valued as an end in
itself. An instrumental job characteristic is valued as a means for a different purpose. The question of interest is: How important to an individual is
the noninstrumental values of working compared to the importance of
instrumental work values? This relative importance will be called *preferability of intrinsic work*. It is indicated by preferences for jobs under the
condition of opposite compositions. That condition is now to be read in the
following sense: The first class of job characteristics is to be thought of as
containing the characteristics which correspond to the noninstrumental
values associated with working; the second class, however, is to be thought
of as containing the characteristics which correspond to the instrumental
values associated with working. Preferability of intrinsic work can range
along a continuum from regarding working as an instrumental activity to
regarding working itself as a terminal value.

To measure preferability of intrinsic work, four job characteristics were
selected: (1) pay, (2) autonomy (or self-direction) at work, (3) ability/job
match, and (4) interesting work. Pay represents an instrumental value
associated with working, while the remaining three characteristics represent intrinsic values associated with working. Recall that the latter three
values loaded on the same factor (termed *expressive values*) in Chapter 4.
These values were operationalized in two carefully constructed sets of job
images. These images can be found in Appendix A3 and include questions
33–40.

In brief, the first four pairs of images include two components:
autonomy and pay. In Job *A*, within this first set of questions (33–36),
autonomy is high and pay is equal to what the respondent currently earns.
Job *B*, in this set of images, always assumes a state of low autonomy. The
pay characteristic in Job *B* assumes one of four states. Beginning with the
first pair of images, these states are pay equal to, 10% greater, 30% greater,
and 50% greater than the respondent currently receives. Thus, in Job *A*,
there is high autonomy and pay equal to present pay, while in Job *B*, there
is low autonomy and pay ranging from the same to 50% more than the
present job.

The second set of job images is similar to this first set, but includes four
(Qs 37–40) pairs of conforming four-component images. Job *A* now consists of high autonomy, ability/job match, and interesting work, while Job
B is low on all three of these components. Job *A* always has pay equal to
the respondent's present job, while Job *B* assumes the same increasing pay
states as described for Qs 33–36.

Results are discussed first for the pair of images in each set which vary in one or three intrinsic characteristics, but are equal in pay. Findings indicate that 88.5% and 85.7% respectively, of the respondents prefer Job *A*. These findings are supportive of the notions of universalism and particularism discussed by Parsons (1951), Blau (1964), and Fararo (1973). According to Blau, particularistic values are unique to a person, while universalistic values tend to be common to large percentages of people. The present findings provide evidence that, for substantial proportions of people, autonomy (or self-direction), ability/job match, and interesting work may be considered universalistic values.

The remaining pairs of job images in each of the two sets satisfy the condition of opposite compositions. That is, responses indicate the preferences of the individual for intrinsic as compared to extrinsic characteristics of jobs. In the first set of images, when pay is increased by 10% and everything else is unchanged, 79.3% of the respondents prefer Job *A*. When pay is increased by 30%, 58.8% of the respondents prefer Job *A*. This preference for Job *A* declines to 38.3% when pay is increased by 50% in Job *B*. The corresponding findings for the second set of images show a decline in preferences for Job *A* from 90.9% to 77.1%, and finally, 57.6%. Based on all the findings presented to this point, the most parsimonious conclusion would seem to be that large proportions of respondents have a preference for both intrinsic *and* extrinsic work outcomes, but that there is no clear preference for one or the other types of outcomes (given the states of each that were utilized in the job images).

Nevertheless, autonomy, ability/job match, and interesting work may be regarded as constituting a sample from the set of job characteristics corresponding to intrinsic values associated with working. Analogously, pay may be considered to represent a sample from the set of job characteristics which correspond to an instrumental value associated with working. Responses to the eight questions about preferences are, therefore, considered as providing an estimate of preferability of intrinsic work.

Responses of any respondent can be represented by an array of eight numbers. Let $UK(i)$ stand for the number of the response category which was checked by the ith respondent at the Kth of the eight questionnaire items $(i = 1, 2, \ldots, 5777)$; namely, 5777 is the number of valid cases from all target group samples. The array of eight numbers representing responses of the ith respondent, that is, the ordered 8-tuple

$$U(i) = [U(i), U2(i), \ldots, U8(i)]$$

will be called *pattern of preferences* of the ith respondent. It is assigned a real number which should be a reasonable measure of preferability of intrinsic work for the ith respondent. We refer to $X(i)$ as *scale value* of the pattern of preferences $U(i)$ and as *score* for the ith respondent. If

$UK(i) < 3$, we may say that the ith respondent weakly prefers Job A to Job B, and if $UK(i) = 2$, we may say that the ith respondent strictly prefers Job A to Job B, when the Kth pair of job images is concerned. Thus, each of the eight questionnaire items (33–40) contains two dichotomous, monotone measurement items—one being about a weak preference, and one being about a strict preference. Each gives a partition of respondents into two equivalence classes: Every item about a weak preference yields a class of respondents who at least weakly prefer Job A to Job B and a class of respondents who do not weakly prefer Job A to Job B; similarly, every item about a strict preference gives a class of respondents who strictly prefer Job A to Job B and a class of respondents who do not strictly prefer Job A to Job B. We want scores $X(i)$ to satisfy the following requirement: For each of 16 partitions of respondents simultaneously, all respondents belonging to the same class should have scores as much alike as possible and as different as possible from scores of respondents who do not belong to that class. Such a requirement is known as *scalogram requirement* or the Guttman (1941) *scaling problem*. It introduces a measure of distance—in our case, the measure of distance between the patterns of preferences. The scale values for the pattern of preferences and scores for respondents are uniquely determined by the scalogram requirement only after an origin and a unit of measurement have been specified. It has been shown that it is possible to obtain scores satisfying the scalogram requirement by performing the principal-components analysis on the dichotomous variables and by taking the first principal component as the scoring component. The dichotomous variables were created by using additive binary coding for responses to the eight questions about preferences. Then, principal-components analysis was performed to obtain scale values for the patterns of preferences.

Table A8.1 in the Appendix shows the patterns of preferences and their scale values for the target group data which were determined in order to satisfy the scalogram requirement. For example, the pattern (2, 3, 3, 3, 2, 2, 3, 3) consists of the following preferences: If, using the pair of job images shown in Question 33 in Appendix A3.1, A is strictly preferred to B, this preference is indicated by the first number in the pattern. If, using the pair of job images shown in Question 34 in Appendix A3.1, B is strictly preferred to A, this preference is indicated by the second number in the pattern, and so on. If B is strictly preferred to A when using the pair of job images shown in Question 40 in Appendix A3.1, this preference is indicated by the last or eighth number in the pattern. As can be seen in Table A8.1, the pattern (2, 3, 3, 3, 2, 2, 3, 3) is assigned the scale value 1.54. We set the origin of the scale at the pattern (3, 3, 3, 3, 3, 3, 3, 3) which consists of eight strict preferences for job images B. Hence, respondents who constantly state that they would prefer Job *B*—no matter which of the eight pairs of job images is introduced—are assigned a 0 score. We specified the unit of measurement so that the difference between scale value of the pattern (2, 3, 3, 3, 2, 3, 3, 3) and scale value of the pattern (3, 3, 3, 3, 3, 3, 3, 3) is equal to unity. Under the scalogram requirement, the maximum scale value is assigned to the pattern (2, 2, 2, 2, 2, 2, 2, 2) which consists of eight strict preferences for job images *A*. This ordering imposed by the scalogram requirement meets the intuitive ordering of the patterns of preferences.

Table 8.1. Descriptive statistics of preferability of intrinsic work scores for combined target group samples within each country and for each target group across all countries

	Mean	Standard deviation	Number of cases
Country			
Belgium	2.52	0.75	880
Germany	2.81	0.58	682
Israel	2.57	0.84	834
Japan	2.47	0.84	1089
Netherlands	2.77	0.63	905
United States	2.53	0.69	847
Yugoslavia	2.67	0.64	540
Target group			
Unemployed	2.46	0.86	539
Retired	2.69	0.76	555
Chemical engineers	2.81	0.53	534
Teachers	2.96	0.49	635
Self-employed	2.91	0.56	654
Toolmakers	2.48	0.72	588
White-collar	2.51	0.68	685
Textile workers	2.13	0.95	554
Temporary workers	2.55	0.65	456
Students	2.49	0.69	577

Table 8.1 shows the means, standard deviations, and sample sizes for the combined target group samples in each country and for each target group combined across all countries. The grand mean for all target samples in all countries is 2.61 and the corresponding standard deviation is 0.74. The highest mean score for the combined target group samples in each country was observed in the German sample and the lowest in the Japanese combined target group sample. The highest mean score for target groups combined across countries was observed for teachers and the lowest mean was observed for textile workers.

A quick perusal of Table 8.1 suggests that there is approximately a one-half standard-deviation difference between the highest and lowest country means and slightly more than a 1 standard-deviation difference between the highest and lowest target groups. The question emerges as to whether the differences in sample means are statistically significant. To answer this question, we performed several types of covariance analyses with preferability of intrinsic work as the dependent variable, target group and country as factors, and age as a covariate. The covariate was entered not only to assess variation in preferability of intrinsic work due to age, but also to correct for age composition of target groups when assessing target group effect on preferability of intrinsic work. Recall that we have target groups of retired persons and students, for whom age is one of the defining characteristics. For the under-30-years-of-age group in the total target group sample, the average preferability of intrinsic work, that is, the corresponding mean score is 2.51, while for the 30–50-years-of-age group, it is 2.67; and for those over 50 years, it is 2.66. The difference between the first and the last two sample means is statistically significant.

Let us turn to the covariance analysis. Since, in the case of Germany and Yugoslavia, data were not collected from all 10 target groups, we decided to perform covariance analyses on two subsets of samples: (1) on samples from all target groups from five countries (Germany and Yugoslavia not included), and (2) on samples from the six fully employed target groups from six countries (Germany not included). As can be seen in Table 8.1, the numbers of (valid) cases in our country target group samples are unequal. Consequently, in covariance analysis, we deal with nonorthogonality of effects: The country factor effect is not orthogonal to the effect of the target group factor, and the two factor effects are not orthogonal to the interaction effect.

Table 8.2. Analysis of covariance of preferability of intrinsic work scores for all target groups from five countries

Source of variation	Regression approach Sum of squares	F	Hierarchical approach Sum of squares	F	DF
Covariate					
Age	4.066	8.28	28.206	57.41	1
Main effects	340.669	53.34	345.181	54.05	13
Country	49.103	24.99	53.487	27.22	4
Target	287.921	65.12	291.693	65.97	9
Two-way interaction					
Country/Target	49.433	2.80	49.432	2.80	36
Explained	422.817	17.21	422.818	17.21	50
Residual	2201.448		2201.447		4481
Total	2624.265		2624.265		4531

Table 8.3. Analysis of covariance of preferability of intrinsic work scores for fully employed target groups from six countries

Source of variation	Regression approach Sum of squares	F	Hierarchical approach Sum of squares	F	DF
Covariate					
Age	1.130	2.60	16.883	38.90	1
Main effects	300.851	69.32	302.879	69.79	10
Country	33.523	15.45	36.483	16.81	5
Target	264.905	122.07	266.395	122.76	5
Two-way interaction					
Country/Target	53.470	4.93	53.470	4.93	25
Explained	373.232	23.89	373.232	23.89	36
Residual	1396.635		1396.636		3218
Total	1769.868		1769.868		3254

Lacking a clear idea of some causal priority between the two factors and the covariate, we tried different designs of covariance analysis. We used a regression and hierarchical approach within the fixed-effect model. The conclusion reached with respect to the significance of the country effect and the target group effect are the same, regardless of the design of covariance analysis. That is, the country effect and the target group effect are both statistically significant but the respective sums of squares suggest that the target group factor is more important (as a source of variation in preferability of intrinsic work) than the country factor. Four covariance analyses are shown in Table 8.2 and Table 8.3. In the hierarchical design exhibited in these two tables, age was assigned the highest priority. Its effect on preferability of intrinsic work was assessed without adjusting for the other effects. After removing age effect, country effect was assessed. After removing country effect—in addition to age effect—target group effect was assessed. After removing the first three effects, interaction effects on the remaining variation in preferability of intrinsic work was assessed.

Multiple classification analyses were performed to examine the patterns of the country and the target group effects on preferability of intrinsic work. The obtained results are shown in Table 8.4 and Table 8.5. The numbers in the second column of the tables are the means for each country and each target group, expressed as unadjusted deviation from the grand mean. The numbers in the third column indicate the means for each country and each target group, again expressed as deviations from the grand mean, but adjusted for the other factor. In calculating the deviations which appear in the fourth column of these tables, the differences in age of

Table 8.4. *Multiple classification analysis of preferability of intrinsic work scores for all target group samples from five countries*

Grand mean = 2.57

Variable + category	N	Unadjusted Deviation	η	Adjusted for independents Deviation	β	Adjusted for independents + covariates Deviation	β
Country							
Belgium	879	−0.05		−0.05		−0.05	
Israel	822	0.01		0.01		0.01	
Japan	1082	−0.10		−0.09		−0.09	
Netherlands	905	0.20		0.19		0.20	
United States	844	−0.04		−0.05		−0.06	
			0.14		0.13		0.14
Target group							
Unemployed	444	−0.15		−0.15		−0.15	
Retired	463	0.13		0.13		0.03	
Chemical engineers	443	0.24		0.23		0.24	
Teachers	439	0.42		0.42		0.42	
Self-employed	464	0.32		0.32		0.29	
Toolmakers	443	−0.13		−0.14		−0.14	
White-collar	492	−0.11		−0.11		−0.08	
Textile workers	435	−0.55		−0.54		−0.54	
Temporary workers	441	−0.03		−0.03		−0.00	
Students	468	−0.14		−0.14		−0.07	
			0.35		0.35		0.34

the samples are also controlled. In the context of country, the highest deviation scores are found for the Netherlands and Japan with the Netherlands deviating upward, and Japan downward. For the target groups, the highest deviation scores are found among teachers and textile workers; teachers deviate upward, and textile workers deviate downward.

Observe, that when the effects of target group and age are statistically controlled, the estimated effect of the country factor on preferability of intrinsic work is not attenuated. The pattern of the estimated target group effect also remains almost unaltered when controlled for country, but some changes in the pattern do occur as we further adjust for the differences in age. This can be viewed as a decomposition of the target group effect into two independent effects: target group and age. Namely, after adjusting for age in addition to country, the mean deviation score corresponding to the category "retired" diminishes, while the mean deviation score corresponding to the category "students" increases, suggesting that age and preferability of intrinsic work are positively related (see Table 8.4). Finally, the squares of statistics η and β in Table 8.5 indicate that the country factor

Table 8.5. *Multiple classification analysis of preferability of intrinsic work scores for fully employed target group samples from six countries*

Grand mean = 2.61

Variable + category	N	Unadjusted Deviation	η	Adjusted for independents Deviation	β	Adjusted for independents + covariates Deviation	β
Country							
Belgium	526	−0.10		−0.10		−0.10	
Israel	486	−0.03		−0.03		−0.03	
Japan	627	−0.13		−0.11		−0.11	
Netherlands	552	0.20		0.19		0.19	
United States	525	0.01		0.00		−0.00	
Yugoslavia	539	0.06		0.06		0.05	
			0.15		0.14		0.14
Target group							
Chemical engineers	533	0.20		0.20		0.20	
Teachers	529	0.33		0.33		0.33	
Self-employed	554	0.29		0.28		0.27	
Toolmakers	534	−0.17		−0.18		−0.18	
White-collar	582	−0.14		−0.14		−0.12	
Textile workers	523	−0.50		−0.50		−0.50	
			0.40		0.40		0.39

explains about 15% of the variation in preferability of intrinsic work for fully employed target groups. Thus, we have some justification for claiming that the net effect of target groups is seven–eight times greater than the country net effect on preferability of intrinsic work.[1] It seems safe to conclude that the country effect, though statistically significant, is relatively unimportant.

Deleting the country factor from analysis and substituting sex, educational attainment, and job experience of autonomy[2] for the target group factor in the regression design of covariance analysis, we obtain the results shown in Table 8.6. An examination of the respective sums of squares in this table suggests that autonomy experience is the most important, education next most important, and sex the least important source of variability in preferability of intrinsic work.

It could be argued that the questionnaire item on job autonomy does not provide an assessment of the actual respondent's latitude to make decisions about his work, but rather, the respondent's subjective assessment of his autonomy at work. It remains open to question whether we would obtain a similar distribution of autonomy assessments, had we an objective measuring device. Nevertheless, as Mortimer and Lorence (1979b) point out in their analysis of job satisfaction, the perception of one's job features can

Table 8.6. *Analysis of covariance of the effects of education, sex and autonomy on preferences for intrinsic work*

Source of variation	Sum of squares	F	DF
Covariate			
Age	6.253	12.93	1
Main effects	234.137	80.68	6
Autonomy	60.465	62.50	2
Sex	3.680	7.61	1
Education	47.458	32.71	3
Two-way interaction	10.561	1.99	11
Autonomy/sex	2.381	2.46	2
Autonomy/education	3.358	1.16	6
Sex/Education	4.417	3.04	3
Three-way interaction			
Autonomy–sex–education	4.243	1.46	6
Explained	306.144	26.37	24
Residual	2444.656		5054
Total	2750.799		5078

NOTE: Student samples were not included in this analysis because job autonomy does not apply to them.

mediate the impact of objective job situation on the psychological response to work (see also Seashore and Taber, 1975).

There is widespread acceptance of the hypothesis that a reciprocal influence exists between work values and occupational experience. The causal path from work values to occupational experience is called the *selection* effect. It reflects an iterative process of job molding, whereby people start their work career by choosing some initial trial job from the set of available jobs on the basis of their values and then continuously mold their work career to converge as closely as possible to their work values. However, work values are not constant over time; but rather, are reshaped by work experiences. The causal path from work experiences to work values is called the *socialization* effect. A number of studies provide evidence for both the selection and the socialization effect (see Mortimer and Lorence, 1979b, for a review). It is beyond the scope of this analysis to estimate separately the selection effect of work values and the socializing impact of occupational experience. We only can hypothesize that the relationship between preferability of intrinsic work and occupational experience of autonomy—the relationship which we assess in this analysis—is a resultant outcome of both selection and socialization effects.

Only one work experience variable, that is, work experience of autonomy, was included in our covariance analysis. The literature, emphasizing the importance of work autonomy, provides considerable justification for such a parsimonious work-related input. Kohn (1969: chapter 10) and Kohn and Schooler (1983), for instance, demonstrate that variation in opportunities for self-direction at work largely account for the social class differences in values and orientation. Mortimer and Lorence (1979b) give substantial evidence for the socialization hypothesis, but only with respect to the autonomy dimension of work.

Table 8.7. Multiple classification analysis of the pattern of effects of sex, education and autonomy on preferences for intrinsic work

Grand mean = 2.62

Variable + category	N	Unadjusted Deviation	η	Adjusted for independents Deviation	β	Adjusted for independents + covariates Deviation	β
Sex							
Male	2805	−0.01		−0.04		−0.04	
Female	2274	0.01		0.05		0.05	
			0.02		0.06		0.07
Education							
1	628	−0.25		−0.16		−0.18	
2	2205	−0.11		−0.09		−0.09	
3	1110	0.13		0.10		0.10	
4	1136	0.22		0.17		0.18	
			0.22		0.17		0.18
Autonomy							
1	721	−0.42		−0.37		−0.36	
2	2515	−0.01		−0.02		−0.02	
3	1843	0.18		0.18		0.17	
			0.26		0.24		0.23

Table 8.7 contains the results of multiple classification analysis, examining the pattern of effects of autonomy, sex, and education on preferability of intrinsic work. Observe that more autonomy at work is associated with higher preferability of intrinsic work. This finding is consistent with that of Mortimer and Lorence (1979a). In Table 8.7, we see that in the initial pattern of deviations from the grand mean, the span of autonomy effect on preferability of intrinsic work is equal to $0.18 - (-0.42) = 0.6$ scale unit. After adjusting for sex and education, the span of autonomy effect diminishes to 0.55 scale unit. In the final pattern—when deviations from the grand mean attributed to variations in opportunities for autonomy at work are adjusted for sex, education, and age—the remaining span of autonomy effect on preferability of intrinsic work is equal to 0.53 scale unit. These changes in the span of the estimated autonomy effect are small; they suggest that the confounding effects of education, sex, and age are weak.

In addition, the F statistics in Table 8.6 show that the three-way interaction effect, as well as the two-way interaction effect, fail to reach statistical significance. The effect of educational attainment is weaker than the corresponding autonomy effect on preferability of intrinsic work. As can be seen in Table 8.7, the net estimated educational effect is equal to 0.36 scale unit. The effect of sex, though statistically significant, is negligible when compared to the autonomy effect. However, the changes in this pattern after adjustments for autonomy and education may indicate that females tend to work in positions with less autonomy or tend to have lower levels of education attainment.

In sum, the target group factor remains the best predictor of preferability of intrinsic work. This is consistent with the conclusion of Samuel and Lewin-Epstein (1979): that the concept of occupational status is a better predictor of workers' values than many other variables. Furthermore, our findings provide some modest support for the hypothesis that there is a reciprocal causal path between occupational experience of autonomy and work values.

The modest relationship leads to the hypotheses that experiences outside the work environment may have an important influence on work culture. Yankelovich (1979) examines societal changes in the last 2 decades and, thereby, identifies some of the non-work experiences which generate a new work culture. He describes developments which, he suggests, have fostered a new work culture in the American society. But it seems safe to generalize some of his arguments. Yankelovich (1979) argues that, for the American society, "the 'constants' suddenly turned into variables"; the symbols of success take on new forms of cultural definition. The traditional sources of contentment expire. Self-fulfillment has been severed from success and has acquired its own cultural meanings, some of which still partly overlap with success, but much of which does not. The labor force participation rate has markedly increased, mainly owing to the large increase in the female propensity to seek gainful employment. Significant shifts, therefore, have occurred in family structure, and the patterns of family life have changed. When a man is the sole wage earner, he will endure hardships to support his family, but the traditional male breadwinner role is being replaced by other roles, reflecting different values.

Yet the prevailing job design fits, at best, the traditional breadwinner role. If the present work institutions do not undergo changes to reach greater congruence with the work culture which our study convincingly reveals, we may witness a "legitimacy crisis." We borrow the notion of legitimacy crisis from Horvat (1979: 54–58). He refers to Lipset's (1963) definition of legitimacy as the capacity of the system to engender and maintain the belief that the existing institutions are the most appropriate.

One of the tantalizing issues raised by Yankelovich (1979: 5) is: So many jobs go begging when so many people are looking for work. This is not an ordinary labor market disequilibrium or an ordinary structural unemployment problem. Rather, it is indicative of a potential incongruity between the work institution and work culture. We can assume that such incongruities have a corroding effect on the system legitimacy.

The foregoing analysis has examined some of the possible antecedents of preferability of intrinsic work. We now turn to one potential consequence of preferability of intrinsic work by investigating its relationship with occupational satisfaction. As an indicator of the respondent's occupational satisfaction, we used Question 50B in Appendix A3.1:

> If you were to start all over again, would you again choose your occupation or would you choose a different one?
> 1. Different occupation.
> 2. Same occupation.

The number of a response category (1 or 2) checked by a respondent can be considered a random variable called Z. Thus, $Z = 2$ designates the event that occurs if a respondent chosen at random happened to check the response category 2. This event is assumed to display occupational satisfaction.

The respondent's score for preferability of intrinsic work is also a random variable called X. The previously discussed questionnaire item about the respondent's autonomy at work yields a third random variable called Y. Thus, $X = x$ denotes the event that occurs if a respondent selected at random is found to have score x, and $X > a$ denotes the event that occurs if that respondent is found to have score greater than some number a. Analogously, $\gamma = 1, \gamma = 2, \gamma = 3$ are the events that occur if a respondent chosen at random is found to have assessed his autonomy at work by a respective response category.

The conditional probability of $Z = 2$, given $X = x$ and $\gamma = y$, written $P[(Z = 2)/(X = x)(\gamma = y)]$, is assumed to reflect a causal structure. The causal structure which we hypothesize consists of the causal path from preferability of intrinsic work to occupational satisfaction, with causation mediated by the experienced work autonomy. Expressed another way, experienced work autonomy appears as a parameter of the causal relationship between preferability of intrinsic work and occupational satisfaction.

From the collected target group data we calculate:

$$P[(Z = 2)/(X = 2.33)(\gamma = 1)] = 0.344$$
$$P[(Z = 2)/(X = 3.26)(\gamma = 1)] = 0.386$$
$$P[(Z = 2)/(X = 2.33)(\gamma = 2)] = 0.504$$
$$P[(Z = 2)/(X = 3.26)(\gamma = 2)] = 0.554$$

$$P[(Z = 2)/(X = 2.33)(\gamma = 3)] = 0.539$$
$$P[(Z = 2)/(X = 3.26)(\gamma = 3)] = 0.633$$

In Table A8.1, we find that a respondent is assigned the score of 2.33 for having the pattern of preferences (2, 2, 3, 3, 2, 2, 2, 3), and the score of 3.26 for having the pattern of preferences (2, 2, 2, 2, 2, 2, 2, 2).

By regression analysis, we obtain:

$$P[(Z = 2)/(X < 1.93)] = 0.415$$
$$P[(Z = 2)/(X = x > 1.93)(\gamma = 1)] = -0.02242\,x + 0.415$$
$$P[(Z = 2)/(X = x > 1.93)(\gamma = 2)] = 0.03482\,x + 0.415$$
$$P[(Z = 2)/(X = x > 1.93)(\gamma = 3)] = 0.06766\,x + 0.415$$

These prediction equations fit the collected target group data roughly since their predictive accuracy is not high. Yet, they are indicative of direction of the relationship. All coefficients appearing in the given prediction equations reach statistical significance. Observe that *higher* preferability of intrinsic work is associated with higher predicted occupational satisfaction, given that respondents assessed *at least some* ($\gamma = 2$ or $\gamma = 3$) latitude to make decisions about their work. If, however, the respondents assessed have *hardly any* ($\gamma = 1$) latitude to make decisions about their work, *higher* preferability of intrinsic work is associated with *lower* predicted occupational satisfaction (as one would expect). Note also the difference in magnitude of the coefficients in the last two prediction equations. When $\gamma = 3$, the increase in predicted probability of occupational satisfaction with the increase of one unit in preferability of intrinsic work is approximately *twice* as great as when $\gamma = 2$.

Preferability of leisure

Another partition of job characteristics into two classes which we examine is derived from the dichotomy working/nonworking (see, for example, Henderson and Quandt, 1958: 23–24). The total amount of time (T) available to an individual can be divided into the amount of time (W) spent at work and the amount of time (L) spent out of work:

$$T = W + L$$

This accounting equation can refer to a day, to a week, or to a longer time interval, that is, $T = 24$ hours, or $T = 7$ days, or T equals a certain number of some other time units. Time L will be called *leisure time*. An interval of time (O, T) can be divided into subintervals ($O, T1$), ($T1, T2$) . . . ($Tn -1$, Tn) according to when work is performed and is not performed. There is also an alternating sequence of time intervals: If ($O, T1$) is a leisure-time interval, then $(T1, T2)$ is a working-time interval, followed by another leisure-time interval $(T2, T3)$, and so on. We are interested in establishing how important the leisure-time activities are for an individual as compared to the importance—to him—of working. In other words, we are concerned with finding out the importance to an individual of goals he wants to achieve or satisfy by the leisure-time activities, as compared to the importance of goals the person wants to gain or satisfy by working. This relative importance will be called *preferability of leisure*. Again, it is indicated by preferences for jobs under the condition of opposite compositions, that is, under the condition of opposite compositions in the following sense: Job characteristics are partitioned into two classes. The first class contains the leisure-time-related characteristics, and the second class contains the characteristics, which are not leisure-time-related.

The job images used to measure preferability of leisure include some of the same characteristics which were used to measure preferability of intrinsic work plus two aggregative characteristics concerned with the impact of jobs on the amount of leisure time. To reveal preferences for jobs which differentially affect leisure time, six pairs of conforming four-component job images were presented in the questionnaires for all target group samples. They consist of questions 41–46 in Appendix A3.1. Again, in every pair, one of the images represents a job called "Job A" and the other image represents a job called "Job B." Each of the six pairs of job images is assumed to satisfy the condition of opposite compositions: Leisure-time characteristics of jobs A and B, presumably, push respondents to prefer Job A, while the other three characteristics of jobs A and B, presumably, push respondents to prefer Job B. The resultant preference for one of the two jobs is indicative of the importance to a respondent of goals achieved by leisure-time activities, as compared to the importance of goals achieved by working.

When jobs A and B are represented by the images shown in Question 41, 65.5% of respondents from target group samples state they would prefer Job A. With successive pairs of images, the percentage of respondents who prefer Job A declines to 11.6, 7.5, and 4.8, respectively. In the final pair of images, when the pay in Job A is increased to a level equal to Job B, the percentage of respondents who prefer Job A increases to 7.9.

These findings may be consistent with those reported by Sessions (1978), but we would not claim that the work ethic is alive and well. We would rather, borrowing from Marcuse's vocabulary, say that they reveal preferences which do not seem to stem from and do not imply the "liberation from work" orientation, but imply the "liberation of work" requirement. It is important to recognize the shifts in preferences. Initially, when better extrinsic rewards were offered in exchange for less leisure time, the probability that a respondent preferred Job *B* was much lower than later, when better intrinsic rewards were offered in exchange for less leisure time. The significance of these differences in probability is so visible that there is no need for statistical testing. This leads to the conclusion that extrinsic work rewards may be traded for leisure, but leisure is not a substitute for intrinsic work rewards.

For further analysis, we developed a measure of preferability of leisure, using the same procedure used to develop the measure of preferability of intrinsic work. Table A8.2 in the Appendix shows the patterns of preferences and scale values used in these analyses. The scale values satisfy the scalogram requirement on the target group data. We set the origin for the scale at the pattern (3, 3, 3, 3, 3, 3) which consists of six strict preferences for job image *B*. Thus, if respondents prefer Job *B* no matter which of the six pairs of job images is presented, they are assigned a score of 0. We determine the unit of measurement so that the difference between scale value of the pattern (2, 2, 3, 3, 3, 3) and scale value of the pattern (3, 3, 3, 3, 3, 3) is equal to unity. The maximum scale value of 10.25 is assigned to the pattern (2, 2, 2, 2, 2, 2). This is the score for respondents who prefer Job *A*, irrespective of which images are presented to them.

Table 8.8. *Preferability of leisure: mean scores by country and target groups*

	Mean	Standard deviation	Number of cases
Country			
Belgium	1.48	2.42	881
Germany	1.54	2.13	685
Israel	1.32	2.34	839
Japan	1.69	2.54	1089
Netherlands	1.32	2.09	901
United States	0.93	1.67	846
Yugoslavia	1.31	2.31	540
Target group			
Unemployed	1.85	2.71	534
Retired	1.34	2.23	545
Chemical engineers	0.95	1.53	538
Teachers	1.09	1.56	641
Self-employed	1.35	2.38	649
Toolmakers	1.46	2.32	581
White-collar	1.36	2.26	687
Textile workers	1.87	2.59	564
Temporary workers	1.46	2.25	457
Students	1.17	1.83	585

Table 8.8 contains the mean scores, which indicate the average preferability of leisure for the combined target groups within each country and for each target group combined across countries. The grand mean equals 1.38; *and* the corresponding standard deviation equals 2.25. The highest mean score for combined target group samples in a country was observed in Japan and the lowest in the United States. The highest mean score for each target group combined across countries was found for textile workers and the lowest for chemical engineers. As can be verified in Table 8.8, all standard deviations are very high when compared to the corresponding mean scores. So, the mean score is not a very good measure of the central tendency in a respective sample.

Table 8.9. Analysis of covariance of the effects of country and target groups on preferability of leisure time

Source of variation	Regression approach Sum of squares	F	Hierarchical approach Sum of squares	F	DF
Covariate					
Age	134.350	27.90	74.692	15.51	1
Main effects	668.228	10.68	675.097	10.79	13
Country	321.708	16.70	318.742	16.55	4
Target	345.144	7.97	356.355	8.22	9
Two-way interaction					
Country/Target	814.169	4.70	814.167	4.70	36
Explained	1563.956	6.50	1563.956	6.50	50
Residual	21580.842		21580.843		4482
Total	23144.799		23144.799		4532

Because of the high standard deviations, a relevant question is whether the country and target group effects vanish as sources of influence on preferability of leisure. The covariance analyses in Table 8.9 address this question. Preferability of leisure is the dependent variable, of course, country and target group are factors, and age is introduced as covariate. Recall that we are confronted with the problem of nonorthogonality of effects. Recall also that, in the case of Germany and Yugoslavia, data were not collected from all 10 target groups. So we performed covariance analyses on samples from all target groups from five countries (Germany and Yugoslavia not included) and on samples from six target groups (unemployed, retired, temporary workers, and students not included) from six countries (Germany not included). The two covariance analyses which are summarized in Table 8.9 were performed on samples from all target groups from five countries. In the hierarchical design, age effect was assessed first. Then, adjusting for age effect, country effect was assessed. After removing country effect, in addition to age effect, target group effect was assessed. Finally, interaction effect of the remaining variation in preferability of leisure was assessed. Regardless of the covariates, all assessed effects are statistically significant.

Multiple classification analysis was used to examine the pattern of additive effects of the two factors and covariate on preferability of leisure. Tables 8.10 and 8.11 report the results. The analyses of covariance showed that the country and target group factors had a statistically significant interaction effect on preferability of leisure. Therefore, it might be argued that it was not appropriate to conduct a multiple classification analysis, which is a multivariate analysis of an additive form. However, the multiple classification analyses yield meaningful patterns of the additive effects. In the fourth column of Table 8.11, we find figures showing the estimated net effect of the country factor. The span of the effect is equal to $0.39 - (-0.46) = 0.85$ scale unit which explains about 1.4% of variation in

Table 8.10. Multiple classification analysis of preferability of leisure scores for all target group samples from five countries

Grand mean = 1.37 Variable + category	N	Unadjusted Deviation	η	Adjusted for independents Deviation	β	Adjusted for independents + covariates Deviation	β
Country							
Belgium	880	0.12		0.11		0.11	
Israel	826	−0.06		−0.06		−0.06	
Japan	1083	0.32		0.32		0.34	
Netherlands	901	−0.04		0.05		−0.02	
United States	843	−0.44		−0.41		−0.47	
			0.11		0.11		0.12
Target group							
Unemployed	439	0.51		0.46		0.46	
Retired	453	−0.07		−0.07		−0.63	
Chemical engineers	447	−0.41		−0.39		−0.38	
Teachers	447	−0.20		−0.19		−0.14	
Self-employed	459	0.12		0.14		0.01	
Toolmakers	436	0.12		0.14		0.12	
White-collar	496	−0.10		−0.11		0.02	
Textile workers	442	0.33		0.32		0.35	
Temporary workers	442	0.09		0.10		0.24	
Students	472	−0.35		−0.35		−0.02	
			0.12		0.12		0.14

Table 8.11. *Multiple classification analysis of preferability of leisure scores for fully employed target group samples from six countries*

Grand mean = 1.34

Variable + category	N	Unadjusted Deviation	η	Adjusted for independents Deviation	β	Adjusted for independents + covariates Deviation	β
Country							
Belgium	529	−0.00		−0.00		0.00	
Israel	507	−0.11		−0.12		−0.11	
Japan	620	0.34		0.35		0.39	
Netherlands	547	0.13		0.13		0.14	
United States	524	−0.41		−0.40		−0.46	
Yugoslavia	539	−0.03		−0.03		−0.04	
			0.10		0.10		0.12
Target group							
Chemical engineers	537	−0.38		−0.38		−0.38	
Teachers	537	−0.23		−0.23		−0.21	
Self-employed	549	0.07		0.07		−0.05	
Toolmakers	527	0.15		0.16		0.16	
White-collar	585	−0.10		−0.12		−0.03	
Textile workers	531	0.51		0.51		0.52	
			0.13		0.13		0.12

preferability of leisure. This column also includes figures which show the estimated net effect of the target group factor. The span of the effect is equal to $0.46 - (-0.63) = 1.09$ scale unit and explains about 2% of variation in preferability of leisure. In addition, from figures in Table 8.9, we calculate that the interaction effect of the two factors accounts for about 3.5% of variation in preferability of leisure. In the pattern of the target group effect, a noticeable change occurs after controlling for age. The deviation score assigned to the retired category changes from −0.07 to −0.63, and the deviation score for the students category changes from −0.35 to −0.02. These changes apparently represent statistically significant differences between age groups. For the under-30-years-of-age group in the grand sample, the mean preferability of leisure score is 1.28; for the 30–50-years-of-age group the mean is 1.39; and for those older than 50 years, the mean is 1.57.

Hence, we find no evidence that target group or country are important sources of variation in preferability of leisure. A remaining question is whether socialization processes or stratification characteristics (which do not covary with the target group variable) are a major source of observed differences in preferability of leisure. To examine this question, we replaced the target group factor with the respondent's job characteristics, educational attainment, and sex. For the purpose of this examination, work schedule, physical, and mental job requirements were used in addition to work autonomy to characterize the respondent's job.[3]

Table 8.12 summarizes the results of a covariance analysis, and Table 8.13 summarizes the results of two multiple classification analyses. Due to the limits of the computer program available to us, estimates of the effects of the six factors were made in two separate analyses. Consequently, the estimated effect of work schedule, physical requirements, and mental requirements are not adjusted for each other. Most of the interaction effects and the effects of sex shown in Table 8.12 fail to reach statistical significance. The pattern of adjusted deviations attributable to work schedule apparently indicates a selection effect (see the respective figures in the fourth column of Table 8.13). The socialization effect of occupational experience appears in the pattern of deviations attributable to the autonomy variable and in the patterns of deviations attributable to the two variables which represent physical and mental job requirements. However,

Table 8.12. Analysis of covariance of the effects of education, sex and autonomy on preferences for intrinsic work

Source of variation	Sum of squares	F	DF
Covariate			
Age	25.570	5.05	1
Main effects	248.155	5.45	9
Work Schedule	44.850	2.95	3
Autonomy	35.419	3.50	2
Education	64.570	4.25	3
Sex	11.199	2.21	1
Two-way interaction	269.200	1.83	29
Work schedule/autonomy	56.585	1.86	6
Work schedule/education	52.988	1.16	9
Work schedule/sex	93.875	6.18	3
Autonomy/education	63.652	2.10	6
Autonomy/sex	16.584	1.64	2
Education/sex	47.874	3.15	3
Three-way interactions	214.671	1.09	39
Work schedule/autonomy/ education	58.841	0.65	18
Work schedule/autonomy/sex	96.919	3.19	6
Work schedule/education/sex	64.860	1.42	9
Autonomy/education/sex	11.056	0.36	6
Explained	1101.328	2.79	78
Residual	25020.729		4942
Total	26122.058		5020

Table 8.13. Multiple classification analysis of pattern of effects of work schedule, autonomy, education, sex, physical, and mental job requirements on preferability of leisure

Variable + Category	N	Unadjusted Deviation	η	Adjusted for independents Deviation	η	Adjusted for independents + covariates Deviation	η
Work schedule							
1	3307	−0.03		0.01		0.01	
2	898	−0.03		0.02		0.01	
3	508	0.35		0.10		0.12	
4	308	−0.19		−0.33		−0.33	
			0.05		0.04		0.04
Autonomy							
1	713	0.38		0.19		0.21	
2	2498	−0.04		−0.02		−0.01	
3	1810	−0.10		−0.05		−0.07	
			0.07		0.03		0.04
Education							
1	626	0.63		0.59		0.55	
2	2164	0.12		0.11		0.12	
3	1104	−0.16		−0.15		−0.15	
4	1127	−0.41		−0.40		−0.39	
			0.14		0.13		0.13
Sex							
Male	2765	−0.02		−0.01		−0.02	
Female	2256	0.02		0.02		0.03	
			0.01		0.01		0.01
Requirement Physical							
1	2983	−0.15		−0.09		−0.09	
2	2066	0.22		0.13		0.12	
			0.08		0.05		0.04
Mental							
1	2216	−0.09		−0.10		−0.09	
2	2833	0.07		0.08		0.07	
			0.03		0.04		0.04

the estimated socialization effects are quite weak. Overall, education turns out to be the best predictor of preferability of leisure. However, the estimated education effect should not be interpreted as indicating that stratification characteristics are an important source of differences in preferability of leisure. Rather, the results of this analysis support the earlier conclusion that intrinsic work—the complement of leisure—is a universalistic value. This interpretation suggests that stratification is not a source of influence on preferability of leisure, but, at most, implies stratification.

Summary

In many work situations, employees are required to make trade-offs, giving up some features of a job or giving up leisure in order to gain other job features or gain work. The purpose of this chapter was to investigate these kinds of trade-offs. There are several reasons why trade-off situations provide insight into peoples' preferences and choices. People tend to evaluate gains and losses relative to some reference point. Further trade-offs are not symmetrical; losses are more important to people than gains.

Within the context of trade-offs, the present findings reveal several interesting results. In the first set of job images it is clear that the increases in pay must be substantial (about 30%) before large numbers of people begin to change their preferences from job A to job B. Too small a pay increment seems to draw a "no deal" or "not enough" response from people. Thus, it would appear that pay increases must be substantial in order to overcome the general tendency of individuals to give greater weight to the autonomy or intrinsic features they are giving up on choosing job B.

Yet it is also clear that pay had a very powerful influence on changes of job choices. Large percentages of people did opt for job B even when it meant that they had to give up large amounts of the intrinsically reinforcing features. This finding is consistent with the role of pay as a generalized conditioned reinforcer.

Third, the person's past history, particularly their prior experience in jobs with high intrinsically satisfying content, and education are related to intrinsic job preferences. This finding is consistent with the reasoning provided in Chapter 2 and elsewhere in this chapter. Common to both these correlates of intrinsic preferences is the exercising of self-direction (Kohn and Schooler, 1983). Both selection and socialization influences could explain this relationship and suggest that people both self select themselves for jobs with lots of autonomy, and good ability/job match and interesting work content, and that the experience of working in such jobs influences their job preference at a later date.

Finally, economists have for some time discussed the trade-off of leisure for pay. Much less commonly investigated is whether workers will trade-off leisure for intrinsic job features. The present findings indicate a slight tendency for people to trade leisure for intrinsic job features, but the trade-off is not as great as occurs in prior research where pay is the alternative. Does this mean that intrinsic job characteristics do not have as large an influence on people's decisions about working as is the case for pay? Perhaps, but before we would draw such a conclusion, we would note that giving up leisure for intrinsic job features confronts people with a very uncertain task. There is a well understood metric for calculating pay increases, but calculating the amount of leisure lost or intrinsic job features gained poses a much more difficult task.

In summary, pay, intrinsic job features and leisure are three types of preferences that pull people in different directions and frequently require that they make trade-offs. The purpose of this chapter was to investigate the choices and preferences that people do make when confronted by a task that required these trade-offs.

Notes

(1) However, the reader should remember that target groups differ in their sex composition, tend to be drawn from different levels in organizations, and differ in educational attainment.

(2) Job experience with autonomy was derived by using responses to Question 9 in Appendix A3.1. Response alternatives range from 1 (hardly any room to make job decisions) to 3 (I decide how to do my work).

(3) The relevant questions for work schedule and physical requirement are Question 6A, Question 6C and Question 16. In the present analysis, questions 6A and 6C were combined with the following four alternatives:

1. Primarily day work and more than half of the weekends free.
2. Primarily day work and less than half of the weekends free.
3. Primarily night work, swing shift, or shift changes regularly and more than half of the weekends free.
4. Primarily night work, swing shift, or shift changes regularly and less than half of the weekends free.

In the present analysis, the two alternatives for physical requirements are:

1. Job never or seldom requires too much physically.
2. Job sometimes or often requires too much physically.

The same procedure was used to construct the mental requirements measure.

Chapter 9

Definitions of Working

Introduction

Working is a central and basic role in the life of the individual as shown in several previous chapters. Consequently, it appears to be of particular interest to examine the way in which this activity, termed "work," is defined by those who engage in working.

Defining the concept of working has been a topic of interest for social scientists from various disciplines for some time. In its theoretical conceptualization, work has been discussed from different perspectives by various authors. These perspectives range from the philosophical to the religious to the individual as discussed in chapters 1 and 2. No wonder then, that the usage of the term "work" has taken on a multiplicity of meanings, ranging from the totally instrumental to purely expressive (Kaplan and Tausky, 1974).

The concept of work is by no means an easy term to define. *The American College Dictionary*, for instance, gives 46 noun and verb definitions of work. Other prominent dictionaries, such as the *Oxford Universal Dictionary* and the *Webster's Third New International Dictionary*, devote over a page of analysis to this topic. Part of the complexity in the definition of work results from the very fact that working does not have the same meaning and function for all people. For some, it is primarily an instrument through which they derive their basic maintenance and survival, while for others, it also serves as a mechanism through which self-expression and other social needs are fulfilled. Another complicating aspect concerning the definition of working is that it may take different meanings at different times, places, societies, and cultures (Tilgher, 1962).

Miller (1980) claims that the context of meaning about work that has most occupied sociologists of work in this century is that of the workplace and is made up of the various activities and relationships found within specific work settings. The social context of the workplace is a particular-istic one within which workers construct meanings and relationships that are often unique (Miller, 1980).

One of the early (and only) attempts to define work empirically was carried out more than 2 decades ago by Weiss and Kahn (1960) in a study of 371 employees. One-fifth of the men interviewed defined work as an activity which requires physical or mental exertion. Warr (1981) also regards employment as providing outlets for physical and mental energy. Work may be defined in the context of a larger task or activity. According to Salz (1955), work is an activity related to the execution of a task or project and the spirit and behavior in which this goal-directed activity is carried out.

A different approach advanced by some writers sees work as contribut-ing to society. Donald and Havighurst (1959) found that one function of work is to serve or to benefit society. A similar definition is suggested by Friedman and Havighurst (1954). Work is also seen as a source of identity and peer/group relations (Friedman and Havighurst, 1954; Steers and Porter, 1975). A somewhat similar approach, but also including a sense of belongingness, is presented by Morse and Weiss (1955) in their classic study on the function and meaning of work, in which interviewees noted that "work gives them a feeling of being tied into the larger society" (p. 191). Work has also been noted for the value it may add to other things. Hence, the authors of *Work in America* provide the following definition of work, "An activity that produces something of value for other people" (Special Task Force, 1973: 3).

Shimmin (1966) claims, in her treatment of work, that one of the distinguishing features of work is that it is not enjoyable. Support for this argument is given by Weiss and Kahn (1960) who define work as an activity one performs but does not enjoy. Firth (1948), however, warned against representing work simply as something which people do not like doing. Others defined work in terms of a duty that has to be done. Hearnshaw (1954), Weiss and Kahn (1960), and Friedman (1961) observe the elements of obligation and restraint when trying to define work.

Firth (1948) points out that any definition of work must be arbitrary to some extent and suggests that "income-producing activity" covers a general use of the term in an occupational sense. Many of the definitions of work focus on it as an economic activity or a means of survival. Friedman and Havighurst (1954) say that one function of work is to maintain a minimum sustenance level of existence. Dubin (1958) claims that by work we mean continuous employment in the production of goods and services for remuneration. His definition contains three elements: (1) that work is continuous; (2) that it results in production of goods and services; and (3) that work is performed for pay. Anderson (1961) defines work as an "activity of some purpose"; in more direct terms, time given to a job for which one is paid. Braude (1975) declares that work may be viewed as that which a person does in order to survive; work is simply the way in which a person earns a living. The first and most dominant thought about work's meaning in *Work in America* (Special Task Force, 1973) is its economic purpose(s). Miller (1980) defines "work as the various ways in which human beings attain their livelihoods."

This conceptual discussion serves as the source for the formulation of our work definition question. It incorporates directly and indirectly, the previous conceptualizations which have attempted to define working. It seems useful to indicate that the definition of working item occured rather late in the questionnaire (see Appendix A3.1, item 49) and that the preceding context suggested that paid employment activities served as the general referent for "working". While this was never directly stated, it seems a likely conclusion on the part of many respondents. The question was stated as follows:

> Not everyone means the same thing when they talk about working. When do you consider an activity as working? Choose four statements from the list below which best define when an activity is "working":
>
> A. If you do it in a working place.
> B. If someone tells you what to do.
> C. If it is physically strenuous.
> D. If it belongs to your task.
> E. If you do it to contribute to society.
> F. If, by doing it, you get the feeling of belonging.
> G. If it is mentally strenuous.
> H. If you do it at a certain time (for instance, from 8AM until 5PM).
> I. If it adds value to something.
> J. If it is not pleasant.
> K. If you get money for doing it.
> L. If you have to account for it.
> M. If you have to do it.
> N. If others profit by it.

From the list of 14 statements, every individual was asked to choose four statements which best define when an activity would be considered "working." We are interested in determining the most dominant definitions of working in the eight participating countries and to look at country similarities and differences in these definitions. Next, we determine whether there are definitions of working which apply mainly to specific target groups. A cluster analysis is performed on a representative sample of the total target group data, stratified by country and target groups to cluster respondents with similar definitions of working together. The derived work

Table 9.1. Comparison of work definitions, rankings and frequency (percentage) chosen in eight countries (national sample data)

Definition of work	Country							
	Belgium N = 450	Germany N = 1278	Israel N = 973	Japan N = 3225	Netherlands N = 996	United States N = 998	Britain N = 806	Yugoslavia[a][c] N = 541
A. Do in working place	(13)12	(2)38	(5)29	(7)22	(11)9	(10)23	(2)59	(6)39
B. Someone tells to do	(12)13	(10)19	(12)14	(12)7	(13)6	(12)16	(10)21	(12)7
C. Physically strenuous	(7)21	(6)27	(9)20	(10)16	(9)17	(11)20	(8)25	(11)9
D. Belongs to task	(1)65	(4)37	(2)50	(2)61	(4)48	(3)48	(3)44	(3)51
E. Contribute to society	(5)33	(12)16	(3)40	(7)22	(2)55	(4)36	(12)18	(3)51
F. Feeling of belonging	(4)44	(5)34	(7)24	(13)6	(5)41	(5)31	(6)26	(8)20
G. Mentally strenuous	(10)18	(9)20	(6)25	(9)17	(7)25	(6)28	(7)28	(9)11
H. Do at certain time	(7)21	(7)25	(10)16	(5)25	(8)20	(7)25	(4)42	(9)11
I. Adds value	(3)46	(8)24	(8)22	(3)53	(3)54	(2)49	NA	(2)55
J. Not pleasant	(14)6	(14)4	(14)1	(13)6	(14)2	(14)8	(13)8	(14)1
K. Get money for it	(2)58	(1)65	(1)68	(1)71	(1)62	(1)54	(1)63	(5)45
L. Account for it	(6)25	(2)38	(13)12	(4)48	(6)37	(9)24	(9)22	(1)56
M. Have to do it	(9)20	(11)18	(10)16	(6)23	(12)8	(13)14	(5)33	(13)6
N. Others profit by it	(11)14	(13)13	(4)34	(11)9	(10)14	(7)25	(11)20	(6)39

NOTE: [a] target group data.
Left: number in parentheses denotes ranking position within a country.
Right: percentage of country's national sample that chose the particular activity as one of the four that best defines working.

definition clusters then are examined in relation with other MOW indices. Finally, it is determined to what extent selected antecedent variables (sex, age, and educational level) are associated with certain work-definition patterns.

International comparison of definitions of working

Rankings of work definitions in the national samples are presented in Table 9.1.

For simplification purposes, only the four most frequently chosen responses are discussed here. As can be observed, the role of money (K) is the most frequently chosen item for defining work in most countries. Yugoslavia and Belgium are the only countries that deviate somewhat from this pattern, ranking fifth and second, respectively. If the activity "belongs to your task" (D) is another component present in the top four definitions for all national samples. In Yugoslavia, Netherlands, Japan, the United States, and Belgium, respondents included "if it adds value to something" (I) among their top four items. An accountability definition (L) was ranked as Number One in Yugoslavia—a significantly higher proportion of their labor force selecting it than in the other countries. However, it was also part of the four top definition statements in Germany and Japan. Contribution to society (E) was also among the top four definition statements and was viewed so by the Netherlands, Yugoslavia, the United States, and Israel. Further, Israelis selected "if others profit by it" (N) among their top four definitions. Britain deviated to some degree from the rest of the countries by placing among its top four definitions, "do it in a working place" (A) which ranked second as well as in Germany, and "do it at a certain time" (H).

Target groups' definitions of working

Rankings of work definitions in the combined samples of target groups (over all countries) are presented in Table 9.2.

Every target group included the financial reward definition (K) among their four most frequently picked definitions of working. It should be noted further that except for chemical engineers and teachers, who ranked it, respectively, second and third, all target groups selected the financial definition item as their first choice. All target groups but textile workers included the item "adds value" (I) in their top four definitions (in the latter group, it was ranked fifth). "Contribution to society" (E) was in the top

Table 9.2. Distribution of work definitions ranking and frequency percentage chosen* for target group samples (combined over countries)

Definition of work	Unemployed N = 555	Retired N = 523	Chemical engineers N = 547	Teachers N = 649	Self-employed N = 657	Tool- & Diemakers N = 595	White-collar N = 693	Textile workers N = 583	Temporary workers N = 464	Students N = 589
A. Do in a working place	(9) 20	(8) 21	(9) 17	(10) 18	(8) 23	(6) 29	(6) 31	(3) 36	(8) 24	(10) 22
B. Someone tells you what to do	(13) 15	(13) 9	(13) 7	(13) 6	(13) 6	(13) 14	(13) 12	(12) 16	(13) 12	(13) 14
C. Physically strenuous	(8) 23	(12) 14	(12) 10	(11) 13	(11) 16	(9) 21	(12) 14	(8) 22	(12) 14	(6) 26
D. Belongs to your task	(2) 45	(2) 54	(3) 53	(1) 58	(3) 50	(2) 47	(2) 46	(2) 48	(2) 47	(2) 45
E. Contribute to society	(5) 29	(3) 50	(5) 39	(4) 44	(5) 32	(4) 35	(5) 32	(4) 34	(6) 28	(4) 31
F. Feeling of belonging	(4) 31	(5) 33	(8) 21	(6) 30	(6) 26	(7) 25	(7) 26	(6) 28	(7) 27	(9) 24
G. Mentally strenuous	(12) 17	(8) 21	(6) 26	(8) 25	(9) 21	(11) 17	(9) 21	(12) 13	(9) 21	(8) 25
H. Do at certain time	(7) 24	(7) 22	(11) 14	(9) 19	(11) 16	(8) 22	(8) 24	(7) 27	(5) 32	(6) 26
I. Adds value	(3) 41	(4) 44	(1) 61	(2) 50	(2) 51	(3) 37	(3) 42	(5) 31	(3) 42	(3) 41
J. Not pleasant	(14) 5	(14) 3	(14) 3	(14) 4	(14) 4	(14) 5	(14) 4	(14) 4	(14) 4	(14) 6
K. Get money for it	(1) 63	(1) 56	(2) 59	(3) 48	(1) 61	(1) 70	(1) 67	(1) 71	(1) 69	(1) 69
L. Account for it	(5) 29	(6) 27	(4) 44	(5) 41	(4) 37	(5) 32	(4) 36	(9) 21	(4) 34	(5) 29
M. Have to do it	(10) 18	(11) 17	(10) 15	(11) 13	(10) 18	(11) 17	(11) 17	(9) 21	(11) 18	(12) 17
N. If others profit by it	(10) 18	(10) 19	(6) 26	(7) 27	(6) 26	(10) 20	(9) 21	(11) 19	(10) 19	(11) 20

* Target groups data were not collected in Britain.
Above: Number in parentheses denotes ranking position within a target group.
Below: Percentage of the target group that chose the particular activity as one which best defines when an activity is working.

four for the retired, teachers, tool- and diemakers, textile workers, and students. The chemical engineers, self-employed, white-collar, and temporary workers, however, selected the item, "have to account for it" (L), as their fourth work definition notion. Finally, two target groups chose in fourth place a rather specific definition item that was not selected by any of the other groups. Unemployed chose "feeling of belonging" (F), whereas textile workers selected "if you do it in a working place" (A).

Identification of work definitions clusters

An approach, which combined hierarchical clustering and multiple discriminant analysis on the 14 definition of working items, was employed to identify work definition patterns and to reduce the number of work definition notions to a smaller meaningful set.

Cluster and multiple discriminant analyses were both performed on a representative, stratified sample of the total target group data. Approximately 14 respondents randomly were selected to represent each target group in each country. The total number of individuals in this sample was 910, and it will be referred to in this chapter as the "original sample." Results from the original sample were cross-validated on a representative sample, stratified per country of the national survey data of Belgium, Israel, Japan, Netherlands, and the United States.[1] The total number of respondents in this sample was 450, and it will be referred to as the "cross-validation sample."

Ward's method of hierarchical clustering was performed on individual respondents' choices on the 14 items of the work definition question (Question 49; see Appendix A3.1). Through this method, respondents who selected similar work definitions items were grouped together to form homogeneous definitional groups differing as much as possible from other groups. Taking into consideration the optimal ratio between loss of variance (error coefficient) and number of clusters, a decision was made to identify only four work definition clusters. Identifying less than four clusters would have resulted in a large loss of variance (Wishart, 1978).[2]

Multiple discriminant analysis was conducted with five groups as criterion; four work definition clusters and one category of ungrouped cases, namely, the rest of the total target group data. In the cross-validation phase, the final category was the rest of the national survey data. The predictors from the multiple discriminant analysis were the choices made on the 14 binary work definition variables. A high percentage (82–88%) of respondents were correctly classified into the appropriate work definition cluster, using their discriminant function scores. Consequently, the four extracted work definition clusters are apparently valid. The ungrouped cases of both the original and the cross-validation samples were distributed over the four clusters with percentages about equal to the representative samples. This illustrates that the work definition clusters are valid in terms of defining items and are generalizable beyond their construction samples.

Empirical work definitions

Work-definition clusters can be described as follows:

The *Concrete* work definition (Cluster 1) groups about 35% of the respondents who defined working in terms of:

(*K*) if you get money for doing it
(*M*) you have to do it
(*A*) you do it in a working place
(*H*) you do it at a certain time
(*J*) it is not pleasant

The *Social* work definition (Cluster 2) groups between 17–22% of respondents for whom working is an activity which:

(*E*) contributes to society
(*F*) by doing it you get the feeling of belonging
(*N*) others profit by it

The *Duty* work definition (Cluster 3) contains between 25–30% of the respondents who define work as an activity which:

(*L*) you have to account for
(*D*) belongs to your task

Work in this cluster seems to be considered as a duty and a moral obligation.

The *Burden* work definition (Cluster 4) groups 19–23% of the respondents who define working in terms of being:

(*C*) physically strenuous
(*G*) mentally strenuous

Table 9.3 presents the distribution of the four work-definition clusters for each country.

Examination of the distributions in Table 9.3 reveals some cross-national similarity in work definition patterns and some country-specific work definition patterns. The *concrete* work definition includes almost half of the Japanese and the German samples, while less than a quarter of Yugoslavian

Table 9.3. Distribution of work definition clusters for countries (national sample data)

| Country | N | Work definition cluster | | | |
		Concrete	Social	Duty	Burden
Belgium	450	29	32	25	14
Germany	1278	45	13	27	15
Israel	973	36	35	18	11
Japan	3226	42	5	45	8
Netherlands	996	23	27	37	13
United States	998	29	29	25	17
Yugoslavia[a]	541	15	25	53	7

[a] target group data.

and Dutch respondents define work in such a manner. Furthermore, about half of the Japanese and Yugoslavian sample population are grouped into the *duty* work definition, whereas a much smaller proportion of respondents from Belgium, Germany, Israel, and the United States were so classified. The *social* work definition attracted relatively similar proportions of individuals in all countries except Japan and Germany, which had much lower membership. Regarding the *burden* work definition, the proportions are approximately the same across countries with the exception of Japan and Yugoslavia, which are low.

Generally, national samples differ considerably in the way their labor forces are distributed among the four work definitional groups. Two countries (Germany and Yugoslavia) are what might be termed "single peak" countries in that they predominantly utilize one definitional type with less frequent use of the other three definitional types. Germany would be classified as a single-peak definitional country of the concrete type while Yugoslavia is a single-peak definitional country of the duty type. The other five countries could be described as "multiple peak" countries in terms of work definition categorization. Japan peaks on duty and concrete definition types, while Israel peaks on concrete and social definitions. Belgium, the Netherlands and the United States are distributed relatively equally across all four definition types.

Turning to an analysis of the work definition clusters distributions for target groups, the findings are presented in Table 9.4.

The results indicate that five of the 10 target groups (unemployed, tool- and diemakers, temporary workers, textile workers and students) would be single-peak groups in that each group predominantly utilizes one definitional type with less frequent use of the other three definitional types.

The five target groups that are single-peak definitional groups uniformly peak on the concrete work definition category. The other five target groups—multiple-peak groups—peak on two, three, or all four definitional

Table 9.4. Distribution of work definition clusters for target groups

| Target group | N | Work definition cluster | | | |
		Concrete	Social	Duty	Burden
Unemployed	555	44[a]	13	27	16
Retired	573	27	27	23	23
Chemical engineers	547	19	32	36	13
Teachers	649	28	25	35	12
Self-employed	657	29	22	37	12
Tool- and diemakers	595	42	22	26	10
White-collar	693	35	18	35	12
Textile workers	583	39	27	26	8
Temporary workers	464	42	16	30	12
Students	589	38	20	21	21

[a] percentage of each target group classified into each work definition cluster.

types. The retired peak on all four definitional types, while teachers and self-employed peak on the concrete, social, and duty definitional types. White-collar employees peak on the concrete and the duty definitional types, while chemical engineers peak on the duty and social definitional types.

Generally, it is observed that there are greater distinctions in how working is defined among countries than among target groups.

Work definition clusters and other meaning of working variables

Table 9.5 presents the average index score (mean T scores) on the central MOW dimensions expressed in linear T scores on several major MOW variables for each definitional type among national samples. It can be observed that all scores on these MOW indices do not depart substantially from the overall average score of 50. Thus, there seems to be no substantial relationship between work definition types and level of MOW central variables. The same analyses reported in Table 9.5 were conducted for each country separately, and the findings are similar. The central MOW variables (as shown in Table 9.5) do not differentiate among the four work definition clusters to any appreciable degree.

Work definition clusters and demographic variables

Distributions of the demographic variables of gender, age, and education within work definition clusters for the combined national samples are

Table 9.5. Meaning of working indices (mean T scores)[a] found for work definition
clusters (national sample data)

Central meaning of working indices	N	Work definition cluster			
		Concrete	Social	Duty	Burden
Work centrality (CW)	7710	50	49	51	49
Interpersonal contact (CONTACT)	4277[b]	49	50	50	50
Self-expression (IR)	7245	49	51	50	50
Economic function (PAY)	4344[b]	53	49	49	50
Obligation (OBL)	7773	50	51	50	50
Opportunity (OPP)	7774	50	51	50	51

NOTE: [a] Mean of 50; standard deviation of 10.
[b] Japanese sample was not included, due to missing data on this MOW index.

exhibited in Table 9.6 (for country specific distributions, see Tables A9.3,
A9.4, and A9.5 in the Appendix).

It is apparent that, considering the combined national samples, males
and females share the same work definitions. Perhaps, males stress the
duty definition of work a bit more, while the reverse is true for the concrete
definition. In Belgium (see Table A9.3), both sexes favored the social work

Table 9.6. Distribution of work definition clusters by gender, age, and education in the
combined national survey data (percentages)

Demographic variable	Work definition cluster			
	Concrete	Social	Duty	Burden
Gender (N = 8447)				
Male	35	17	36	12
Female	38	18	33	11
Age (N = 8440)				
30 years	34	19	35	12
30–50 years	36	17	36	11
50 years	38	18	34	10
Education (N = 8414)				
Primary	43	23	24	10
Secondary	39	17	33	11
Some college	30	22	35	13
University	28	15	47	10

definition more than the three other definitions. So did American males; however, females evenly selected the concrete and duty definitions. In Israel, the concrete work definition was selected most frequently by males, while females selected the social definition. Japanese males were classified mainly into the duty definition, whereas a majority of females were grouped into the concrete definition cluster. The latter was also the most dominant definition found for both sexes in Germany. Finally, the duty definition was overwhelmingly chosen in the Netherlands and Yugoslavia (target group sample) by both sexes. Overall, the general conclusion is that there is no substantial gender difference in the way people define the activity of working.

Age seems to have little or no effect on how people define working (work definition types) in the total national samples. Some slight age trends can be noted for specific countries (see Table A9.4 in the Appendix), but they are small and not consistent in direction among countries so little interpretation can be made here.

Educational level is linearly related to membership in the concrete work definition cluster for all countries except in Belgium (see Table 9.6, and Table A9.4 in the Appendix). Generally, the higher the educational level, the lower the percentage of respondents who are in the concrete cluster. In contrast, a trend in the opposite direction is noted in the duty work definition cluster: The higher the educational level, the greater the selection of the duty work definition by the respondents. Educational level, then, seems to be correlated more highly with the way individuals define their work than is the case for gender or age.

Conclusions

The activity which is commonly referred to as "working" takes on multiple meanings in the present study—as it has historically. From the various analyses reported here, it is evident that some definition statements most frequently are chosen in all countries with approximate similarity in rankings. The role of money is clearly most significant cross nationally in terms of how working is defined (in Yugoslavia, "money" assumed somewhat less importance; nevertheless, it was found among its top five definitions). Other frequently chosen definitional statements were: "if it belongs to your task" (D), "if it adds value to something" (I), "if you do it to contribute to society" (E), and "if you have to account for it" (L).

The pattern among target groups in choice of definitional statements resembled that observed for national samples. Similar definitions were found in the top of the list selected by target groups, with money chosen most often. Blue-collar and low-skill-level groups frequently chose this definition (e.g., textile workers, 71%, tool- and diemakers, 70%). On the other hand, teachers ranked it only third, and chemical engineers, second. An observation worth noting is the fact that only the target group of unemployed ranked the definition of "if by doing it, you get the feeling of belonging" (F) among their top selected definitions (number four). None of the other target groups saw it as important; hence, this may indicate an important function that working has for people who cannot obtain gainful employment. Not being employed may affect individuals psychologically through a feeling of being rejected by organizations as well as society.

Through cluster analysis, the previously identified 14 work definition notions were reduced to a smaller set of categorized definitions. These were: (1) concrete cluster—including various tangible and practical aspects associated with work (questionnaire subitems K, M, A, H, J); (2) the social cluster—although difficult to name—comprising definitional characteristics through which one may get a feeling of belonging and relate to society (E, F, N); (3) the duty cluster—containing definitions implying one's sense of task relatedness and accountability (L, D); and (4) the burden cluster—incorporating definitions denoting physical as well as mental strain related to work (C, G).

National differences are considerably more evident than are target group differences in the distributions of work definition types. Likewise, educational differences are more pronounced than are gender or age differences in work definition classification. The way in which the activity called "working" is defined seems more a function of aspects of living in a certain country and education level and much less a function of age, sex, or standing on work meaning variables such as work centrality, societal norms about working, or preferred work goal characteristics.

Notes

(1) National sample for Britain had some missing data for the work definitions question, and the national German data were not available when this analysis was carried out; therefore, both countries were not represented in the cross-validation procedure.

(2) To define the four clusters, one has to examine the ratio percentage of occurrence of an item in a cluster versus the percentage of overall occurrence. This ratio is termed the binary frequency ratio (BFR). The general criterion for use of one of the 14 items in defining a cluster, is the largest possible deviation from 1.0 (either positive or negative) for the BFR. We chose, however, to label the clusters by the positive deviation of BFR from 1.0. Finally, the inclusiveness of each work definition cluster is expressed by the percentage of respondents grouped together in the cluster. Tables 9.1 and 9.2 in the Appendix respectively present the cluster solutions for both the total target groups data (original sample) and the national samples (cross-validation sample).

Chapter 10

Meaning of Working Patterns

Introduction

In Chapter 2, separate meaning of working concepts included in our heuristic model were identified and described. Our measures of these concepts were discussed in Chapter 3, and the factor analysis results presented in Chapter 4 provide some support for the validity of our measures of the concepts. Subsequent chapters developed each of the concepts in greater depth and provided evidence for some major sources of variation in peoples' scores on measures of these concepts.

But the totality of meaning assigned to working by people may be lost in isolated examinations of individual dimensions of meaning. Indeed, in Chapter 2, we discussed the conceptual interrelatedness of the various meanings of working and indicated that we sought to provide a more idiographic view of individuals as one important goal. Theoretically, the core meaning of working variables do not operate independently within an individual, but rather form a *gestalt* or pattern. From a practical point of view as well, it would be difficult to work only with a single meaning of working dimension when focusing on important issues such as the design of jobs. From a broader company policy perspective, concern for the motivation of employees, knowledge of what meaning of working dimensions "hang together" and form a pattern would seem to be an important issue.

The purpose of this chapter is to focus on the question of how the particular meaning of working dimensions combine and form patterns of meanings. We seek to identify and describe meaning of working patterns and determine how generalizable these patterns are in different countries and target groups. The following two chapters examine the antecedents and consequences of these patterns of work meanings.

Developing meaning of working patterns

A pattern of work meanings consists of the combination of scores of individuals on several different meaning dimensions. Six separate indices of work meanings were used in the development of MOW patterns (indices are abbreviated in parentheses).

- Work centrality (CW): the evaluative belief that work is important and significant in one's life.
- Entitlement norm (ENT): the normative belief that all individuals should be provided certain outcomes in terms of working as a matter of right.
- Obligation norm (OBL): the normative belief that all individuals have a duty to contribute to society through work and working.
- Economic function of working (PAY): valued working outcome preference for income.
- Intrinsic or expressive working outcomes (IR): valuing working that allows for self-expression.
- Interpersonal contact through working (CONTACT): valuing good social relations in a work setting.

Procedure for the formation and validation of MOW patterns

We used hierarchical cluster and multiple discriminant analyses in the construction of MOW patterns that are important, definable, distinguishable, stable, valid, and generalizable. Cluster analysis is based on the assumption that, when the similarities of people or objects on certain variables are greater than the dissimilarities, clusters of those people or objects will be formed. Through cluster analysis, we group those respondents who have a similar combination of scores on the six MOW dimensions. Each group formed is relatively homogeneous but maximally different when compared to the other groups which are formed. Ward's method of hierarchical clustering was performed on the individual respondents' scores on the six central MOW indices. To arrive at usable MOW patterns, the following cluster analysis results are taken into account: loss of variance versus number of clusters; stability of dimensions in a cluster; mean score on dimensions in a cluster versus grand mean and grand standard deviation; and number of respondents in each cluster.

Multiple discriminant analysis was performed with the clusters (from the cluster analysis) as the criterion and the individuals' scores on the six central MOW indices as the predictors. Through multiple discriminant analysis, we initially tested the power of the separate MOW dimensions to detect groups of respondents with different MOW patterns. We used the discriminant function coefficients and the distances between group centroids along the discriminant functions to identify the MOW dimensions that contributed the most to cluster differentiation. Then, multiple discriminant analysis was used to assess the validity of the identified patterns. The purpose was to determine whether respondents grouped in a particular MOW pattern through cluster analysis were correctly classified into that MOW pattern by using their scores on the discriminant functions as predictors. Finally, multiple discriminant analysis served as a control on the generalizability of the MOW patterns by allocating respondents with unknown MOW patterns to a certain cluster based on their scores on the discriminant functions.

Both cluster and multiple discriminant analyses were, due to computer program limitations, performed on a representative stratified sample of the total target group data. Fourteen respondents were randomly selected from each country and target group to form the developmental sample.[1] The total number of respondents in the representative sample was 901. A second stratified representative sample of equal size was used in cross validation.

Identification of MOW patterns

Five clusters provide the optimal grouping with fewer clusters of respondents yielding an unacceptable loss of variance. Four of these five clusters were affirmed through cross validation in terms of stability of the dimensions and of specific mean scores on the dimensions. The conclusion from extensive analysis is that we have constructed stable and definable MOW patterns. Respondents are fairly evenly distributed over four patterns, while the fifth grouping is marginal and included about 10% of the respondents. Thus, the MOW patterns include large groupings of people.

There are several distinguishable features of the patterns of work meanings.

1. All central MOW dimensions have power to discriminate between clusters, with only work centrality providing slightly less discrimination in the cross validation sample.
2. A high percentage (about 80%) of respondents with a particular MOW pattern are correctly classified into that pattern using their discriminant function scores. Therefore, we conclude that the MOW patterns are valid.

3. It is possible to allocate each respondent with unknown MOW pattern to a certain pattern by using his discriminant functions' scores.

Thus, the MOW patterns are generalizable over large numbers of respondents.

Since the fifth marginal pattern was not confirmed in cross-validation and, moreover, also lacks discriminatory power, we added respondents with that pattern to the group with an unknown MOW pattern. Following this procedure, check of the percentage of correct classifications shows an increase. Further, the discriminatory power of the six central MOW dimensions between the four usable patterns remains high, as does the generalizability. With this evidence, we restrict our consideration to the four cross-validated MOW patterns.

The identified MOW patterns involve the three MOW dimensions that are the most stable and contribute the most to the definition of each pattern. However, over the four patterns, all six central MOW dimensions contributed to pattern definition. Among the work meaning dimensions, two kinds of contrasts emerge. The first contrast is between the economic function and both intrinsic valued working outcomes and work centrality. The second contrast is between the societal norms about working and the interpersonal contact dimension of working.

Figures 10.1–10.4 show the identified MOW patterns for both the original and cross-validation samples. Each pattern includes the mean score for the three defining dimensions expressed in linear T score in relation to the grand mean and the grand standard deviation. Since few significant differences (at the .05 level) between cluster means and grand mean occur, we used the following cross-validated rule to aid labeling of the patterns: high (T scores > 54); medium (T scores, 46–54); low T scores < 46).

> The *instrumental MOW pattern* (Figure 10.1) includes about 30% of the respondents. For these people, the income working provides is particularly important. Work does not occupy a very central place in their lives; but rather, is an instrument to obtain income. They place a low value on intrinsic aspects in their work.
> The *expressive work centrality MOW pattern* (Figure 10.2) includes about 25% of the respondents. People with this pattern stress the importance of working where they can express themselves; work is central in their lives. Income or pay is not stressed as an important outcome of working; indeed, it has a very low position in this respect.
> The *entitlement and contact orientation MOW pattern* includes about 20% of the respondents (Figure 10.3). People with this pattern are rather high on the right to work as contrasted with the duty to work

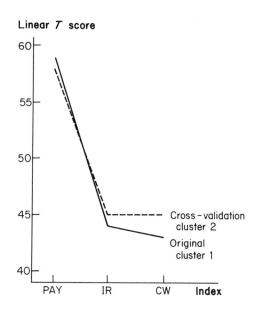

Figure 10.1. *Instrumental MOW pattern.*

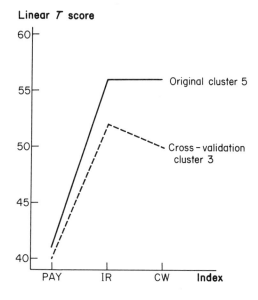

Figure 10.2. *Expressive work centrality MOW pattern.*

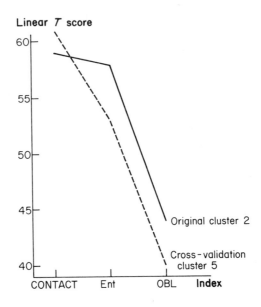

Figure 10.3. Entitlement and contact orientation MOW pattern.

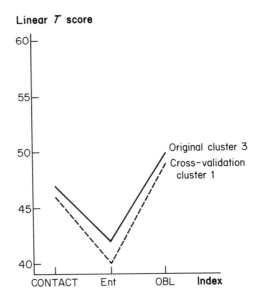

Figure 10.4. Low entitlement MOW pattern.

and place high value on the social contact dimension of working as an important outcome.

The *low entitlement MOW pattern* (Figure 10.4) includes approximately 25% of the respondents. The defining feature for these people is an extremely low entitlement orientation to working which is only slightly counterbalanced by a medium obligation orientation.

Distribution of national representative samples on the MOW patterns

An important issue concerns the distribution of national representative samples among the four MOW patterns. To address this issue, we extend our analysis and discussion to the national representative samples in five of the countries. The British data were excluded because of lack of information on some of the items used to form the defining indices of clusters. Some of the relevant questions also were excluded from the national survey in Japan. Therefore, the combined Japanese and Yugoslavian target group samples are included for comparative purposes.

The coefficients developed in the multiple discriminant analysis on the target groups were applied to the index scores of all respondents in the representative samples to assign them to one of the four MOW patterns. The results of this analysis are shown in Table 10.1. The size of the national representative samples are included to aid understanding. The percentages shown for each country indicate the percentage frequency of a particular MOW pattern among the national samples from Belgium, Germany,

Table 10.1. Distribution of national labor force samples on the four MOW patterns (in percentages)

	Instrumental pattern	Expressive work centrality pattern	Entitlement and contact orientation pattern	Low entitlement pattern
Belgium (450)	30	20	26	24
Germany (1268)	35	28	14	23
Israel (955)	26	41	8	25
Japan* (1098)	18	29	11	42
Netherlands (991)	28	21	31	20
United States (998)	16	22	10	52
Yugoslavia* (528)	20	48	7	25

* Target group data for comparison purposes.

Israel, the Netherlands, and the United States. Again, Japanese and Yugoslavian target group data are presented for comparison purposes.

There are some conclusions that can be drawn from the distibutions shown in Table 10.1.

- There is a clear modal MOW pattern in the Israeli and the United States national samples. For Israel, the modal pattern is expressive work centrality, and for the United States, the low entitlement orientation pattern is modal.
- There is a clear modal MOW pattern for the target groups used for comparison purposes in Japan and Yugoslavia. For the Japanese target groups, the modal MOW pattern is low entitlement orientation, and for Yugoslavian target groups, the expressive work centrality pattern is modal.
- Belgian and Dutch national samples are fairly evenly distributed across four MOW patterns.
- The German national representative sample is mainly concentrated in the instrumental and expressive work centrality patterns.

MOW patterns among target groups

Having presented the results from the national sample distributions on the MOW patterns, we return to the target group samples and present findings on the distribution of these groups over the four MOW patterns. Table 10.2 presents the target groups' distribution over the four MOW patterns. All target groups are represented in each pattern to some extent, but there are some notable differences in the distributions of the groups on the patterns.

However, before discussing these differences in distributions, it is important to register notes of caution necessary in interpreting these findings. First, as indicated in the previous section, there are differences in the distribution of the national representative samples on these four patterns. We do not know the extent to which these national differences were cancelled out by merging the target groups over countries for the present analysis, but undoubtedly some cancelling-out probably occurred. Second, the composition of the target groups is an important consideration in interpreting findings. (The composition of the groups was discussed in Chapter 3.) Recall, as an example, that half the students are male and half are female and the samples were drawn from vocational trade schools. The males were training for skilled trade jobs with tool- and diemaking being an example of a later job for them. The female students were training for

Table 10.2. Target group distribution for each MOW pattern (in percentages)

	Instrumental pattern	Expressive work centrality pattern	Entitlement and contact orientation pattern	Low entitlement pattern
Unemployed (536)	27	25	20	28
Retired (556)	20	39	11	30
Chemical engineers (545)	11	32	14	43
Teachers (646)	8	41	33	18
Self-employed (649)	13	36	10	41
Tool- and diemakers (582)	36	22	7	35
White-collar (689)	27	22	18	33
Textile workers (569)	35	25	6	34
Temporary workers (456)	29	23	23	25
Students (588)	26	20	22	32

white-collar clerical and office work. These target group features again influence interpretation of findings.

There are five conclusions drawn from the distribution of target groups over the patterns:

- There is a modal MOW pattern that characterizes chemical engineers, which is low entitlement orientation.
- Teachers tend to be concentrated in either the expressive work centrality pattern or the entitlement and contract orientation pattern.
- Both the retired and the self-employed tend to be concentrated in either the expressive work centrality pattern or the low entitlement pattern.
- Tool- and diemakers, white-collar workers, and textile workers tend to be concentrated in either the instrumental pattern or low entitlement pattern.
- Unemployed, temporary workers, and students are fairly evenly distributed over the four MOW patterns.

Summary

At the beginning of this chapter, we suggested that people do not perceive and interpret the world of work through the use of a series of relatively independent dimensions of work meanings. Rather, based on the communications of experiences and interpretation of these experiences from others, and based on their own experiences, people form a gestalt—an integrated pattern that allows for a unique perception and interpretation of work-related events and experiences. From this point of view, each MOW pattern can be thought of, initially, as a hypothetical set of glasses. The patterns are like prisms: ground and shaped by events, experiences, and social influences to provide clear but distinct ways of attending, and responding, to working as a life role.

The patterns can also be thought of as a "chunking" device; patterns may be capable of storing more information and assigning meaning to a wider range of experiences than isolated MOW dimensions. The instrumental pattern, as an example, may be characteristic of people who prefer highly visible and externally mediated behavior/reward relationships as a feed-back device for controlling and adjusting subsequent behavior. In contrast, the expressive work centrality pattern could suggest self-monitoring and personal mediation as a feedback device for regulating behavior. The entitlement and contact orientation and low entitlement patterns may signal different combinations of norms of distributive justice. The former pattern would suggest a view of distributive justice with priority given to rights over duties and social contact as a medium for gaining information used in assigning normative meanings. The latter pattern would suggest a view of distributive justice that assigns a modest priority to duties over rights and a lesser priority to social contact as a medium for gaining information used in assigning normative meaning.

While the four patterns provide a parsimonious set of hypothetical models for the assignment of meaning to working, there is a great deal of diversity in the distribution of these models in different countries and for different target groups. This diversity is particularly pronounced within countries such as Belgium and the Netherlands where there is no distinct modal MOW pattern indicated in national representative labor force samples. In these countries, the diversity of patterns may indicate that these are societies in transition or societies in which the meaning of work is highly segmented and quite different for large proportions of the labor force. This may present particular problems and require a great deal of imagination in formulating labor policies and practices. Similar lines of argument may be applied to the other countries.

The implications of the present findings would seem to differ for different target groups viewed against the backdrop of the more prevailing patterns of the particular country or, in some cases, other target groups. Students, as an example, are fairly evenly distributed over the four MOW patterns. This may suggest one of two general implications. First, the students have varied preconceptions of work based upon anticipatory socialization and will likely respond in quite different ways to initial work experiences. Remember that in the student group half are males and half are females; so, an anticipatory socialization interpretation may be gender-related. Alternatively, the diverse MOW patterns of students may suggest that they are particularly open to the influence of early work experiences which will alter their patterns of work meanings. The male students were receiving training for skilled trade jobs such as tool- and diemaking. Thus, based on subsequent experiences, either an instrumental or low entitlement pattern of meaning may develop in the future. With the female students, their training was for jobs such as those represented by the white-collar group. This may again suggest that with experience, they may develop either an instrumental or low entitlement MOW pattern.

Additionally, two other frames of reference are likely to shape and influence the formation of MOW patterns. First, some patterns are much less or much more likely in some target groups than in others. In general, the instrumental pattern is much less likely to be found among chemical engineers than among textile workers or tool- and diemakers. Thus, the development of MOW patterns partially may relate to specific job settings or occupational circumstances. But, in addition, the modal pattern in a society also can act as a frame of reference in the development of MOW patterns. As an example, the instrumental pattern is not very widely held in the United States labor force, while the low entitlement MOW pattern is the modal pattern. This modal pattern also is one of the two major patterns for both tool- and diemakers and textile workers. This modal pattern in the labor force may suggest that these target groups in the United States would be more likely to develop a low entitlement pattern than an instrumental pattern. Thus, the MOW patterns may act as a device for organizing and assigning meaning to diverse work experiences. But the development of these patterns, and changes in the patterns are likely to be influenced by these experiences, by occupational MOW patterns as frames of reference, and by societal MOW patterns as frames of reference. The picture is one of both parsimony and diversity.

Notes

(1) This sample is not the same sample that was drawn for analysis in Chapter 9. The sampling parameters were the same but the samples were separately drawn.

Chapter 11

Antecedents of Meaning of Working Patterns

Introduction

In Chapter 10, we identified and described four meaning of working profiles. The purpose of the present chapter is to extend the discussion of these patterns. Specifically, we examine antecedents of these patterns. These antecedents are organized into three major areas: biographical variables, the work history, and the present job situation. These three categories generally fall into the personal background, the work history, and job situation influences on the meaning of working shown in the model (Figure 2.1 in Chapter 2). In addition, some presentation of regression-analysis results relating antecedents to each of the MOW core variables are discussed when they add understanding to the major analysis.

Biographical variables

In this section, we investigate the relations between biographical variables and the MOW patterns. Three groups of biographical variables are distinguished: personal characteristics, family situation, and upbringing. The results are presented in Table 11.1. For each pattern, the mean score of a variable was calculated. In case of nominal variables, the table entry is the percentage of people per MOW pattern having a particular characteristic (i.e., the percentage male respondents and the percentage married of those who have an instrumental pattern). To test the significance of the differences between patterns, an overall F test was calculated where appropriate. The magnitude of the differences between the MOW patterns is judged by means of the Tukey test.[1] For nominal variables, a χ square is used.

Table 11.1. MOW patterns and biographical variables (percentages and mean scores)

MOW Patterns	Instrumental	Entitlement and Contact Orientation	Low Entitlement	Expressive Work Centrality	Significance
Personal characteristics					
• Age	33.8	32.8	36.7	39.0	$p < .001$
• Education[a]	2.1	2.8	2.5	2.7	$p < .001$
• Percentage male	55.9	40.2	62.5	50.5	$p < .001$
• Percentage with religion: close contact	15.1	11.6	17.5	19.4	ns
Home situation					
• Percentage married	64.8	50.0	66.7	65.8	$p = .003$
• Number of persons financially supported	1.9	1.8	2.1	2.1	ns
• present community: percentage city	64.5	73.3	64.2	74.0	ns
Upbringing					
• Education father[a]	1.9	2.1	1.9	2.0	$p = .03$
• Education mother[a]	1.6	1.8	1.7	1.6	$p = .04$
• Percentage religious education	53.5	55.2	55.6	58.3	ns
• Community childhood: percentage city	48.9	59.4	50.2	52.2	ns

[a] Means indicated for respondent education and for father's and mother's education are the average-response category. The response alternatives for parent's education are (1) primary school, (2) secondary school, (3) some college, and (4) university degree.

Personal characteristics

Among the personal characteristics taken into consideration are education, age, sex, and association with a religion. The level of education clearly differentiates between the instrumental pattern and the other three patterns. People with less education are more instrumentally oriented than people with more education.

The age differences between the patterns are also significant. The patterns can be ordered from a high to a low mean age, but adjacent MOW patterns in the ranking process are not significantly different. The ordering in terms of average age of persons in the pattern is expressive work centrality (39.0 years), low entitlement (36.7 years), instrumental (33.8 years), and entitlement and contact orientation (32.8 years). Inglehart (1979) found that younger people in the Netherlands, Great Britain, the United States, West Germany, and Austria were also well represented in a value pattern similar to the entitlement and contact orientation pattern.

The literature on the preference for intrinsic versus instrumental/ extrinsic aspects of work generally report a positive correlation between age and instrumental work orientation (Andrisani and Miljus, 1977; Jurgensen, 1978). We expect, accordingly, that those people with the instrumental pattern will be somewhat older in average age. We also expect a relatively higher mean age for those who adhere to the low entitlement pattern, since this pattern reflects more traditional work norms. Our findings indicate that people with the low entitlement pattern tend to be older and agrees with the findings of other studies (Sessions, 1978; Yankelovich, 1981).

The overall test of sex differences between patterns also is significant. A relatively high percentage of those with the entitlement and contact orientation pattern are females, while a high percentage of the instrumental and low entitlement MOW patterns are males. The expressive work centrality pattern includes equal percentages of females and males. Generally, research findings indicate that women are more intrinsically oriented than men (Jurgensen, 1978; Stake, 1978), although Brief and Oliver (1976) claimed that these differences were confounded by occupation and organizational level. The target groups that are heavily represented in the expressive work centrality pattern (see Chapter 10, Table 10.2) include particular occupational and higher-level jobs such as teachers (all women), chemical engineers (all males), and self-employed (all males).

The patterns do not differ to the extent that respondents are associated with a religion. This might be due to the fact that all religions were combined in our operationalization. An analysis by particular religious background may have been more revealing, particularly as a correlate of the low entitlement pattern.

Regression-analysis results also bear out the generality of the relationship between biographical variables and MOW pattern. As an example, sex, generally, was not related to work centrality or to intrinsic values in most countries and is consistent with the finding that both sexes are equally represented in the expressive work centrality pattern. Educational attainment was related negatively to pay values in all seven countries included in the analysis. This finding is consistent with the higher percentage of less-educated people in the instrumental pattern. The finding that women are more heavily represented in the entitlement and contact orientation pattern likely is due to their greater valuation of social contacts than is the case for men. Regression findings indicate no general relationship (mean differences) between sex and entitlement norms. But, in all seven countries where regression analyses were performed, women's social contact values were higher than those of men. Finally, regression-analysis findings indicate that age is positively related to both work centrality and obligation norms in all six countries where it was performed. It is likely that the higher proportion of older people in the expressive work centrality and low entitlement (moderate obligation norms) patterns are due to these age-related values, preferences, and beliefs.

Home and community situation

The discussion in Chapter 2 posited that financial responsibility for others would relate to various MOW variables. A positive correlation was predicted between financial responsibilities and the obligation and entitlement norms, and income as a valued working outcome. Additionally, a negative correlation with work centrality was predicted. Therefore, a relationship between financial responsibility and the instrumental pattern would be expected, because the PAY index is high, work centrality scores low, and respondents who have this pattern feel, to some extent, that working is something one is entitled to. Contrary to expectation, it appears from Table 11.1, that the differences between the mean number of financially dependent persons per MOW pattern are not statistically significant.

A relatively low percentage of those with the entitlement and social contact orientation pattern are married. However, this finding can be understood in connection with the prior finding that respondents with this pattern are younger.

There is a line of psychological research, rooted in the work of Turner and Lawrence (1965) and Hulin and Blood (1968), which investigated the relationship between community characteristics and work-related values. Those living in rural areas would adhere to middle-class norms, while those in urban areas were supposed to be alienated from these norms. In our research, there appears to be no significant relationship between MOW patterns and the percentage of persons living in a large city. This finding is not surprising, in view of the conclusion that, "The rural-urban dichotomy is a sociological construct attached to communities. It is not clear what, if any, relationship it has to growth need strength or any other psychological construct attached to individuals". (Roberts and Glick, 1981.)

Upbringing

Work values result partly from a developmental process which starts with early socialization. Significant others (i.e., parents, teachers, and peers) pass on their values and norms during the formative years (Sewell *et al.*, 1970). This point of view is in accordance with traditional sociology. The symbolic interactionist perspective stresses the adaptation of individuals to the various social situations they meet. They see socialization as a continuous learning process and individual differences are acknowledged (White, 1977).

To investigate the influence of upbringing on the meaning of working, various variables were included in our research. The variables included are education of the father and mother, religious education, and community size during childhood. Findings relating these variables to the MOW patterns results are presented in Table 11.1. Only the education of the father and mother differentiate significantly between the patterns. In particular, the parents of respondents with an instrumental pattern tend to be less educated than the parents of respondents with the entitlement and contact orientation pattern, although the differences are small. The mean educational levels per pattern for the father and the mother are similar, although the educational attainment of the mother is consistently lower than the father's.

The influence of father's occupation and preference for intrinsic or extrinsic factors was investigated by Saleh and Singh (1973). Their operationalizations of father's occupation in three categories (unskilled, technical, and professional) is highly correlated with the educational levels of the father we used. A relationship between father's occupation and intrinsic job orientation was found only among the low-salaried group: the lower the level of the father's occupation, the less the intrinsic orientation appeared to be. Andrisani and Miljus (1977) found no relationship between socioeconomic status of family background and intrinsic preferences. They used an index based on fathers' and mothers' education as well as on several other indicators.

Inglehart (1979) constructed an index based on the occupation and the education of the father. In the four countries included in his sample, a positive relationship between the socioeconomic status of the father and a pattern of work values resembling the entitlement and social contact orientation was observed. Our results also suggest this relationship between family background and work values and favors the traditional stratification-oriented perspective of socialization processes.

Our findings regarding the relationship between childhood community characteristics and MOW patterns are consistent with Adler, Aranya and Amernic (1981), who conclude that, "Relevant early socialization influences stemming from community size may exist, but they are offset by later socialization influences on work need development." However, as was discussed in the preceding section, the influence of rural or urban environment during later socialization seems not to exist either.

In view of the commonly held assumption of an association between religion (particularly Protestantism) and work ethic, it is surprising that the patterns are not significantly different with reference to religious education. As we have seen before and explained to some extent, there is no relationship between the present religious association and patterns, which may be due to the fact that our questions did not specify which religion.

Age, education, sex, and the MOW patterns

From the results presented so far, we conclude that age, education, and sex are the most powerful biographical discriminants of MOW patterns. In this section, we shift focus and study the distribution of patterns over age, educational, and sex groups.

For purposes of this analysis, we dichotomize age and education. Two age groups are formed by distinguishing those above and below the mean age of our sample of target groups (36.3 years). The two educational levels used in the analysis are a low level, which compromises primary and secondary school; and a high level, which combines some college and a university degree. For both males and females, the percentage distribution of the MOW patterns of each age by education group was calculated.

Figure 11.1 presents a summary for the male respondents. We observe that:

- The *younger* and *less*-educated the males, the *greater* the frequency of the instrumental and low entitlement patterns.
- The *younger* and *more* educated the male respondents, the *more likely* they are to adhere to the low entitlement pattern.
- The *older* and *less* educated the male respondents, the *more* likely they are to adhere to the low entitlement patterns, followed by the expressive work centrality and instrumental patterns.
- The *older* and *more* educated the males, the *more* likely they are to adhere to the low entitlement and expressive work centrality patterns.

In summary, the instrumental pattern is relatively frequent among the younger and less-educated males. In contrast, more than one-third of the

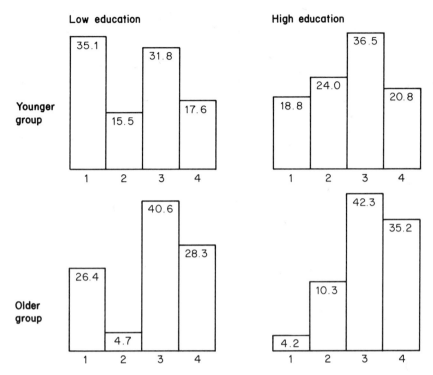

Figure 11.1. Percentage distribution of MOW patterns for men on education by age.

NOTE: MOW patterns are as follows. 1 = instrumental. 2 = entitlement and contact orientation. 3 = low entitlement. 4 = expressive work centrality.

older males who attained a higher educational level adhere to the expressive work centrality pattern and only 4% adhere to the instrumental pattern. Compared to the younger groups, the older age groups have more divergent distributions on the four patterns. The largest differences between the more- and less-educated males are on the entitlement and contact orientation and instrumental MOW patterns.

The picture for the female respondents is different (see Figure 11.2).

• Among the less-educated females, the instrumental pattern is the most frequent for both age groups, followed by the low entitlement pattern. Regardless of age, less-educated females adhere to the instrumental pattern to an extent similar to males younger than the mean age.

• The more-educated female groups in both age categories adhere most frequently to the expressive work centrality pattern. Younger

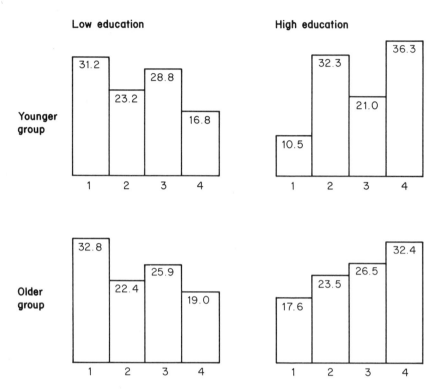

Figure 11.2. Percentage distribution of MOW patterns for women on education by age.

NOTE: MOW patterns are as follows. 1 = instrumental. 2 = entitlement. 3 = low entitlement. 4 = expressive work centrality.

women also adhere frequently to the entitlement and contact orientation pattern. Note that this younger age group grew up after World War 2 (because the division point is at 36 years). The major differences in women's rights and protective legislation would support a cohort effect instead of maturation effect in accounting for the differences between younger and older more-educated women.

If we compare both sexes, we observe that, for the higher-educated males, the low entitlement pattern is more frequent, while the females adhere more often to the entitlement and contact orientation, and expressive work centrality (especially for younger, more-educated women) patterns. The less-educated women are more evenly distributed over the four patterns when compared to the less educated male respondents.

Work history, job, and organizational characteristics

Career history

From the perspective of the individual, the meaning of working is not invariable. The values and cognitions about working acquired during childhood and adolescence are modified as a result of working experiences. Work history has been captured in this research by the unemployment history, mobility in work history, and career progress. Theoretical considerations and research evidence discussed in Chapter 2, lead to the following expectations about relationships between unemployment or turbulent careers and separate MOW dimensions. Unemployment and turbulent careers are related to:

1. Increased valuation of economic factors.
2. Decreased valuation of intrinsic outcomes.
3. Stronger belief in entitlement norms, lower adherence to obligation norms.

From this, it follows that the instrumental work pattern should be more frequent among unemployed and people who experience turbulent working careers.

Mobility in work history was operationalized by the percentage of people still working in their first job, the percentage describing their careers as having ups and downs and the index of mobility of work history (MWH; see Chapter 3). Experience with unempolyment was measured as the percentage of respondents who experienced unemployment during the last 5 years.

Table 11.2 shows that neither unemployment history nor career turbulence differentiate significantly between the patterns, so our expectations were not supported. Since career progress was expected to relate to higher work centrality, we had some reason to believe that people indicating substantial career progress would adhere more frequently to the expressive work centrality pattern, and relatively less frequent to the instrumental MOW pattern. This hypothesis is confirmed (see Table 11.2). In particular, people with substantial career progress tend to have either a low entitlement or an expressive work centrality pattern, while people marked by little career progress tend to have an instrumental pattern. People with an instrumental pattern also tend to be less satisfied with their careers than people in the other patterns.

The number of years one works in the present job can be interpreted as an inverse measure of mobility in work history. The longer one stays in the

Table 11.2. *Pattern scores on career history variables (percentages and mean scores)*

MOW Patterns	Instrumental	Entitlement and Contact Orientation	Low Entitlement	Expressive Work Centrality	Significance
Unemployment					
• Percentage respondents which have been unemployed in last 5 years	24	33	25	22	ns
Career turbulence					
• Percentage still working in first job	32	41	37	43	ns
• mobility in work[a] history (MWH)	38	36	40	34	ns
• Percentage which evaluated career as having ups and downs	41	49	48	41	ns
Progress					
• Respondents'[b] judgment of progress	2.7	2.9	3.0	3.0	$p = .02$
Evaluation					
• Satisfaction[c] with career	3.3	3.7	3.7	3.8	$p = .001$
Present job					
• Years in present job	8.0	6.4	7.7	9.7	$p = .02$

[a] MWH is the number of jobs multiplied by 100 and divided by the number of years worked. Range is from 3 to 167, standard deviation is 26.7.
[b] Question 26 asks about work history in relationship to where the person started. The responses are: (1) marked by some decline, (2) approximately where I started, (3) improved somewhat, and (4) improved a great deal. Standard deviation is .95.
[c] Response alternatives are (1) very dissatisfied, (2) somewhat dissatisfied, (3) neutral, (4) somewhat satisfied, and (5) very satisfied. Standard deviation is 1.16.

job, the less mobility in the work history. It appears that people with the entitlement and contact orientation pattern work a relatively short time in their present job, while those with the expressive work centrality pattern have the longer tenure. This result also reflects the correlation between age and tenure, so an appropriate conclusion is that maturational and tenure explanations account for this finding. We also note that some models of work socialization (e.g., Van Maanen and Schein, 1979) suggest that job tenure is positively related to opportunities for individualistic expression in work. The relationship between job tenure and the expressive work centrality pattern seems to be consistent with expectations derived from these models of work socialization and individual selfexpression.

The present job

Throughout this chapter, the influence of socialization on the formation of values has been stressed. In particular, the influence of experiences during childhood and adolescence seems to result in relatively stable work values. However, it is assumed that characteristics of one's present job also exert influences on what a person considers as desirable and preferable in working. The MOW patterns are based on dimensions, which reflect both values and preferences. We expect them to be related to variables which capture not only socialization influences, but also variables which measure the influence of characteristics of the present work environment. That is, present work values and preferences are related to past influences and, therefore, are stable but are related to present influences and reflect continued adaptation.

The importance of the income-producing function of working for instance, as measured by the PAY index, is related to gender, as well as the quality of the present work. Gender includes different socialization processes which result in different value patterns for men and women. In many instances, men are still brought up with the idea that they have to earn the family income and, consequently, value income more than women. On the other hand, they may prefer income more because they have a low-quality job, for which the compensation can only be financial.

Job characteristics, income, and hours of work

The characteristics of the present job captured in this research mainly center around the concept of the quality of work. The quality of work is measured by an index based on the amount of variety, autonomy, responsibility, learning possibilities, and skill utilization. Results shown in Table 11.3 indicate that people with low-quality work tend to adhere to an instrumental MOW pattern, while people with high-quality jobs tend to adhere to the expressive work centrality pattern. These findings are consistent with expectations discussed in Chapter 2. Regression analyses results (not reported here) support the generalizability of this relationship between quality of work and work centrality. In five of six countries (Germany excepted) where the regression analyses were carried out,

Table 11.3. Pattern scores on present job variables (percentages and mean scores)

MOW Patterns	Instrumental	Entitlement and Contact Orientation	Low Entitlement	Expressive Work Centrality	Significance
Job characteristics					
• Quality of work[a]	9.5	10.3	10.4	11.0	$p < .001$
• Aggravating working[a] conditions	1.2	0.7	0.9	1.0	$p = .007$
• Mentally demanding[b]	2.3	2.4	2.6	2.6	$p = .001$
• Job level: percentage supervision	21.0	45.8	38.3	36.2	$p < .001$
• Income[c]	2.7	3.0	2.9	2.8	ns
• Hours working (per week)	41.7	42.3	44.5	44.8	$p = .03$
Organizational characteristics					
• Sector: percentage private sector	74.5	52.3	76.8	48.7	$p < .001$
• Size[d]	2.4	2.0	2.2	2.1	$p = .05$

[a] The construction of the indices on quality of work and aggravating working conditions is discussed in Chapter 3. The quality of work index ranges from 5 to 15, standard deviation is 2.31 (in the sample used here). The aggravating working conditions index ranges from 0 to 4. Standard deviation is 1.10.
[b] Question 16: Does your job require *too* much of you mentally? Response options are (1) never, (2) seldom, (3) sometimes, and (4) often. Standard deviation 1.01.
[c] Scores based on monthly net income. Five intervals of about 20% of the income distribution. Range is from 1 to 5. Standard deviation 1.29.
[d] Response options are (1) under 100 employees, (2) 100–299 employees, (3) 300–999 employees, and (4) 1000 or more employees. Standard deviation is 1.26.

quality of work was found to be related positively to work centrality. The relationship between intrinsic work goals (see Chapter 3, Index IR) and quality of work was significantly positive in all six countries, as was the negative relationship between pay values and quality of work.

Table 11.3 also shows that respondents with an instrumental work pattern tend to have the most aggravating working conditions. That is, their job is physically demanding, and they tend to engage in work that is dangerous or carried out in unhealthy circumstances. Finally, those who adhere to the instrumental pattern usually do not have a supervisory job and their work tends to be less mentally demanding.

Conversely, those with the entitlement and contact orientation have jobs with the most favorable physical working conditions. Their jobs also tend not to be mentally demanding. A large percentage of those with the entitlement and contact orientation have a supervisory job. Income does not differentiate significantly between the patterns. Finally, those with the low entitlement and expressive work centrality patterns work more hours per week than those who adhere to the instrumental and entitlement and contact orientation patterns.

At this point, it is useful to recall the distribution of the patterns over the target groups (Table 10.2). If we examine only the employed target groups, the following results shed more light on the present findings:

1. There is a relatively high percentage of tool- and diemakers, textile workers, and white-collar employees who have the instrumental MOW pattern (low quality of work, high on aggravating working conditions, low on mentally demanding, few supervisory jobs).
2. The entitlement and contact orientation pattern includes a relatively high percentage of teachers (average on quality of work, low on physically demanding working conditions, many supervisory jobs).
3. The low entitlement pattern frequently is found among all employed target groups except teachers (average scores on most variables, but high on mentally demanding and hours working).
4. The expressive work centrality pattern includes large percentages of chemical engineers, teachers, and self-employed (high quality of work, mentally demanding jobs, high average hours working).

Therefore, the job characteristics and job conditions that relate to MOW patterns, generally, helps us to better understand the nature of the jobs and work conditions of the employed target groups.

Organizational characteristics

From the many possible relevant organizational characteristics, two macro-level variables were chosen, namely, organization size and sector. By sector, we mean whether the organization is public or private. Since material rewards in the public sector are more secure and less dependent upon achievement, public-sector workers are expected to be more concerned with intrinsic work aspects. Andrisani and Miljus (1977) found, however, that, "Public sector employees are less likely than average to cite intrinsic factors as the most satisfying aspects of work." Smith and Nock (1980) concluded the same for white-collar government employees, who also were less satisfied with social relationships. Blue-collar government workers, on the other hand, tend to be more satisfied with intrinsic factors.

In our data, we find that people who work in the public sector tend to have either the entitlement and contact orientation or expressive work centrality patterns. In contrast, people who work in the private sector tend to have either instrumental or low entitlement patterns (see Table 11.3). The differences between the patterns are highly significant. Thus, this finding partially supports previous studies to the extent that the expressive work centrality pattern includes an intrinsic dimension. Finally, respondents in large organizations tend to be oriented instrumentally, while large percentages of respondents who work in smaller organizations tend to have an entitlement and contact orientation pattern.

Quality of work, sector, and the MOW patterns

We choose to measure the characteristics of the present job mainly through the quality of the work. Work quality should be taken in a broad sense,

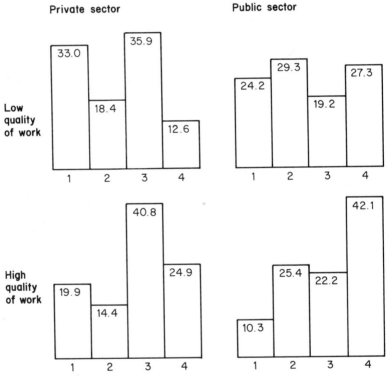

Figure 11.3. Percentage distribution of MOW patterns among people who vary in quality of work and sector.

NOTE: MOW patterns are as follows. 1 = instrumental. 2 = entitlement and contact orientation. 3 = low entitlement. 4 = expressive work centrality.

encompassing the work itself, as well as working conditions. From the previous analysis, we know that the quality of the work as operationalized by the amount of autonomy and responsibility discriminates strongly between the patterns. Organizational sector (public or private) also accounts for important differences in MOW patterns.

Therefore, we present a summary which looks at these characteristics simultaneously. Figure 11.3 shows the pattern distribution within quality of work and sector groups. The quality of work dimension is split at the mean in a low and high quality of work group. Regardless of sector, the instrumental pattern includes relatively high percentages of individuals with low work quality. However, nearly twice as many people in the private sector with high-quality jobs have an instrumental pattern when compared to those in the public sector with high-quality jobs. Among the private workers with a high quality of work, the low entitlement pattern is dominant, while the expressive work centrality pattern is dominant among public-sector jobs with high quality. Finally, public-sector employees with low-quality work tend to have an entitlement and contact orientation pattern to a much greater extent than employees in the private sector with low-quality work.

Conclusions

In this chapter, antecedent variables are related to meaning of working concepts as well as MOW patterns. As far as the *MOW concepts* are concerned, only a limited number of independent variables are entered in the analysis, because of the use of multiple regression analysis. Biographical variables and characteristics of the present job appear to be independently related to the MOW dimensions under consideration, namely work centrality, social norms, and three valued working outcomes: income, contacts, and the work itself. In particular, age, education, and sex as well as quality of work are the most important predictors of MOW indices.

The biographical variables—age, education, and sex—and the job variables—quality of work and organizational sector—relate strongly to the *MOW patterns*. This is to be expected, since the MOW patterns are based on the same MOW indices which were the dependent variables in the regression analysis reported in this chapter. Of particular interest are the variables which do not discriminate between the MOW patterns. This applies to aspects of upbringing: Neither religious education nor community size during childhood is significantly related to the patterns. Nor is the present association with a religion related to the MOW patterns. The characteristics of the home situation included in our research appear not to differ per pattern either, except for marital status. Contrary to expectations, it appears that two important aspects of the career history, namely unemployment history and career turbulence do not differentiate significantly between the patterns. Finally, income, which is considered as a feature of the present job, is not related to the MOW patterns.

Turning to the relationships which are demonstrated in our data and which are generally in line with other research results, it seems that our findings can be described by two general notions: socialization and adaptation to the work environment.

It has been hypothesized at the outset of our research that work values and cognitions result from an individual developmental process. This process begins with early socialization. The educational level of the parents, which is also indicative for their socioeconomic status, is an important factor in early socialization and appears to have an impact on work meanings. Highly correlated with this is the education of the respondents themselves. Educational attainment has a strong effect on the formation of values, in particular, the preference for intrinsic or instrumental outcomes and social norms with regard to working. Education also shapes the opportunities for the level and type of the occupational career.

Men and women are socialized in different roles. This results, according to our findings, in differences in work centrality and the outcomes of working which they value. On the other hand, the work opportunities which are available differ greatly for men and women. Once one enters "the world of work," the work environment influences the acquired values and cognitions. Among these environmental factors are the quality of work, the actual working conditions, job level, and the organizational type and size. The revised or reaffirmed meanings of working and the available work opportunities result in job change or continuation, which, in turn, may lead to further changes in the meaning of working.

Whether the influence of biographic age on the meaning of working is a cohort or a maturation effect cannot be determined on the basis of our research. It is likely, however, that these two explanatory positions are not mutually exclusive but must be seen as describing factors that interact in intricate ways to bring about different work-related values in different social groups.

Notes

(1) Subsets of groups were formed, in which the highest and lowest means do not differ by more than the significance range for a subset of that size.

Chapter 12

The Consequences of the Meaning of Working

Introduction

In this chapter, we look at the consequences of holding patterns of beliefs, values and preferences, which we call "the meaning of working." Among the basic questions we raise are: Why do people work? What are the correlates of working, and what might explain different levels of working intensity? These are important questions in industrial societies because they are critical for the efficient functioning of the economic system (March and Simon, 1958). We do not want to suggest that, for most people in our study, there is a substantial choice about whether to work or not to work. While there are certainly choices at the beginning (by remaining shorter or longer in the educational system) and at the end of a career (by taking earlier or later retirement), one might expect country difference in choices to work or not to work during mid-career. However, once people are working, certain decisions are open to them such as preferences for job content and rewards. How do these decisions differ, depending on people's work values and the intensity of their values? Given differences in the content of jobs and rewards from jobs, what job-decision preferences do people with different work values make? Finally, we need to recognize the complexities of both individuals and work. Not only do people assign a variety of meanings to work, but working also has multiple facets and consequences. Recognizing this raises additional questions about the consequences of work meanings. In particular, how do individuals with contrasting patterns on several work meanings differ on multiple consequences of work?

In this chapter, we provide some answers to these questions by investigating the relationship between work meanings and work consequences. The evidence presented is relational and, therefore, consquences do not necessarily imply causality. However, an assumption guiding this research and, indeed, a fundamental assumption in most behavioral science research, is that many people have some freedom of choice relating to certain aspects of work; for instance, the intensity of the effort they make, how to arrange or sequence their work (but not in mass production industry), how to handle their social relationships with people on their own level and others, what rewards to choose (under cafeteria schemes), and when to work (under flexible time arrangements).

The choices made by individuals provide an indication of the range of consequences associated with the meanings they assign to work.

Meaning of working and involvement with work for national labor force samples

In this section, we look at two aspects of decisions relating to work. One is whether, once the economic necessity for working is removed, people would choose to continue working. The second decision concerns the extent of involvement with working. The first issue uses the lottery question. The justification for this task stems from the theory of labor supply which recognizes that the supply of labor is increasingly influenced by non-economic factors, (e.g., psychological and sociological) as the influences of economic factors for working approaches zero. Observation seems to support this economic theory. One of the reasons that the labor force participation rate of older workers (both those below and above mandatory retirement age) has declined in most industrial countries over the past several decades may be due to the increased prevalence of public and private pension plans. This does not imply, of course, that all early retirement is based exclusively on voluntary reasons.

The lottery question was first used by Morse and Weiss (1955) and has been included subsequently in several large survey studies in the United States, Europe, and Japan (Davis, 1980; Quinn and Staines, 1979; Takeuchi, 1975; Vecchio, 1980; Warr, 1982). It asks a person to imagine they had won a lottery or inherited a large sum of money which would allow them to live comfortably for the rest of their life without working. What would the person do concerning work—stop working, continue working, or continue working but with changed conditions? Responses to the second and third alternatives were combined and used as a measure of work continuation in the present study.

There are four meaning of work variables that we expect to correlate with individuals' preferences about continuing to work: work centrality,

obligation norm, pay or economic valued working outcomes, and expressive valued working outcomes. The properties of work centrality discussed
in Chapter 2 include identification with work, involvement with work, and
commitment to work. Our expectation is that individuals at increasingly
higher levels of work centrality will indicate they would continue to work
even when it is not economically necessary. Individuals who feel it is an
obligation or a duty of societal members to work also are more likely to
indicate they would continue work than people who do not subscribe
strongly to this norm. We also expect persons who increasingly value
expressive outcomes from work such as autonomy, a match between their
skills and their work, interesting work, and variety in their work are more
likely to indicate that they would continue working. These work values
traditionally have been satisfied in work settings; not to have these values
satisfied probably would activate a search process resulting in a return to
work (March and Simon, 1958). Collectively, these expressive values
suggest that work provides a challenge (mental activation) or avenue for
self-expression through continued work involvement. Conversely, people
who value pay or for whom economic values are particularly strong are
unlikely to indicate they would continue working once the economic
necessity to work has been removed. In summary, we expect work centrality, obligation norms, and expressive valued working outcomes to correlate
positively, and pay valued working outcomes to correlate negatively with
the people's response to the lottery question indicating that they would
continue working.

Once individuals are at work, they have some room to make decisions
about the amount of time to devote to work. In practice, there are many
limitations on this due to national labor and tax policies, union contracts,
employer policies, the requirements of shift work in some sectors, and
legally entered contracts for repayments of mortgages and other loans.
Nevertheless, we believe that in many jobs, individual preferences can
influence the amount of time people devote to work. Gechman and Weiner
(1975) support this expectation. They found a moderate relationship
between teachers' work involvement score and personal time devoted to
work-related activities outside the normal work day. Similar considerations
may apply to other professional or semiprofessional jobs. Conceptually,
however, we recognize a reciprocal causal relationship between the meaning of working and measures of time involvement in work. That is, time
involvement in work is both influenced by, and influences the meaning of,
working.

There are five meaning of work variables that we expect to relate to
hours of work.

1. Work centrality should correlate positively with hours of work. Individuals who identify with work, are involved in work, and are committed to work for whatever reason are likely to devote more hours to work.

2. Individuals who value pay as a work outcome are likely to devote more time to work. Since the amount of regular and overtime pay is frequently determined by hours spent working, people who value pay are likely to participate more in work to obtain more of this reward.

3. Individuals who value expressive outcomes from work (variety, autonomy, interesting work, and a match between their skills and their work) are likely to work more hours.

4. Valuation of interpersonal contacts and social interaction can also constitute an important factor related to the extent of involvement to work. However, as Vroom (1964) recognized, the direction of relationship between interpersonal value and involvement to work may depend on situational factors that affect the amount and kind of social interaction permitted or required by work roles.

5. Norms of obligation can influence the extent of work involvement. The felt sense of social duty or responsibility can be used as an evaluative standard in assessing work inputs, such as the extent of involvement. Individuals who adhere more strongly to this norm would be expected to work longer to fulfill their standard of social duty and responsibility.

In summary, the amount of time people spend at work as indicated by the length of the average work week will depend on how central work is to the person, values toward pay, self-expression, interpersonal contacts, and level of agreement with obligation norms.

Table 12.1 presents the results when the involvement variables are regressed on the specified MOW variables. The squared multiple correlations (R^2) shown in the table indicate the percentage of variance in the attachment measures which is accounted for by the MOW variables. The numbers below each MOW variable are the standardized (beta) weights. The size of the weight indicates the relative contribution of that MOW variable to the prediction of the involvement score of the respondents in that country. The sign (β) of the beta weight indicates the direction of contribution of the MOW variable to the prediction of the involvement score. Negative-signed beta weights indicate that the higher the MOW variable, the *less* likely the person would be to continue working and the *more* likely they would be to work fewer hours.

While modest, several of the specific findings are consistent with theoretical expectations. The best predictors of continued work involvement or non-involvement are work centrality and pay-oriented work

Table 12.1. Relationship between MOW variables and measures of work involvement in national labor force samples

	R^2	Work Centrality	Obligation Norm	Pay	Expressive	Interpersonal Contact
		Standard Regression (Beta) Weights				
Lottery						
Belgium	.064**	0.107**	0.035	−0.166**	0.020	0.068
Israel	.091**	0.168**	0.076**	−0.181**	0.041	−0.009
Netherlands	.048**	0.086**	0.054	−0.165**	0.033	−0.016
United States	.076**	0.177**	0.076**	−0.120**	0.079**	−0.048
Yugoslavia	.016	0.069	0.076	−0.059	−0.050	−0.019
Britain	.058**	0.115**	0.040	−0.172**	0.002	0.006
W. Germany	.100**	0.181**	0.050	−0.155**	0.110**	−0.057
Japan	.030**	0.104**	0.041**	−0.064**	0.069**	−0.006
Hours work* per Week						
Belgium	.129**	0.112**	0.180**	0.071	0.233*	−0.104**
Israel	.097**	0.217**	0.044	0.307**	0.125**	0.051
Netherlands	.127**	0.137**	0.131**	−0.162**	0.170**	−0.151**
United States	.042**	0.129**	0.121**	−0.084**	0.115**	0.052
Yugoslavia	.080**	0.163**	−0.014	0.073	0.199**	−0.080
W. Germany	.102**	0.187**	0.005	0.080**	0.235**	−0.117**
Japan	.053**	0.184**	0.050**	0.038	0.099**	−0.008

* This question was not included in the British survey.
** Equals $< .05$

values. The results indicate that the *higher* the work centrality of the respondent, the *more* they would continue to work even if they become wealthy. In contrast, the *higher* the respondent values pay, the *less* likely they would be to continue working. Results are much less consistent for the remaining MOW variables. People with higher norms of obligation to employers and society indicate a greater likelihood of work continuation in Israel, the United States, and Japan. People with higher expressive work values indicate a greater likelihood of work continuation in the United States, West Germany, and Japan. In summary, the most general model of a person who would remain involved with work in these national labor force samples is a person with high work centrality and low pay work values. To this general model, we would add people with high obligation norms in Israel, the United States, and Japan, and people with high expressive values in the United States, West Germany, and Japan.[1]

The general model—with regard to the extent of labor market involvement in terms of hours of work—is slightly more differentiated. For this measure of extent of involvement, work centrality and expressive work values provide the most consistent findings. In all seven countries, people with increasingly higher work centrality and higher expressive work values work longer hours. To this general model, we add that people with higher obligation norms tend to work longer hours in Belgium, the Netherlands, the United States, and Japan. In addition, people with higher pay-oriented work values tend to work longer hours in Israel, the Netherlands, the United States and West Germany. Finally, people with higher inter-personal contact work values tend to work *fewer* hours in Belgium, the Netherlands, and West Germany. In summary, the most consistent model of a person in the national labor force samples with more extensive involvement to working is someone who is higher in work centrality and expressive work values. To this general model, we need to add people with higher obligation norms and pay-oriented work values, and people with lower interpersonal contact values in some countries.

Valued working outcomes and preferences for jobs/national labor force comparisons

Before examining the findings concerned with the consequences of speci-fied valued working outcomes, we need to extend the theory and concepts of valued working outcomes beyond that found in Chapter 2. We concen-trate on work values as they relate to choices of jobs which differ in reward features. In this review, we draw heavily from Locke's (1969; 1976) theory of job satisfaction, Mahoney's (1979a) extension of Locke's theory, and Mahoney's (1979b) discussion of job features in relationship to pay.

There are properties of values for work outcomes that have conceptual importance for choice behavior. First, values have content; they pertain to what a person wants to gain and/or keep. This property of values serves as a standard used in making value judgments about the desirability of job characteristics. In making these judgments, two other features of the choice process are important: perceptions of some feature or combination of features of the job and the relationship between one's perceptions of job features and one's values. In this sense, job choices are estimates of the perceived characteristics of jobs in relationship to one's value standards.[2]

But part of the process of making decisions also depends on importance of the valued outcome for the person. By importance, we mean the intensity of a work value relative to the intensity of values for other outcomes from work. Here, we recognize that values for work outcomes are held in a hierarchy and that people differ in the degree to which they value particular features of work. When making job choices, we can consider one to be making estimates of the gap between perceived features of jobs and one's value standards *and* the importance of that standard in relationship to other standards.

There is one other property of values that is important for the present study: Values may have an equilibrium or optimal point. The importance of a value may vary as a function of the amount already possessed. For example, pay may be important up to some increment of increase, but further pay increments may be valued less than specific changes in other characteristics of jobs which are judged in relationship to other personal value standards. As a corollary, there is a distinction between one's value of pay and the specific amount of pay a person will seek before they give up features of a job which are evaluated against other values. This amount of additional pay depends upon the importance of pay relative to the importance of values for other features of work.

The size of the increment in pay necessary to observe a change of preferences for jobs also is an important consideration. This pay increment, as well as values toward pay relative to values for other job features, must be taken into account when investigating job preferences. The best estimate of the size of the pay increment needed to change the job preferences of people is a 30% increase (Jacques, 1965; Kuethe and Levenson, 1964; Mahoney, 1979b). Since this increment is an average, we expect there will be substantial individual differences, depending partially on the importance of pay relative to the importance of other job features. This effect of pay importance should be observed by changes in the slope of the line indicating job preferences when increases in pay are used to offset the removal of other job features (i.e., autonomy, interesting work, and match between personal characteristics and job). That is, the slope of the line for the percentage of people preferring a job will depend on the importance of their values for the contrasting features of jobs and the size of the increment of one job feature used to offset the removal of other job features.

These are the aspects of the theory of values for work outcomes which we tested in each of six countries. Initially, we measured individuals' values for different features of work and jobs by asking them to rank—or rate and rank—these features on an importance scale. For each person, we then were able to calculate a difference between their values for features of jobs—for example, the difference between their values for pay relative to autonomy. Then, people were grouped into seven categories, depending on the difference score: from those for whom pay was a very important value and autonomy a very unimportant value to the reverse position of these values in a person's value hierarchy. We note that the middle category of people is conceptually important as it includes people who are balanced in their values; they value pay and autonomy about equally. This middle category is the value range from which we begin to speak of increasing values of one job characteristic (e.g., pay or autonomy) relative to other job features. Our expectation is that this balanced values group will have a preference function for a job with increasing increments of pay, but no autonomy, which lies between the functions for those groups valuing one feature more than the other.

We should also note that these values of people for work or job features and outcomes were not selected at random. Findings presented in Chapter 4 indicate that values for aspects of self-expression in jobs (i.e., autonomy, abilities/job match, and interesting work) are found among significant numbers of people in different countries. The same can be said with regard to values toward pay.

We should mention that the images are used in the present analysis in a different manner than was the case with an analysis of images in Chapter 8. In the present analysis, we disaggregate the job images data and consider the images to be a series of job preference decisions. In Chapter 8, the images were aggregated and a general analysis was performed. In addition, in the present analysis, individual differences in work values are considered to be a major influence on job preference choices of individuals. Individual differences in work values were treated more implicitly in Chapter 8. Finally, the subsequent analysis draws on somewhat different theoretical bases than Chapter 8.

The results from these analyses are shown in figures 12.1 and 12.2. These figures show the general pattern, which was similar in the national labor force samples from each of the six countries. The results in Figure 12.1 are for the first set of images, where both the jobs and the work values contrast pay and autonomy. There are several findings illustrated in the figure that require discussion.

First, individual differences in the relative importance of pay and autonomy are associated with large differences in preferences for jobs that differ in these characteristics. With a 30% pay increment the difference between the two extreme groups (7–10 and −7–10) in their preference for Job *B* is approximately 40%. At the 50% pay increment, the difference between these two groups in preferences for Job *B* increased to approximately 50%. The change in preferences for Job *B* from pay equal to the present pay to pay 50% more than present pay for the group with the highest pay/autonomy score (7–10) was about 72%. The change in preferences for Job *B* over the four images for the group with the highest autonomy/pay score (−7–10) was approximately 30%. In both figures 12.1 and 12.2, the group with equally strong preferences for pay and either autonomy or expressive characteristics has a preference function for Job *B* that falls between the preference functions for the groups with unequal work values.

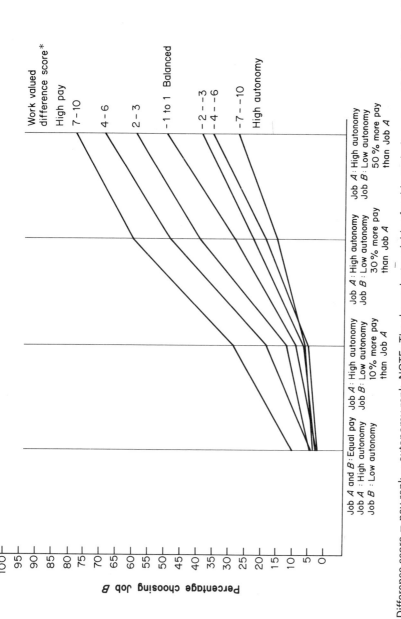

* Difference score = pay rank − autonomy rank. NOTE: The dependent variables for this analysis were not included in the German and British surveys.

Figure 12.1. Percentage of national samples at each level of valued working outcomes who choose Job B with each increase in pay: general patterns for workers in six countries.

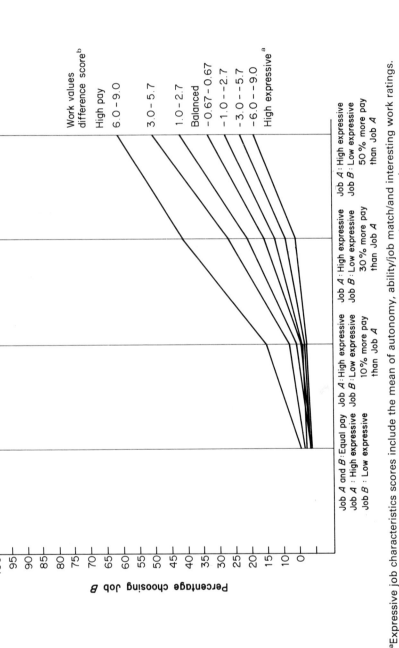

Work values
difference score[b]

High pay

6.0 – 9.0

3.0 – 5.7

1.0 – 2.7

Balanced

-0.67 – 0.67

-1.0 – -2.7

-3.0 – -5.7

-6.0 – -9.0

High expressive [a]

Percentage choosing Job B

100
95
90
85
80
75
70
65
60
55
50
45
40
35
30
25
20
15
10
0

Job A and B: Equal pay
Job A : High expressive
Job B : Low expressive

Job A : High expressive
Job B : Low expressive
10% more pay
than Job A

Job A : High expressive
Job B : Low expressive
30% more pay
than Job A

Job A : High expressive
Job B : Low expressive
50% more pay
than Job A

[a]Expressive job characteristics scores include the mean of autonomy, ability/job match/and interesting work ratings.
[b]Difference score = Pay score – X̄ (Autonomy + Skill match + Interesting work values scores)
NOTE: The dependent variables for this analysis were not included in the German and British surveys.

Figure 12.2. Percentage of national samples at each level of valued working outcomes who choose Job B with each increase
in pay (general pattern for workers in six countries (variables not included in German and British surveys).

A second general finding shown in Figure 12.1 is that the slope of the job preference line for groups that value pay more than autonomy increases dramatically at a 30% pay increment. This supports the expectation that relative value importance can be observed in terms of the slope of the preference line. In contrast, and as expected, the slope of the job preference lines is not as steep for all three groups that value autonomy more than pay.

There is also evidence in both figures that supports an equilibrium view of values and motivation, in the sense that current importance of a work value depends partially on the amount of an outcome presently possessed. In both figures, the slope of the job preference line increases at a greater rate—between a 10–30% pay increment—for the groups valuing pay more than autonomy or the average of the three features. But between a 30–50% pay increment, the slope of the preference lines for these groups *decreases*. In contrast, the slope of the job preference line increases some between 10–30% increments for the groups valuing autonomy alone or autonomy, match, and interesting work more than pay. But the slope of the preference lines for these expressive groups *increases* even more between a 30–50% pay increment. We interpret this finding as an indication of substitution effects. For groups in the relatively high pay bracket, the attractiveness of additional pay increases may be limited by the increased preference for autonomy alone or the three expressive job features. For groups relatively high on autonomy or the three expressive characteristics, a 50% pay increment is valued enough to increase the rate of substitution of pay for a loss of autonomy alone or the three expressive job characteristics.

We would also like to draw attention to one more specific, but important, finding shown in the figures. First, a majority of the people in each of the groups that value autonomy alone, or autonomy, job requirements/competence match, and interesting work more than pay do not switch their job preferences from Job *A* to Job *B* even with a 50% pay increase. We interpret this finding as providing support for the central role that occupational self-direction plays in Kohn and Schooler's (1983) research. These values appear to be a powerful set of valued working outcomes for a significant percentage of workers in all six countries. Within practical limits, pay increments would not seem to substitute for a loss of autonomy or autonomy, job/competence match, and interesting work in the job preferences for many workers. Most powerful of all in terms of preferences and choice of jobs would be jobs with high autonomy or the three expressive characteristics and high pay increments. This is a situation often found in compensation practices for managerial and professional jobs where pay and pay increases are based on features of decision autonomy (i.e., decision frequency, decision size in terms of resources or time commitment of decisions, and decision responsibility).

In summary, the relative values of individuals for pay and autonomy alone or autonomy, skill match, and interesting work do relate to their stated choices of jobs. The slope of the preference line for jobs with increasing increments of pay used to offset the loss of autonomy or the three expressive features depends, to a significant extent, on the relative importance of the work values for the person as well as the magnitude of the pay increase. These conclusions similarly hold for national labor force samples in Belgium, the Netherlands, Israel, the United States, Japan, and the combined target group sample in Yugoslavia.

Complex man: patterns of work meanings and patterns of consequences

One of the major conclusions that can be drawn from the present research is that not only do people assign many meanings to working, but the patterning of those meanings also varies. Previous chapters have documented that the patterns of work meanings differ, depending on characteristics of the individual, the characteristics and quality of their career experience, their occupation, and other antecedents. What emerges is a picture of complex man with a complex pattern of work meanings. This is to be expected. Schein (1980), for many years, has advanced this view of complex man with patterns of work meanings and values changing with age, stage of vocational development, changes in jobs and work environments, and other influences. In this section, we extend the earlier discussion of the patterns of work meanings and the pattern antecedents to the multiple consequences associated with these patterns. The beginning point in the present analysis was the four major meaning of work patterns that were identified and described in Chapter 10.

There are five major classes of consequences that we include in this analysis. The first class includes two measures: the lottery question and average length of the person's work week. The second class of consequences are the person's preferences for the jobs described in the immediately previous section of this chapter. Here, we restrict the consequences to the preferences of the person when pay was 30% greater than present pay in each set of decisions. The decision to include only responses at the 30% increase was based on the theoretical reasoning provided by Mahoney (1979b)—described in the last section—and because the job preferences begin to differ greatly at this pay-increase level for people with contrasting work values.

The third class of consequences includes three affective/emotional measures. The first is a measure of occupational satisfaction. This is based on the person's responses to two questions concerned with whether they would choose the same or a different occupation if they were to start over or whether they would recommend their occupation to their children. The first of these questions has been used in a study of 3000 workers in 16 industries conducted by the Roper organization in the United States—with results reported by Kahn (1981). The second of the measures asked the person to indicate how frequently they worried about work in their free time. The third of the measures asks individuals about their reaction to a situation in which they would work fewer hours and draw commensurately less pay. The fourth class of consequences is concerned with social participation and asks people whether they would participate in company-organized group activities outside of working hours. The fifth and final class of consequences is future-, rather than present-oriented, and asks the person how important work will be to them in the next 5–10 years as compared to the importance of work at the present time. In summary, the consequences we relate to patterns of work meanings include those concerned with attachment to work, preferences for jobs, affective/emotional responses to work and work policies, social participation, and future importance of work. Our task, in subsequent sections is initially, to identify and describe the MOW patterns and then to examine differences in the multiple consequences associated with each pattern.

MOW patterns

Cluster analysis was performed on a representative stratified sample of employed target group from each country. Fourteen respondents were selected from each employed target group per country. Each of the employed target groups from Germany and Yugoslavia included two more cases than in the other countries to compensate for the absence of chemical

Table 12.2. MOW patterns for employed target group samples from seven countries*

	Cluster 1	Cluster 2	Cluster 3	Cluster 4
Work centrality	55.3	45.7	51.8	41.1
Entitlement norm	49.4	49.0	50.2	51.6
Obligation norm	51.5	51.5	50.2	40.8
Pay values	52.3	57.0	41.6	45.5
Expressive values	49.6	47.7	52.9	47.2
Contact values	46.7	50.0	52.9	58.2

* Numbers are the T-scores in relation to the grand mean and grand standard deviation.

214 The meaning of working

engineers or part-time workers in the samples from these countries. Thus, a total of 686 cases were selected from the seven countries. Fifty-six of these cases were eliminated because of incomplete data on some of the consequences included in the analysis. These fifty-six cases were about equally distributed across the seven countries and the employed target groups. Final sample size for the cluster analysis consisted of 630 cases.

The optimal number of clusters of respondents identifying patterns of MOW was found to be five, with fewer groupings resulting in a substantial loss of variance. Four of the clusters were retained for analysis in this chapter because they tend to show opposite MOW patterns on several variables. Table 12.2 shows the T scores for each variable used to describe the MOW patterns. Cluster 1 is defined by high work centrality, moderate obligation norms and pay values, and low interpersonal contact values. Cluster 2 is defined by high pay values, low work centrality, and low expressive values. Cluster 3 is defined by moderate work centrality, expressive and interpersonal contact values, and by low pay values. Finally, Cluster 4 is defined by low work centrality and obligation norms, moderate entitlement norms, and high interpersonal contact values. Clusters 1 and 4 represent contrasting MOW patterns as do clusters 2 and 3. Of the 630 cases included in the present solution, 31% are in Cluster 1, 22% in Cluster 2, 31% in Cluster 3, and 7% in Cluster 4, respectively.

These four clusters show considerable similarity to the clusters discussed in Chapter 10. Cluster 1 in the present solution is similar to the fourth pattern in Chapter 10 with the exception of the moderate pay values. Cluster 2 is similar to the first cluster in Chapter 10. Cluster 3 is similar to the second cluster in Chapter 10 with the exception of the moderate interpersonal contact values. Cluster 4 is similar to the third cluster in Chapter 10 with the exception of the low work centrality score. The T scores for each variable can be used to describe the MOW patterns shown in Table 12.2.

Table 12.3. Classes of consequences associated with meaning of work patterns for employed target groups from seven countries*

MOW Variables	Cluster 1	Cluster 4	Cluster 2	Cluster 3
Work centrality	High	Low	Low	Moderate
Entitlement/opportunity norm	—	Moderate	—	—
Obligation norm	Moderate	Low	—	—
Pay values	Moderate	Low	High	Low
Expressive values	—	—	Low	Moderate
Interpersonal contact values	Low	High	—	—

Table 12.3 (continued)

MOW Variables	Cluster 1	Cluster 4	Cluster 2	Cluster 3	Significance test/level of significance
Consequences					
1. Work involvement (percentage)					
A. Lottery question					
Stop work	7.7	18.6	18.4	6.2	$F = 7.35$
Continue—same job	48.0	25.6	30.2	48.2	$p < 0.0001$
Continue—different job	44.4	55.8	51.5	45.4	
B. Average work week (hours)	45.5	35.5	43.4	43.1	$F = 7.84$ $p < 0.0001$
2. Job preferences (percentage)					
A. 30% higher pay or autonomy					
Prefer Job A	61.7	72.1	51.5	77.8	$\chi^2 = 46.17$
Prefer Job B	33.2	27.9	39.0	20.1	$p < 0.0001$
B. 30% higher pay or autonomy, match, and interesting work					
Prefer Job A	81.2	86.1	69.1	91.8	$\chi^2 = 37.22$
Prefer Job B	16.3	9.3	25.7	7.7	$p < 0.0001$
3. Occupation satisfaction Percentage choosing or recommending same occupation	39.5	36.1	30.5	58.5	$F = 8.21$ $p < 0.0001$
4. Attitudes – emotional (percentage) reaction to working less hours for less pay					
Against/indifferent	62.3	30.2	69.4	51.5	$F = 9.14$
Moderately for/in favor	37.7	69.8	31.7	49.5	$p < 0.0001$
Worry about work in free time?					
Never/occasionally	45.8	25.4	33.3	28.3	$F = 9.22$
Often/very often	21.5	50.7	34.5	35.1	$p < 0.0001$
5. Social participation in company-sponsored activities outside work hours (percentage)					
No	17.9	7.0	25.7	11.9	$F = 2.19$
Maybe	42.9	46.5	33.8	41.2	$p < 0.07$
Yes	39.3	46.5	40.4	46.9	
6. Future Importance of work (percentage)					
Less important	9.7	14.0	9.6	8.8	$F = 1.69$
Same as MOW	61.7	74.4	65.4	71.7	$p < 0.15$
More important	28.6	11.6	25.0	19.6	

* No target group survey was conducted in Britain.

The similarities between the four clusters identified here and the four clusters identified in Chapter 10 are especially noteworthy. The differences that do occur result from two differences in procedure between the present solution and the solution in Chapter 10. Only employed target groups were used in the present analysis rather than all target groups, and only respondents with information on all the consequences were included in the final sample of the present solution. These similarities in the clusters in each solution increase our confidence in the replicability of the four MOW patterns, which are also important since they include 91% of the cases used in the present solution.

Classes of consequences associated with contrasting MOW patterns

The classes of consequences associated with each of the two contrasting sets of MOW patterns are shown in Table 12.3. Adjectives, rather than T scores, have been used to represent each MOW pattern, and the clusters have been reordered so contrasting patterns are adjacent to each other. Clusters 1 and 4 contrast with each other and so do clusters 2 and 3. An examination of the table indicates that there were overall differences between the four clusters on all classes of consequences except social participation and the future importance of work.

The most notable differences in consequences between respondents in Cluster 1 and Cluster 4 are found on the work involvement, job preference, and attitude/emotional measures. Approximately 2.5 times as many respondents in Cluster 4 as in Cluster 1 would quit working if they suddenly became wealthy. In addition, a much smaller percentage of the Cluster 4 than Cluster 1 respondents would continue to work in the same job if they become wealthy. Respondents in Cluster 4 also work about 10 hours less per week than those in Cluster 1. Work centrality and, to a lesser extent, obligation norms probably contribute to these differences in the work attachment decisions. Cluster 1 respondents show a somewhat greater preference for the higher paying job (Job B) than Cluster 4 respondents. The higher pay values of the Cluster 1 respondents in comparison to the Cluster 4 respondents probably contribute to these differences in job preferences. A much greater percentage of Cluster 1 than Cluster 4 respondents are against working fewer hours and receiving less pay. The higher-level work centrality and pay values among Cluster 1 than Cluster 4 respondents probably contributes to their less-favorable reaction. Finally, Cluster 1 respondents report that they worry about work much less frequently than Cluster 4 respondents. The higher level of work centrality and obligation norms among Cluster 1 than among Cluster 4 respondents may contribute to these differences. In summary, the differences in the pattern of work centrality, obligation norms, and pay values of respondents in clusters 1 and 4 probably contribute to the observed differences on work attachment, job preference, and affective/emotional classes of consequences.

The differences in consequences between respondents in clusters 2 and 3 are especially notable on the lottery questions, job preferences, and occupation satisfaction. Approximately three times as many respondents in Cluster 2 than in Cluster 3 would stop working if they become wealthy, although a larger percentage of those who would continue to work would want to work in a different job. Conversely, a much higher percentage of respondents in Cluster 3 than in Cluster 2 indicate that they would continue to work in the same job if they become wealthy. The differences in pay and expressive work values of respondents in these two clusters probably contribute to the differences in job preferences. As would be expected, the Cluster 2 respondents with high pay and low expressive work values more frequently choose the high-paying job (Job B), while Cluster 3 respondents more frequently choose the job with greater autonomy, or greater autonomy, skill match, and interesting work (Job A).

Finally, respondents in Cluster 3, consistent with their higher work centrality levels, would choose their same occupation again and would recommend their occupation to their children. Cluster 2 respondents would—much less frequently—choose or recommend their occupation to their children. In summary, differences in work centrality, pay work values, and expressive work values probably contribute to the observed differences in the decision to work or not to work, the job preferences, and the occupational satisfaction of respondents in clusters 2 and 3.

We conclude, based on this evidence, that contrasting MOW profiles tend to be associated with differences on multiple work outcomes. To paraphrase Schein (1980), man assigns several meanings to work and these multiple meanings form complex patterns. Contrasts between complex patterns of work meanings are likely to be associated with differences in whole patterns of work consequences, rather than just with isolated consequences. We have sought to provide evidence for this more holistic perspective of contrasting patterns of work meanings being associated with contrasting patterns of consequences.

Summary

We began this chapter by posing a series of questions about the relationship between the meaning of work and the consequences of working. In relationship to the lottery question, which deals with attachment or non-attachment to work, people can make decisions about whether they would continue to work if they no longer had to for financial reasons. People also have some choice relating to the amount of time to devote to work.

As we have seen, these two decisions are not the same, particularly in terms of the meaning of work correlates of each decision. But the same general model of MOW variables that contribute to each decision were observed in the national labor force samples of the eight countries. In each country (except Yugoslavia), the model of the person who would continue to work was someone for whom work centrality was high and pay work values low.

To this general model, more country-specific findings add that people who say they would continue to work—even with the removal of financial incentives to do so—were people with somewhat higher obligation norms and with somewhat higher values for autonomy, variety, interesting work, and work that lets them use their skills and abilities.

There is also a general, though somewhat different, model that explains people's extent of attachment in terms of hours of work. Again, work centrality is a part of this general model; people higher in work centrality work longer hours. In addition, people who have higher expressive work values tend to work longer hours. This is a model that is generalizable to seven of the countries in our study. To this general model, more specific national models of the worker working longer hours would include a person with high norms of obligation, a high valuation of pay, and placement of a lower valuation on interpersonal contact.

Having considered work attachment as a major consequence of the meaning of working, we then turned to a major decision for people: the type of job they prefer. Here, individual differences in the work values of people would seem to make a major contribution. From the descriptive data presented in Chapter 7, we observe that, for the national labor force samples, two prominent work values are expressive and pay values. These work values include the most important work goals in the national surveys in the countries included. We find that the relative importance of these two sets of values contributes to the job preferences of people in all six countries. Further, a general pattern that best fits the preferences for all countries was presented. As expected, the more important the pay values of individuals relative to their expressive values, the more they chose the job in which they forego expressive characteristics for pay increases. But even with people who have very high pay values relative to expressive values, a significant pay increase (10–30%) may be needed to induce many of them to forego autonomy, interesting work, and a good skill match. Further, for these relatively high-pay-oriented value groups, there is some evidence that their preferences function reaches an equilibrium point. Beyond a 30% pay increase, the rate of substitution of Job B for Job A decreases.

For the majority of the relatively high expressive value groups, they do not prefer a job with much greater pay if they have to forego what they value more in work. But there is an increasing rate of preference among these groups for the high-paying job with a 30–50% pay increase indicating the power of pay. We conclude that both pay and expressive characteristics of jobs are powerful work values. Both contribute in major ways to the job preferences of people in the six countries included in the analysis. A case can be made for the use of both as major motivational factors in the job preferences of people, while recognizing the role of individual differences.

Finally, we sought—with the MOW profiles—to put people back together rather than taking them apart and examining various pieces of them. We find this more idiographic or holistic picture of workers with the multiple meanings they assign to working to be more satisfying, albeit more difficult to understand than the relationships with the multiple consequences of working. The contrasting MOW patterns help in organizing the multiple consequences of working. We find large differences between contrasting MOW clusters of respondents and work attachment, job preferences, occupation satisfaction, and affective/emotional responses to work. Industrial man and the consequences of working in industrial societies both have multiple dimensions. To identify and describe the contrasting patterns formed by the multiple meanings of work is an interesting and important research task. To extend our understanding by identifying the multiple and contrasting work consequences associated with replicable and important MOW patterns makes the task even more rewarding. Finally, the multiple patterns of work meanings and the consequences associated with each pattern provide a general set of models of complex man which apply to labor force samples in each country.

Notes

(1) Later in this chapter, under the heading MOW patterns, we show that people who say they would continue to work if they win a lottery, very frequently would not want to have the same job they presently hold.

(2) We argued similarly in Chapter 8 and, in fact, our subsequent analysis uses the same items of our questionnaire although we rely here on a different analytic approach.

Chapter 13

International Comparison of the Relationships between MOW Variables

Introduction

When making international comparisons, it is important to consider response frequency distributions and averages. This, however, is not sufficient, and in some instances, may lead to erroneous or incomplete interpretations. In a hypothetical case, 100 Japanese and 100 Americans are asked if they agree with each of two statements, A and B. The results show that 60% of each sample agrees and 40% disagrees with both statements. In this case, is it safe to conclude that there are no differences between the two countries with regard to the two statements? The answer is obvious from a hypothetical cross-tabulation table (Table 13.1).

As the table shows, in Japan, individuals who agree (disagree) with A also tend to agree (disagree) with B. Conversely, in the United States, those who agree (disagree) with A tend to disagree (agree) with B. These

Table 13.1. Comparisons of Japanese and American response frequency distribution and averages

	Agree with B	Disagree with B	Total
Japan			
Agree with A	50%	10%	60%
Disagree with A	10	30	40
Total	60	40	100

	Agree with B	Disagree with B	Total
United States			
Agree with A	20%	40%	60%
Disagree with A	40	0	40
Total	60	40	100

tendencies cannot be discovered from the simple distribution of A (or B). Not only that, but if the conclusions obtained from the distribution of A alone are linked to the conclusions obtained from the distribution of B alone simply using "and," there is a chance that an erroneous conclusion or, at least an incomplete conclusion, will be reached: In the above example, that both Japanese and Americans tend to agree with both statements A and B.

A configural view may be especially relevant when the number of questions being considered increases and when several content domains are covered by the items. As the number of items (and content domains) increases, the interrelationships become more diversified, and it is from the nature of those interrelationships that we may discover characteristics of each country. This is the perspective from which we conducted a comparative analysis of the interrelationships among the MOW variables. The data used for this comparative analysis were from the national representative samples in the seven countries which had such samples (all countries but Yugoslavia).

Quantification on response pattern

The analytical technique used is *quantification on response pattern*, developed by Hayashi (1950, 1956). This technique was developed for the analysis of interrelationships among multivariate categorical data. The categories used in the present analysis were defined as shown in Table 13.2. Table 13.3 shows the data matrix for the Japanese national sample as an example. Quantification on response pattern treats each category and each subject to satisfy maximally the following criteria. If many of the subjects who belong to Category W2 (assign 20–39 points to work) also belong to Category AF (interesting work is ranked first, second, or third), then similar numerical values are assigned to these two categories. Conversely, if most of the subjects belonging to Category W2 do not belong to Category AF, disparate values are assigned to the two categories. At the same time, if Individuals 1 and 2 share many of the same categories, they are assigned similar numerical values. Conversely, if two individuals do not share many categories, disparate values are assigned to them. In this way, the technique calculates a set of quantifications for all categories and for all individuals that maximally satisfy the criteria.

The first set of quantifications is called *Axis I*. If the quantifications of Axis I do not explain sufficiently the interrelationships among the data, another set of quantifications that satisfy these criteria can be obtained (Axis II). If needed, Axis III, Axis IV, and so on can be obtained. In this

Table 13.2 Category definitions for "quantification on response pattern"

Categories			Questions	
LS*	Leisure	(20 points or more)	Q28	Assign a total of 100 points to indicate how important the following areas are in your life at the present time.
CM	Community	(20 points or more)		
W1	Work	(0 through 19 points)		1. My leisure (like hobbies, sports, recreation, and contacts with friends).
W2	Work	(20 through 39 points)		
W3	Work	(40 through 59 points)		2. My community (like voluntary organizations, union and political organizations).
W4	Work	(60 points or more)		3. My work.
RL	Religion	(20 points or more)		4. My religion (like religious activities and beliefs).
FM	Family	(20 points or more)		5. My family.
			Q49	Not everyone means the same thing when they talk about working. When do you consider an activity as *working*? Choose *four* statements from the list which best define when an activity is "working".
DA	If you do it in a working place			
DB	If someone tells you what to do			Note: When an item is chosen, it will take "1" as value, and "O" if not.
DC	If it is physically strenuous			
DD	If it belongs to your task			
DE	If you do it to contribute to society			
DF	If, by doing it, you get the feeling of belonging			
DG	If it is mentally strenuous			
DH	If you do it at a certain time (for instance, from 8 until 5)			
DI	If it adds value to something			
DJ	If it is not pleasant			
DK	If you get money for doing it			
DL	If you have to account for it			
DM	If you have to do it			
DN	If others profit by it			

Table 13.2 Category of definitions for "quantification on response pattern" (continued)

Categories		Questions	
AA	A lot of opportunity to learn new things	Q32	What about the nature of your working life?
AB	Good interpersonal relations (supervisors, coworkers)		How important to *you* is it that your work life contains the following. Please rank the following items from "1" to
AC	Good opportunity for upgrading or promotion		"11," noting that 1 is the most important item and 11 the
AD	Convenient work hours		least one.
AE	A lot of variety		
AF	Interesting work (work that you really like)		Note: When an item is ranked from "1" to "3," it will take
AG	Good job security		"1" as value, and "0" if not.
AH	A good match between job requirements and your abilities and experience		
AI	Good pay		
AJ	Good physical working conditions (such as light, temperature, cleanliness, low noise level)		
AK	A lot of autonomy (you decide how to do your work)		
NA	If a worker's skills become outdated, his employer should be responsible for retraining and reemployment.	Q47	Here are some work-related statements that people might make. We would like you to decide whether you agree or disagree with each of these statements depending on
NB	It is the duty of every able-bodied citizen to contribute to society by working.		your personal opinions. If you strongly agree with a statement, please circle the number 4; if you agree
NC	The educational system in our society should prepare every person for a good job if they exert a reasonable amount of effort.		somewhat with the statement, circle the number 3; and so on.
ND	Persons in our society should allocate a large portion of their regular income toward savings for their future.		1. Strongly disagree. 2. Disagree
NE	When a change in work methods must be made, a supervisor should be required to ask workers for their suggestions before deciding what to do.		3. Agree. 4. Strongly agree.

Categories		Questions
NF	A worker should be expected to think up better ways to do his or her job.	Q47 (continued)
NG	Every person in our society should be entitled to interesting and meaningful work.	Note: When the responses "strongly agree" or "agree" have been chosen, these will be valued as "1", and "0" if the responses "strongly disagree" or "disagree" have been chosen.
NH	Monotonous, simplistic work is acceptable as long as the pay compensates fairly for it.	
NI	A job should be provided to every individual who desires to work.	
NJ	A worker should value the work he or she does even if it is boring, dirty, or unskilled.	
L1	I would stop working.	Q48A Imagine that you won a lottery or inherited a large sum of money and could live comfortably for the rest of your life without working. What would you do concerning working?
L2	I would continue to work in the same job.	
L3	I would continue to work but with changed conditions.	
X1	1 (one of the least important things in my life) or 2	Q29 How important and significant is working in your *total* life? (7-point scale)
X2	3, 4 (of medium importance in my life), or 5	
X3	6 or 7 (one of the most important things in my life)	

* Identification symbols for each category which are consistently used in the tables, figures, and discussion throughout the chapter. For example, LS is the category of responses which includes assigning 20 or more points to leisure on Question 28.

Table 13.3. Example of data matrix submitted to the quantification on response pattern (Japanese national sample)

Individual number	Category LS	CM	W1	W2	W3	W4	RL	FM	DA	DB	-----	AA	AB	-----	NA	NB	-----	L1	L2	L3	X1	X2	X3
1	0	0	0	1	0	0	1	0	0	0	---	0	1	---	1	1	---	0	1	0	0	0	1
2	0	0	1	0	0	0	0	1	0	0	---	1	0	---	1	1	---	0	1	0	0	0	1
3	1	0	1	0	0	0	1	0	0	0	---	0	1	---	1	1	---	0	1	0	1	0	0
4	0	0	0	1	0	1	0	0	0	0	---	0	0	---	1	1	---	0	0	1	1	0	0
5	0	1	0	0	1	0	0	0	0	0	---	1	1	---	1	1	---	0	0	1	0	0	1
6	1	1	1	0	0	0	1	1	0	1	---	0	0	---	1	1	---	0	1	0	0	1	0
7	0	1	0	0	0	1	0	1	1	0	---	0	1	---	1	0	---	0	1	0	1	0	0
8	1	0	0	1	0	0	0	0	0	0	---	1	0	---	0	0	---	1	0	0	0	1	0
9	1	0	0	0	1	0	0	0	0	0	---	0	0	---	1	1	---	1	0	0	0	1	0
10	1	0	1	0	0	0	1	1	1	0	---	0	0	---	1	1	---	1	0	0	1	0	0
.	.	.	.	.	.	.	.	.	.	.	.	.	.	.	.	.	.	.	.	.	.	.	.
.	.	.	.	.	.	.	.	.	.	.	.	.	.	.	.	.	.	.	.	.	.	.	.
.	.	.	.	.	.	.	.	.	.	.	.	.	.	.	.	.	.	.	.	.	.	.	.
3220	0	0	0	0	0	1	0	0	1	0	---	0	0	---	1	0	---	1	0	0	0	1	0
3221	0	0	0	1	0	0	1	1	0	0	---	0	1	---	1	1	---	1	0	0	1	0	0
3222	0	0	1	0	0	1	0	0	0	0	---	0	0	---	1	1	---	0	1	0	0	1	0
3223	1	0	0	1	0	0	1	1	0	0	---	0	0	---	1	1	---	0	0	1	0	0	1
3224	0	0	0	0	1	0	0	1	0	1	---	0	0	---	1	1	---	0	1	0	0	0	1
3225	0	1	0	0	0	0	1	0	0	0	---	0	1	---	1	1	---	0	0	0	0	0	1
3226	0	0	0	0	0	0	0	0	0	0	---	0	0	---	1	1	---	0	1	0	0	0	1

NOTE: This is only a part of the Japanese data matrix:
1: When the score corresponds to the given limit, or a given item has been chosen.
0: When the score does not correspond to the given limit, or a given item has not been chosen.

respect, quantification on response pattern is similar to principal component analysis.

A more detailed mathematical explanation of quantification on response pattern is provided in Appendix A13. Here, we address the question of why the more commonly used techniques of factor analysis and principal component analysis were not utilized. The variables used in this study—with the exception of a few categorical variables (work definition items)—were continuous variables such as those measured by distribution of points (work centrality), variables measured by ranking (importance of various work aspects), and variables measured by rating scales (societal norms about working). Data of this kind usually are analyzed by using factor analysis and principal component analysis. However, it is well known that the use of factor analysis and principal component analysis is based on the condition that the relationship between the variables is a linear one. Non-linear relationships cannot be identified by factor analysis or principal component analysis. When relationships are non-linear, even continuous variables need to be broken down into several levels and analyzed categorically.

The correlation coefficients (representing the linear relationships between pairs of variables) for the continuous variables shown in Table 13.2, before being transformed into categorical variables, were uniformly low in the MOW study. Most were less than 0.2 and the largest were less than 0.4. Thus, it may be inappropriate to hypothesize a linear relationship between these variables. As a matter of fact, results from applying quantification on response pattern indicate that the tendency in some countries to value interesting work (AF in Table 13.2) and autonomy (AK) was stronger for people with medium work centrality than for those with high or low work centrality. In other words, a non-linear relationship was discovered between the importance attached to interesting work (or autonomy) and the centrality of work. The reason, then, that we used quantification on response pattern (based on categorical data), was to discover the relationships between the variables without being constrained by the condition that there be a linear character to those relationships—a condition we felt was not totally appropriate to our data.

We now turn to the results of applying quantification on response pattern to the categories shown in Table 13.2.

Results of quantification on response pattern

The quantifications of each category on Axis I and Axis II are plotted by country in figures 13.1–13.7. Each of the country's samples also is

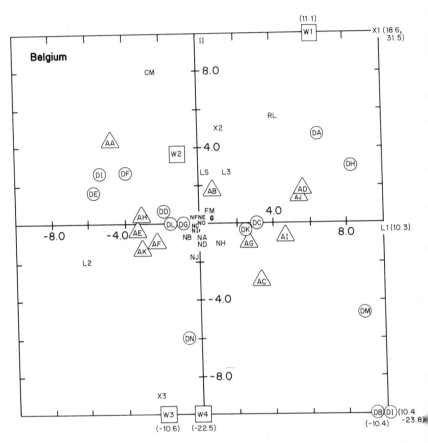

Figure 13.1. Configuration of each category plotted with Axis I and Axis II (Belgium). For identification of symbols see Table 13.2.

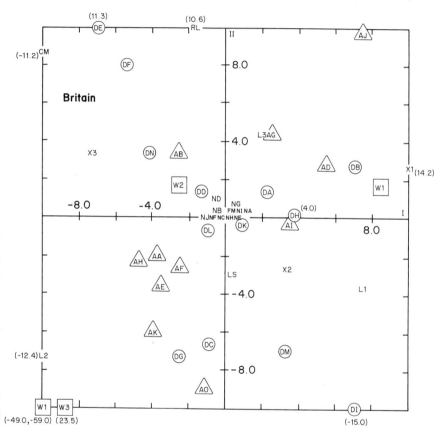

Figure 13.2. Configuration of each category plotted with Axis I and Axis II (Britain). For identification of symbols see Table 13.2.

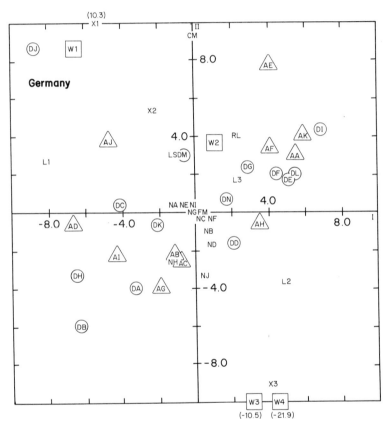

Figure 13.3. Configuration of each category plotted with Axis I and Axis II (Germany). For identification of symbols see Table 13.2.

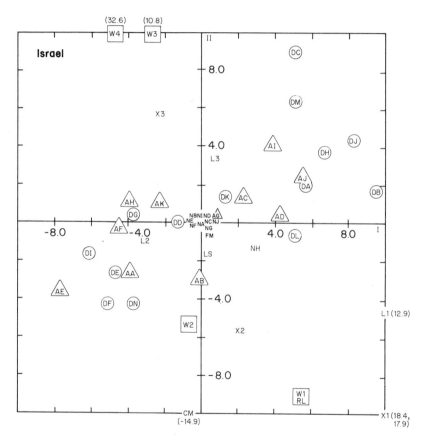

Figure 13.4. Configuration of each category plotted with Axis I and Axis II (Israel). For identification of symbols see Table 13.2.

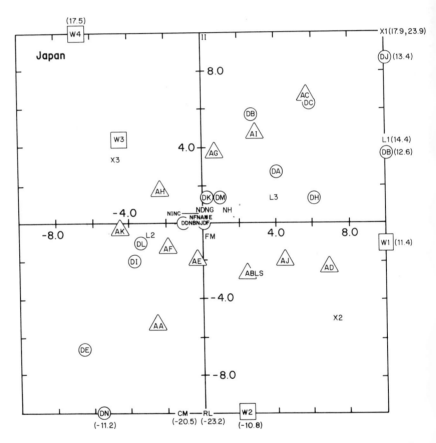

Figure 13.5. Configuration of each category plotted with Axis I and Axis II (Japan). For identification of symbols see Table 13.2.

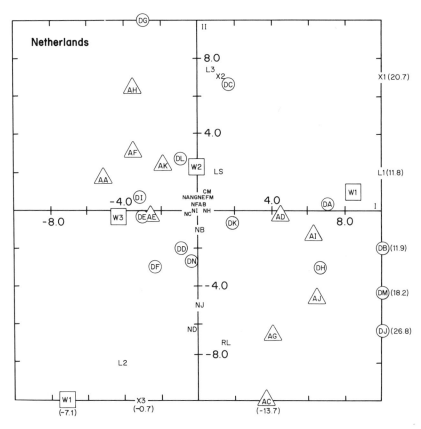

Figure 13.6. Configuration of each category plotted with Axis I and Axis II
(The Netherlands). For identification of symbols see Table 13.2.

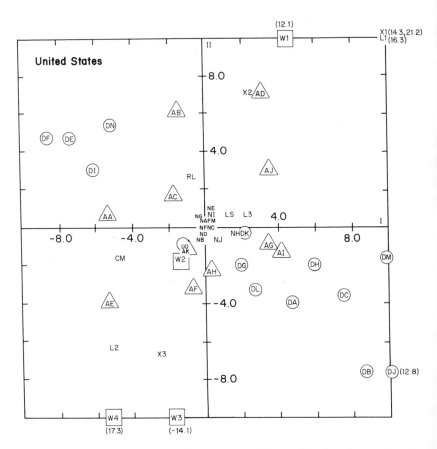

Figure 13.7. Configuration of each category plotted with Axis I and Axis II (U.S.A.). For identification of symbols see Table 13.2.

divided into subsamples of sex, age, education, occupation, and status. (Subject scores are obtained by adding the scores assigned to each category and dividing by number of checked categories.)

Relationships between categories on axis I

First, we consider the values assigned to each category on Axis I. The categories that were assigned plus values and the categories that were assigned minus values on Axis I were nearly identical in the seven countries. In West Germany, the categories that had plus (or minus) values in the other countries had minus (or plus) values; that is, the direction of the values of Axis I was opposite that of the other countries. However, this does not create any problem in considering the interrelationships between categories. Therefore, we reverse the plus and minus signs of West German values in the present discussion.

Looking at the work definition categories (DA–DN) and the categories on the work goals or valued aspects of work (AA–AK), we see that the categories with plus values are practically the same in each country, and likewise for minus values. The categories with plus values in all countries and those with minus values are listed separately in Table 13.4. We see that

Table 13.4. Categories of work definition and work goals which had plus and minus values on the first axis in all seven countries of the "Quantification on Response Pattern"

Plus values	Minus Values
Work definition	DD If it belongs to your task
DA If you do it in a working place	DE If you do it to contribute to
DB If someone tells you what to do	society
DC If it is physically strenuous	DF If, by doing it, you get the feeling
DH If you do it at a certain time	of belonging
DJ If it is not pleasant	DI If it adds value to something
DK If you get money for doing it	DN If others profit by it
DM If you have to do it	
Work Goals	AA A lot of opportunity to learn new
AD Convenient work hours	things
AG Good job security	AE A lot of variety
AI Good pay	AF Interesting work
AJ Good physical working conditions	AH A good match between job
	requirements and your abilities and
	experience
	AK A lot of autonomy

NOTE: In Britain, DC had a minus value, but the value was almost zero.

for both work definitions and work goals, there is an obvious contrast in content between the categories that have plus values and those that have minus values. Considering work definitions first, the group of categories with plus values imply a somewhat negative definition of working: Working is something forced on you by someone else; something you have to do; something that is not pleasant. On the other hand, the group of categories with minus values are indicative of a positive definition of work: Working is an activity that produces value and contributes to society. With regard to the importance of various work goals, the categories with plus values are those related to the economic and material conditions of work such as good pay, convenient hours, and good physical working conditions. On the other hand, the categories with minus values are concerned with the expressive characteristics of work such as autonomy, the chance to use one's abilities, and the opportunity to learn new things.

These results reveal a similar pattern of responses in each country: The first set of responses suggests that work is something that has to be done, is forced upon one, and importance is placed on good economic and material conditions of work. The second set of responses suggests that work is something that produces social value and importance is placed on the self-expressive characteristics of working. When we consider that this tendency was revealed on Axis I, it seems safe to conclude that the framework is an important one for a general classification of work meanings in each country.

Next, we consider the values taken on Axis I by the categories of work centrality, the importance of life areas other than work, and societal norms concerning working.

In considering the work centrality categories (W1–W4), we measured by distributing 100 points among five life areas. In each country, W1 (less than 20 points assigned to work) had a plus value. In every country except Japan, W2 (20–39 points), W3 (40–59 points), and W4 (over 60 points) had a minus value. In Japan, W1 and W2 had plus values, while W3 and W4 had minus value. The same tendency was seen in the categories measuring work centrality on a 7-point scale (X1–X3). That is, the categories X1 (working is one of the least important things in my life) and X2 (medium importance) received plus values, while X3 (working is one of the most important things) received minus values. In general, we can see that low work centrality responses group with defining work negatively and placing importance on economic and material work conditions. High work centrality responses group with defining work positively and placing importance on expressive aspects of working.

Although the relationship between work centrality and work definitions in the first instance and valued work goals in the second are similar in a general sense among the seven countries as described, there are differences between countries in the strength of the relationships. Upon closer inspection, we found that what we described as the characteristics associated with low work centrality are salient characteristics of people belonging to Category W1, and what we called the characteristics associated with high work centrality are salient in people belonging to Category W2 (in Japan and the Netherlands, W3), rather than W3 and W4. We discuss this point in more detail later in our treatment of Axis II.

Let us look at the values on Axis I of categories other than work—leisure, community, religion, and family. FM (more than 20 points given to family) had a value of close to 0 in all countries, even on Axis II. This shows that in all countries, a majority of people gave more than 20 points to family. LS (more than 20 points to leisure) had a plus value, but it was very small. Defining work negatively and placing importance on economic and material conditions was slightly related to placing importance on leisure. CM (more than 20 points to community) had a minus value or one close to 0. Placing importance on community is, for the most part, independent of work definitions and valued work aspects, or slightly associated with defining work positively and placing importance on expressive aspects of working.

There were differences between countries in the values obtained by RL (more than 20 points to religion). This category was a plus in Israel and Belgium; a minus in Germany; and close to 0 in Japan, the United States, the Netherlands and Britain. In Israel and Belgium, placing importance on religion is related to defining work negatively and placing importance on economic and material labor conditions. In West Germany, on the other hand, placing importance on religion is related to defining work positively and placing importance on expressive aspects of working. In Japan, the United States, the Netherlands, and Britain, there is no strong relationship between the importance placed on religion, and the definition of work or the importance of various work goals. It can be seen from figures 13.1–13.7 that these two factors are closer to being independent in these latter four countries.

Similar values were obtained on Axis I in all countries on the question of what one would do if one won a lottery and could live comfortably (financially) without working (Question 48A). In all countries, L1 (stop working) was a plus value, and L2 (continue working in the present job) was a minus. In West Germany, L3 (continue working but under different conditions) had a minus value, but in all other countries, it had a plus value. In each country, the descending order of the values these categories received on Axis I is L1, −L3, −L2.

Finally, the group of categories concerning societal norms about work

(NA–NJ on Question 47) had values close to 0 in every country. This held true even on Axis II because, in each country, a majority of the people agree with these norms. Thus, the relationship between agreement or disagreement with these norms and work definitions or importance of various work goals is small.

Relationships among categories on axes I and II

As seen in the previous section, there is much in common among countries in the values taken by each response category on Axis I. However, when we look further to the interrelationships among categories on Axis II, we find several differences between countries. We consider now these differences as shown in figures 13.1–13.7.

First of all, we see a common trend in West Germany, Belgium, the United States, and Israel. The values of the categories on work centrality are in the ascending (or descending) order W1, −W2, −W3, −W4 on Axis II. A line connecting the cluster of categories of negative work definitions and valuing economic and material work conditions to the cluster of categories of positive work definitions and valuing expressive aspects of working intersects almost perpendicularly with a line connecting W1, −W2, −W3, −W4. This indicates that in these countries, although there is a connection between work centrality on the one hand and work definitions and valued work goals on the other, it is not strong and the relationship, rather, is one of mutual independence.

Japan, the Netherlands, and Britain, however, show a closer relationship between work centrality and work definitions and importance of work goals. In these three countries, W1 had large plus values on Axis I, while W3 and W4 had large minus values. Axis I seems mainly to reflect the degree of work centrality in these three countries. Thus, the similarity and dissimilarity of work meanings among these three countries are primarily determined by the degree of work centrality rather than by work definitions and/or importance placed on various work goals.

As indicated, Japan, the Netherlands, and Britain are similar in that Axis I reflects the degree of work centrality. The meaning of Axis II, however, is different in each country. First, in Japan, W2 had a large minus value, and W4 a large plus value. This suggests that not only is there a quantitive difference among the four categories—W1, W2, W3, and W4—in Japan, but additionally, there is the possibility of a difference in another dimension in which W2 and W4 are on opposite poles. We discuss this point in more detail when we consider the results of analysis of certain questions that were used only in Japan.

In the Netherlands, the categories RL (more than 20 points given to religion), ND (should save for the future), NJ (should value one's work), L2 (would continue work in same job even with no financial need), and X3 (high importance of work measured on a 7-point scale) had large minus values. On the other hand, the categories DG (definition of work as mentally strenuous), DC (definition of work as physically strenuous), L3 (if no financial need, would continue to work but under different conditions), and X2 (medium importance of work measured on a 7-point scale) had large plus values. Thus, in the Netherlands, the group of categories having minus scores on Axis II indicates a grouping of responses that place importance on religion, show a strong sense of duty, and have high work centrality.

In Britain, the group of categories that had minus values on Axis I were further divided on Axis II. Categories that had plus values on Axis II were categories relating to an attitude that places importance on religion and society, such as RL (importance on religion), DE (definition of work as something that contributes to society), and DF (definition of work as something that gives the feeling of belonging). On the other hand, categories that had minus values on Axis II were DG, DC (definition of work as something physically and mentally strenuous), AC (importance on upgrading or promotion), and AK (importance on autonomy). Thus, Axis II distinguishes two groups of responses in Britain: (1) placing importance on religion and on working for society, and (2) working for individual reasons and for personal advancement.

Relationships among sex, age, education, occupation, status, and MOW variables

In the previous sections, we discussed the similarities and dissimilarities among categories of variables, based on their values on Axes I and II as determined by quantification on response pattern. The technique of quantification on response pattern assigns a numerical value to each category according to its similarity in response pattern with other categories. At the same time, it assigns a numerical value to each individual. The numerical value assigned to each individual is verified by being equivalent to the sum of the values of each of the categories to which the individual belongs, divided by the number of those categories. Thus, if a particular individual belongs to many categories that have a plus value on Axis I, that individual's value on Axis I also is a plus. In this section, we analyze the data by sex, age, education, occupation, and organizational level for each country. If the mean value of a particular sample group (e.g., men, college graduates) on Axis I is a large plus value, for example, that would mean that most of the group belong to categories with plus values on Axis I. A group of samples that takes the same position as that taken by a group of categories as shown in figures 13.1–13.7 can be said to have a strong affinity for those categories. We discuss each attribute and its characteristics in each country.

Sex

There is almost no difference between the sexes on both axes in Belgium and the United States. On the other hand, in Japan, the difference is great. In Japan, many men have high work centrality and place importance on expressive aspects of working, while many women have low work centrality and place importance on the economic and material conditions of work. West Germany, Britain, the Netherlands, and Israel show similar, but less salient, tendencies as those found in Japan.

Age

In every country, there is a strong tendency for older people to have high work centrality, to define work positively, and to place importance on expressive aspects of working. In the Netherlands, West Germany, and Belgium, the older the person, the greater the tendency to have a strong obligation norm toward work. In Japan, there was a clear tendency for work centrality to decline after 60 years of age.

Education

In Belgium, West Germany, the Netherlands, and Israel, work meanings are associated with educational level. In these countries, there is an obvious tendency for people of low educational level to define work negatively and place importance on the economic and material conditions of work, while many people of high educational level define work positively, and place importance on expressive aspects of working. Although this tendency also can be seen to some extent in the United States, variation in work meanings according to educational level is relatively small. Japan is different from the other countries in that graduates from 2-year colleges are closer in work meanings to junior high and high school graduates than to graduates of 4-year universities.

Occupation

There is a common trend in all countries except Israel. The trend is for specialists, administrators, and working proprietors to have high work centrality, define work positively, and place importance on expressive aspects of working, while production workers, sales and service workers, and clerical workers have low work centrality, define work negatively, and place importance on the economic and material conditions of work. Israel differed in that clerical workers showed the former tendency while working proprietors showed the latter.

Organizational level

In each country, as organizational level increases, the tendency is to have high work centrality, define work positively, and place importance on expressive aspects of working.

Inclusion of question items from survey on National Character (Japan)

The Japanese questionnaire included questions specific to Japan, in addition to the common questions used in all countries. These are listed in Table 13.4 and are from the *Survey on the Japanese National Character* undertaken every 5 years since 1953 by the Institute for Statistical Mathematics. The questions primarily deal with one's outlook on life and social attitudes.

Quantification of response pattern on these categories was done for the Japanese sample. These results are similar to those obtained from analysis of the common categories alone: categories defining work positively and categories indicating importance of expressive characteristics of working had minus values on Axis I, while categories defining work negatively and categories relating to the economic and material conditions of work had plus values. Of the categories in Table 13.4, T1 (concern with getting a good salary), E1 (preference for manager who makes no unreasonable work demands but does not get involved with your personal life) and S4 (live each day as it comes, cheerfully and without worrying) had plus values. On the other hand, S2 (desire to study hard and make a name for oneself), and T4 (desire for a job that gives a sense of achievement) had minus values. These results coincide well with the results obtained concerning definition of work and importance of various work goals.

On Axis 2, U1 (other people are out to make use of you), S1 (attitude toward life of "work hard and get rich"), T2 (desire for a job with no fear of bankruptcy or unemployment), and G2 (always best to be on your guard) had large plus values. In contrast, the categories G1 (people can be trusted), H1 (most people try to help one another), and T3 (concerned about having workmates you get on well with) had large minus values. There is one set of responses indicative of not easily trusting others and intently striving for economic security. There is another set of responses indicative of trusting other people and placing importance on human relationships. The category W4 is located near the cluster of categories characteristic of the first set of responses and W2 is located near the cluster of categories characteristic of the latter set of responses. This suggests that people with work centrality of 20–30 points have a strong tendency to trust others, while people with the highest work centrality of 60 points or more have a strong tendency not to trust others and to strive intently for economic security. In Japan, the set of categories, W1, $-$W2, $-$W3, $-$W4, does not simply reflect a quantitative difference in work centrality but includes a second dimension of meaning which includes attitudes toward life, work, and other people.

Characteristics of people with high, medium, and low work centrality

In the previous sections, we analyzed the interrelationships between the MOW variables in each country in a general way. In this section, we focus on the categories of work centrality, W1–W4. By looking at the kinds of categories that are located in the area of each of the work centrality categories, we consider the characteristics of the people at each level of work centrality.

1. Category W1, along with the categories relating to a negative definition of work and those relating to the economic and material conditions of work, had a relatively large plus value on Axis I. In all countries, many people who gave less than 20 points to work think of work as something they are forced to do and have to do, and place importance on the economic and material conditions of work. However, there is a difference between countries in the strength of this tendency. In Japan, the Netherlands, and Britain, the tendency is strong. In Belgium, West Germany, Israel, and the United States, the relationship between work centrality and the other aspects mentioned can be characterized as more independent.

2. Although people belonging to Category W1 assign less than 20 points to work, they do not rate work as "one of the least important things in my life" (X1) on a 7-point scale of work importance. Quantification of response pattern shows that W1 is located between X1 and X2 (medium importance), or even closer to X2. Furthermore, West Germany, the country with the highest percentage of people in the X1 category, had only 6% in this category—a very small proportion. Thus, we see that even for people who assign work only 20 or less points as a life role, work is still considered to be of medium importance in their lives.

So far, we have considered the characteristics of people belonging to category W1 that are common to all of the countries surveyed. Now, we consider the characteristics peculiar to certain countries:

- West Germany had the highest percentage of people belonging to W1 who defined work as something not pleasant (DJ). However, the number of people defining work this way is not large, only 56 out of 1278.
- In Israel, W1 and RL (more than 20 points to religion) have almost the same position. This shows that many people with low work centrality also place importance on religion.

Next, we consider the characteristics of people belonging to Category W2. In Belgium, West Germany, Israel, and Britain, many people belonging to Category W2 define work positively as something that produces social value, and place importance on expressive aspects of working. In the United States as well, many people in this category place importance on expressive aspects of working. In the Netherlands, the categories W2 and W3 are relatively close, and appear to be quite similar. They share the characteristics of W2 in Belgium, West Germany, Israel, and Britain.

In Japan, it is W3 that has the characteristics of W2 in Belgium, West Germany, Israel, and Britain. As mentioned previously, people belonging to W2 in Japan have the characteristic of trusting others.

Finally, we consider the characteristics of people with high work centrality, those belonging to categories W3 and W4. Unfortunately, not much can be said from the results of this analysis. We mention the weak relationships that were discovered, however.

In the Netherlands, on Axis II—where X3 and W4 had high minus values—the social norm categories ND (persons in our society should allocate a large portion of their regular income toward savings for their future) and NJ (a worker should value the work he or she does even if it is boring, dirty, or unskilled) also had relatively high minus values. In West

Germany as well, these categories had minus values, although not as great as in the Netherlands. In Belgium, there is also a slight, but similar, tendency. In Belgium, the category DN (work is something that others profit by) also had a relatively high minus value. Although not completely substantiated by the data, the findings indicate that, in the Netherlands, West Germany, and Belgium, many people with high work centrality of over 40 points have a strong obligation norm toward work.

The characteristics of people belonging to categories W3 and W4 in the United States are not revealed in Figure 13.7. However, in response to the question, "Suppose people were able to work less hours for the same pay in the future, which alternative would be most preferable to you?" more people belonging to W3 chose "a year off for further study about every 10 years" than did people belonging to W1 or W2. W3 also has a greater percentage of people with high educational and organizational level. From the results, it could be inferred that many Americans with the high work centrality of over 40 points are members of the social elite.

In Britain, W3 had a large minus score on Axis II. This suggests a weaker sense of working for the benefit of society than was the case for category W2 but a stronger sense of working for enjoyment and advancement. Many people in this category may be, as in the United States, part of the social elite.

In Japan, as was already mentioned, many people in the Category W4 do not readily trust others and work intently for economic security.

This suggests the possibility that, in each country, the people who have the highest work centrality have different characteristics than those with work centrality of 20–39 (in Japan and the Netherlands, 40–59) points. It is, therefore, probably not appropriate to simply extrapolate that as work centrality increases, work is defined more positively and more importance is placed on expressive characteristics of working. People who assign over 40 or even over 60 points to work—relative to the generally hard-to-neglect areas of family and leisure—must have unique social norms, social status orientations, and attitude toward life. The data suggest that it may be on the characteristics of the people with such high work centrality that countries differ most.

Summary

The results of the present analysis clearly differentiate between people who define work negatively as something they have to do and are forced to do and who place importance on the economic and material conditions of work in contrast to people who define work positively as an activity that produces something of value for society and who place importance on self-expressive aspects of working. This major classification framework is appropriate to all countries surveyed. The former group contains many people with low work centrality, the latter group contains many people with high work centrality. In Belgium, West Germany, Israel, and the United States, however, this tendency is weaker than in Japan, the Netherlands, and Britain, and the relationship between the dimensions of the framework and work centrality is more independent.

By creating four categories of work centrality (less than 20 points, 20–39, 40–59, and more than 60 points) and analyzing the characteristics of the people belonging to each category, we conclude the following.

In all countries, many people assigning less than 20 points to work defined work negatively and placed importance on the economic and material conditions of work. Many people giving 20–39 points to work (40–59 in Japan, 20–59 in the Netherlands) defined work positively and placed importance on self-expressive aspects of working. People who gave 40 points or more to work (more than 60 in Japan and the Netherlands) had unique attitudes toward life (Japan), social norms (Belgium, West Germany, the Netherlands) or social status (the United States and Britain). It is suggested further that the characteristics of people belonging to this group may reveal important differences between countries.

Chapter 14

The Meaning of Working; Overview and Implications

Introduction

This research addressed the topic of what working means to people. Our conceptual framework posited that the meaning of working to an individual should be defined (and assessed) in terms of:

- The general degree of importance and value of working in one's life
- Normative beliefs and expectations about "rights" and "duties" attached to the role and process of working
- Valued working outcomes and work goals sought and preferred by individuals in their working lives

Stated in question form, we were trying to determine:

- How attached people are to working
- What level of "rights" and "duties" beliefs about working exist in various labor forces
- What are the general outcomes and/or opportunities people are seeking from working and what are their relative importances

We have told the story of a large scale, complex study which included about 15,000 respondents from eight countries and which kept an international team of 14 colleagues busy for several years. A great variety of findings are presented in the preceding chapters. Some may be primarily of interest to social scientists inasmuch as they reflect conceptual or methodological advances in the context of received theory and research. Although it is difficult to anticipate properly the eclectic curiosity of our social scientific readers, we do provide a general summary or overview of these findings here. Additionally, since social science findings often feed public debates in perplexing ways, it seems appropriate to point out what *we* believe some of our main findings imply. We will do so at varying levels, sometimes stressing individual, sometimes organizational, and sometimes societal implications.

The general structure of MOW

The general structure of "meaning of working" which emerges from our conceptualization and measurement *and* which survives as important through our analyses is represented in Figure 14.1. We place work central-ity in the center of a series of concentric circles to reflect its fundamental and genotypical importance in understanding the meaning of working. We believe that the general assessment or measurement of work centrality

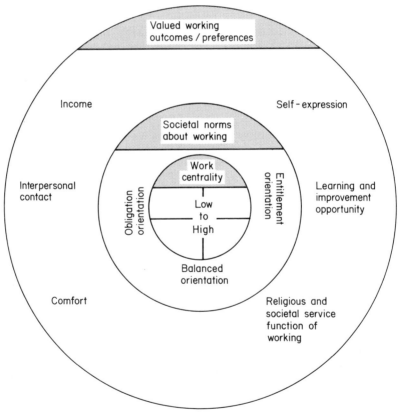

Figure 14.1. Structure representation of the meaning of working.

should encompass all possible reasons why work could be important to individuals but not be partial to any particular reason. In short, it should represent a generalized measure of how attached (in a value sense) one is to working as a life role.

Societal norms about working represent normative beliefs and expectations connected to the role of working in one's life. Conceptually, there could be a wide range of content categories subsumed under this heading. The societal norms about working which have been developed in the MOW research project concentrate on two notions that have a long and important history in discussion and analysis of working. We have named these two notions entitlement orientation and obligation orientation. They also are characterized as "rights" and "duties" connected to the working role which are viewed by individuals as just, fair and socially legitimized. Additionally, it would seem reasonable to view these two normative orientations as an expression of equitable exchange rules concerning what should be received from working (outcomes) and what should be provided to organizations and society through working (inputs). Thus, our conceptualizations and our analyses include the notion of a balance between entitlements and obligations. The most salient issues which comprise working "rights" and "duties" will probably change over time in given societies at different rates and in different ways. It is also likely, however, that global markets for the products and services of work and worldwide communication networks operate as forces toward a degree of standardization of working rights and duties. Societal norms about working are placed in the second concentric circle in Figure 14.1 because they function in a society to express equitable exchange rules between individuals and collectivities in the process of working. As· such, they are general in character and constitute a major set of work meanings.

Valued working outcomes and work goal preferences probably have been studied and examined more than any other domain shown in Figure 14.1. It is this domain, however, which is the most open-ended and in some respects the most difficult in which to identify the relevant constructs and move from construct to measurement. This difficulty rests on two interrelated facts. First, the domain theoretically can include any outcome, preference, incentive, goal, need, or value which any individual desires from his/her working life, thus encompassing a potentially enormous and idiosyncratically identified set. Secondly, the possible levels of abstraction run from the most specific and minute notion to the most abstract such as self-expression through working. Chapters 2, 4, 7 and 8 allow the reader to observe some of the difficulties in the development of this domain. In Chapter 7, we identified two levels of abstraction for considering valued working outcomes. The most general or abstract level was that which identified a *dominant rationale for working* or the basic reasons why individuals are working. We found that the economic rationale for working was predominant for slightly over half of the total national sample respondents and was nearly three times as frequently dominant as the next most frequent rationale. Clearly, the dominant underlying reason why people work is to secure and maintain an income to purchase needed and/or desired goods and services. The second and less abstract level of valued working outcomes includes work goal dimensions which people prefer to find or obtain in their work. Here, the expressive dimension of work goals was preferred by about half of our combined national sample respondents and was nearly two times as frequently preferred as the economic dimension. The opportunity to express oneself through working leads the list of dimensions which people prefer to obtain in their working situation. This apparent (but we think not real) contradiction nicely illustrates one major reason for the diversity of findings in the literature dealing with the work goal domain of the meaning of working.

Figure 14.1 presents those valued working outcomes which emerge as most relevant in our data set and through our analyses. They represent a mid-range in terms of level of abstraction. We clearly recognize that one can move up or down in terms of level of abstraction depending upon one's purpose. Indeed, Chapter 7 reports data on individual work goals, on empirically developed work goal dimensions and on dominant rationales—thus spanning three levels of abstraction. Though multidimensional, complex, and idiosyncratic in nature, valued working outcomes are a major component of the meaning of working.

There is a qualitative similarity of 75–90% in the structure of work meanings across the countries studied in the MOW project as reported in Chapter 4. This degree of common structure does not imply the absence of level differences among countries on the various work meanings, but it does indicate that there is sufficient structural similarity to make country comparisons meaningful.

Individual variability in meaning of working

We have found that there actually is a great deal of individual variability on major MOW variables in every country, occupation, age group, educational level or sex group. For example, in every country there are individuals who have each Work Centrality Index score from the lowest possible score (2) to and including the highest score (10).[1] As indicated in Chapter 5, a score of 2 means that working is evaluated as the least important of the five life roles *and* is rated no higher than three on the 7-

point scale of work importance. A score of 10, on the other hand, means that working is the most important of the five life roles *and* is scored as seven on the 7-point work importance scale. The score range from 2 to 10 covers work centrality levels that are vastly different in both conceptual and actual meaning. In the case of societal norms about working, there are individuals in every country who strongly disagree, disagree, agree and strongly agree with each one of the five entitlement items and with each one of the five obligation items. In the valued working outcomes domain, there are individuals in every country who rank each of the 11 work goals as being most important, least important and every rank between the two extremes.

The same basic observation is true whether we look at countries as in the above examples or at occupations, age groups, sex groups or educational level groups. Thus, there are individuals who have every possible measurement value on every one of the major MOW variables. Individual variability on the major MOW variables is reduced by about 20% in some cases when controlled on the aforementioned categories, but it is never eliminated and individual differences remain dominant. The meaning of working is both complex in structure and highly differentiated at the level of the individual. This is, we believe, a picture of reality and not a function of measurement artifacts.

Attachment to working

A general view of the level of attachment that there is to working as a life role among our eight countries can be discerned by considering the following lines of evidence.

- The combined national sample data from the eight countries shows the Work Centrality Index to be distributed as follows:

	Very low work centrality	Moderately low work centrality	Moderately high work centrality	Very high work centrality
WCI score range	2, 3, 4	5, 6	7, 8	9, 10
Percentage distribution	8.5%	26.5%	35.2%	29.8%

- Eighty-six percent of the combined national sample say they would continue to work even if they had enough money to live comfortably for the rest of their life without working.

- Work is second only to family in life role importance. In the combined national samples, 39.5% place family as most important while 26.5% place working as most important among the five life roles (family, working, community, religion and leisure).
- In the combined national samples, about 1 in 8 says work will be *less* important to them in the next five to ten years, 5 in 8 say work will be *equally* important to them, and 2 in 8 say work will be more important to them in the next five to ten years.

Our general interpretation of these findings is that approximately two out of every three individuals has a strong attachment to working as a life role while one out of every three individuals has a relatively weak attachment to working. However, this analysis is a broad generalization and an alternative interpretation in terms of country and occupational differences, education and job quality will be briefly treated at the end of this chapter. These contingencies are carefully analyzed in chapters 5, 11 and 13 and they show that the degree of work centrality shows significant variations as a function of these variables.

From a cross-sectional study one cannot legitimately infer what future trends will be, but the multivariate analysis in Chapter 13 shows that, for the population sample, age was a significant contingency. In general, older people have higher work centrality than younger people (in Japan, however, work centrality declines after 60). It would be useful to monitor this result every decade to identify trends.

Normative expectations about working

When we view the societal norms about working as a general expression of equitable exchange rules concerning what should be received from working versus what should be contributed through the process of working, two important observations stand out. First, it seems clear that the level of endorsement of the two norms and the extent of balance between them are most appropriately understood as national level phenomena. The logic of the constructs and their development as well as our analytic results indicate that national level interpretations predominate. The reader will remember from Chapter 6 that most occupational groups in each country show the same basic exchange rules concerning rights and duties about working as did their respective national sample.

In four countries (Japan, Britain, Yugoslavia and Israel), rights and duties are roughly balanced. In the Netherlands, the Federal German Republic and Belgium, the national samples have societal norms about working which reflect relatively higher levels of endorsement of working rights than of working duties. This tendency is considerably stronger in the case of the Netherlands. The labor force in the United States has societal norms about working which reflect relatively higher levels of endorsement of duties than of rights.

Secondly, as pointed out in Chapter 6, there is little indication in our data that entitlement or rights orientations differ for various age groups, educational groups and sex groups.[2] Obligation or duty orientation, however, is significantly related to these bio-categories whether we look within countries or within our total sample. Males, older employees and those with less education are more obligation oriented. It thus seems likely that the changing demographic composition of labor forces (which are generally moving toward more highly educated workers and toward greater female labor force participation) would bring some reduction in the level of obligation or duty orientation over time. Thus, *it might be argued* that the exchange rules concerning work and working at the societal level are changing and will likely continue to change in the future. While this may happen, we would argue that it is a change in the nature or context surrounding the attachment to working and not in the actual *level* of attachment to working itself. We would make the same argument if there were changes in obligation orientation which were a function of cohort or generation differences. As pointed out earlier, this distinction between level of attachment and the nature or context of attachment is important and is based upon a differentiated model of the meaning of working, such as the present one. Again, we would point out the critical need for longitudinal study of societal norms about working within countries for a clearer view of changes actually taking place and their likely causes.

The nature of a desirable working life

In a real sense, assessment of the importance of different work goals or work outcomes to individuals (as obtained in the MOW project) is a strong composite statement about the nature of desirable working lives in industrial societies. Neglecting for the moment our concern about the validity of broad generalizations and the very real problems in this domain of meaning of working relative to various levels of abstraction, it seems useful to highlight what our work goal data suggest about the nature of desirable working lives as expressed by employed labor forces in eight industrialized nations. It should be remembered that each individual was responding at a given point in their working life and that the full range of job types, backgrounds, and work situations that exist in each society were represented. Also, our instructions asked respondents to focus on their total working life as opposed to only their present job situation.

As reported in Chapter 7, *interesting work (work that you really like)* was the most important element that individuals wanted in their working life. The margin by which this element stood out as the most preferred characteristic of working life is impressive. In four of the eight countries, it was the most preferred element across the whole labor force; it was second in preferability in three countries and third in one country. It was the most important working life element in each age group and for both males and females. It also led the list for eight of the ten target groups. Perhaps it is both more instructive and more meaningful to note that interesting work was among the *three most important* work goals for four out of every ten individuals in the combined national sample, while it was among the *three least important* work goals for only one of every ten individuals. The closest rival to interesting work was the work goal, *good pay*, which also was among the three most important work goals for about four of every ten individuals but it was among the three least important work goals for about two of every ten individuals.

For such an important work goal as *interesting work (work that you really like)*, it would seem imperative to identify and understand what constitutes, makes up, or leads to the state of viewing your work as interesting. We do know that interesting work is part of the self-expression dimension which also included the work goals, *a good match between your job requirements and your abilities and experience, a lot of autonomy (you decide how to do your work)* and *a lot of variety*. However, this is far from identifying those personal states and working situations which lead one to perceive his work as interesting. Additionally, we would need to know the relative frequency of various paths to "interesting work" in work force populations. We believe that this issue constitutes a major research question which is suggested by results from the eight country data. Clearly, the issue has enormous significance to individuals, to work design specialists within organizations and to societies that are increasingly becoming more highly educated. It is an area that may be destined to become a major mismatch between the nature of preferred and available work for large numbers of individuals during the early part of the 21st century.

If we look at the relative preferences for work goals other than *interesting work* and *good pay* in the combined national samples, the following general picture emerges:

- For the work goals *Good interpersonal relations, a good match between job requirements and skills and abilities, good interpersonal relations* and *good job security*, approximately three of ten individuals include each among their three most important work goals while two of ten individuals include each among their three least important work goals.

- For the work goals *a lot of opportunity to learn new things, a lot of variety*, and *convenient work hours*, approximately two of ten individuals include each among their three most important work goals while about three of ten individuals include each among their three least important work goals.
- For the work goal *good physical working conditions*, approximately one in ten individuals includes it among their three most important work goals while about four of ten individuals includes it among their three least important work goals.
- At the bottom of the preference list is the work goal, *good opportunity for upgrading or promotion*, where one in ten individuals includes it among their three most important work goals while five in ten individuals includes it among their three least important work goals.

There seems to be a growing consensus that the inherent flexibility of new technologies, particularly those based on microelectronics, is far greater than the constraints and necessities they impose for specific, unalterable working conditions (Sorge, Hartmann and Warner, 1983). This may present a unique opportunity and challenge to the design of jobs to make them maximally compatible with the diversity of human needs, expectations and preferences which clearly exist. The issue, however, is not only a matter of intent. It also is an issue of knowledge and competence of work designers concerning what is a "more appropriate job" and for how many is it appropriate. Our data provides reasonable hints as to those work goals and dimensions that might be considered, as well as some evidence about the frequency or incidence of various preference levels. Few studies from which such criteria or guides have been derived in the past command the scope or have a data base comparable to the present MOW project.

Meaning of working patterns

When we view the meaning of working patterns as holistic or integrated descriptions of the multiple meaning that large numbers of people assign to working, three observations stand out. First, it is clear that there are large quantitative and qualitative differences in the combination of MOW variables that define the patterns described in chapters 10 and 12. Second, there are substantial national and target group differences in the relative frequency of MOW pattern representation. Third, the different MOW patterns are associated with substantial differences in patterns of consequences.

In Chapter 10, the instrumental pattern and the expressive work centrality pattern are both defined by pay and expressive work goals and by work
centrality, but differ in the quantitative level of each variable. The entitlement and contact orientation pattern and the low entitlement MOW
pattern differ in their quantitative level on contact work goals and on the
societal norms. There is a clear *qualitative* difference, however, between
the two sets of contrasting patterns.

The modal MOW pattern for Japan and the United States is low
entitlement, while for Israel and Yugoslavia the modal pattern is expressive work centrality. In contrast, there is no clear modal pattern among the
Belgian and Dutch samples, while the German sample tends to be concentrated most heavily in the instrumental pattern. Tool- and diemakers,
textile and white-collar workers tend toward the instrumental pattern while
professionals (chemical engineers, teachers) and self-employed are concentrated in the low entitlement and/or expressive work centrality pattern.

In Chapter 12, the different MOW patterns are shown to have substantial differences in patterns of consequences. Pattern 1 is associated with
consequences of high job involvement (longer work week, a lower percent
indicating they would stop working on the lottery question and continuation on the same job), a more negative reaction to working fewer hours for
less pay and tend to worry less frequently about work in their free time.
The consequences for pattern 4 members is just the opposite. There also
are large quantitative differences in the pattern of consequences associated
with MOW pattern 2 as compared to pattern 3. Pattern 2 members prefer a
job with greater pay but substantially lower autonomy or expressive features to a much greater extent than do pattern 3 members. Pattern 2
members also register much lower occupational satisfaction than pattern 3
members. Thus MOW patterns that differ only in quantitative level in their
defining features also differ in a quantitative manner on consequences. But
where the differences between MOW patterns is qualitative there is also a
qualitative difference in the consequences.

In chapters 9, 10, 11, 12 and 13, analytic methods were used to group
individuals on various MOW and/or work definition variables. This
strategy of analysis differs from the strategy of earlier chapters that concentrated on one domain of MOW or particular MOW variables. What should
not be overlooked is that these analytic methods yield findings at different
levels of abstraction. At one level of analysis in earlier chapters, we dealt
with individual differences in which the configuration of MOW variables
could potentially number in the thousands. At a much higher level of
abstraction almost all of our national combined sample were characterized
as belonging to one of two polar opposite patterns (Chapter 13). Between
these extremes are the four pattern solutions discussed in chapters 10
through 12.

These various levels of abstraction have importance not only as heuristic devices, but in their practical implications as well. Decision makers are constantly confronted with making choices involving trade-offs in the strengths and weaknesses associated with different levels of abstraction in seeking solutions to problems involving work systems. At higher levels of abstraction of human characteristics, more general solutions can be designed which encompass larger groups of people that share similar characteristics to some degree. Both the diagnosis of problems and the design of solutions is more tractable and economically feasible when these levels of abstraction are appropriate.

However, there is a cost involved in adopting such a strategy which can be traced to the loss of information about individuals and this cost becomes potentially greater at increasingly higher levels of abstraction. The loss of information reduces the accuracy or fidelity of decision making and hence the quality of the decisions from the point of view of specific individuals. Decisions that require high recognition of individuality thus suffer. However, solutions to work system problems that require characteristics of people at a more differentiated level run a serious risk of being more intractable, more difficult to explain and economically costly.

The choice of the level of generality of specification of human characteristics in decisions concerning work systems remains as one of the most persistent and major challenges for present and future decision makers as they seek solutions to the effective utilization of human resources in work systems. The success with which they meet the challenge has widespread implications for the continued viability of industrial societies.

Definitions of working

The criteria and rationales which individuals use to decide when an activity is considered "working" is more an attribution about working than a major MOW variable and therefore should be viewed as parallel to, rather than as an intrinsic part of, MOW. This distinction was made in our heuristic research model in Figure 2.1 in Chapter 2 and is again reinforced in Figure 14.1 in the present chapter. In both cases, the *definition of working* is not presented as one of the major MOW variables. As shown in Chapter 9, however, it is useful to consider this attribution about working.

When presented with 14 statements about activities which were drawn from previous work-related literature, respondents do show rather clearly what statements or ideas identify an activity as working in their view. Chapter 9 contains the data and analyses on the work defining power of each statement as well as major types of work definitions. As might be expected by the predominant economic rationale for working previously described, the statement "if you get money for doing it" had the greatest defining power of working and was chosen by two out of every three individuals in the combined national sample. At the other extreme, "if it is not pleasant" was selected by only one in 20 respondents.

Pattern analysis of work definition statements reveals that about three of eight individuals define working primarily in terms of *concrete* notions (e.g., getting money, doing it at a certain time, having to do it). There are large differences in the percentage of national labor forces who are concretists in defining working as well as some educational level and occupational differences.

About three of every eight individuals define work largely in *duty* terms (e.g., if you have to account for it, if it belongs to your task). Here, work seems to be viewed in terms of accountability and role prescriptions. There are large differences in the percentage of national labor forces who define work in duty terms and some educational influence is also noted.

Slightly more than one of eight individuals has a *social* definition of working which encompasses three notions (if you do it to contribute to society, if by doing it you get the feeling of belonging, if others profit by it). National level differences in *social* definitions of working are large and some occupational and educational differences are noted.

Slightly less than one in eight individuals defines working in *burden* terms which encompass the notions, if it is physically strenuous, if it is mentally strenuous. There are country differences in the incidence of burden definitions but very little variability by occupation, gender, age, or education level.

Three conclusions stand out based on our examination of the definitions people assign to working. First, we conclude that working as an unenjoyable or burdensome activity is only a minor definitional element when people attempt to elaborate the features that distinguish working from other activities or experiences in their lives. This finding is contrary to the claims made by Shimmin (1966) and Weiss and Kahn (1960) that one of the distinguishing features of working activities is that people perform them but do not enjoy them. Rather it would seem that when most people elaborate the distinguishing features of working they utilize concrete formal features that regulate their activities, working as an avenue of social integration or duty and control.

A second conclusion is that there is no relationship between the four definitional patterns of working and the MOW variables. As previously noted, one reason for this finding is that the two measure different conceptual domains. The MOW variables measure people's reactions to their (often lengthy) working experiences. The definitional features measure the aspects of working activities that distinguish them from other life activities.

For example, the concrete working definitions include working features mediated by others (the exchange of work for money), compulsion (having to work) and formalized or regulated features (the location of activities and the time when they occur). The social definitions seem to be concerned with working as an avenue for social integration including contributing something of value that people profit from and deriving a feeling of belonging. Finally, the duty definitional elements are concerned with working as activities and outcomes for which people are held accountable by others or activities that are part of formal role prescriptions.

Third, the conclusion that the defining features of working are character-istics which distinguish work from other life activities helps in providing an understanding of national differences on the work definition clusters. We would suggest that the national samples in the countries differ in the definitions they emphasize because the characteristics of work systems between countries differ in their emphasis. For example, the Japanese work system would seem to have a company level emphasis on concrete features such as social pressure to engage in particular behavior and highly formalized and regulated settings. In addition, there would seem to be a high degree of personal accountability and strong role prescriptions. These key features of Japanese work systems may be one reason why the Japan-ese national sample emphasizes the concrete and duty definitional features of work. In contrast, the more equal emphasis on all four work definition patterns among the United States and Belgian national samples may stem from work systems that are more idiosyncratic and variable at the company level and are therefore less universal or focused in emphasis than is the Japanese work system.

Working and societies

Berger and Offe, (1984) note that any society is faced with the twofold task of ensuring a viable distribution of work among those able to work and an equitable distribution of the fruits of this work among those who work and those who legitimately do not work. This double allocational problem is both intensified and complicated as global competition and technological developments highlight differing national advantages and disadvantages in the production of goods and services which are economically viable. Work-ing, as a paid activity, constitutes a fundamental mechanism in literally all industrialized nations for both the creation and the distribution of existen-tial and social benefits: income and economic security, identity and status and options for leisure time activities. Thus it is certainly necessary to consider work and working as both a "private good" and a "public good."

There is intense ideological debate both within nations and between nations about what constitutes a reasonably balanced view of working as both a private and public good and it extends far beyond the scope of our inquiry. We do believe, however that the debate in each nation could be instructed by a thorough understanding of the MOW results in their own country as viewed against results found in other countries. Indeed, this is one major reason for conducting cross-national inquiry and encompasses our rationale for the large number of by-country analyses reported in earlier chapters.

Ensuring a viable distribution of work to those able to work has long been attempted through the establishment of norms regarding working time. Roughly within the timespan of a century, the average working hours per week have been reduced to almost one half in many countries; in the Federal German Republic, for example, from 72 hours in 1881 to 41.6 hours in 1980 (Schneider, 1984). Today, some debate entering the 39 or 35 hour week. Concurrently with these developments, our societies have undergone dramatic social changes, shifting from basically agrarian structures to industrial ones, and increasingly more so to those that are characterized as economies with a strong service sector. The change of economic bases from agrarian production to goods-producing industries and then to information processing services (labelled as the advent of post-industrial society—Bell, 1972) implied significant changes in the structure of the workforce, e.g. expansion of labor market participation, changing occupational and competence structures, expansion of employment in private profit and in public non-profit services (paid through public budgets). While increases of the labor force in the non-profit service sector seems to have reached its fiscally feasible limits in most Western countries, technological innovations and their accompanying productivity gains make themselves already strongly felt in the industrial sectors by creating redundancies. Besides, they begin to make their inroads in the service sector (Friedrichs and Schaff, 1982). Our MOW results emphasize the need to strive toward *an increase in employment opportunities*. The findings are quite unequivocal as to the continued subjective significance and value of working to individuals irrespective of some differentiations according to different social groups or with respect to certain aspects of work meanings. Thus they contradict the thesis of a widespread "decentering" of working as a life role (Offe, 1984). The subjective significance of working also persists so far in spite of the existing transfer payments in most industrialized countries. Strategies to reallocate worktime (in its various forms, e.g. early retirement, part-time arrangements, job sharing, prolonged vacation, leave of absence for educational and training purposes) should be considered seriously provided they give sufficiently balanced concern to both personal preferences and requirements of productive output from working.

Another direction to which our research may contribute relates to a more fundamental aspect of desirable *change of social values* and the *concept of working* itself. A crucial facet for defining an activity as working is, as we have shown (Chapter 9), "to be paid for it." Since most responsible citizens will agree that a lot still remains to be done in our societies (better educational systems, more livable cities, improved environmental protection, more cultural activities, more opportunity for development of individuals' abilities and interests and more humane treatment of older citizens—to name only a few) and since we seem to be facing a mismatch between this unfinished business and a looming lack of traditionally defined (paid) jobs to do it, it seems useful to consider extending the notion of working to also include those needs and to provide corresponding financial incentives for them. Such a prospect seems totally congruent with the way most individuals define working and it is equally congruent with the diversity of meanings of working. The achievement of such an extension of the concept of work will not be easily accomplished and will require a great deal of imagination, thought and analysis. We have no ready-made recipes but hope to have provided some ingredients for informed discussion.

Working and the fruits of working remain as central elements in humankind's existence and have far-reaching significance to individuals as well as to collectivities. We hope that our eight-nation inquiry into the meaning of working provides useful conceptual notions, methodological contributions and relevant findings to better illuminate people's relationship to working.

Alternative interpretations

As has already been indicated, there are several ways of interpreting our data and the reader will have to draw his own conclusions. It is a study that involves values both in the formulation of the research and in the evaluation of answers. This can be brought out clearly by focusing on the notion of work centrality, but applies also to other variables in the model.

If one takes the view that working, in one form or another, is virtually inescapable for the vast majority of men and women except those who have unemployment imposed upon them, then average high scores on work centrality are a foregone conclusion. After all, most people spend at least eight hours out of an approximately 16-hour waking day on something called work, without which few people can obtain either the necessities or the luxuries of life.

From this perspective, an aggregated or average work centrality score for the total sample of 15,000 respondents is an academic curiosity and has few practical policy implications. The important questions relate to the factors that distinguish relatively high from relatively low scores. Our data shows that at least two major antecedents have to be considered. One is country, and this could involve variations in norms derived from historic and cultural factors. The other is based on the nature of the job itself, its level in the hierarchy, the freedom of choice it allows and the amount of skill and education required to carry it out. Our data shows that both are significant explanatory factors.

Country analysis in Chapter 5 points to some startling differences in work centrality scores. Japan has by far the highest score and Britain the lowest. This was not unexpected, but who would have predicted that Germany has the second lowest work centrality score and that Yugoslavia has the next highest after Japan? The American sample occupies a middle position.

It is clear that these findings do not support the work ethic explanations put forward by Weber (1930) who saw it as an offspring of Calvinist protestantism. Though Tawney's judgment was more cautious, he still thought that the work ethic found in later puritanism "a tonic which braced its energies and fortified its already vigorous temper" (Tawney, 1926: 227). With Japan and Yugoslavia heading the work centrality list in the 1980s, we must search out other explanations, but this requires further studies. However, the data suggests that we should ask the question whether high and low work centrality are to some extent a function of industrialization. The Industrial Revolution started in Britain around the 1750s, while Japan and Yugoslavia moved from largely agricultural to industrial economies as recently as the 1950s. If this were part of the explanation, we would have to expect a fall in work centrality for several of the countries in our sample over the next century.

The second important contingency is the nature of the job. Chapters 11 and 13 address themselves to this issue. People who have a high-quality job (meaning variety, autonomy, responsibility and opportunity to use their competence) have relatively high work centrality scores, expressive rather than instrumental orientations and intrinsic goal orientation, and they put pay incentives significantly lower than the average respondent. People who have poor working conditions, and repetitive, demanding, dangerous and unhealthy work show the opposite pattern.

The relationship between occupation and MOW patterns is consistent in all countries except Israel. Administrators, managers, specialists and proprietors have high work centrality, define work positively and place importance on expressive values. In contrast, production, sales, service and clerical workers have the opposite characteristics. The same contrast exists between people who occupy high or low levels in organizations.

We have already seen that work centrality is to some extent a function of age; older people think it is more important than younger people. We cannot tell whether this signals a general shift which would make future generations less likely to value work highly compared with other life interests, or whether the change in work centrality is simply a function of getting old. In either case there are policy implications which longitudinal research will have to identify.

Older people define work more positively and stress expressive rather than instrumental aspects of working. There are also significant differences between the sexes in six out of the eight countries. Belgium and the USA are the exceptions; in the other countries and most noticably in Japan, women have low work centrality.

Finally, education is an important contingency, but the effect is a little more complex than with the other variables. For both men and women, low education is associated with an instrumental MOW pattern. Expressive work orientation is relatively strong among the more highly educated groups. These differences are much more marked among women than men (Chapter 11).

The conclusions one draws from such a contingency or situational analysis of our research are different from those based on global aggregate data. From a policy standpoint, there may not be very much one can suggest that would change the low centrality of the UK or West Germany to the high centrality of Japan, but the contingency findings have practical implications at the level of organizational policy. It is useful to think about the reasons for the significant differences between age groups, males and females and the more or less highly educated. Future research should address itself to these issues.

However, by and large, our findings, particularly on occupational levels and differences between high and low quality jobs strongly support the large area of research sometimes summarized under the heading of QWL (quality of working life). In particular they support the importance of job design, increases in autonomy, decentralized participative decision making, flatter organizational patterns and greater attention to the utilization of existing competence.

Notes

(1) The only exception to this statement is that no score of 2 on the work centrality index occurred in Japan.

(2) This finding severely questions interpretations which are based on the belief that "entitlement" is the dimension that has greatly increased in salience during the past 20–30 years.

Item Level Response Distribution Data for National Samples and for Target Groups

The reader should refer to the MOW Questionnaire (Appendix A3.1) for exact item wording. Items are shortened and/or abbreviated for response distribution presentation.

The first section of this Appendix presents data for the national representative sample in each country.

The second section of this Appendix presents data for each target group. The sample for each target group consists of the respondents (from Target Group Sampling) belonging to that specified target group in all countries.

MOW National Sample Responses — '**' Indicates Data Missing and/or Unavailable

		Country of Residence							
		Belgium	Britain	Germany	Israel	Japan	Netherlands	U.S.A.	Yugoslavia
—Total Sample Size—	Number of Responses	450	840	1278	973	3226	996	1000	542
Q1: Type of Work									
**Missing Data	Percent	0.2	100.0	0.2	2.6	0.0	0.8	0.7	0.0
Chemists	Percent	2.2	**	0.0	0.4	0.8	0.0	0.5	15.5
Teachers	Percent	3.1	**	0.0	10.7	3.2	5.4	5.8	16.6
Other Prof	Percent	12.7	**	0.9	7.0	12.8	17.9	19.3	0.6
Admin and MGR	Percent	5.6	**	20.0	6.2	11.6	13.1	14.7	0.9
Clerical	Percent	15.1	**	29.3	21.0	21.8	18.8	16.7	16.6
Prop—Whlsale & Retail	Percent	7.8	**	5.6	2.2	15.7	0.0	2.7	0.0
Sales	Percent	5.6	**	1.3	1.6	5.2	6.6	5.6	0.0
Prop—Cater & Lodging	Percent	0.2	**	0.0	1.5	5.3	0.0	0.1	0.0
Service	Percent	10.2	**	6.0	12.7	7.6	7.6	12.7	0.0
Agriculture	Percent	4.0	**	1.4	2.6	0.2	2.6	2.3	0.0
Spinners & Weavers	Percent	2.2	**	1.6	0.9	0.2	0.7	0.8	16.6
Blacksmiths—Toolers	Percent	4.9	**	11.9	0.9	0.9	6.7	1.6	16.6
Construction—Equipment	Percent	20.2	**	17.2	14.2	9.2	19.8	12.1	0.0
Armed Forces	Percent	0.9	**	0.0	3.2	0.1	0.0	1.1	0.0
Other	Percent	5.1	**	4.4	12.3	5.5	0.0	3.3	16.6
Q2: Supervisory Status									
**Missing Data	Percent	0.7	5.5	100.0	2.9	0.8	1.4	0.0	1.1
Non-Super	Percent	59.3	64.5	**	46.8	64.6	62.9	56.0	73.4
Super	Percent	26.2	17.4	**	32.0	8.6	28.6	22.1	14.2
Managerial	Percent	13.8	12.6	**	18.4	26.1	7.1	21.9	11.3

MOW National Sample Responses — '**' Indicates Data Missing and/or Unavailable (continued)

		Country of Residence							
		Belgium	Britain	Germany	Israel	Japan	Netherlands	U.S.A.	Yugoslavia
Q3A: Union Member?									
**Missing Data	Percent	0.4	5.1	100.0	8.9	1.4	0.8	0.0	0.9
No	Percent	58.2	60.5	**	30.0	74.5	64.4	84.4	21.0
Yes	Percent	41.3	34.4	**	61.0	24.1	34.8	15.6	78.0
Q3B: Prof Assn Member?									
**Missing Data	Percent	0.9	6.7	100.0	100.0	2.4	0.8	0.3	1.1
No	Percent	76.0	85.1	**	**	91.9	85.1	74.4	65.7
Yes	Percent	23.1	8.2	**	**	5.8	14.1	25.3	33.2
Q3C: Employers Assn Member?									
**Missing Data	Percent	0.9	7.9	100.0	18.8	2.3	0.8	0.2	100.0
No	Percent	96.0	91.2	**	71.7	89.6	96.9	94.1	**
Yes	Percent	3.1	1.0	**	9.5	8.1	2.3	5.7	**
Q4: Hours Worked per Week	Number of Responses	447	0	1269	933	3131	982	998	537
	Mean	44.3	**	39.9	42.0	48.9	40.9	42.6	44.9
	STD	13.5	**	11.8	14.6	13.0	10.8	10.8	7.4
Q5: Travel Time To & From Work (minutes)	Number of Responses	428	0	0.0	896	0.0	967	0.0	539
	Mean	44.6	**	**	53.3	**	42.5	**	46.6
	STD	46.6	**	**	40.9	**	40.7	**	38.1
Q6A: Shift Worked									
**Missing Data	Percent	100.0	4.2	100.0	0.5	100.0	0.8	100.0	0.2
Day	Percent	**	76.3	**	87.6	**	78.1	**	62.9
Night	Percent	**	4.5	**	1.1	**	1.2	**	0.0
Swing Shift	Percent	**	11.2	**	6.6	**	12.1	**	1.7
Shift Changes	Percent	**	3.8	**	4.2	**	7.7	**	35.2
Q6B: Work Hours									
**Missing Data	Percent	100.0	3.1	100.0	0.1	100.0	0.8	100.0	0.0
Regular	Percent	**	73.8	**	82.1	**	79.6	**	95.6
Varied	Percent	**	23.1	**	17.8	**	19.6	**	4.4

MOW National Sample Responses — '**' Indicates Data Missing and/or Unavailable (continued)

		Country of Residence							
		Belgium	Britain	Germany	Israel	Japan	Netherlands	U.S.A.	Yugoslavia
Q6C: Worked Weekends Past Year?									
**Missing Data	Percent	100.0	6.9	100.0	0.0	100.0	0.0	100.0	0.4
No	Percent	**	64.5	**	36.3	**	80.6	**	61.8
Yes	Percent	**	28.6	**	62.9	**	18.6	**	37.8
Q7A: Unemployed Last 5 Years?									
**Missing Data	Percent	100.0	5.6	0.5	2.3	100.0	0.0	100.0	1.3
No	Percent	**	75.0	84.6	84.8	**	83.3	**	96.3
Yes	Percent	**	19.4	14.9	12.9	**	15.9	**	2.4
Q7B: If Unemp. NUM Mos 5 years	Number of Responses	0.0	158	0.0	98	0.0	151	0.0	11
	Mean	**	11.3	**	16.4	**	11.3	**	6.5
	STD	**	13.5	**	15.8	**	12.8	**	4.5
Q7C: If Unem. NUM Mos Past Year	Number of Responses	0.0	154	0.0	50	0.0	96	0.0	6
	Mean	**	7.6	**	5.4	**	5.2	**	1.8
	STD	**	3.5	**	3.6	**	4.0	**	1.9
Q8: Level of Variety in Job									
**Missing Data	Percent	100.0	1.9	0.9	1.1	1.6	1.8	0.1	0.4
Much Repetition	Percent	**	30.6	28.8	40.0	27.5	23.1	18.9	25.6
Some Variety	Percent	**	32.3	39.5	32.5	43.6	31.4	27.6	32.3
Wide Variety	Percent	**	35.2	30.8	26.4	27.2	43.7	53.4	41.7
Q9: Level of Autonomy in Job									
**Missing Data	Percent	100.0	100.0	0.6	0.3	100.0	1.3	0.0	0.0
No Decision Making	Percent	**	**	25.7	18.4	**	7.3	8.3	13.8
Some Decisions	Percent	**	**	48.8	43.7	**	47.8	52.5	51.5
My Own Decisions	Percent	**	**	24.8	37.6	**	43.6	39.2	34.7

MOW National Sample Responses — '**' Indicates Data Missing and/or Unavailable (continued)

		Country of Residence							
		Belgium	Britain	Germany	Israel	Japan	Netherlands	U.S.A.	Yugoslavia
Q10: Level of Responsibility in Job									
**Missing Data	Percent	100.0	2.9	1.0	1.7	100.0	1.9	0.2	0.0
Mistakes — Little Cons	Percent	**	30.4	29.4	35.1	**	27.4	15.7	20.3
Some Consequences	Percent	**	34.4	44.2	39.1	**	36.5	40.5	53.5
Serious Consequences	Percent	**	32.4	25.4	24.0	**	34.1	43.6	26.2
Q11: Level of New Learning in Job									
**Missing Data	Percent	100.0	2.1	100.0	0.6	1.5	1.5	0.1	0.4
No Learning	Percent	**	20.1	**	24.8	9.4	13.7	6.5	10.0
Some Learning	Percent	**	39.6	**	31.6	55.7	31.1	26.0	43.0
Learn Many Things	Percent	**	38.1	**	43.1	33.5	53.7	67.4	46.7
Q12: Interpersonal Contact in Job									
**Missing Data	Percent	100.0	100.0	100.0	0.6	100.0	1.3	100.0	0.4
Work Alone	Percent	**	**	**	15.8	**	24.0	**	20.1
Work with Some	Percent	**	**	**	31.1	**	20.9	**	41.0
Work Much with Others	Percent	**	**	**	52.4	**	53.8	**	38.6
Q13: Non — Job Conversation in Job									
**Missing Data	Percent	100.0	100.0	100.0	0.9	100.0	1.2	100.0	0.0
No Non-Business Talk	Percent	**	**	**	19.8	**	8.3	**	32.3
Some Non-Business Talk	Percent	**	**	**	43.9	**	32.7	**	45.0
Often Non-Business Talk	Percent	**	**	**	35.4	**	57.7	**	22.7

MOW National Sample Responses — '**' Indicates Data Missing and/or Unavailable (continued)

		Country of Residence							
		Belgium	Britain	Germany	Israel	Japan	Netherlands	U.S.A.	Yugoslavia
Q14: Work in Dangerous Circumstances									
**Missing Data	Percent	100.0	100.0	100.0	4.3	100.0	0.8	100.0	0.2
No	Percent	**	**	**	70.7	**	75.1	**	70.8
Yes	Percent	**	**	**	25.0	**	24.1	**	29.0
Q15: Work in Unhealthy Circumstances									
**Missing Data	Percent	100.0	100.0	100.0	4.4	100.0	0.8	100.0	0.0
No	Percent	**	**	**	71.1	**	74.4	**	53.5
Yes	Percent	**	**	**	24.5	**	24.8	**	46.5
Q16: Job require too much physically?									
**Missing Data	Percent	100.0	100.0	100.0	1.6	100.0	2.2	100.0	0.0
Never	Percent	**	**	**	38.6	**	49.1	**	26.6
Seldom	Percent	**	**	**	14.8	**	20.8	**	22.5
Sometimes	Percent	**	**	**	22.4	**	21.6	**	37.6
Often	Percent	**	**	**	22.5	**	6.3	**	13.3
Q17: Job require too much mentally?									
**Missing Data	Percent	100.0	100.0	100.0	1.6	·100.0	1.0	100.0	0.0
Never	Percent	**	**	**	21.1	**	42.2	**	12.4
Seldom	Percent	**	**	**	13.5	**	16.6	**	22.5
Sometimes	Percent	**	**	**	29.7	**	29.1	**	44.3
Often	Percent	**	**	**	34.1	**	11.1	**	20.8

MOW National Sample Responses — '**' Indicates Data Missing and/or Unavailable (continued)

		Country of Residence							
		Belgium	Britain	Germany	Israel	Japan	Netherlands	U.S.A.	Yugoslavia
Q18: Skills and Abilities Used?									
**Missing Data	Percent	100.0	5.2	100.0	1.2	100.0	1.4	0.0	0.0
Very Little	Percent	**	16.2	**	13.5	**	4.3	13.7	4.4
Little	Percent	**	17.1	**	11.4	**	11.7	13.0	11.8
A Lot	Percent	**	31.5	**	38.6	**	42.1	37.0	40.4
Almost All	Percent	**	29.9	**	35.3	**	40.5	36.3	43.4
Q19: How Does Supervisor Make Decisions?									
**Missing Data	Percent	100.0	2.7	10.2	11.6	100.0	13.5	100.0	8.1
No Inform—Decisions	Percent	**	19.6	13.9	9.0	**	4.7	**	5.4
Inform After Decisions	Percent	**	0.0	33.6	19.1	**	18.8	**	23.6
Asks for Advice	Percent	**	26.2	19.3	19.0	**	12.2	**	18.8
Decide Jointly	Percent	**	28.6	12.5	27.9	**	28.6	**	28.0
I Decide	Percent	**	22.9	10.4	13.4	**	22.2	**	16.1
Q20: Is your present job your first?									
**Missing Data	Percent	100.0	100.0	100.0	6.0	100.0	0.8	0.0	0.4
No	Percent	**	**	**	46.4	**	72.4	87.5	52.2
Yes	Percent	**	**	**	47.7	**	26.8	12.5	47.4

MOW National Sample Responses — '**' Indicates Data Missing and/or Unavailable (continued)

					Country of Residence				
		Belgium	Britain	Germany	Israel	Japan	Netherlands	U.S.A.	Yugoslavia
Q23A 1: Why Chose Your Present Job?									
**Missing Data	Percent	100.0	100.0	100.0	13.8	100.0	1.6	100.0	8.7
Good Pay	Percent	**	**	**	8.6	**	7.4	**	6.1
Good Conditions	Percent	**	**	**	4.5	**	1.6	**	3.0
Location	Percent	**	**	**	1.7	**	3.1	**	7.7
Hours	Percent	**	**	**	1.4	**	0.9	**	1.5
Interesting	Percent	**	**	**	26.6	**	21.6	**	27.9
Opportunity to Learn	Percent	**	**	**	0.9	**	2.0	**	0.6
Opportunity for Promotion	Percent	**	**	**	2.3	**	2.1	**	0.7
More Responsibility	Percent	**	**	**	0.1	**	0.6	**	0.4
Challenge	Percent	**	**	**	1.8	**	0.6	**	0.6
Trained for it	Percent	**	**	**	11.3	**	7.1	**	6.6
Job Security	Percent	**	**	**	0.7	**	6.0	**	0.2
Necessity	Percent	**	**	**	4.1	**	6.2	**	7.4
No Choice	Percent	**	**	**	13.9	**	9.0	**	20.1
Recommended	Percent	**	**	**	1.8	**	2.3	**	0.2
Parent Chose	Percent	**	**	**	2.9	**	1.0	**	1.8
Image of Firm	Percent	**	**	**	0.8	**	0.0	**	0.4
Independence	Percent	**	**	**	1.2	**	1.3	**	3.0
Military Draft	Percent	**	**	**	0.0	**	0.2	**	0.0
Health	Percent	**	**	**	0.9	**	1.4	**	0.4
Temporary to Fill Time	Percent	**	**	**	0.3	**	0.2	**	0.0
Temporary for Freedom	Percent	**	**	**	0.1	**	0.4	**	0.0
Other	Percent	**	**	**	0.0	**	23.2	**	3.0

MOW National Sample Responses — '**' Indicates Data Missing and/or Unavailable (continued)

		Country of Residence							
		Belgium	Britain	Germany	Israel	Japan	Netherlands	U.S.A.	Yugoslavia
Q23B: Years at Present Job	Number of Responses	450	0	0	836	3166	963	1000	524
	Mean	11.2	**	**	11.3	12.6	9.9	6.8	12.1
	STD	10.3	**	**	10.3	10.7	9.8	7.9	10.0
Q23C: Monthly Income (Note at Table End)	Number of Responses	430	0	1219	891	2380	988	965	516
Q24: Where Started Your Work Career?	Mean	29530	**	1735	3241	340	1824	1396	1299
**Missing Data	Percent	100.0	100.0	100.0	4.7	100.0	1.9	100.0	2.6
Lower	Percent	**	**	**	19.6	**	56.7	**	26.8
Same	Percent	**	**	**	61.7	**	26.5	**	68.1
Higher	Percent	**	**	**	14.0	**	14.9	**	2.6
Q25A: Has Your Career Had Ups and Downs?									
**Missing Data	Percent	100.0	100.0	100.0	4.7	100.0	0.8	100.0	2.6
No	Percent	**	**	**	62.6	**	56.1	**	64.8
Yes	Percent	**	**	**	32.7	**	43.1	**	32.7
Q25B: Size of Ups and Downs									
**Missing Data	Percent	100.0	100.0	100.0	68.3	100.0	56.9	100.0	65.5
Small	Percent	**	**	**	18.4	**	18.7	**	29.0
Large	Percent	**	**	**	13.3	**	24.4	**	5.5
Q26: My Work History Trend									
**Missing Data	Percent	100.0	100.0	100.0	9.9	100.0	1.7	100.0	2.6
Some Decline	Percent	**	**	**	6.0	**	7.5	**	1.8
Same Level	Percent	**	**	**	17.2	**	16.2	**	21.4
Some improve	Percent	**	**	**	30.0	**	23.2	**	60.1
Much Improve	Percent	**	**	**	37.0	**	51.4	**	14.0

MOW National Sample Responses — '**' Indicates Data Missing and/or Unavailable (continued)

		Country of Residence							
		Belgium	Britain	Germany	Israel	Japan	Netherlands	U.S.A.	Yugoslavia
Q27: Satisfaction with Work History									
**Missing Data	Percent	100.0	100.0	100.0	5.4	100.0	1.3	100.0	2.8
Dissatisfied	Percent	**	**	**	4.6	**	4.5	**	3.5
Some Dissatisfaction	Percent	**	**	**	7.3	**	7.8	**	12.9
Neutral	Percent	**	**	**	11.5	**	7.8	**	9.2
Some Satisfaction	Percent	**	**	**	45.2	**	33.2	**	55.2
Very Satisfactory	Percent	**	**	**	25.9	**	45.3	**	16.4
Q28A1: Points—Status &	Number of Responses	447	471	1278	940	3180	979	989	522
Prestige	Mean	6.9	10.9	15.7	8.5	5.6	4.9	11.9	9.3
	STD	8.1	8.5	23.2	11.1	8.1	7.0	9.5	11.2
Q28A2: Points—Income	Number of Responses	447	471	1278	940	3180	979	989	522
	Mean	35.5	34.4	41.7	31.1	45.4	26.2	33.1	34.1
	STD	22.2	17.9	21.0	23.5	23.3	18.7	18.7	20.9
Q28A3: Points—Keeps	Number of Responses	447	471	1278	940	3180	979	989	522
Occupied	Mean	8.7	11.0	16.1	9.4	11.5	10.6	11.3	11.7
	STD	9.7	7.6	20.8	12.0	11.1	10.8	9.6	11.8
Q28A4: Points—Interesting	Number of Responses	447	471	1278	940	3180	979	989	522
Contacts	Mean	17.3	15.3	16.8	11.1	14.7	17.9	15.3	9.8
	STD	13.2	8.6	19.6	11.6	12.5	12.8	9.3	9.3
Q28A5: Points—Way to Serve	Number of Responses	447	471	1278	940	3180	979	989	522
Society	Mean	10.2	10.5	13.9	13.6	9.3	16.7	11.5	15.1
	STD	10.2	7.9	24.0	15.4	10.2	13.1	9.4	13.3
Q28A6: Points—Interesting	Number of Responses	447	471	1278	940	3180	979	989	522
& Satisfying	Mean	21.3	18.0	19.5	26.2	13.4	23.5	16.8	19.8
	STD	15.4	11.7	19.1	20.0	13.4	15.1	12.2	18.1

MOW National Sample Responses — '**' Indicates Data Missing and/or Unavailable (continued)

		Country of Residence							
		Belgium	Britain	Germany	Israel	Japan	Netherlands	U.S.A.	Yugoslavia
Q29: Importance of Work to Your Life									
**Missing Data									
1: One of the Least....	Percent	0.0	6.5	0.2	5.7	0.8	1.0	0.0	2.6
2: (on 1–to–7 scale)	Percent	0.4	1.9	2.0	1.0	0.4	0.9	0.9	0.6
3: (on 1–to–7 scale)	Percent	1.3	2.7	4.0	0.9	0.3	1.6	0.9	2.0
4: Cf Medium Importance	Percent	6.7	5.0	8.3	1.2	1.4	5.8	2.5	1.3
5: (on 1–to–7 scale)	Percent	26.0	25.7	21.4	21.8	22.4	28.4	14.5	20.5
6: (on 1–to–7 scale)	Percent	26.7	23.3	25.8	17.4	14.0	23.1	27.3	16.6
7: One of the Most....	Percent	24.9	19.0	24.3	22.8	16.3	24.6	23.7	25.5
	Percent	14.0	15.7	14.0	29.2	44.4	14.6	30.2	31.0
Q30A: Points—Import of Leisure	Number of Responses	446	423	1278	944	3165	985	996	521
	Mean	24.6	22.3	22.7	18.2	19.7	24.2	18.1	19.5
	STD	16.3	12.8	15.9	15.6	15.8	15.9	12.2	16.4
Q30B: Points—Community Import	Number of Responses	446	423	1278	944	3165	985	996	521
	Mean	6.0	7.8	7.3	4.5	5.3	7.5	9.9	7.5
	STD	8.2	6.0	8.9	8.9	8.0	9.8	6.9	8.9
Q30C: Points—Work	Number of Responses	446	423	1278	944	3165	985	996	521
	Mean	29.9	21.5	28.0	28.3	36.1	29.6	24.5	36.7
	STD	16.6	10.0	16.4	18.6	20.1	16.6	13.3	18.6
Q30D: Points—Religion	Number of Responses	446	423	1278	944	3165	985	996	521
	Mean	4.9	8.6	5.2	4.9	3.7	4.9	14.0	1.1
	STD	6.8	8.6	7.0	11.6	8.3	8.7	12.0	3.3
Q30E: Points—Family	Number of Responses	446	423	1278	944	3165	985	996	521
	Mean	34.7	40.1	35.7	43.9	35.1	33.7	33.6	35.3
	STD	17.7	14.9	18.6	20.5	19.8	18.6	15.6	18.9
Q31A: Tasks Rank	Number of Responses	440	0.0	1278	820	0.0	972	998	517
	Mean	3.5	**	3.9	3.9	**	3.9	3.2	4.2
	STD	1.5	**	1.5	1.7	**	1.4	1.6	1.6

MOW National Sample Responses — '**' Indicates Data Missing and/or Unavailable (continued)

		Country of Residence							
		Belgium	Britain	Germany	Israel	Japan	Netherlands	U.S.A.	Yugoslavia
Q31B: Company Rank	Number of Responses	440	0.0	1278	820	0.0	972	998	517
	Mean	2.5	**	2.5	2.7	**	2.3	2.9	2.5
	STD	1.6	**	1.6	1.6	**	1.5	1.6	1.6
Q31C: Product or Service Rank	Number of Responses	440	0.0	1278	820	0.0	972	998	517
	Mean	3.5	**	2.8	3.7	**	3.2	3.8	4.2
	STD	1.7	**	1.6	1.7	**	1.7	1.6	1.6
Q31D: Type of People Rank	Number of Responses	440	0.0	1278	820	0.0	972	998	517
	Mean	3.8	**	3.7	3.4	**	3.9	3.8	2.9
	STD	1.5	**	1.6	1.5	**	1.5	1.5	1.5
Q31E: Type of Occupation Rank	Number of Responses	440	0.0	1278	820	0.0	972	998	517
	Mean	3.8	**	3.8	3.6	**	3.9	3.4	3.4
	STD	1.6	**	1.7	1.7	**	1.7	1.7	1.6
Q31F: Money Rank	Number of Responses	448	0.0	1278	885	0.0	987	1000	517
	Mean	3.9	**	4.3	3.8	**	3.9	3.9	3.7
	STD	1.8	**	1.7	1.7	**	1.8	1.9	1.8
Q32A: Learn New Things Rank	Number of Responses	448	742	1258	930	2959	987	996	512
	Mean	5.8	5.5	5.0	6.0	6.3	5.4	6.2	6.6
	STD	3.0	2.9	2.9	3.0	2.8	3.0	3.1	3.1
Q32B: Interpers Relations Rank	Number of Responses	447	742	1269	937	2951	983	999	512
	Mean	6.3	6.3	6.4	6.8	6.4	7.2	6.1	7.5
	STD	2.9	2.8	2.9	2.6	2.8	2.7	2.9	3.1
Q32C: Promotion Opportunity Rank	Number of Responses	448	742	1263	906	2909	982	996	512
	Mean	4.5	4.3	4.5	5.4	3.3	3.3	5.1	4.0
	STD	3.1	3.0	3.0	3.0	2.7	2.6	3.1	2.9
Q32D: Convenient Hours Rank	Number of Responses	448	742	1270	924	2969	982	995	512
	Mean	4.7	6.1	5.7	5.7	5.6	5.6	5.3	5.0
	STD	3.2	3.2	3.0	3.0	3.3	3.1	3.2	2.9

MOW National Sample Responses — '**' Indicates Data Missing and/or Unavailable (continued)

		Country of Residence							
		Belgium	Britain	Germany	Israel	Japan	Netherlands	U.S.A.	Yugoslavia
Q32E: Variety Rank	Number of Responses	449	742	1267	913	2924	988	999	512
	Mean	6.0	5.6	5.7	5.1	5.1	6.9	6.1	5.6
	STD	2.8	2.7	2.8	2.7	2.6	2.7	2.7	2.7
Q32F: Interesting Work Rank	Number of Responses	447	742	1267	916	2971	988	998	512
	Mean	8.3	8.0	7.3	6.9	7.4	7.6	7.4	7.5
	STD	2.8	2.8	2.8	2.6	2.8	2.8	2.7	2.9
Q32G: Job Security Rank	Number of Responses	448	742	1269	906	2977	984	997	512
	Mean	6.8	7.1	7.6	5.4	6.8	5.7	6.3	5.2
	STD	3.0	3.1	3.1	2.8	3.0	3.2	3.2	3.1
Q32H: Good Match Rank	Number of Responses	448	742	1268	905	2992	990	998	512
	Mean	5.8	5.6	6.1	5.7	7.9	6.2	6.2	6.5
	STD	2.7	2.9	2.9	2.7	2.7	2.9	3.0	2.8
Q32I: Pay Rank	Number of Responses	447	742	1270	920	2961	981	998	512
	Mean	7.1	7.8	7.8	6.7	6.6	6.3	6.0	6.7
	STD	3.0	2.8	2.9	2.9	3.1	3.2	3.3	3.0
Q32J: Working Conditions Rank	Number of Responses	448	742	1265	919	2915	985	995	512
	Mean	4.2	4.9	4.4	5.4	4.2	5.1	4.8	5.9
	STD	2.7	2.9	2.8	2.8	2.6	3.0	3.1	3.0
Q32K: Autonomy Rank	Number of Responses	448	742	1263	920	2984	992	996	512
	Mean	6.6	4.7	5.7	6.1	7.0	7.6	5.8	5.4
	STD	3.2	3.2	3.2	2.9	3.2	2.9	3.5	3.3
Q33: Job Choice Number 1									
** Missing Data	Percent	0.0	100.0	100.0	1.7	0.2	0.0	0.0	0.2
Either Job	Percent	4.2	**	**	4.1	11.0	2.1	0.2	5.0
Prefer Job A	Percent	93.3	**	**	89.1	85.5	95.3	97.3	89.3
Prefer Job B	Percent	2.4	**	**	5.0	3.3	2.6	2.5	5.5

MOW National Sample Responses — '**' Indicates Data Missing and/or Unavailable (continued)

		Country of Residence							
		Belgium	Britain	Germany	Israel	Japan	Netherlands	U.S.A.	Yugoslavia
Q34: Job Choice Number 2									
**Missing Data	Percent	0.0	100.0	100.0	2.1	0.2	0.0	0.1	0.2
Either Job	Percent	3.3	**	**	3.4	12.2	1.5	0.1	5.4
Prefer Job A	Percent	84.2	**	**	81.1	75.6	90.2	88.0	81.5
Prefer Job B	Percent	12.4	**	**	13.5	12.1	8.3	11.8	12.9
Q35: Job Choice Number 3									
**Missing Data	Percent	0.0	100.0	100.0	2.4	0.3	0.0	0.1	0.4
Either Job	Percent	3.3	**	**	2.8	13.6	2.8	0.1	4.4
Prefer Job A	Percent	57.6	**	**	65.4	55.3	69.2	61.7	62.9
Prefer Job B	Percent	39.1	**	**	29.5	30.8	28.0	38.1	32.3
Q36: Job Choice Number 4									
**Missing Data	Percent	0.0	100.0	100.0	2.9	0.4	0.0	0.1	0.4
Either Job	Percent	2.4	**	**	2.8	10.6	2.7	0.1	5.0
Prefer Job A	Percent	38.2	**	**	49.9	39.5	48.9	41.7	40.6
Prefer Job B	Percent	59.3	**	**	44.4	49.5	48.4	58.1	54.1
Q37: Job Choice Number 5									
**Missing Data	Percent	0.0	100.0	100.0	1.8	0.2	0.0	0.0	0.2
Either Job	Percent	0.4	**	**	2.8	6.2	1.0	0.0	0.9
Prefer Job A	Percent	98.0	**	**	91.5	91.1	96.8	99.2	98.0
Prefer Job B	Percent	1.6	**	**	3.9	2.4	2.2	0.8	0.9
Q38: Job Choice Number 6									
**Missing Data	Percent	0.0	100.0	100.0	1.7	0.3	0.0	0.0	0.2
Either Job	Percent	0.9	**	**	2.6	8.1	1.7	0.0	1.1
Prefer Job A	Percent	94.2	**	**	84.7	85.1	93.4	96.2	95.8
Prefer Job B	Percent	4.9	**	**	11.0	6.5	4.9	3.8	3.0

MOW National Sample Responses — '**' Indicates Data Missing and/or Unavailable (continued)

		Country of Residence							
		Belgium	Britain	Germany	Israel	Japan	Netherlands	U.S.A.	Yugoslavia
Q39: Job Choice Number 7									
**Missing Data	Percent	0.0	100.0	100.0	1.7	0.3	0.0	0.0	0.2
Either Job	Percent	1.3	**	**	3.0	11.7	1.4	0.1	3.5
Prefer Job A	Percent	80.2	**	**	72.8	69.1	80.1	85.0	80.8
Prefer Job B	Percent	18.4	**	**	22.5	18.8	18.5	14.9	15.5
Q40: Job Choice Number 8									
**Missing Data	Percent	0.0	100.0	100.0	2.7	0.5	0.0	0.0	0.2
Either Job	Percent	2.4	**	**	2.9	10.3	2.7	0.0	5.0
Prefer Job A	Percent	60.2	**	**	58.5	52.1	61.4	68.7	58.1
Prefer Job B	Percent	37.3	**	**	36.0	37.0	35.8	31.3	36.7
Q41: Job Choice Number 9									
**Missing Data	Percent	100.0	100.0	100.0	5.8	100.0	0.0	100.0	0.2
Either Job	Percent	**	**	**	8.7	**	7.8	**	8.9
Prefer Job A	Percent	**	**	**	58.5	**	69.5	**	64.2
Prefer Job B	Percent	**	**	**	27.0	**	22.7	**	26.8
Q42: Job Choice Number 10									
**Missing Data	Percent	100.0	100.0	100.0	6.4	100.0	0.0	100.0	0.4
Either Job	Percent	**	**	**	6.1	**	9.0	**	6.8
Prefer Job A	Percent	**	**	**	40.5	**	46.1	**	38.2
Prefer Job B	Percent	**	**	**	47.1	**	44.9	**	54.6
Q43: Job Choice Number 11									
**Missing Data	Percent	100.0	100.0	100.0	2.3	100.0	0.0	100.0	0.2
Either Job	Percent	**	**	**	4.0	**	2.7	**	2.6
Prefer Job A	Percent	**	**	**	18.6	**	13.5	**	11.1
Prefer Job B	Percent	**	**	**	75.1	**	83.8	**	86.2

MOW National Sample Responses — '**' Indicates Data Missing and/or Unavailable (continued)

		Country of Residence							
		Belgium	Britain	Germany	Israel	Japan	Netherlands	U.S.A.	Yugoslavia
Q44: Job Choice Number 12									
**Missing Data	Percent	100.0	100.0	100.0	2.3	100.0	0.0	100.0	0.2
Either Job	Percent	**	**	**	2.7	**	1.2	**	2.0
Prefer Job A	Percent	**	**	**	11.7	**	8.6	**	7.7
Prefer Job B	Percent	**	**	**	83.4	**	90.2	**	90.0
Q45: Job Choice Number 13									
**Missing Data	Percent	100.0	100.0	100.0	2.1	100.0	0.0	100.0	0.2
Either Job	Percent	**	**	**	2.0	**	1.2	**	1.1
Prefer Job A	Percent	**	**	**	9.4	**	5.7	**	5.0
Prefer Job B	Percent	**	**	**	86.6	**	93.1	**	93.7
Q46: Job Choice Number 14									
**Missing Data	Percent	100.0	100.0	100.0	1.8	100.0	0.0	100.0	0.2
Either Job	Percent	**	**	**	3.7	**	2.4	**	1.8
Prefer Job A	Percent	**	**	**	13.4	**	8.5	**	7.9
Prefer Job B	Percent	**	**	**	81.1	**	89.1	**	90.0
Q47A: Employer Responsible for Retraining									
**Missing Data	Percent	0.2	2.6	0.2	0.3	1.5	1.2	0.1	0.2
Strongly Disagree	Percent	3.3	1.2	5.4	1.4	0.6	4.3	1.5	2.6
Disagree	Percent	18.4	10.6	15.7	5.9	5.0	7.8	17.8	7.4
Agree	Percent	55.8	53.3	42.3	44.8	61.5	51.6	58.4	45.4
Strongly Agree	Percent	22.2	32.3	36.4	47.6	31.4	35.0	22.2	44.5

MOW National Sample Responses — '**' Indicates Data Missing and/or Unavailable (continued)

		Country of Residence							
		Belgium	Britain	Germany	Israel	Japan	Netherlands	U.S.A.	Yugoslavia
Q47B: Duty of Every Able Citizen to Work									
**Missing Data	Percent	0.0	2.9	0.1	0.4	1.7	0.9	0.1	0.2
Strongly Disagree	Percent	4.4	1.7	2.4	1.4	1.3	4.1	2.1	0.2
Disagree	Percent	16.9	14.4	10.9	9.5	10.1	11.2	13.5	1.7
Agree	Percent	45.8	48.9	34.7	41.5	60.5	31.0	40.5	26.0
Strongly Agree	Percent	32.9	32.1	51.9	47.2	26.3	52.7	43.8	72.0
Q47C: Society Obliged to Educate for Job									
**Missing Data	Percent	0.0	2.9	0.2	0.9	2.1	1.3	0.0	0.4
Strongly Disagree	Percent	0.4	0.5	1.0	0.6	1.1	2.6	1.2	0.6
Disagree	Percent	7.8	3.9	5.9	4.8	10.0	7.7	6.4	1.8
Agree	Percent	51.3	58.9	35.9	49.8	59.3	44.8	57.7	30.1
Strongly Agree	Percent	40.4	33.8	57.0	43.8	27.5	43.6	34.7	67.2
Q47D: Persons Should Save for Future									
**Missing Data	Percent	0.0	3.1	0.1	1.1	1.8	1.3	0.3	0.4
Strongly Disagree	Percent	5.8	3.0	9.9	1.3	1.6	11.5	1.1	9.0
Disagree	Percent	32.0	45.6	30.5	10.9	21.7	49.8	21.9	34.1
Agree	Percent	43.8	41.2	39.0	46.5	62.0	29.5	58.6	42.1
Strongly Agree	Percent	18.4	7.1	20.5	40.2	12.9	7.8	18.1	14.4
Q47E: Super Should Consult Workers re Changes									
**Missing Data	Percent	0.2	2.4	0.3	0.6	1.3	1.1	0.1	0.2
Strongly Disagree	Percent	1.1	0.6	3.2	3.5	0.9	1.9	1.4	2.2
Disagree	Percent	6.4	9.0	14.9	10.5	8.4	4.1	18.9	3.7
Agree	Percent	47.6	61.9	41.7	49.6	62.5	36.2	54.3	37.1
Strongly Agree	Percent	44.7	26.1	39.8	35.8	26.9	56.6	25.3	56.8

MOW National Sample Responses — '**' Indicates Data Missing and/or Unavailable (continued)

		Country of Residence							
		Belgium	Britain	Germany	Israel	Japan	Netherlands	U.S.A.	Yugoslavia
Q47F: Worker Should Improve Work Methods									
**Missing Data	Percent	0.0	2.9	0.2	1.0	2.0	1.3	0.2	0.2
Strongly Disagree	Percent	0.9	1.7	2.5	0.4	0.4	0.9	0.9	4.6
Disagree	Percent	14.4	17.9	13.7	3.6	2.1	5.2	9.8	14.8
Agree	Percent	54.9	63.7	45.3	44.6	55.7	48.9	66.3	57.6
Strongly Agree	Percent	29.8	13.9	38.3	50.4	39.9	43.7	22.8	22.9
Q47G: All Entitled to Meaningful Work									
**Missing Data	Percent	0.0	3.3	0.1	1.2	1.9	1.2	0.2	0.6
Strongly Disagree	Percent	0.2	0.6	1.4	1.5	0.9	1.6	1.8	0.2
Disagree	Percent	6.9	15.2	4.9	9.1	12.0	7.5	21.5	4.6
Agree	Percent	49.6	59.8	31.6	45.1	62.5	40.0	61.4	47.2
Strongly Agree	Percent	43.3	21.1	62.1	43.0	22.8	49.7	15.1	47.4
Q47H: Monot Work OK if Pay Compensates									
**Missing Data	Percent	0.0	3.6	0.1	1.0	3.2	1.2	0.3	0.2
Strongly Disagree	Percent	5.1	2.9	12.2	17.0	3.3	6.6	4.8	2.6
Disagree	Percent	22.2	17.4	25.9	39.5	35.3	23.7	34.2	17.2
Agree	Percent	60.9	64.8	34.0	34.1	48.6	46.1	55.6	53.1
Strongly Agree	Percent	11.8	11.4	27.8	8.4	9.7	22.4	5.1	26.9

MOW National Sample Responses — '**' Indicates Data Missing and/or Unavailable (continued)

		Country of Residence							
		Belgium	Britain	Germany	Israel	Japan	Netherlands	U.S.A.	Yugoslavia
Q47I: Job Should Be Provided Everyone									
**Missing Data	Percent	0.0	2.7	0.0	0.9	1.9	1.0	0.0	0.4
Strongly Disagree	Percent	0.7	1.0	0.7	0.7	0.7	0.8	1.7	0.6
Disagree	Percent	0.4	7.1	1.8	6.2	5.1	1.9	17.5	1.3
Agree	Percent	34.7	52.7	18.9	37.9	57.6	32.1	60.1	25.3
Strongly Agree	Percent	64.2	36.4	78.6	54.3	34.8	64.2	20.7	72.5
Q47J: Worker Should Value Any Work Done									
**Missing Data	Percent	0.0	2.6	0.2	1.6	1.7	1.1	0.1	0.6
Strongly Disagree	Percent	21.1	4.9	15.9	10.7	9.3	19.7	4.5	5.0
Disagree	Percent	30.2	22.5	28.6	27.1	34.7	35.3	25.1	19.0
Agree	Percent	30.2	53.2	33.6	39.5	43.2	25.4	53.4	41.1
Strongly Agree	Percent	18.4	16.8	21.7	21.1	11.2	18.5	16.9	34.3
Q48A: If You Had Money Would You Work									
**Missing Data	Percent	0.0	20.7	0.4	3.1	0.9	0.0	0.3	0.2
Stop	Percent	15.8	24.6	29.8	12.1	6.5	13.7	11.9	3.7
Continue Same Job	Percent	36.9	12.9	30.8	48.7	65.6	42.4	39.0	62.0
Continue—Different Conditions	Percent	47.3	41.8	39.0	36.1	27.0	44.0	48.8	34.1
Q49A–N: Is An Activity Work . . .	Number of Responses	450	840	1278	973	3226	996	1000	542
Q49A: . . . If in a Working Place?									
**Missing Data	Percent	0.0	4.0	0.0	0.1	0.0	0.0	0.2	0.2
No, Is Not Work	Percent	87.8	39.3	62.5	70.8	77.9	91.0	76.6	61.1
Yes, Is Work	Percent	12.2	56.7	37.5	29.1	22.1	9.0	23.2	38.7

MOW National Sample Responses — '**' Indicates Data Missing and/or Unavailable (continued)

		Country of Residence							
		Belgium	Britain	Germany	Israel	Japan	Netherlands	U.S.A.	Yugoslavia
Q49B: If Told To Do It?									
**Missing Data	Percent	0.0	4.0	0.0	0.1	0.0	0.0	0.2	0.2
No, Is Not Work	Percent	86.7	75.6	80.8	86.1	93.1	94.0	83.4	93.4
Yes, Is Work	Percent	13.3	20.4	19.2	13.8	6.9	6.0	16.4	6.5
Q49C: . . . If Phys Strenuous?									
**Missing Data	Percent	0.0	4.0	0.0	0.1	0.0	0.0	0.2	0.2
No, Is Not Work	Percent	78.9	71.7	73.3	79.7	83.6	83.0	80.0	91.3
Yes, Is Work	Percent	21.1	24.3	26.7	20.2	16.3	17.0	19.8	8.5
Q49D: . . . If Part of Task?									
**Missing Data	Percent	0.0	4.0	0.0	0.0	0.0	0.0	0.2	0.2
No, Is Not Work	Percent	34.2	53.6	63.3	49.6	38.7	51.6	51.6	48.9
Yes, Is Work	Percent	65.8	42.4	36.7	50.4	61.3	48.4	48.2	50.9
Q49E: . . . If Contributes to Society?									
**Missing Data	Percent	0.0	4.0	0.0	0.0	0.0	0.0	0.2	0.2
No, Is Not Work	Percent	67.1	78.8	84.4	59.6	78.1	45.4	63.0	48.7
Yes, Is Work	Percent	32.9	17.1	15.6	40.4	21.9	54.6	36.0	51.1
Q49F: . . . If Feeling Of Belonging?									
**Missing Data	Percent	0.0	4.0	0.0	0.0	0.0	0.0	0.2	0.4
No, Is Not Work	Percent	56.2	70.7	66.3	76.1	94.3	58.8	69.3	79.5
Yes, Is Work	Percent	43.8	25.2	33.7	23.9	5.7	41.2	30.5	20.1
Q49G: . . . If Ment Strenuous?									
**Missing Data	Percent	0.0	4.0	0.0	0.0	0.0	0.0	0.2	0.4
No, Is Not Work	Percent	82.0	68.9	79.8	74.8	83.5	75.5	71.7	88.4
Yes, Is Work	Percent	18.0	27.0	20.2	25.2	16.5	24.5	28.1	11.3

MOW National Sample Responses — '**' Indicates Data Missing and/or Unavailable (continued)

		Country of Residence							
		Belgium	Britain	Germany	Israel	Japan	Netherlands	U.S.A.	Yugoslavia
Q49H: . . . If At Certain Time?									
**Missing Data	Percent	0.0	4.0	0.0	0.0	0.0	0.0	0.2	0.4
No, Is Not Work	Percent	78.7	56.1	75.0	84.0	75.0	80.4	75.3	88.7
Yes, Is Work	Percent	21.3	39.9	25.0	16.0	25.0	19.6	24.5	10.9
Q49I: . . . If It Adds Value?									
**Missing Data	Percent	0.0	100.0	0.0	0.0	0.0	0.0	0.2	0.2
No, Is Not Work	Percent	54.0	**	76.2	77.8	47.5	46.4	51.2	44.8
Yes, Is Work	Percent	46.0	**	23.8	22.2	52.5	53.6	48.6	55.0
Q49J: . . . If Not Pleasant?									
**Missing Data	Percent	0.0	4.0	0.0	0.0	0.0	0.0	0.2	0.2
No, Is Not Work	Percent	94.2	88.2	95.6	98.6	94.3	98.4	91.9	98.5
Yes, Is Work	Percent	5.8	7.7	4.4	1.4	5.7	1.6	7.9	1.3
Q49K: . . . If You Get Money?									
**Missing Data	Percent	0.0	4.0	0.0	0.0	0.0	0.0	0.2	0.2
No, Is Not Work	Percent	42.2	35.5	34.6	31.8	29.0	38.2	46.0	55.4
Yes, Is Work	Percent	57.8	60.5	65.4	68.2	71.0	61.8	53.8	44.5
Q49L: . . . If You Must Account?									
**Missing Data	Percent	0.0	4.0	0.0	0.0	0.0	0.0	0.2	0.2
No, Is Not Work	Percent	74.7	75.0	61.6	87.6	52.1	62.8	75.5	44.5
Yes, Is Work	Percent	25.3	21.0	38.4	12.4	47.9	37.2	24.3	55.4
Q49M: . . . If You Must Do It?									
**Missing Data	Percent	0.0	4.0	0.0	0.0	0.0	0.0	0.2	0.2
No, Is Not Work	Percent	80.4	64.4	81.8	83.8	77.0	92.5	85.8	93.5
Yes, Is Work	Percent	19.6	31.5	18.2	16.2	23.0	7.5	14.0	6.3

MOW National Sample Responses — '**' Indicates Data Missing and/or Unavailable (continued)

		Country of Residence							
		Belgium	Britain	Germany	Israel	Japan	Netherlands	U.S.A.	Yugoslavia
Q49N: . . . If Others Profit?									
**Missing Data	Percent	0.0	4.0	0.0	0.0	0.0	0.0	0.2	0.4
No, Is Not Work	Percent	86.0	76.7	87.0	66.4	90.7	86.3	75.3	60.3
Yes, Is Work	Percent	14.0	19.3	13.0	33.6	9.3	13.7	24.5	39.3
Q50A: Would Choose Occupation Again?									
**Missing Data	Percent	100.0	3.9	3.2	3.1	100.0	1.3	0.0	0.6
Different Occupation	Percent	**	52.9	35.1	37.5	**	39.4	45.8	42.4
Same Occupation	Percent	**	43.2	61.7	59.4	**	59.3	54.2	57.0
Q50B: Would Recommend Occupation to Your Child?									
**Missing Data	Percent	100.0	4.4	100.0	5.4	100.0	1.8	0.2	0.9
No	Percent	**	58.6	**	31.0	**	39.7	40.5	72.5
Yes	Percent	**	37.0	**	63.5	**	59.0	59.3	26.6
Q51A: Will Your Work Attitude Change?									
**Missing Data	Percent	100.0	100.0	100.0	8.1	100.0	0.0	100.0	1.3
No	Percent	**	**	**	44.8	**	18.9	**	43.7
Yes	Percent	**	**	**	47.1	**	81.1	**	55.0
Q52: Preference—Job vs Organization									
**Missing Data	Percent	100.0	100.0	100.0	25.5	100.0	22.1	0.5	33.9
Stay With Different Job	Percent	**	**	**	45.9	**	34.8	55.7	42.4
Same Job Different Organ	Percent	**	**	**	28.6	**	43.1	43.8	23.6

MOW National Sample Responses — '**' Indicates Data Missing and/or Unavailable (continued)

		Country of Residence							
		Belgium	Britain	Germany	Israel	Japan	Netherlands	U.S.A.	Yugoslavia
Q53: Leisure-activity Unrelated to Work									
**Missing Data	Percent	100.0	100.0	100.0	1.1	100.0	0.3	100.0	0.2
Never	Percent	**	**	**	10.0	**	7.3	**	10.0
Only Occasionally	Percent	**	**	**	10.1	**	20.1	**	24.4
Sometimes	Percent	**	**	**	26.0	**	22.2	**	34.7
Often	Percent	**	**	**	23.4	**	15.8	**	18.8
Very Often	Percent	**	**	**	29.4	**	34.3	**	12.0
Q54: Partic in Co Activities Cuts of Work?									
**Missing Data	Percent	100.0	100.0	100.0	9.4	100.0	0.7	100.0	3.3
No	Percent	**	**	**	17.5	**	21.7	**	6.3
Maybe	Percent	**	**	**	26.9	**	11.4	**	49.1
Yes	Percent	**	**	**	46.2	**	66.2	**	41.3
Q55: Worry About Work in Free Time?									
**Missing Data	Percent	100.0	100.0	100.0	0.8	100.0	0.1	100.0	0.2
Never	Percent	**	**	**	17.2	**	28.1	**	4.4
Only Occasionally	Percent	**	**	**	14.2	**	20.2	**	11.6
Sometimes	Percent	**	**	**	30.3	**	30.2	**	38.6
Often	Percent	**	**	**	21.2	**	16.4	**	33.0
Very Often	Percent	**	**	**	16.3	**	5.0	**	12.2
Q56A: Change—Or Start—Job in Next Year?									
**Missing Data	Percent	100.0	100.0	100.0	4.4	100.0	0.0	100.0	1.1
No	Percent	**	**	**	81.9	**	85.0	**	90.2
Yes	Percent	**	**	**	13.7	**	15.0	**	8.7

MOW National Sample Responses — '**' Indicates Data Missing and/or Unavailable (continued)

		Country of Residence							
		Belgium	Britain	Germany	Israel	Japan	Netherlands	U.S.A.	Yugoslavia
Q57: Easy to Find Job?									
**Missing Data	Percent	100.0	100.0	100.0	19.3	100.0	9.4	100.0	17.2
Difficult	Percent	**	**	**	24.0	**	35.4	**	22.3
Not So Easy	Percent	**	**	**	19.6	**	27.3	**	29.2
Somewhat Easy	Percent	**	**	**	9.8	**	8.4	**	11.4
Easy	Percent	**	**	**	17.7	**	13.3	**	14.9
Very Easy	Percent	**	**	**	9.6	**	6.1	**	5.0
Q58A: Willing To Retrain?									
**Missing Data	Percent	100.0	100.0	100.0	3.5	100.0	0.0	100.0	0.6
Under No Conditions	Percent	**	**	**	44.0	**	24.0	**	16.8
Only if Necessary	Percent	**	**	**	22.3	**	43.7	**	43.2
Under Certain Conditions	Percent	**	**	**	30.2	**	32.3	**	39.5
Q59: Intend To Retrain—Different Job—This Year?									
**Missing Data	Percent	100.0	100.0	100.0	2.3	100.0	0.0	0.4	0.0
No	Percent	**	**	**	86.6	**	90.6	75.4	94.5
Yes	Percent	**	**	**	11.1	**	9.4	24.2	5.5
Q60: Intend To Retrain—This Job—This Year?									
**Missing Data	Percent	100.0	100.0	100.0	1.8	100.0	0.0	0.3	0.6
No	Percent	**	**	**	58.3	**	73.3	42.7	62.4
Yes	Percent	**	**	**	33.8	**	17.5	49.3	19.6
Already Training	Percent	**	**	**	6.1	**	9.2	7.7	17.5
Q61: Try to Be Promoted This Year?									
**Missing Data	Percent	100.0	100.0	100.0	4.0	100.0	9.7	0.2	17.2
No	Percent	**	**	**	46.8	**	70.8	63.7	55.2
Yes	Percent	**	**	**	49.2	**	19.5	36.1	27.7

MOW National Sample Responses — '**' Indicates Data Missing and/or Unavailable (continued)

		Country of Residence							
		Belgium	Britain	Germany	Israel	Japan	Netherlands	U.S.A.	Yugoslavia
Q62A: Significant Plans re Work—5 Years?									
**Missing Data	Percent	100.0	100.0	100.0	3.0	100.0	0.0	100.0	0.2
No	Percent	**	**	**	64.9	**	75.3	**	69.9
Yes	Percent	**	**	**	32.2	**	24.7	**	29.9
Q63: Worse Employment Situation?									
**Missing Data	Percent	100.0	100.0	100.0	5.0	100.0	0.0	100.0	0.6
No	Percent	**	**	**	73.5	**	57.0	**	76.9
Yes	Percent	**	**	**	21.5	**	43.0	**	22.5
Q64: Improved Employment Situation?									
**Missing Data	Percent	100.0	100.0	100.0	6.7	100.0	0.0	100.0	1.1
No	Percent	**	**	**	55.4	**	76.0	**	63.3
Yes	Percent	**	**	**	37.9	**	24.0	**	35.6
Q65: Level of Pay Expectations									
**Missing Data	Percent	100.0	100.0	100.0	2.2	100.0	0.8	100.0	0.4
Go Down	Percent	**	**	**	5.9	**	18.8	**	20.1
Stay Same	Percent	**	**	**	46.8	**	64.8	**	71.2
Go Up	Percent	**	**	**	45.2	**	15.7	**	8.3

MOW National Sample Responses — '**' Indicates Data Missing and/or Unavailable (continued)

		Country of Residence							
		Belgium	Britain	Germany	Israel	Japan	Netherlands	U.S.A.	Yugoslavia
Q66A: Imp To You Of Work— Next 5–10 Years									
**Missing Data	Percent	100.0	100.0	100.0	3.2	100.0	0.0	0.2	0.0
Less Imp	Percent	**	**	**	8.8	**	11.0	14.9	6.6
Equal in Imp	Percent	**	**	**	67.7	**	77.9	39.8	74.0
More Imp	Percent	**	**	**	20.2	**	11.0	45.1	19.4
Q67: Alternative if Same Pay/ Less Hours?									
**Missing Data	Percent	0.0	4.4	0.8	3.8	4.9	0.4	0.2	0.0
More Hoildays	Percent	24.0	16.7	22.8	19.9	36.0	20.0	12.3	14.4
Less Working Hours	Percent	17.1	18.2	19.4	36.7	28.0	21.0	19.1	31.7
A Free Aft Per Week	Percent	16.9	8.5	9.9	8.6	10.9	14.3	14.7	2.6
More Ed B4 Work	Percent	3.8	2.7	2.1	4.7	3.0	1.5	7.9	1.1
Year of Study Per 10	Percent	6.7	6.0	3.0	11.0	5.4	3.5	15.8	3.1
Less Hours For Older	Percent	9.6	9.5	9.9	5.0	10.6	15.2	7.0	10.1
Early Retirement	Percent	22.0	34.0	32.0	10.2	1.1	24.2	23.0	36.9
Q68: Less Hours/Less Pay— Attitude									
**Missing Data	Percent	100.0	2.9	0.7	1.7	100.0	0.3	100.0	0.0
Against Them	Percent	**	43.7	53.0	47.3	**	46.8	**	40.2
Dont Care	Percent	**	9.5	13.4	22.1	**	14.9	**	4.6
Moderately in Favour	Percent	**	36.0	27.6	14.7	**	28.1	**	38.0
In Favour	Percent	**	8.0	5.3	14.2	**	9.9	**	17.2
Q69: Your Age									
**Missing Data	Percent	0.2	1.1	0.0	1.5	0.2	0.0	0.0	0.2
30 & Under	Percent	41.6	29.5	31.3	30.3	22.3	33.8	37.3	31.0
31–50	Percent	42.7	46.4	45.5	46.0	55.6	51.0	46.8	58.5
Over 50	Percent	15.6	23.0	23.2	22.1	21.9	15.2	15.9	10.3

MOW National Sample Responses — '**' Indicates Data Missing and/or Unavailable (continued)

		Country of Residence							
		Belgium	Britain	Germany	Israel	Japan	Netherlands	U.S.A.	Yugoslavia
Q70: Highest Formal Education									
**Missing Data	Percent	0.0	1.5	0.4	1.1	0.8	0.3	0.2	0.2
Primary School	Percent	16.0	18.0	17.4	18.9	1.7	13.1	5.4	16.8
Secondary School	Percent	47.6	28.7	65.3	45.5	57.3	60.3	34.8	57.7
Some College or Votech	Percent	24.4	42.1	6.7	18.3	13.6	21.9	29.8	8.3
University Degree	Percent	12.0	9.6	10.3	16.1	26.6	4.4	29.8	17.0
Q71: Religious Education?									
**Missing Data	Percent	100.0	100.0	0.3	0.8	100.0	0.0	100.0	0.6
No	Percent	**	**	32.3	45.4	**	27.2	**	35.6
Yes	Percent	**	**	67.4	53.8	**	72.8	**	63.8
Q72: Present Association with Religion									
**Missing Data	Percent	100.0	100.0	0.3	0.3	100.0	0.5	100.0	0.6
No Contact	Percent	**	**	27.1	45.7	**	51.3	**	66.1
Loose Contact	Percent	**	**	53.8	39.9	**	31.1	**	29.7
Close Contact	Percent	**	**	18.8	14.1	**	17.1	**	3.7
Q73A: Highest Ed—Father									
**Missing Data	Percent	100.0	100.0	7.0	12.4	100.0	9.6	100.0	1.5
Primary School	Percent	**	**	75.7	46.7	**	43.5	**	41.1
Secondary School	Percent	**	**	13.6	27.4	**	34.0	**	48.3
Some College or Votech	Percent	**	**	1.1	4.7	**	10.1	**	4.8
University Degree	Percent	**	**	2.6	8.7	**	2.7	**	4.2
Q73B: Highest Ed—Mother									
**Missing Data	Percent	100.0	100.0	6.5	15.0	100.0	6.5	100.0	0.6
Primary School	Percent	**	**	81.4	52.9	**	57.8	**	70.1
Secondary School	Percent	**	**	11.0	24.5	**	29.3	**	26.6
Some College or Votech	Percent	**	**	0.9	4.7	**	5.9	**	2.2
University Degree	Percent	**	**	0.2	2.9	**	0.4	**	0.6

MOW National Sample Responses — '**' Indicates Data Missing and/or Unavailable (continued)

		Country of Residence							
		Belgium	Britain	Germany	Israel	Japan	Netherlands	U.S.A.	Yugoslavia
Q74: Size of Childhood Community									
**Missing Data	Percent	100.0	100.0	0.3	1.0	100.0	5.6	100.0	0.2
City	Percent	**	**	31.8	71.6	**	53.0	**	21.6
Village	Percent	**	**	29.0	14.5	**	31.2	**	31.2
Rural	Percent	**	**	38.9	12.8	**	10.1	**	47.0
Q75: Size of Present Community									
**Missing Data	Percent	100.0	100.0	0.2	0.6	100.0	0.1	100.0	0.0
City	Percent	**	**	41.0	83.8	**	52.6	**	43.4
Village	Percent	**	**	28.9	10.6	**	37.4	**	36.3
Rural	Percent	**	**	29.9	5.0	**	9.8	**	20.3
Q76A: Married or Partnership?									
**Missing Data	Percent	0.4	3.2	0.0	0.8	0.4	0.0	0.1	0.4
No	Percent	24.4	29.0	31.2	18.3	19.8	20.9	35.5	24.0
Yes	Percent	75.1	67.7	68.8	80.9	79.8	79.1	64.4	75.6
Q76B: If Yes Is Partner Employed?									
**Missing Data	Percent	100.0	100.0	31.7	21.8	100.0	20.9	100.0	24.7
Not Employed	Percent	**	**	28.6	27.0	**	45.7	**	6.8
Part Time Employ	Percent	**	**	7.7	10.9	**	12.1	**	2.2
Full Time	Percent	**	**	23.8	38.2	**	17.2	**	64.2
Other	Percent	**	**	8.2	2.1	**	4.1	**	2.0

MOW National Sample Responses — '**' Indicates Data Missing and/or Unavailable (continued)

		Country of Residence							
		Belgium	Britain	Germany	Israel	Japan	Netherlands	U.S.A.	Yugoslavia
Q78: General Life Satisfaction									
**Missing Data	Percent	0.0	100.0	100.0	2.6	0.4	0.4	0.0	0.4
1: Very Dissatisfied	Percent	0.4	**	**	1.2	2.8	0.2	0.7	1.7
2: (On 1–to–9 scale)	Percent	0.7	**	**	0.2	1.1	0.3	0.7	1.3
3: (On 1–to–9 scale)	Percent	0.9	**	**	1.3	5.6	0.4	1.2	1.8
4: (On 1–to–9 scale)	Percent	0.9	**	**	1.7	7.4	0.9	2.4	2.2
5: (On 1–to–9 scale)	Percent	8.0	**	**	10.3	48.0	5.0	6.2	15.5
6: (On 1–to–9 scale)	Percent	14.7	**	**	8.9	10.5	5.9	8.3	15.9
7: (On 1–to–9 scale)	Percent	31.6	**	**	22.3	15.5	27.0	31.6	24.0
8: (On 1–to–9 scale)	Percent	22.9	**	**	21.6	5.1	30.1	22.2	17.7
9: Very Satisfied	Percent	20.0	**	**	29.8	3.5	29.7	26.7	19.6
Q82: Sex of Resp									
**Missing Data	Percent	0.0	0.6	0.0	1.2	0.1	0.0	0.0	0.2
Male	Percent	68.0	47.5	64.9	56.7	66.5	73.3	53.4	49.8
Female	Percent	32.0	51.9	35.1	42.0	33.4	26.7	46.6	50.0
Q84A: Ownership of Work Organization									
**Missing Data	Percent	100.0	100.0	0.0	21.9	100.0	0.8	0.0	3.1
Public	Percent	**	**	21.6	41.4	**	28.6	31.0	80.3
Private	Percent	**	**	78.4	36.7	**	70.6	69.0	16.6

MOW National Sample Responses — '**' Indicates Data Missing and/or Unavailable (continued)

		Country of Residence							
		Belgium	Britain	Germany	Israel	Japan	Netherlands	U.S.A.	Yugoslavia
Q84B: Size of Work Organization									
**Missing Data	Percent	100.0	9.4	22.8	5.1	100.0	1.9	0.2	17.0
Under 100 Employees	Percent	**	60.8	46.9	47.2	**	56.2	60.8	31.0
100–299	Percent	**	11.4	11.3	10.7	**	16.3	13.3	8.7
300–999	Percent	**	10.6	6.7	10.3	**	13.1	12.5	27.7
1000 or More	Percent	**	7.7	12.2	26.7	**	12.6	13.2	15.7
	Number of Responses	450	0.0	1278	888	0.0	981	997	541
Q85: Length of Interview	Mean	41.2	**	30.4	42.3	**	60.0	30.7	47.8
(Minutes)	STD	17.0	**	10.1	12.6	**	14.8	7.7	16.6

YUGOSLAVIAN DATA NOTE: Yugoslavia did not collect data on a national sample and so the target group sample is used here for purposes of comparisons with other countries.

Q23C NOTE: Values for monthly net income in the currency of the respective countries: Belgian francs, German marks, Israeli pounds, Japanese yen (thousands), Dutch guilders, American dollars, and Yugoslavian dinar (tens).

MOW Target Group Sample Responses — '**' Indicates Data Missing and/or Unavailable

		Unemployed	Retired	Chemical Engineers	Teachers	Self-Employed	Tool and Die	White-Collar	Textile	Temporary	Students
-Total Sample Size-	Number of Responses	556	573	549	652	665	598	695	588	465	592
Country of Residence											
Belgium	Number of Responses	100.0	90.0	90.0	90.0	90.0	83.0	92.0	90.0	82.0	90.0
	Percent	18.0	15.7	16.4	13.8	13.5	13.9	13.2	15.3	17.6	15.2
Germany	Number of Responses	91.0	92.0	0.0	103.0	99.0	51.0	102.0	33.0	14.0	114.0
	Percent	16.4	16.1	0.0	15.8	14.9	8.5	14.7	5.6	3.0	19.3
Israel	Number of Responses	90.0	90.0	90.0	90.0	90.0	91.0	90.0	90.0	90.0	90.0
	Percent	16.2	15.7	16.4	13.8	13.5	15.2	12.9	15.3	19.4	15.2
Japan	Number of Responses	134.0	125.0	99.0	99.0	103.0	93.0	143.0	116.0	101.0	118.0
	Percent	24.1	21.8	18.0	15.2	15.5	15.6	20.6	19.7	21.7	19.9
Netherlands	Number of Responses	90.0	86.0	90.0	90.0	103.0	98.0	88.0	84.0	88.0	90.0
	Percent	16.2	15.0	16.4	13.8	15.5	16.4	12.7	14.3	18.9	15.2
U.S.A.	Number of Responses	51.0	90.0	90.0	90.0	90.0	90.0	90.0	85.0	90.0	90.0
	Percent	9.2	15.7	16.4	13.8	13.5	15.1	12.9	14.5	19.4	15.2
Yugoslavia	Number of Responses	0.0	0.0	90.0	90.0	90.0	92.0	90.0	90.0	0.0	0.0
	Percent	**	**	16.4	13.8	13.5	15.4	12.9	15.3	**	**
Q2: Supervisory Status											
**Missing Data	Percent	3.4	1.6	0.5	2.8	6.0	0.2	0.7	1.9	1.9	**
Non-Super	Percent	66.4	44.2	51.5	61.8	21.4	83.6	81.2	81.8	87.1	100.0
Super	Percent	19.6	28.8	32.2	26.8	22.1	12.4	14.1	11.9	6.9	**
Managerial	Percent	10.6	25.5	15.7	9.0	50.5	3.8	4.0	4.4	4.1	**
Q3A: Union Member?											
**Missing Data	Percent	5.0	5.1	1.6	1.1	3.0	2.0	1.6	1.4	1.7	100.0
No	Percent	59.9	55.3	46.4	32.7	86.5	36.0	47.3	23.8	78.1	**
Yes	Percent	35.1	39.6	51.9	66.3	10.5	62.0	51.1	74.8	20.2	**

MOW Target Group Sample Responses — '**' Indicates Data Missing and/or Unavailable (continued)

					Target Group						
		Unemployed	Retired	Chemical Engineers	Teachers	Self-Employed	Tool and Die	White-Collar	Textile	Temporary	Students
Q3B: Prof Assn Member?											
**Missing Data	Percent	19.6	19.4	20.8	15.8	14.6	17.6	17.8	20.6	21.1	100.0
No	Percent	77.5	59.7	35.5	57.2	52.5	76.9	77.0	78.1	75.9	**
Yes	Percent	2.9	20.9	43.7	27.0	32.9	5.5	5.2	1.4	3.0	**
Q3C: Employers Assn Member?											
**Missing Data	Percent	10.8	9.9	27.3	21.6	15.3	25.1	24.6	25.5	12.7	100.0
No	Percent	84.9	85.0	69.4	75.3	68.1	73.6	73.5	74.5	86.7	**
Yes	Percent	4.3	5.1	3.3	3.1	16.5	1.3	1.9	0.0	0.6	0
Q4: Hours Worked Per Week	Number of Responses	531	567	545	647	662	593	691	582	444	**
	Mean	43.3	44.0	45.0	41.0	56.5	44.9	43.0	42.5	33.6	**
	STD	11.6	11.9	7.0	11.5	15.0	6.7	10.0	6.9	10.6	**
Q5: Travel Time To & From Work (Minutes)	Number of Responses	536	546	546	649	606	595	691	579	444	0.0
	Mean	55.7	55.5	62.1	42.8	31.0	61.0	58.6	35.3	69.6	**
	STD	42.7	42.3	41.7	31.4	34.1	41.7	40.3	30.4	49.1	**
Q6A: Shift Worked											
**Missing Data	Percent	2.2	0.3	0.2	0.6	1.8	0.0	0.0	0.2	1.9	100.0
Day	Percent	77.3	86.9	97.3	88.7	76.8	87.3	95.8	45.7	91.6	**
Night	Percent	3.2	0.9	0.0	0.2	1.2	0.2	0.3	1.4	1.9	**
Swing Shift	Percent	7.6	6.6	0.9	2.9	11.3	1.2	1.9	5.3	3.0	**
Shift Changes	Percent	9.7	5.2	1.6	7.7	8.9	11.4	2.0	47.4	1.5	**
Q6B: Work Hours											
**Missing Data	Percent	2.9	0.7	0.2	0.3	0.5	0.2	0.1	0.3	1.5	100.0
Regular	Percent	78.2	84.1	93.8	96.0	73.8	92.5	94.7	82.1	83.9	**
Varied	Percent	18.9	15.2	6.0	3.7	25.7	7.4	5.2	17.5	14.6	**

MOW Target Group Sample Responses — '**' Indicates Data Missing and/or Unavailable (continued)

		Target Group									
		Unem-ployed	Retired	Chemical Engineers	Teachers	Self-Employed	Tool and Die	White-Collar	Textile	Tempo-rary	Students
Q6C: Worked Weekends Past Year?											
**Missing Data	Percent	2.5	1.2	0.5	0.6	0.6	0.2	1.2	0.9	2.6	100.0
No	Percent	69.2	71.2	87.6	76.2	40.6	81.4	85.2	79.4	88.0	**
Yes	Percent	28.2	27.6	11.8	23.2	58.8	18.4	13.7	19.7	9.5	**
Q7A: Unemployed Last 5 Years?											
**Missing Data	Percent	2.7	1.9	0.5	0.5	1.5	1.5	0.7	0.5	2.4	100.0
No	Percent	16.0	85.0	93.8	89.9	91.4	85.5	89.1	80.6	48.2	**
Yes	Percent	81.3	13.1	5.6	9.7	7.1	13.0	10.2	18.9	49.5	**
Q7B: If Unemployed, Num	Number of Responses	429	63	30	59	42	73	68	95	217	0.0
Mos 5 Years	Mean	19.3	39.3	4.4	14.6	8.9	4.8	7.8	9.5	11.0	**
	STD	16.1	23.7	4.6	16.8	9.5	9.3	9.2	10.1	10.4	**
Q7C: If Unemployed, Num	Number of Responses	423	56	26	55	32	65	62	88	201	0.0
Mos Past Year	Mean	8.2	9.4	0.3	1.9	0.7	1.3	1.3	3.7	4.0	**
	STD	3.8	4.3	0.7	3.4	2.0	2.1	2.4	2.9	3.1	**
Q8: Level of Variety In Job											
**Missing Data	Percent	3.6	1.7	0.7	0.6	1.5	1.3	0.1	0.5	2.6	100.0
Much Repetition	Percent	33.8	30.0	5.5	2.9	23.9	10.7	37.7	63.4	40.9	**
Some Variety	Percent	35.3	30.5	33.7	39.0	29.9	39.0	38.4	23.1	36.8	**
Wide Variety	Percent	27.3	37.7	60.1	57.5	44.7	49.0	23.7	12.9	19.8	**
Q9: Level of Autonomy in Job											
**Missing Data	Percent	2.3	0.7	0.9	0.5	0.6	1.2	0.1	0.7	2.4	100.0
No Decision Making	Percent	23.0	12.9	2.6	0.8	1.7	6.5	17.7	35.9	34.2	**
Some Decisions	Percent	49.6	41.5	57.0	62.3	10.1	57.0	64.0	50.5	49.7	**
My Own Decisions	Percent	25.0	44.9	39.5	36.5	87.7	35.3	18.1	12.9	13.8	**

MOW Target Group Sample Responses — '**' Indicates Data Missing and/or Unavailable (continued)

						Target Group					
		Unemployed	Retired	Chemical Engineers	Teachers	Self-Employed	Tool and Die	White-Collar	Textile	Temporary	Students
Q10: Level of Responsibility In Job											
**Missing Data	Percent	2.9	1.2	1.1	1.2	0.9	1.5	0.3	0.7	3.4	100.0
Mistakes—Little Cons	Percent	37.1	37.7	10.4	15.8	30.5	19.2	17.3	32.1	30.8	**
Some Consequences	Percent	33.3	32.3	50.3	50.2	29.5	43.1	50.5	36.6	50.1	**
Serious Consequences	Percent	26.8	28.8	38.3	32.8	39.1	36.1	31.9	30.6	15.7	**
Q11: Level of New Learning In Job											
**Missing Data	Percent	2.3	0.9	0.7	0.5	0.9	1.5	0.0	1.0	2.4	100.0
No Learning	Percent	21.4	13.6	1.5	1.1	8.7	5.5	10.9	35.4	15.1	**
Some Learning	Percent	41.4	33.5	27.0	28.8	32.3	50.8	49.5	42.2	48.6	**
Learn Many Things	Percent	34.9	52.0	70.9	69.6	58.0	42.1	39.6	21.4	34.0	**
Q12: Interpersonal Contact In Job											
**Missing Data	Percent	2.2	0.3	0.0	0.6	0.5	0.0	0.3	1.0	2.8	100.0
Work Alone	Percent	24.5	19.7	7.7	13.2	26.0	32.1	16.7	28.2	27.7	**
Work With Some	Percent	35.3	30.4	34.8	40.5	25.7	38.8	38.0	32.7	41.9	**
Work Much With Others	Percent	38.1	49.6	57.6	45.7	47.8	29.1	45.0	38.1	27.5	**
Q13: Non-Job Conversation In Job											
**Missing Data	Percent	1.8	0.9	0.0	0.6	0.5	0.0	0.0	1.0	2.6	100.0
No Non-Business Talk	Percent	15.3	19.9	6.7	35.3	5.9	10.5	12.1	37.6	10.5	**
Some Non-Business Talk	Percent	44.4	41.7	45.4	48.9	37.6	49.0	49.9	36.1	43.7	**
Often Non-Business Talk	Percent	38.5	37.5	47.9	15.2	56.1	40.5	38.0	25.3	43.2	**

MOW Target Group Sample Responses — '**' Indicates Data Missing and/or Unavailable (continued)

		Target Group									
		Unem-ployed	Retired	Chemical Engineers	Teachers	Self-Employed	Tool and Die	White-Collar	Textile	Tempo-rary	Students
Q14: Work in Dangerous Circumstances?											
**Missing Data	Percent	2.0	0.5	0.2	0.5	0.6	0.7	0.0	1.0	1.7	100.0
No	Percent	62.2	81.0	55.2	93.6	80.8	56.2	93.7	69.9	95.5	**
Yes	Percent	35.8	18.5	44.6	6.0	18.6	43.1	6.3	29.1	2.8	**
Q15: Work In Unhealthy Circumstances											
**Missing Data	Percent	2.5	0.3	0.4	0.5	0.6	0.8	0.1	0.9	1.1	100.0
No	Percent	60.1	82.5	47.4	82.1	73.5	47.7	85.5	58.7	87.7	**
Yes	Percent	37.4	17.1	52.3	17.5	25.9	51.5	14.4	40.5	11.2	**
Q16: Job Require Too Much Physically?											
**Missing Data	Percent	2.3	0.9	0.2	0.8	0.2	0.0	0.0	1.2	1.5	100.0
Never	Percent	23.6	39.4	40.8	24.1	26.9	15.1	49.2	18.2	55.5	**
Seldom	Percent	19.2	21.8	39.7	29.8	25.4	30.8	27.1	15.8	23.2	**
Sometimes	Percent	30.2	29.5	17.7	35.3	34.9	43.8	20.4	42.2	17.6	**
Often	Percent	24.6	8.4	1.6	10.1	12.6	10.4	3.3	22.6	2.2	**
Q17: Job Require Too Much Mentally?											
**Missing Data	Percent	2.5	0.5	0.5	0.5	0.5	0.0	0.0	0.9	1.7	100.0
Never	Percent	22.7	27.7	12.2	12.6	24.1	15.4	19.6	27.0	28.8	**
Seldom	Percent	19.2	16.8	31.9	18.6	16.7	27.9	26.2	17.2	29.7	**
Sometimes	Percent	35.1	30.4	39.3	40.5	37.9	41.5	37.8	38.6	29.9	**
Often	Percent	20.5	24.6	16.0	27.9	20.9	15.2	16.4	16.3	9.9	**

MOW Target Group Sample Responses — '**' Indicates Data Missing and/or Unavailable (continued)

		Target Group									
		Unem-ployed	Retired	Chemical Engineers	Teachers	Self-Employed	Tool and Die	White-Collar	Textile	Tempo-rary	Students
Q18: Skills and Abilities Used?											
**Missing Data	Percent	2.0	0.5	0.2	0.2	0.3	0.5	0.1	1.4	1.3	100.0
Very Little	Percent	27.0	12.0	5.5	8.9	10.2	5.2	25.2	26.7	26.0	**
Little	Percent	30.0	21.8	28.1	20.9	18.0	24.6	35.1	24.1	30.5	**
A Lot	Percent	29.5	38.7	47.2	37.9	34.0	39.1	30.2	31.6	27.5	**
Almost All	Percent	11.5	26.9	19.1	32.2	37.4	30.6	9.4	16.2	14.6	**
Q19: How Does Supervisor Make Decisions?											
**Missing Data	Percent	5.8	7.3	2.9	3.4	82.7	1.3	0.3	1.5	6.5	100.0
No Inform–Decisions	Percent	14.6	3.3	2.4	1.2	1.1	5.9	7.2	10.9	21.3	**
Inform After Decision	Percent	35.6	24.3	18.8	27.5	0.9	27.8	45.6	48.3	43.4	**
Asks For Advice	Percent	12.8	16.1	24.0	17.3	1.2	18.1	18.8	12.1	9.9	**
Decide Jointly	Percent	20.7	30.2	32.6	36.8	3.2	27.8	19.3	20.2	12.5	**
I Decide	Percent	10.6	18.8	19.3	13.8	11.0	19.2	8.8	7.0	6.5	**
Q20: Is Your Present Job Your First?											
**Missing Data	Percent	2.9	1.0	1.3	1.2	2.9	1.2	1.0	2.2	1.9	100.0
No	Percent	67.8	64.7	51.2	45.1	68.9	57.9	52.4	55.6	78.7	**
Yes	Percent	29.3	34.2	47.5	53.7	28.3	41.0	46.6	42.2	19.4	**
Q23A1: Why Chose Your Present Job?											
**Missing Data	Percent	16.0	9.4	7.1	5.2	8.0	9.7	8.5	6.1	12.9	100.0
Good Pay	Percent	10.4	6.8	4.6	1.2	6.3	11.0	11.4	10.2	4.5	**
Good Conditions	Percent	1.4	2.8	3.5	3.7	2.6	3.0	2.7	2.0	6.5	**
Location	Percent	2.7	1.7	6.0	7.1	0.8	2.7	3.9	9.4	2.2	**
Hours	Percent	1.4	1.0	0.2	1.2	0.0	0.8	3.2	4.4	6.5	**
Interesting	Percent	19.2	20.8	36.8	46.6	23.0	28.9	21.9	10.4	13.1	**

MOW Target Group Sample Responses — '**' Indicates Data Missing and/or Unavailable (continued)

		Target Group									
Q23A1: Why Choose Your Present Job? (continued)		Unem-ployed	Retired	Chemical Engineers	Teachers	Self-Employed	Tool and Die	White-Collar	Textile	Tempo-rary	Students
Opportunity to Learn	Percent	0.7	0.9	3.1	1.1	1.2	2.5	1.7	0.5	2.4	**
Opportunity for Promotion	Percent	0.9	4.0	3.8	0.5	0.8	1.3	3.2	0.7	0.4	**
More Responsibility	Percent	0.5	0.5	1.3	0.6	0.8	0.3	0.4	0.2	0.0	**
Challenge	Percent	2.3	1.4	1.5	3.2	1.2	1.2	1.7	0.0	0.2	**
Trained For It	Percent	7.4	9.4	9.5	6.9	5.9	9.5	4.3	3.1	5.2	**
Job Security	Percent	2.2	3.3	2.0	1.2	2.7	3.8	5.9	2.0	0.6	**
Necessity	Percent	9.2	5.9	1.1	1.2	2.7	2.7	4.7	9.7	5.6	**
No Choice	Percent	12.8	9.4	11.5	7.7	5.4	9.4	11.9	26.5	14.0	**
Recommended	Percent	3.2	5.8	1.1	2.0	1.7	3.7	1.6	6.3	4.9	**
Parent Chose	Percent	1.4	4.2	0.4	1.1	10.5	1.2	0.7	2.2	0.4	**
Image of Firm	Percent	0.4	0.5	0.9	0.6	0.0	1.8	0.7	0.5	0.4	**
Independence	Percent	1.1	0.5	0.0	0.3	19.2	0.0	0.4	0.2	0.6	**
Military Draft	Percent	0.2	0.0	0.0	0.0	0.0	0.0	0.0	0.0	0.0	**
Health	Percent	1.1	2.4	0.0	1.7	1.8	1.5	1.0	1.0	0.4	**
Temp to Fill Time	Percent	0.4	0.2	0.0	0.2	0.0	0.2	0.1	0.0	3.9	**
Temp For Freedom	Percent	0.0	0.2	0.0	0.0	0.0	0.0	0.0	0.0	8.4	**
Other	Percent	5.0	8.7	5.8	6.7	5.6	4.7	9.9	4.6	6.9	**
Number of Responses		473	552	520	631	628	555	657	570	377	0.0
Mean		3.7	17.8	6.7	8.2	11.8	9.0	5.2	10.2	1.6	**
STD		5.4	14.0	6.8	7.5	11.6	8.6	5.8	10.0	2.2	**
Q24: Where Started Your Work Career?											
**Missing Data	Percent	6.5	3.3	1.8	1.5	7.2	1.3	1.3	1.4	4.1	100.0
Lower	Percent	32.4	28.8	16.6	16.7	30.1	32.1	26.6	29.6	28.6	**
Same	Percent	50.5	57.2	75.4	77.6	43.9	60.0	65.9	60.9	53.3	**
Higher	Percent	10.6	10.6	6.2	4.1	18.8	6.5	6.2	8.2	14.0	**

MOW Target Group Sample Responses — '**' Indicates Data Missing and/or Unavailable (continued)

		Target Group									
		Unemployed	Retired	Chemical Engineers	Teachers	Self-Employed	Tool and Die	White-Collar	Textile	Temporary	Students
Q25A: Has Your Career Had Ups and Downs?											
**Missing Data	Percent	4.3	0.7	2.0	0.9	1.8	0.8	1.2	0.5	1.5	80.1
No	Percent	38.3	52.4	61.9	58.7	39.8	54.0	62.2	60.4	50.1	**
Yes	Percent	57.4	46.8	35.9	40.3	57.7	44.6	36.7	38.3	46.7	**
Q25B: Size of Ups & Downs											
**Missing Data	Percent	40.2	50.6	62.6	58.6	42.1	54.1	62.2	61.5	51.6	100.0
Small	Percent	31.3	25.1	26.0	26.7	26.5	31.6	27.9	25.7	29.5	**
Large	Percent	28.4	24.3	11.3	14.7	31.4	14.2	9.9	12.8	18.9	**
Q26: My Work History Trend											
**Missing Data	Percent	7.6	2.1	2.6	4.1	4.1	1.3	1.7	2.0	5.4	100.0
Some Decline	Percent	22.7	8.9	5.8	5.4	8.4	5.0	6.0	9.5	15.9	**
Same Level	Percent	26.8	12.2	14.8	24.7	8.3	14.2	20.1	31.6	22.6	**
Some Improve	Percent	25.5	30.9	41.5	35.3	32.3	44.0	42.3	35.4	28.2	**
Much Improve	Percent	17.4	45.9	35.3	30.5	46.9	35.5	29.8	21.4	28.0	**
Q27: Satisfaction with Work History											
**Missing Data	Percent	3.4	0.3	1.3	2.1	1.8	0.5	1.0	1.4	3.0	100.0
Dissatisfied	Percent	18.3	3.1	2.7	1.5	3.9	4.8	2.7	6.1	8.8	**
Some Dissatisfaction	Percent	20.3	5.4	18.0	6.9	4.8	13.7	12.5	14.1	15.3	**
Neutral	Percent	23.4	15.0	13.8	10.3	14.3	22.4	23.3	23.6	23.7	**
Some Satisfaction	Percent	23.2	29.8	42.6	43.1	34.7	39.0	40.1	35.0	28.4	**
Very Satisfied	Percent	11.3	46.2	21.5	36.0	40.5	19.6	20.3	19.7	20.9	**
Q28A1: Points—Status &	Number of Responses	539	559	541	643	647	581	682	570	454	585
Prestige	Mean	7.5	8.5	8.8	6.0	7.7	8.5	8.9	7.7	6.7	9.1
	STD	10.3	10.4	8.9	8.6	9.6	9.3	10.5	9.5	8.0	8.2

MOW Target Group Sample Responses — '**' Indicates Data Missing and/or Unavailable (continued)

		Target Group									
		Unem-ployed	Retired	Chemical Engineers	Teachers	Self-Employed	Tool and Die	White-Collar	Textile	Tempo-rary	Students
Q28A2: Points—Income	Number of Responses	539	559	541	643	647	581	682	570	454	585
	Mean	35.1	29.8	29.7	22.5	33.4	39.4	35.6	40.6	31.1	29.8
	STD	23.2	20.8	16.6	16.4	21.0	21.0	20.7	22.4	20.5	17.5
Q28A3: Points—Keeps Occupied	Number of Responses	539	559	541	643	647	581	682	570	454	585
	Mean	11.0	9.2	7.7	9.7	9.1	9.9	10.7	12.2	12.7	12.0
	STD	11.2	9.8	9.1	10.6	10.3	9.6	10.7	11.4	11.9	9.4
Q28A4: Points—Interesting Contacts	Number of Responses	539	559	541	643	647	581	682	570	454	585
	Mean	17.0	14.9	12.3	17.1	15.1	11.9	16.9	14.0	20.6	19.3
	STD	13.8	11.5	9.5	12.6	13.2	9.1	12.0	11.8	12.6	10.4
Q28A5: Points—Way to Serve Society	Number of Responses	539	559	541	643	647	581	682	570	454	585
	Mean	10.6	16.0	13.5	17.0	10.7	11.1	9.8	11.4	8.4	11.3
	STD	11.5	13.9	11.5	13.3	11.9	10.7	10.0	11.9	8.6	8.6
Q28A6: Points—Interesting & Satisfying	Number of Responses	539	559	541	643	647	581	682	570	454	585
	Mean	18.8	21.5	28.1	27.7	24.0	19.2	18.0	13.9	20.4	18.3
	STD	15.9	16.1	16.7	16.5	18.7	13.9	14.3	12.6	14.4	11.5
Q29: Importance of Work to Your Life											
**Missing Data	Percent	4.3	3.7	1.1	0.8	3.5	2.0	0.9	2.7	2.2	0.8
1: One of the Least...	Percent	2.5	1.0	0.5	0.2	1.2	2.3	1.0	0.9	1.7	0.5
2: (On 1-to-7 Scale)	Percent	2.2	0.3	1.5	0.5	2.1	2.2	1.9	2.2	4.1	1.4
3: (On 1-to-7 Scale)	Percent	6.3	2.6	2.0	1.8	4.5	3.0	6.3	4.3	9.0	5.1
4: Of Medium Importance	Percent	21.9	16.8	15.3	23.5	17.3	23.6	27.8	22.6	32.9	22.0
5: (On 1-to-7 Scale)	Percent	17.1	15.7	27.5	29.4	18.9	23.4	23.2	14.1	21.9	28.4
6: (On 1-to-7 Scale)	Percent	18.3	20.4	32.8	25.6	25.3	17.7	22.4	19.4	15.7	26.7
7: One of the Most....	Percent	27.3	39.4	19.3	18.3	27.2	25.8	16.5	33.8	12.5	15.2
Q30A: Points—Import of Leisure	Number of Responses	540	554	540	645	643	586	688	578	454	589
	Mean	25.3	21.4	20.0	20.0	19.1	24.0	25.6	20.5	27.1	31.8
	STD	19.5	17.1	12.7	13.0	17.0	16.3	17.2	17.5	16.9	16.4

MOW Target Group Sample Responses — '**' Indicates Data Missing and/or Unavailable (continued)

		Target Group									
		Unem-ployed	Retired	Chemical Engineers	Teachers	Self-Employed	Tool and Die	White-Collar	Textile	Tempo-rary	Students
Q30B: Points—Community Import	Number of Responses	540	554	540	645	643	586	688	578	454	589
	Mean	8.6	10.1	6.0	6.6	6.1	6.4	5.4	6.5	5.4	9.5
	STD	11.6	12.5	7.2	8.1	9.0	8.3	7.4	8.5	7.9	8.5
Q30C: Points—Work	Number of Responses	540	554	540	645	643	586	688	578	454	589
	Mean	28.8	19.4	35.8	33.9	37.6	28.0	28.8	28.5	26.5	23.1
	STD	19.0	19.9	14.4	15.3	20.4	15.0	16.7	17.6	15.3	12.4
Q30D: Points—Religion	Number of Responses	540	554	540	645	643	586	688	578	454	589
	Mean	5.3	9.7	4.0	5.2	4.9	4.6	4.4	6.1	5.0	6.6
	STD	9.2	13.5	7.1	9.2	9.8	8.9	8.5	10.2	9.8	8.6
Q30E: Points—Family	Number of Responses	540	554	540	645	643	586	688	578	454	589
	Mean	32.1	39.5	34.3	34.3	32.3	36.9	35.8	38.3	36.1	28.9
	STD	20.3	22.0	15.1	17.8	18.6	19.1	18.2	18.6	19.6	13.9
Q31A: Tasks Rank	Number of Responses	503	523	532	618	607	573	671	543	445	572
	Mean	3.7	3.7	4.1	4.1	3.3	3.8	3.7	3.6	3.8	3.5
	STD	1.7	1.7	1.6	1.4	1.6	1.6	1.7	1.6	1.6	1.7
Q31B: Company Rank	Number of Responses	503	523	532	618	607	573	671	543	445	572
	Mean	2.5	2.8	2.5	2.1	3.5	2.4	2.7	2.8	2.3	2.5
	STD	1.6	1.7	1.6	1.4	1.9	1.5	1.6	1.5	1.5	1.5
Q31C: Product or Service Rank	Number of Responses	503	523	532	618	607	573	671	543	445	572
	Mean	3.3	3.8	3.6	4.3	3.9	3.3	3.2	3.4	3.1	2.9
	STD	1.6	1.6	1.8	1.6	1.6	1.7	1.7	1.5	1.7	1.7
Q31D: Type of People Rank	Number of Responses	503	523	532	618	607	573	671	543	445	572
	Mean	3.8	3.4	3.4	3.9	3.3	3.3	3.7	3.4	4.1	4.0
	STD	1.4	1.5	1.5	1.6	1.5	1.5	1.6	1.5	1.5	1.5
Q31E: Type of Occupation Rank	Number of Responses	503	523	532	618	607	573	671	543	445	572
	Mean	3.7	3.6	3.8	3.7	3.3	3.5	3.5	3.2	3.8	4.2
	STD	1.7	1.7	1.8	1.7	1.7	1.6	1.7	1.7	1.6	1.7

MOW Target Group Sample Responses — '*' Indicates Data Missing and/or Unavailable (continued)

		Target Group									
		Unemployed	Retired	Chemical Engineers	Teachers	Self-Employed	Tool and Die	White-Collar	Textile	Temporary	Students
Q31F: Money Rank	Number of Responses	503	523	532	618	607	573	671	543	445	572
	Mean	4.0	3.7	3.6	2.9	3.8	4.7	4.2	4.7	3.9	3.9
	STD	1.8	1.9	1.6	1.5	1.7	1.5	1.6	1.7	1.7	1.5
Q32A: Learn New Things Rating	Number of Responses	527	548	541	633	642	573	675	558	441	568
	Mean	10.1	9.5	11.1	10.5	9.8	10.1	10.4	9.0	10.7	10.5
	STD	3.7	4.0	3.2	3.3	3.6	3.5	3.5	4.1	3.3	3.4
Q32B: Interpers Relations Rating	Number of Responses	528	553	538	637	640	578	677	564	445	574
	Mean	10.0	10.3	10.5	11.1	9.4	10.3	10.7	10.4	10.8	9.9
	STD	3.4	3.4	3.0	3.0	4.0	3.3	3.4	3.5	3.2	3.5
Q32C: Promotion Opportunity Rating	Number of Responses	522	545	540	628	636	580	681	549	440	569
	Mean	8.1	8.0	8.9	5.5	6.7	9.2	9.4	8.5	7.7	9.9
	STD	4.0	4.1	3.4	3.8	4.5	3.8	3.7	4.2	4.1	3.4
Q32D: Convenient Hours Rating	Number of Responses	527	546	540	638	649	578	682	566	449	575
	Mean	9.1	8.2	6.8	9.1	7.7	9.0	9.2	10.0	9.8	8.9
	STD	3.8	3.7	3.2	3.4	4.3	3.5	3.4	3.5	3.7	3.5
Q32E: Variety Rating	Number of Responses	523	544	541	634	648	579	676	551	438	574
	Mean	8.5	8.2	9.4	9.4	9.2	9.1	9.0	7.8	8.8	9.5
	STD	3.9	3.7	3.3	3.8	4.0	3.3	3.4	3.6	4.1	3.6
Q32F: Interesting Work Rating	Number of Responses	523	549	542	638	652	570	679	555	443	573
	Mean	11.3	11.1	12.4	12.7	11.8	10.9	11.0	9.8	11.1	11.6
	STD	3.4	3.4	2.7	2.7	3.2	3.2	3.3	3.6	3.4	3.4
Q32G: Job Security Rating	Number of Responses	530	544	540	623	635	575	673	558	438	571
	Mean	10.0	10.0	8.2	8.9	8.5	10.1	9.5	11.0	7.7	9.7
	STD	3.7	3.5	3.4	3.4	4.2	3.6	3.7	3.3	3.7	3.5
Q32H: Good Match Rating	Number of Responses	508	545	539	635	648	570	672	550	437	571
	Mean	8.8	9.5	9.6	10.3	9.6	9.1	8.9	8.5	8.8	8.9
	STD	3.6	3.7	3.5	3.3	3.7	3.5	3.5	3.8	3.9	3.7

MOW Target Group Sample Responses — '***' Indicates Data Missing and/or Unavailable (continued)

		Target Group									
		Unemployed	Retired	Chemical Engineers	Teachers	Self-Employed	Tool and Die	White-Collar	Textile	Temporary	Students
Q32I: Pay Rating	Number of Responses	535	549	541	634	651	583	682	572	453	580
	Mean	10.5	10.2	10.2	8.6	10.7	12.3	10.9	12.1	10.2	10.7
	STD	3.6	3.5	2.9	3.4	3.6	2.9	3.2	2.9	3.4	3.1
Q32J: Working Conditions Rating	Number of Responses	523	554	544	639	645	574	678	565	446	577
	Mean	9.1	8.6	7.3	8.6	8.9	9.5	8.3	10.0	8.5	9.0
	STD	3.6	3.5	3.3	3.4	4.0	3.4	3.5	3.5	3.5	3.3
Q32K: Autonomy Rating	Number of Responses	526	547	539	638	651	577	682	557	444	582
	Mean	8.8	8.9	9.2	9.9	11.4	8.8	8.3	7.8	8.9	8.8
	STD	4.0	4.0	3.7	3.5	4.1	3.8	3.7	3.7	3.9	3.9
Q33: Job Choice Number 1											
**Missing Data	Percent	0.9	0.9	0.2	0.9	0.6	1.0	0.4	1.5	0.9	0.2
Either Job	Percent	11.0	5.6	2.7	2.0	2.0	6.4	7.8	9.4	8.4	8.4
Prefer Job A	Percent	81.7	90.4	95.6	95.6	95.6	88.3	88.8	76.7	85.2	84.8
Prefer Job B	Percent	6.5	3.1	1.5	1.5	1.8	4.3	3.0	12.4	5.6	6.6
Q34: Job Choice Number 2											
**Missing Data	Percent	0.7	1.2	0.2	1.2	0.9	1.2	0.4	2.6	0.9	0.3
Either Job	Percent	8.3	4.5	3.3	2.8	1.5	5.5	5.8	6.5	8.4	6.3
Prefer Job A	Percent	71.4	82.9	92.3	92.2	92.3	78.1	77.0	56.8	72.9	73.8
Prefer Job B	Percent	19.6	11.3	4.2	3.8	5.3	15.2	16.8	34.2	17.8	19.6
Q35: Job Choice Number 3											
**Missing Data	Percent	1.4	1.7	0.2	1.1	0.9	1.2	0.4	2.9	1.1	0.8
Either Job	Percent	7.2	5.8	7.5	3.5	2.9	5.9	5.0	3.1	8.6	5.4
Prefer Job A	Percent	54.1	63.2	67.0	79.6	80.6	51.5	50.1	38.6	49.9	48.3
Prefer Job B	Percent	37.2	29.3	25.3	15.8	15.6	41.5	44.5	55.4	40.4	45.4

MOW Target Group Sample Responses — '***' Indicates Data Missing and/or Unavailable (continued)

		Unemployed	Retired	Chemical Engineers	Teachers	Self-Employed	Tool and Die	White-Collar	Textile	Temporary	Students
Q36: Job Choice Number 4											
**Missing Data	Percent	1.1	1.4	0.7	1.4	0.9	1.2	0.6	2.9	1.1	1.2
Either Job	Percent	4.7	4.7	5.1	2.8	5.0	5.2	4.0	1.9	5.8	3.7
Prefer Job A	Percent	36.9	51.3	40.8	62.4	57.9	28.3	25.0	26.0	26.5	23.6
Prefer Job B	Percent	57.4	42.6	53.4	33.4	36.2	65.4	70.4	69.2	66.7	71.5
Q37: Job Choice Number 5											
**Missing Data	Percent	1.3	1.2	0.5	0.6	0.8	1.2	0.4	1.9	0.6	0.7
Either Job	Percent	3.8	2.6	0.4	0.2	0.8	2.8	1.3	1.9	1.3	0.5
Prefer Job A	Percent	91.2	93.7	98.7	98.3	97.7	94.5	97.1	89.6	97.0	98.5
Prefer Job B	Percent	3.8	2.4	0.4	0.9	0.8	1.5	1.2	6.6	1.1	0.3
Q38: Job Choice Number 6											
**Missing Data	Percent	1.4	1.7	0.2	0.9	0.6	1.3	0.3	2.0	0.9	0.2
Either Job	Percent	4.0	3.5	0.4	0.5	0.6	2.7	2.2	2.2	1.7	0.8
Prefer Job A	Percent	83.6	88.7	98.0	97.1	96.1	89.8	91.9	75.3	94.4	93.4
Prefer Job B	Percent	11.0	6.1	1.5	1.5	2.7	6.2	5.6	20.4	3.0	5.6
Q39: Job Choice Number 7											
**Missing Data	Percent	1.6	1.7	1.1	1.4	0.6	1.5	0.4	3.9	0.9	0.8
Either Job	Percent	5.4	3.1	2.6	1.8	3.2	3.7	4.2	2.7	3.4	2.9
Prefer Job A	Percent	69.8	77.1	86.7	90.6	87.1	68.9	74.2	57.1	79.8	78.4
Prefer Job B	Percent	23.2	18.0	9.7	6.1	9.2	25.9	21.2	36.2	15.9	17.9
Q40: Job Choice Number 8											
**Missing Data	Percent	1.4	1.7	0.5	0.8	0.8	1.5	0.1	2.0	1.1	0.8
Either Job	Percent	3.8	3.8	3.1	2.1	5.3	4.3	4.0	2.0	4.1	6.4
Prefer Job A	Percent	52.0	62.3	66.3	78.5	69.6	45.8	49.8	45.4	55.9	47.8
Prefer Job B	Percent	42.8	32.1	30.1	18.6	24.4	48.3	46.0	50.5	38.9	44.9

MOW Target Group Sample Responses — '**' Indicates Data Missing and/or Unavailable (continued)

		Target Group									
		Unem-ployed	Retired	Chemical Engineers	Teachers	Self-Employed	Tool and Die	White-Collar	Textile	Tempo-rary	Students
Q41: Job Choice Number 9											
**Missing Data	Percent	2.0	2.6	0.9	1.1	1.2	1.8	0.4	2.2	1.1	0.8
Either Job	Percent	11.2	12.9	7.1	7.4	10.4	9.4	8.6	9.5	7.7	9.1
Prefer Job A	Percent	62.8	57.8	73.0	78.8	64.4	62.5	67.9	53.1	70.3	64.4
Prefer Job B	Percent	24.1	26.7	18.9	12.7	24.1	26.3	23.0	35.2	20.9	25.7
Q42: Job Choice Number 10											
**Missing Data	Percent	2.3	3.0	0.9	1.5	1.2	2.0	0.9	2.7	0.6	0.3
Either Job	Percent	8.8	9.4	7.7	8.1	8.6	9.0	7.6	6.1	9.7	7.4
Prefer Job A	Percent	40.1	39.1	37.5	59.0	45.3	31.9	40.1	31.8	46.9	35.5
Prefer Job B	Percent	48.7	48.5	53.9	31.3	45.0	57.0	51.4	59.4	42.8	56.8
Q43: Job Choice Number 11											
**Missing Data	Percent	2.2	3.3	0.7	0.6	0.6	1.8	0.4	2.2	0.9	0.3
Either Job	Percent	7.4	4.5	2.4	1.4	1.5	4.8	2.6	4.8	3.0	3.5
Prefer Job A	Percent	17.4	9.9	6.2	5.4	10.7	13.4	10.6	19.4	12.0	11.5
Prefer Job B	Percent	73.0	82.2	90.7	92.6	87.2	79.9	86.3	73.6	84.1	84.6
Q44: Job Choice Number 12											
**Missing Data	Percent	2.0	3.0	1.1	0.5	1.1	1.8	0.3	2.9	0.6	0.2
Either Job	Percent	5.4	3.1	1.1	0.9	0.8	3.2	1.9	3.9	1.3	1.9
Prefer Job A	Percent	11.2	7.3	3.8	3.2	7.5	9.0	8.2	12.1	8.6	4.7
Prefer Job B	Percent	81.5	86.6	94.0	95.4	90.7	86.0	89.6	81.1	89.5	93.2
Q45: Job Choice Number 13											
**Missing Data	Percent	2.0	3.0	1.3	0.5	0.5	2.0	0.1	2.7	0.6	0.2
Either Job	Percent	3.8	2.3	0.5	0.5	0.9	2.0	0.7	2.6	0.9	0.8
Prefer Job A	Percent	7.9	4.7	1.5	2.5	6.0	4.3	5.0	9.0	4.7	2.4
Prefer Job B	Percent	86.3	90.1	96.7	96.6	92.6	91.6	94.1	85.7	93.8	96.6

MOW Target Group Sample Responses — '**' Indicates Data Missing and/or Unavailable (continued)

				Target Group							
		Unem-ployed	Retired	Chemical Engineers	Teachers	Self-Employed	Tool and Die	White-Collar	Textile	Tempo-rary	Students
Q46: Job Choice Number 14											
**Missing Data	Percent	2.5	2.3	0.5	0.5	0.8	1.8	0.1	2.2	1.1	0.0
Either Job	Percent	4.7	4.2	1.6	1.2	2.3	3.0	2.9	3.9	1.7	2.4
Prefer Job A	Percent	9.9	5.2	3.5	2.8	7.5	10.4	8.6	15.0	9.5	7.1
Prefer Job B	Percent	82.9	88.3	94.4	95.6	89.5	84.8	88.3	78.9	87.7	90.5
Q47A: Employer Responsible for Retraining											
**Missing Data	Percent	1.1	1.7	0.4	0.5	1.5	1.7	0.7	2.0	1.3	0.3
Strongly Disagree	Percent	2.5	1.7	1.1	2.0	6.9	2.8	2.4	2.2	1.5	1.0
Disagree	Percent	7.4	8.4	11.8	8.4	17.7	11.0	7.1	7.0	11.2	9.5
Agree	Percent	48.9	47.6	54.8	50.0	41.5	51.8	52.8	45.2	54.0	61.7
Strongly Agree	Percent	40.1	40.5	31.9	39.1	32.3	32.6	37.0	43.5	32.0	27.5
Q47B: Duty of Every Able Citizen to Work											
**Missing Data	Percent	0.9	0.5	0.5	0.5	0.6	1.8	0.6	1.4	0.9	0.3
Strongly Disagree	Percent	7.0	1.6	2.2	4.4	4.8	3.2	4.0	2.9	6.2	4.7
Disagree	Percent	12.9	4.9	11.3	16.6	9.6	7.7	13.2	7.3	25.2	17.6
Agree	Percent	48.7	36.3	39.0	39.9	28.7	41.6	41.4	44.6	44.9	43.2
Strongly Agree	Percent	30.4	56.7	47.0	38.7	56.2	45.7	40.7	43.9	22.8	34.1
Q47C: Society Obliged To Educate for Job											
**Missing Data	Percent	1.6	0.9	0.7	1.1	1.4	1.5	0.3	1.4	0.9	0.7
Strongly Disagree	Percent	2.3	1.2	1.3	1.5	2.0	0.7	0.7	0.7	1.3	2.5
Disagree	Percent	7.9	5.1	9.7	8.3	7.2	5.4	5.8	9.4	8.0	9.1
Agree	Percent	46.6	43.1	54.6	42.6	40.0	52.3	51.1	47.3	52.3	49.8
Strongly Agree	Percent	41.5	49.7	33.7	46.5	49.5	40.1	42.2	41.3	37.6	37.8

MOW Target Group Sample Responses — '**' Indicates Data Missing and/or Unavailable (continued)

					Target Group					
		Unemployed	Retired	Chemical Engineers	Teachers	Self-Employed	Tool and Die	White-Collar	Textile	Temporary	Students
Q47D: Persons Should Save For Future											
**Missing Data	Percent	2.0	0.5	1.5	0.5	0.9	1.7	0.1	1.9	1.9	0.5
Strongly Disagree	Percent	11.7	3.3	6.6	8.3	8.4	7.4	6.3	5.8	7.5	10.1
Disagree	Percent	28.6	16.4	37.3	38.7	25.9	33.8	32.4	23.1	33.3	35.8
Agree	Percent	41.4	47.3	46.3	41.4	41.2	39.6	45.3	46.4	42.4	41.9
Strongly Agree	Percent	16.4	32.5	8.4	11.2	23.6	17.6	15.8	22.8	14.8	11.7
Q47E: Super Should Consult Workers re Changes											
**Missing Data	Percent	1.3	0.9	0.4	0.0	1.4	1.3	0.1	1.5	0.9	0.3
Strongly Disagree	Percent	0.7	2.1	2.6	0.2	3.8	1.3	0.4	2.7	1.1	1.0
Disagree	Percent	7.6	8.7	14.6	3.5	13.4	6.4	8.5	11.1	8.4	6.6
Agree	Percent	48.7	47.8	50.1	37.9	47.2	46.8	39.3	41.5	46.2	43.9
Strongly Agree	Percent	41.7	40.5	32.4	58.4	34.3	44.1	51.7	43.2	43.4	48.1
Q47F: Worker Should Improve Work Methods											
**Missing Data	Percent	1.8	0.9	0.4	0.3	1.1	1.5	0.3	2.6	1.1	0.3
Strongly Disagree	Percent	1.8	0.5	1.3	0.5	2.4	0.7	0.4	3.2	0.4	1.0
Disagree	Percent	9.2	4.7	8.2	10.4	6.3	6.7	8.2	8.2	9.9	13.9
Agree	Percent	52.9	48.3	57.9	54.9	47.2	55.9	55.5	54.6	57.0	57.6
Strongly Agree	Percent	34.4	45.5	32.2	33.9	43.0	35.3	35.5	31.5	31.6	27.2

MOW Target Group Sample Responses — '**' Indicates Data Missing and/or Unavailable (continued)

		Target Group									
		Unemployed	Retired	Chemical Engineers	Teachers	Self-Employed	Tool and Die	White-Collar	Textile	Temporary	Students
Q47G: All Entitled to Meaningful Work											
**Missing Data	Percent	1.3	0.9	1.3	0.6	1.2	1.5	0.6	1.5	1.1	0.8
Strongly Disagree	Percent	1.8	1.9	2.2	0.3	3.5	1.3	1.6	0.9	1.3	0.7
Disagree	Percent	7.9	12.9	18.8	8.4	11.4	9.2	12.4	10.0	13.8	9.3
Agree	Percent	43.7	48.0	51.2	42.0	45.3	50.0	51.2	45.7	48.6	45.9
Strongly Agree	Percent	45.3	36.3	26.6	48.6	38.6	38.0	34.2	41.8	35.3	43.2
Q47H: Mon ot Work OK If Pay Compensates											
**Missing Data	Percent	2.0	1.7	1.1	0.8	1.5	2.7	0.3	2.2	1.7	1.9
Strongly Disagree	Percent	11.9	9.6	4.6	10.0	9.6	6.4	7.6	6.1	11.6	13.5
Disagree	Percent	30.8	25.7	36.6	35.9	27.7	29.9	35.4	21.8	32.7	29.4
Agree	Percent	41.2	48.9	47.7	44.0	45.9	47.2	43.3	48.3	43.4	44.6
Strongly Agree	Percent	14.2	14.1	10.0	9.4	15.3	13.9	13.4	21.6	10.5	10.6
Q47I: Job Should Be Provided Everyone											
**Missing Data	Percent	1.3	1.4	0.7	0.2	0.9	1.7	0.1	1.2	0.4	0.3
Strongly Disagree	Percent	0.5	0.9	2.0	0.6	1.5	1.2	0.6	0.5	1.5	1.5
Disagree	Percent	3.4	3.8	9.1	3.4	4.4	2.7	4.0	3.4	4.7	6.3
Agree	Percent	29.3	38.7	47.2	35.4	41.2	40.5	43.2	35.2	42.6	39.9
Strongly Agree	Percent	65.5	55.1	41.0	60.4	52.0	54.0	52.1	59.7	50.8	52.0
Q47J: Worker Should Value Any Work Done											
**Missing Data	Percent	1.6	1.2	0.9	0.6	1.5	1.7	0.4	1.2	1.5	0.7
Strongly Disagree	Percent	19.4	8.6	14.0	21.0	15.2	9.9	15.7	8.3	16.6	24.3
Disagree	Percent	28.2	26.5	33.2	34.0	23.6	29.1	31.5	20.4	32.9	31.1
Agree	Percent	31.3	44.0	37.5	30.1	34.0	42.8	36.4	41.5	33.1	31.9
Strongly Agree	Percent	19.4	19.7	14.4	14.3	25.7	16.6	16.0	28.6	15.9	12.0

MOW Target Group Sample Responses — '**' Indicates Data Missing and/or Unavailable (continued)

		Target Group									
		Unem-ployed	Retired	Chemical Engineers	Teachers	Self-Employed	Tool and Die	White-Collar	Textile	Tempo-rary	Students
Q48A: If You Had Money Would You Work											
**Missing Data	Percent	3.2	1.9	0.9	0.0	1.4	1.7	0.7	1.7	0.2	1.4
Stop	Percent	13.1	15.9	5.5	10.9	7.8	13.0	14.0	18.7	15.1	9.3
Continue Same Job	Percent	32.0	52.0	45.0	49.1	45.3	37.6	44.2	43.5	34.2	42.9
Continue—Diff Conditions	Percent	51.6	30.2	48.6	40.0	45.6	47.7	41.2	36.1	50.5	46.5
Q49A–N: Is An Activity	Number of Responses	556	573	549	652	665	598	695	588	465	592
Q49A: . . . If In A Working Place? Work											
**Missing Data	Percent	0.2	0.0	0.4	0.3	1.2	0.5	0.1	0.9	0.2	0.5
No, Is Not Work	Percent	80.2	79.4	82.5	81.6	75.6	71.1	68.9	63.4	75.5	77.7
Yes, Is Work	Percent	19.6	20.6	17.1	18.1	23.2	28.4	30.9	35.7	24.3	21.8
Q49B: . . . If Told To Do It?											
**Missing Data	Percent	0.2	0.0	0.4	0.3	1.2	0.5	0.1	0.9	0.2	0.5
No, Is Not Work	Percent	85.3	90.8	92.9	94.2	92.5	85.6	87.9	83.2	88.0	86.0
Yes, Is Work	Percent	14.6	9.2	6.7	5.5	6.3	13.9	11.9	16.0	11.8	13.5
Q49C: . . . If Phys Strenuous?											
**Missing Data	Percent	0.2	0.0	0.4	0.3	1.2	0.5	0.1	0.9	0.2	0.5
No, Is Not Work	Percent	76.4	85.9	89.8	86.3	83.0	78.4	86.2	77.2	85.8	73.8
Yes, Is Work	Percent	23.4	14.1	9.8	13.3	15.8	21.1	13.7	21.9	14.0	25.7
Q49D: . . . If Part Of Task?											
**Missing Data	Percent	0.2	0.0	0.4	0.3	1.2	0.5	0.1	1.0	0.2	0.5
No, Is Not Work	Percent	55.2	46.4	47.0	41.7	49.8	52.3	53.5	51.9	53.1	54.4
Yes, Is Work	Percent	44.6	53.6	52.6	58.0	49.0	47.2	46.3	47.1	46.7	45.1

MOW Target Group Sample Responses — '***' Indicates Data Missing and/or Unavailable (continued)

		Target Group									
		Unemployed	Retired	Chemical Engineers	Teachers	Self-Employed	Tool and Die	White-Collar	Textile	Temporary	Students
Q49E: . . . If Contributes To Society?											
**Missing Data	Percent	0.2	0.0	0.4	0.3	1.4	0.5	0.1	0.9	0.2	0.5
No, Is Not Work	Percent	70.7	49.9	61.0	56.3	67.5	65.1	67.6	65.1	72.0	68.4
Yes, Is Work	Percent	29.1	50.1	38.6	43.4	31.1	34.4	32.2	34.0	27.7	31.1
Q49F: . . . If Feeling Of Belonging?											
**Missing Data	Percent	0.2	0.0	0.4	0.5	1.4	0.7	0.1	0.9	0.2	0.5
No, Is Not Work	Percent	69.1	66.7	78.7	70.1	72.6	74.9	73.7	71.3	73.1	75.2
Yes, Is Work	Percent	30.8	33.3	20.9	29.4	26.0	24.4	26.2	27.9	26.7	24.3
Q49G: . . . If Ment Strenuous?											
**Missing Data	Percent	0.2	0.0	0.4	0.5	1.2	0.5	0.3	0.9	0.2	0.5
No, Is Not Work	Percent	82.7	79.4	74.0	74.8	77.9	82.9	78.8	86.6	78.9	74.7
Yes, Is Work	Percent	17.1	20.6	25.7	24.7	20.9	16.6	20.9	12.6	20.9	24.8
Q49H: . . . If At Certain Time?											
**Missing Data	Percent	0.2	0.0	0.4	0.5	1.2	0.5	0.3	0.9	0.2	0.5
No, Is Not Work	Percent	76.1	77.8	86.0	81.1	82.9	77.6	75.4	72.6	67.5	74.0
Yes, Is Work	Percent	23.7	22.2	13.7	18.4	15.9	21.9	24.3	26.5	32.3	25.5
Q49I: . . . If It Adds Value?											
**Missing Data	Percent	0.2	0.2	0.4	0.3	1.2	0.5	0.1	1.0	0.4	0.7
No, Is Not Work	Percent	59.0	56.2	39.2	49.5	48.4	63.0	58.1	68.2	57.6	59.0
Yes, Is Work	Percent	40.8	43.6	60.5	50.2	50.4	36.5	41.7	30.8	41.9	40.4
Q49J: . . . If Not Pleasant?											
**Missing Data	Percent	0.2	0.0	0.4	0.3	1.2	0.5	0.3	0.9	0.2	0.7
No, Is Not Work	Percent	94.8	96.9	96.5	96.2	94.9	94.1	95.7	94.9	96.1	93.6
Yes, Is Work	Percent	5.0	3.1	3.1	3.5	3.9	5.4	4.0	4.3	3.7	5.7

MOW Target Group Sample Responses — '**' Indicates Data Missing and/or Unavailable (continued)

		Target Group									
		Unem-ployed	Retired	Chemical Engineers	Teachers	Self-Employed	Tool and Die	White-Collar	Textile	Tempo-rary	Students
Q49K: . . . If You Get Money?											
**Missing Data	Percent	0.2	0.0	0.4	0.3	1.4	0.5	0.3	0.9	0.2	0.7
No, Is Not Work	Percent	37.1	43.6	41.2	51.7	38.5	30.3	33.4	28.6	30.5	30.4
Yes, Is Work	Percent	62.8	56.4	58.5	48.0	60.2	69.2	66.3	70.6	69.2	68.9
Q49L: . . . If You Must Account?											
**Missing Data	Percent	0.2	0.0	0.4	0.3	1.2	0.5	0.3	0.9	0.2	0.5
No, Is Not Work	Percent	71.2	73.3	55.4	58.7	62.6	67.6	63.5	77.9	65.6	71.1
Yes, Is Work	Percent	28.6	26.7	44.3	41.0	36.2	31.9	36.3	21.3	34.2	28.4
Q49M: If You Must Do It?											
**Missing Data	Percent	0.2	0.0	0.4	0.3	1.2	0.5	0.3	0.9	0.2	0.5
No, Is Not Work	Percent	81.7	82.9	85.1	86.3	81.2	82.4	83.2	77.9	81.9	82.3
Yes, Is Work	Percent	18.2	17.1	14.6	13.3	17.6	17.1	16.5	21.3	17.8	17.2
Q49N: . . . If Others Profit?											
**Missing Data	Percent	0.2	0.2	0.4	0.5	1.2	0.5	0.3	0.9	0.2	0.5
No, Is Not Work	Percent	82.4	81.3	74.1	72.7	73.1	79.4	78.4	80.8	80.6	79.6
Yes, Is Work	Percent	17.4	18.5	25.5	26.8	25.7	20.1	21.3	18.4	19.1	19.9
Q50A: Would Choose Occupation Again?											
**Missing Data	Percent	3.2	2.3	1.8	2.8	2.0	2.7	1.3	1.7	2.6	4.4
Different Occupation	Percent	61.9	33.7	45.0	28.7	36.4	50.8	54.0	64.1	61.7	38.0
Same Occupation	Percent	34.9	64.0	53.2	68.6	61.7	46.5	44.7	34.2	35.7	57.6
Q50B: Would Recommend Occupation to Your Child?											
**Missing Data	Percent	4.3	2.3	2.0	4.3	3.3	2.8	1.6	1.7	4.5	100.0
No	Percent	64.9	52.5	52.5	51.1	53.4	64.9	63.2	86.1	66.7	**
Yes	Percent	30.8	45.2	45.5	44.6	43.3	32.3	35.3	12.2	28.8	**

MOW Target Group Sample Responses — '**' Indicates Data Missing and/or Unavailable (continued)

		Unem-ployed	Retired	Chemical Engineers	Teachers	Self-Employed	Tool and Die	White-Collar	Textile	Tempo-rary	Students
Q51A: Will Your Work Attitude Change?											
**Missing Data	Percent	3.2	5.6	2.4	3.8	3.2	2.7	2.4	3.6	3.4	1.0
No	Percent	34.7	29.0	42.8	35.3	29.9	40.5	48.3	43.5	42.2	45.9
Yes	Percent	62.1	65.4	54.8	60.9	66.9	56.9	49.2	52.9	54.4	53.0
Q52: Preference—Job vs Organization											
**Missing Data	Percent	100.0	100.0	4.4	100.0	100.0	6.2	3.3	4.1	14.2	100.0
Stay With Different Job	Percent	**	**	45.2	**	**	48.8	72.1	70.9	51.6	**
Same Job Diff Organization	Percent	**	**	50.5	**	**	45.0	24.6	25.0	34.2	**
Q53: Leisure—Activity Unrelated To Work											
**Missing Data	Percent	100.0	100.0	0.2	0.3	1.4	1.2	0.3	0.5	0.4	3.0
Never	Percent	**	**	1.6	3.7	6.5	6.0	6.3	9.9	3.7	4.1
Only Occasionally	Percent	**	**	9.7	18.7	17.4	13.2	10.9	12.4	3.2	9.6
Sometimes	Percent	**	**	25.5	29.0	26.3	24.6	18.8	19.9	13.8	25.5
Often	Percent	**	**	34.2	33.7	25.3	33.9	30.6	20.6	31.2	34.8
Very Often	Percent	**	**	28.8	14.6	23.2	21.1	32.9	36.7	47.7	23.0
Q54: Partic In Co Activities Out Of Work?											
**Missing Data	Percent	100.0	100.0	0.5	0.9	27.1	0.7	0.6	0.5	0.4	3.2
No	Percent	**	**	15.8	11.7	10.7	16.6	13.8	20.1	27.5	5.2
Maybe	Percent	**	**	43.2	41.1	21.4	46.0	43.9	31.8	39.4	44.3
Yes	Percent	**	**	40.4	46.3	40.9	36.8	41.7	47.6	32.7	47.3

MOW Target Group Sample Responses — '**' Indicates Data Missing and/or Unavailable (continued)

					Target Group					
		Unemployed	Retired	Chemical Engineers	Teachers	Self-Employed	Tool and Die	White-Collar	Textile	Temporary	Students
Q55: Worry About Work in Free Time?											
**Missing Data	Percent	7.7	100.0	0.2	1.1	2.3	1.2	0.6	0.3	0.6	0.5
Never	Percent	9.2	**	5.3	5.4	10.2	17.2	10.1	19.0	23.7	8.3
Only Occasionally	Percent	10.1	**	20.8	7.4	13.2	24.2	21.6	15.5	28.0	19.3
Sometimes	Percent	21.4	**	41.3	29.1	24.2	37.1	41.9	37.8	28.8	41.7
Often	Percent	28.2	**	26.2	38.8	28.7	16.1	20.7	19.0	13.8	23.5
Very Often	Percent	23.4	**	6.2	18.3	21.4	4.2	5.2	8.3	5.2	6.8
Q56A: Change—Or Start—Job In Next Year?											
**Missing Data	Percent	8.3	100.0	3.3	0.3	1.7	1.3	0.4	0.5	3.0	4.6
No	Percent	38.8	**	83.8	93.3	94.0	87.5	85.9	88.1	47.3	25.2
Yes	Percent	52.9	**	12.9	6.4	4.4	11.2	13.7	11.4	49.7	70.3
Q57: Easy To Find Job?											
**Missing Data	Percent	8.3	100.0	2.2	4.8	100.0	2.7	1.7	2.0	3.2	4.2
Difficult	Percent	39.9	**	32.1	40.2	**	22.7	33.1	53.1	24.3	19.9
Not So Easy	Percent	29.1	**	30.4	26.8	**	27.8	31.7	24.1	23.9	42.7
Somewhat Easy	Percent	9.2	**	13.3	11.8	**	15.2	14.1	7.5	15.9	18.6
Easy	Percent	8.1	**	13.5	11.8	**	18.2	13.2	9.0	18.1	9.6
Very Easy	Percent	5.4	**	8.6	4.6	**	13.4	6.2	4.3	14.6	4.9
Q58A: Willing To Retrain?											
**Missing Data	Percent	10.1	100.0	0.4	1.2	2.9	1.7	0.7	1.0	3.2	2.2
Under No Conditions	Percent	9.5	**	8.6	24.7	31.6	12.5	12.7	22.3	9.0	10.3
Only If Necessary	Percent	27.0	**	45.5	31.4	45.6	48.0	42.3	43.7	29.7	46.6
Under Certain Conditions	Percent	53.4	**	45.5	42.6	20.0	37.8	44.3	33.0	58.1	40.9

MOW Target Group Sample Responses — '**' Indicates Data Missing and/or Unavailable (continued)

		Target Group									
		Unemployed	Retired	Chemical Engineers	Teachers	Self-Employed	Tool and Die	White-Collar	Textile	Temporary	Students
Q59: Intend To Retrain—Different Job—This Year?											
**Missing Data	Percent	11.2	100.0	0.4	1.7	3.2	2.0	0.9	1.4	4.1	100.0
No	Percent	44.6	**	93.4	92.9	92.3	87.6	87.5	85.7	67.5	**
Yes	Percent	44.2	**	6.2	5.4	4.5	10.4	11.7	12.9	28.4	**
Q60: Intend to Retrain—This Job—This Year?											
**Missing Data	Percent	9.2	100.0	0.4	0.9	3.0	1.7	0.7	1.4	1.1	1.9
No	Percent	63.7	**	40.1	32.7	65.1	61.9	47.5	72.8	68.6	48.5
Yes	Percent	21.6	**	43.0	41.3	26.0	29.6	37.8	17.9	22.8	48.3
Already Training	Percent	5.6	**	16.6	25.2	5.9	6.9	14.0	8.0	7.5	1.4
Q61: Try To Be Promoted This Year?											
**Missing Data	Percent	100.0	100.0	0.9	2.0	100.0	2.5	0.7	1.5	4.3	5.2
No	Percent	**	**	54.8	75.8	**	55.5	56.1	59.5	54.6	33.4
Yes	Percent	**	**	44.3	22.2	**	42.0	43.2	38.9	41.1	61.3
Q62A: Significant Plans re Works—5 Years?											
**Missing Data	Percent	100.0	100.0	1.3	0.5	1.7	1.8	0.7	1.5	1.7	1.5
No	Percent	**	**	61.2	70.9	59.4	73.2	69.1	83.2	66.5	62.3
Yes	Percent	**	**	37.5	28.7	38.9	24.9	30.2	15.3	31.8	36.1
Q63: Worse Employment Situation?											
**Missing Data	Percent	9.9	100.0	0.9	2.8	5.7	2.7	4.2	6.8	2.8	2.0
No	Percent	38.5	**	63.6	70.9	61.7	70.2	73.5	49.0	55.1	53.2
Yes	Percent	51.6	**	35.5	26.4	32.6	27.1	22.3	44.2	42.2	44.8

MOW Target Group Sample Responses — '**' Indicates Data Missing and/or Unavailable (continued)

						Target Group					
		Unem-ployed	Retired	Chemical Engineers	Teachers	Self-Employed	Tool and Die	White-Collar	Textile	Tempo-rary	Students
Q64: Improved Employment Situation?											
**Missing Data	Percent	10.3	100.0	1.6	2.6	5.6	3.2	1.7	2.6	5.4	4.1
No	Percent	61.5	**	64.5	74.2	64.1	59.9	66.2	64.1	66.2	55.1
Yes	Percent	28.2	**	33.9	23.2	30.4	37.0	32.1	33.3	28.4	40.9
Q65: Level of Pay Expectations											
**Missing Data	Percent	7.7	100.0	0.4	0.5	2.9	1.7	0.1	1.0	1.7	1.5
Go Down	Percent	12.1	**	17.5	23.2	16.2	9.4	8.6	11.7	6.2	4.2
Stay Same	Percent	52.0	**	64.3	63.0	56.5	59.9	61.0	67.5	64.1	56.3
Go Up	Percent	28.2	**	17.9	13.3	24.4	29.1	30.2	19.7	28.0	38.0
Q66A: Imp to You Of Work— Next 5–10 Years											
**Missing Data	Percent	8.1	100.0	0.4	0.3	1.7	3.5	0.7	0.9	1.3	10.8
Less Imp	Percent	13.8	**	10.2	14.6	15.0	9.7	12.4	12.2	15.9	8.6
Equal In Imp	Percent	43.0	**	68.5	73.8	64.8	61.2	61.7	56.3	56.3	34.3
More Imp	Percent	35.1	**	20.9	11.3	18.5	25.6	25.2	30.6	26.5	46.3

MOW Target Group Sample Responses — '**' Indicates Data Missing and/or Unavailable (continued)

		Target Group									
		Unem- ployed	Retired	Chemical Engineers	Teachers	Self- Employed	Tool and Die	White- Collar	Textile	Tempo- rary	Students
Q67: Alternative If Same Pay/ Less Hours?											
**Missing Data	Percent	5.9	100.0	0.2	0.6	2.7	1.7	0.6	0.7	0.2	1.7
More Holidays	Percent	18.9	**	35.0	13.0	23.0	23.9	29.8	21.6	31.4	32.4
Less Working Hours	Percent	32.2	**	18.2	33.3	24.7	27.6	33.2	23.8	35.3	29.1
A Free Aft Per Week	Percent	8.5	**	13.3	11.0	12.6	11.2	12.7	10.7	14.4	14.4
More Ed B4 Work	Percent	4.7	**	2.2	1.5	3.5	1.7	2.7	3.9	3.0	4.1
Year of Study Per 10	Percent	4.1	**	17.1	10.3	4.8	3.0	3.3	2.7	4.7	4.9
Less Hours For Older	Percent	12.4	**	5.1	10.4	10.7	8.7	4.3	9.7	5.8	4.9
Early Retirement	Percent	13.3	**	8.9	19.8	18.0	22.2	13.4	26.9	5.2	8.6
Q68: Less Hours/Less Pay— Attitude											
**Missing Data	Percent	5.8	100.0	0.5	0.5	2.0	1.5	0.6	0.5	0.6	1.2
Against Them	Percent	34.4	**	46.3	36.0	41.8	62.7	48.5	61.2	39.1	50.0
Dont Care	Percent	12.9	**	9.8	12.4	13.8	9.5	9.4	9.5	16.8	17.2
Moderately In Favour	Percent	24.5	**	24.8	36.5	28.0	19.1	33.1	18.5	30.5	23.0
In Favour	Percent	22.5	**	18.6	14.6	14.4	7.2	8.5	10.2	12.9	8.6
Q69: Your Age											
**Missing Data	Percent	2.2	0.3	0.2	0.5	0.2	1.0	0.1	0.9	0.2	0.5
30 & Under	Percent	41.7	0.0	28.8	39.0	14.1	36.3	66.4	39.5	66.2	99.3
31–50	Percent	39.6	0.2	63.0	53.5	56.4	51.5	28.2	45.7	29.5	0.2
Over 50	Percent	16.5	99.5	8.0	7.0	29.3	11.2	5.3	13.9	4.1	0.0
Q270: Highest Formal Education											
**Missing Data	Percent	2.0	0.5	0.0	0.0	0.2	1.0	0.1	0.5	0.0	5.7
Primary School	Percent	20.9	18.3	0.0	0.3	11.7	6.2	4.5	49.8	3.4	24.3
Secondary School	Percent	53.8	35.4	2.0	8.9	54.6	79.9	63.9	42.3	42.2	52.7
Some College or Votech	Percent	18.2	29.1	11.7	50.8	16.8	12.2	17.6	6.3	33.3	16.9
University Degree	Percent	5.2	16.6	86.3	40.0	16.7	0.7	14.0	1.0	21.1	0.3

MOW Target Group Sample Responses — '***' Indicates Data Missing and/or Unavailable (continued)

		Target Group									
		Unemployed	Retired	Chemical Engineers	Teachers	Self-Employed	Tool and Die	White-Collar	Textile	Temporary	Students
Q71: Religious Education?											
**Missing Data	Percent	1.4	0.5	0.5	0.3	0.8	2.0	0.6	0.7	0.9	5.7
No	Percent	47.3	40.7	52.6	43.9	42.9	43.8	50.8	38.3	48.8	51.0
Yes	Percent	51.3	58.8	46.8	55.8	56.4	54.2	48.6	61.1	50.3	43.2
Q72: Present Association With Religion											
**Missing Data	Percent	2.0	0.3	0.4	0.3	0.3	1.7	0.4	1.0	1.9	5.4
No Contact	Percent	49.8	28.8	53.0	47.5	43.9	46.5	53.8	40.5	51.2	38.3
Loose Contact	Percent	35.6	42.4	29.1	30.2	41.2	42.6	32.9	43.2	34.0	48.3
Close Contact	Percent	12.6	28.4	17.5	21.9	14.6	9.2	12.8	15.3	12.9	7.9
Q73A: Highest Ed—Father											
**Missing Data	Percent	8.6	4.2	0.2	2.1	3.9	5.0	1.3	5.8	3.9	12.8
Primary School	Percent	41.2	56.0	27.0	28.5	41.1	50.7	32.7	64.1	23.9	25.0
Secondary School	Percent	33.3	25.7	39.5	39.4	38.8	37.3	46.8	26.5	40.6	45.1
Some College or Votech	Percent	10.4	9.1	13.1	16.4	9.2	4.5	10.2	2.6	14.8	11.0
University Degree	Percent	6.5	5.1	20.2	13.5	7.1	2.5	9.1	1.0	16.8	6.1
Q73B: Highest Ed—Mother											
**Missing Data	Percent	7.6	3.8	0.5	1.7	4.2	5.0	1.2	4.9	2.2	12.7
Primary School	Percent	48.9	69.3	35.5	37.9	51.0	62.5	41.3	68.2	30.8	28.4
Secondary School	Percent	36.2	19.5	47.9	44.6	35.8	29.4	47.5	25.3	48.8	46.1
Some College or Votech	Percent	5.4	6.5	8.9	11.8	6.5	2.3	7.6	1.4	11.6	9.8
University Degree	Percent	2.0	0.9	7.1	4.0	2.6	0.7	2.4	0.2	6.7	3.0
Q74: Size of Childhood Community											
**Missing Data	Percent	1.6	0.3	0.0	0.3	0.2	1.5	0.4	0.5	0.0	1.7
City	Percent	59.5	43.6	51.2	48.5	50.2	36.3	55.8	28.1	62.2	56.3
Village	Percent	23.2	32.6	32.8	28.4	28.0	33.8	27.5	41.3	28.8	29.9
Rural	Percent	15.6	23.4	16.0	22.9	21.7	28.4	16.3	30.1	9.0	12.2

MOW Target Group Sample Responses — '**' Indicates Data Missing and/or Unavailable (continued)

		Unem-ployed	Retired	Chemical Engineers	Teachers	Self-Employed	Tool and Die	White-Collar	Textile	Tempo-rary	Students
Q75: Size of Present Community											
**Missing Data	Percent	1.1	0.5	0.0	0.0	0.2	1.0	0.3	0.3	0.4	1.2
City	Percent	84.0	76.8	57.7	74.1	70.2	45.8	68.6	41.2	79.1	58.1
Village	Percent	13.1	19.5	33.0	18.3	23.5	36.1	22.9	42.2	17.0	28.2
Rural	Percent	1.8	3.1	9.3	7.7	6.2	17.1	8.2	16.3	3.4	12.5
Q76A: Married or Partnership?											
**Missing Data	Percent	2.0	1.2	0.0	0.3	0.3	1.2	0.4	0.5	0.4	24.3
No	Percent	48.2	26.9	17.9	33.1	13.5	25.3	40.3	29.4	43.9	70.6
Yes	Percent	49.8	71.9	82.1	66.6	86.2	73.6	59.3	70.1	55.7	5.1
Q76B: If Yes is Partner Employed?											
**Missing Data	Percent	51.4	31.6	18.0	34.2	14.3	27.3	40.9	30.4	45.6	95.1
Not Employed	Percent	14.2	44.7	34.1	1.4	28.4	27.8	12.5	20.6	1.5	0.0
Part Time Employ	Percent	5.4	4.5	13.8	4.0	17.4	15.6	4.3	10.2	2.6	0.2
Full Time	Percent	22.1	8.2	30.8	55.1	34.0	26.3	38.3	34.9	44.1	4.4
Other	Percent	6.8	11.0	3.3	5.4	5.9	3.2	4.0	3.9	6.2	0.3

MOW Target Group Sample Responses — '**' Indicates Data Missing and/or Unavailable (continued)

					Target Group					
		Unem- ployed	Retired	Chemical Engineers	Teachers	Self- Employed	Tool and Die	White- Collar	Textile	Tempo- rary	Students
Q78: General Life Satisfaction											
**Missing Data	Percent	3.8	1.6	1.3	0.6	1.2	1.3	0.4	0.7	0.9	3.4
1: Very Dissatisfied	Percent	5.9	1.4	0.7	0.5	1.4	1.5	1.0	1.2	0.4	1.7
2: (On 1–to–9 Scale)	Percent	3.1	0.7	1.1	0.5	0.6	1.0	0.9	1.7	0.6	1.7
3: (On 1–to–9 Scale)	Percent	5.0	1.6	3.6	1.5	3.0	2.8	2.3	3.2	4.1	3.4
4: (On 1–to–9 Scale)	Percent	6.8	1.9	2.4	3.8	2.7	2.7	4.3	4.4	4.1	3.5
5: (On 1–to–9 Scale)	Percent	24.1	18.0	12.0	10.1	13.7	17.1	15.8	21.1	13.8	12.7
6: (On 1–to–9 Scale)	Percent	11.0	8.4	10.9	12.0	9.8	10.9	14.5	10.7	10.8	9.8
7: (On 1–to–9 Scale)	Percent	17.1	20.2	30.1	27.9	21.7	25.4	24.5	14.3	24.7	20.3
8: (On 1–to–9 Scale)	Percent	11.2	16.6	27.7	23.2	18.9	16.7	19.3	15.5	17.4	25.8
9: Very Satisfied	Percent	12.1	29.7	10.2	19.9	27.1	20.6	17.0	27.2	23.2	17.7
Q82: Sex of Resp											
**Missing Data	Percent	0.9	1.6	0.4	0.2	0.2	0.7	1.2	0.3	0.0	1.0
Male	Percent	51.6	52.4	90.9	0.0	95.6	98.5	44.6	49.7	1.7	54.7
Female	Percent	47.5	46.1	8.7	99.8	4.2	0.8	54.2	50.0	98.3	44.3
Q83B: Type of Self Employment											
**Missing Data	Percent	100.0	100.0	100.0	100.0	2.7	100.0	100.0	100.0	100.0	100.0
Craftsman	Percent	**	**	**	**	19.8	**	**	**	**	**
Service	Percent	**	**	**	**	28.7	**	**	**	**	**
Commercial	Percent	**	**	**	**	48.7	**	**	**	**	**
Q84A: Ownership of Work Organization											
**Missing Data	Percent	63.5	32.8	5.5	9.5	7.5	9.7	2.3	8.5	8.0	100.0
Public	Percent	11.9	32.1	30.2	81.3	2.9	17.6	27.9	21.6	31.8	**
Private	Percent	24.6	35.1	64.3	9.2	89.6	72.7	69.8	69.9	60.2	**

MOW Target Group Sample Responses — '**' Indicates Data Missing and/or Unavailable (continued)

					Target Group					
		Unem-ployed	Retired	Chemical Engineers	Teachers	Self-Employed	Tool and Die	White-Collar	Textile	Tempo-rary	Students
Q84B: Size of Work Organization											
**Missing Data	Percent	64.2	32.1	12.2	13.0	17.6	4.7	2.6	2.0	18.7	100.0
Under 100 Employees	Percent	23.7	35.6	10.2	80.1	82.1	24.9	26.9	21.9	29.9	**
100–299	Percent	4.5	7.3	10.0	3.7	0.2	16.7	11.8	27.2	13.3	**
300–999	Percent	3.2	5.2	21.1	0.5	0.0	9.7	28.1	24.8	10.5	**
1000 or More	Percent	4.3	19.7	46.4	2.8	0.2	44.0	30.6	24.0	27.5	**
Number of Responses		506	527	476	593	606	551	651	540	369	572
Q85: Length of Interview (Minutes)											
Mean		65.1	74.4	53.3	61.8	64.3	59.7	55.1	61.3	55.1	55.7
STD		22.0	28.6	15.6	26.8	25.3	19.2	17.1	21.2	18.8	25.1

Appendix A3.1

MOW Interview Schedule

The following interview schedule (Form A) is for data collection among target group samples. A slightly altered version (Form B) is for data collection with retired and unemployed samples. Form C represents a somewhat shorter version for student samples. Due to space limitations the latter two versions are not presented. The deleted or changed questions are indicated in Form A.

```
************************************************************
*                                                          *
*    PLEASE CIRCLE THE NUMBER BESIDE THE RESPONSE          *
*       OF YOUR CHOICE AND FILL IN THE BLANKS,             *
*               WHERE APPROPRIATE.                         *
*                                                          *
************************************************************
```

First, some questions about your present work situation.[1]

1. What type of work (job) do you presently do? _____
    _____

2. Is your position primarily:
    1 Non-Supervisory
    2 Supervisory
    3 Managerial

3. Are you a member of the following types of organizations?
         NO   YES
    3A   1   2   Trade Union
    3B   1   2   Professional Association
    3C   1   2   Employers Association

4. On the average, how many hours a week do you work (including
    overtime)?
         __ __ hours

5. On the average, how much time do you spend travelling to and from
    work (both ways) each day?
         __ __ __ minutes

6. Now about your working schedule:
6A Is your work schedule primarily:
    1 day
    2 night
    3 swing shift (partly day, partly night)
    4 shift changes regularly
6B Are your work hours primarily
    1 regular
    2 varied
6C During the last 12 months, have you worked weekends at least half of
    the time?
    1 no
    2 yes

7A Have you been unemployed in the last 5 years?
    1   no
    2   yes
7B If yes, for how many months in the past 5 years?
    _ _ months
7C If yes, for how many months in the past 12 months?
    _ _ months

Now, some questions about your present job.

---

8.   Which statement best describes your present job? (Please circle <u>one</u> number)
     1   I often do the same things over and over or use the same piece of equipment or procedure almost all the time.
     2   There is some variety in my job. I use different pieces of equipment or procedures.
     3   I do many different things, use a wide variety of equipment or procedures.

9.   Which statement best describes your present job? (Please circle <u>one</u> number)
     1   There is hardly any room for me to make decisions about my work and its procedures.
     2   I make some of the decisions about my work and some are made for me.
     3   I decide myself how to do my work.

10. Which statement best describes your present job? (Please circle <u>one</u> number)
     1   Mistakes in my work do not have serious consequences for the organization or for other people.
     2   Mistakes in my work may have somewhat serious consequences for the organization or for other people.
     3   Mistakes in my work may have serious consequences for the organization or for other people.

11. Which statement best describes your present job? (Please circle <u>one</u> number)
     1   Doing my job I really can't learn something new.
     2   Sometimes I can learn something new doing my job.
     3   My work gives me the opportunity to learn many new things.

12.   Which statement best describes your present job? (Please circle <u>one</u> number)
    1   In fact, I do my work alone.
    2   I work with some other people, but this is not a big part of my job.
    3   Working with other people is a very big part of my job.

13.   Which statement best describes your present job? (Please circle <u>one</u> number)
    1   There is almost no chance during the work day to talk to other people about non-business topics.
    2   Sometimes I do have the opportunity during the work day to talk to other people about non-business topics.
    3   There is almost always an opportunity during the work day to talk to other people about non-business topics.

14.[2]   Do you sometimes have to do your work in dangerous circumstances?
    1   no
    2   yes

15.[2]   Do you sometimes have to do your work in unhealthy circumstances?
    1   no
    2   yes

16.[2]   Does your job require <u>too</u> much of you physically?
    1   It never does.
    2   It seldom does.
    3   It sometimes does.
    4   It often does.

17.[2]   Does your job require <u>too</u> much of you mentally?
    1   It never does.
    2   It seldom does.
    3   It sometimes does.
    4   It often does.

18.[2]   How much of your past experience, skills and abilities can you make use of in your present job?
    1   Very little.
    2   A little.
    3   Quite a lot.
    4   Almost all.

19.[2] Which of the following statements best describes your relationship with your supervisor?
    1 He does not inform me at all about his decisions.
    2 He informs me after he has made his decisions.
    3 He usually asks for my advice before making decisions.
    4 We usually make decisions jointly.
    5 He allows me to make most decisions on my own.

Now we would like to ask you some questions about jobs you have held in the past and about your work history.

20.[2] Is your present job your first job?
    1 no
    2 yes (If yes, go to question 23.)

21.* Let's start with your first full time job that lasted 12 months or longer.

21A __ __ What type of occupation was it? _____

_____

21B __ __ What made you choose this job? _____

_____

21C __ __ What was the name of the organization or company where you worked? _____

_____

21D   How long did you work in this job?
       __ __ years.

22.* Now, for each full time job after your first job and up to but not including your present job, could you provide the following information:

22A Second Job

22A1 __ __ • Type of job (occupation) _____

_____

22A2 __ __ • Length of time on the job __ __ years

*NOTE: For temporary workers, Questions 21 and 22 refer only to full time steady jobs that lasted 12 months or longer. If no steady job has been held, go to Question 23.

22A3 __ __ • Major reasons for leaving the job _____
_____

22B   Third Job
22B1 __ __ • Type of job (occupation) _____
_____
_____

22B2 __ __ • Length of time on the job __ __ years
22B3 __ __ • Major reasons for leaving the job _____
_____

22C   Fourth Job
22C1 __ __ • Type of job (occupation) _____
_____
_____

22C2 __ __ • Length of time on the job __ __ years
22C3 __ __ • Major reasons for leaving the job _____
_____

22D   Fifth Job
22D1 __ __ • Type of job (occupation) _____
_____
_____

22D2 __ __ • Length of time on the job __ __ years
22D3 __ __ • Major reasons for leaving the job _____
_____

22E   Sixth Job
22E1 __ __ • Type of job (occupation) _____
_____
_____

22E2 __ __ • Length of time on the job __ __ years
22E3 __ __ • Major reasons for leaving the job _____
_____

22F   Seventh Job
22F1 __ __ • Type of job (occupation) _____
_____
_____

22F2 __ __ • Length of time on the job __ __ years
22F3 __ __ • Major reasons for leaving the job _____
_____

23.   Now considering your present job (occupation):
23A __ __ • What made you choose this job? _____
__ __ _____
__ __ _____

23B   • How long have you worked in your present job?

             __ __ years

23C   • What is your monthly <u>net</u> income from your present job?

             __ __ __ __ (dollars) per month

Now, looking at your total working history as a whole, please describe it in the following aspects.

---

24. Compared to your present occupational group (colleagues), where did you start your work career?

     1   Lower than my occupational group.

     2   About the same as my occupational group.

     3   Higher than my occupational group.

25. Would you describe your work career as having ups and downs (either large or small)?

25A   1   no

        2   yes

25B If yes, were the ups and downs:

     1   small

     2   large

26. Considering my whole work history until today in relation to where I started:

     1   It is marked by some decline

     2   It has remained approximately on the level where I started

     3   It has improved somewhat

     4   It has improved a great deal

27. On the whole, how satisfied are you with your work history until now?

     1   Very dissatisfied

     2   Somewhat dissatisfied

     3   Neutral

     4   Somewhat satisfied

     5   Very satisfied

For the next set of questions, we would like you to think about what working means to you at the present time. Please remember we are not referring only to your present situation. We are interested in knowing what beliefs and values you personally have regarding working as a result of your total working life.

28B ● First of all, I would like you to tell me, in your own words, what is most important to you about working.

— — _____

— — _____

_____

_____

28C ● Is there anything about working that really bothers you?

— — _____

— — _____

_____

_____

28. To help explain what working means to you, please assign a total of 100 points, in any combination you desire, to the following six statements. The more a statement expresses your thinking, the more points you should assign to it. Please read all the statements before assigning points.

28A1 __ __ Working gives you status and prestige.

28A2 __ __ Working provides you with an income that is needed.

28A3 __ __ Working keeps you occupied.

28A4 __ __ Working permits you to have interesting contacts with other people.

28A5 __ __ Working is a useful way for you to serve society.

28A6 __ __ Working itself is basically interesting and satisfying to you.
(100 Total)

29. How important and significant is working in your total life?

One of the least
important things   1 2 3 4 5 6 7
in my life

One of the most
important things
in my life

of medium
importance
in my life

30. Assign a total of 100 points to indicate how important the following areas are in your life at the present time.

30A   __ __ My leisure (like hobbies, sports, recreation and contacts with friends)

30B   __ __ My community (like voluntary organizations, union and political organizations)

30C   __ __ My work

30D   __ __ My religion (like religious activities and beliefs)

30E   __ __ My family

(100 Total)

31.   When you think of your working life, which of the following aspects of working seem <u>most</u> significant and important to you? Please rank these items from 6 = most significant to 1 = least significant.

31A   __ The tasks I do while working

31B   __ My company or organization

31C   __ The product or service I provide

31D   __ The type of people with whom I work

31E   __ The type of occupation or profession I am in

31F   __ The money I receive from my work

32.   What about the nature of your working life? How important to <u>you</u> is it that your work life contains the following:

		Do not write in this space
32A	–A lot of opportunity to LEARN new things	32A __ __
32B	–Good INTERPERSONAL relations (supervisors, co-workers)	32B __ __
32C	–Good opportunity for upgrading or PROMOTION	32C __ __
32D	–CONVENIENT work hours	32D __ __
32E	–A lot of VARIETY	32E __ __
32F	–INTERESTING work (work that you really like)	32F __ __
32G	–Good job SECURITY	32G __ __
32H	–A good MATCH between your job requirements and your abilities and experience	32H __ __
32I	–Good PAY	32I __ __
32J	–Good physical working CONDITIONS (such as light, temperature, cleanliness, low noise level)	32J __ __
32K	–A lot of AUTONOMY (you decide how to do your work)	32K __ __

<u>First,</u>   Look over the items above to get an idea of what they are.

Second, Determine which of the items is <u>most</u> important in your work life. Then write the capitalized portion of that item on the line of the rating scale which represents its importance in your work life.

Third, Cross the first item you selected off the list.

Fourth, Select the item which is <u>least</u> important in your work life. Decide how important it is in your work life and write the capitalized portion of that item on the line of the rating scale which represents its importance in your work life. Cross out that item.

Fifth, Now from the remaining list, select the item which is most important to your work life and repeat the process. Then select the item that is least important to your work life and repeat the process for that item. Do this until <u>all</u> of the items are written on the scale and all are checked off the list.

Note: You may choose to write <u>more than one item</u> on a line if you decide that they are of equal importance to your work life.

Extremely Important	15	_____
	14	_____
	13	_____
Very Important	12	_____
	11	_____
	10	_____
Important	9	_____
	8	_____
	7	_____
Of Some Importance	6	_____
	5	_____
	4	_____
Of Little Importance	3	_____
	2	_____
	1	_____

Now, we would like you to tell us which choice you would make in the following situations.

33. Imagine that two jobs are available to you. Let's call them job A and job B. You have to take one of them.

JOB A	JOB B
If you take this job, you will have the same pay as you have now.	If you take this job, you will have the same pay as you have now.
You will decide yourself how to do your work.	There will be hardly any room for you to make decisions about your work and its procedures.

  1 It would be more or less the same to me to have either job.
  2 I would prefer job A.
  3 I would prefer job B.
*IF JOB B IS PREFERRED, GO TO QUESTION 37.

34. Now let's say you have to take one of these two jobs.

JOB A	JOB B
If you take this job, you will have the same pay as you have now.	If you take this job, you will have 10% higher pay than you have now.
You will decide yourself how to do your work.	There will be hardly any room for you to make decisions about your work and its procedures.

  1 It would be more or less the same to me to have either job.
  2 I would prefer job A.
  3 I would prefer job B.
*IF JOB B IS PREFERRED, GO TO QUESTION 37.

35.   Now imagine that you have to take one of these two jobs:

JOB A	JOB B
If you take this job, you will have the same pay as you have now.	If you take this job, you will have 30% higher pay than you have now.
You will decide yourself how to do your work.	There will be hardly any room for you to make decisions about your work and its procedures.

1   It would be more or less the same to me to have either job.
2   I would prefer job A.
3   I would prefer job B.
*IF JOB B IS PREFERRED, GO TO QUESTION 37.

36.   Now let's say you have to take one of these two jobs:

JOB A	JOB B
If you take this job, you will have the same pay as you have now.	If you take this job, you will have 50% higher pay than you have now.
You will decide yourself how to do your work.	There will be hardly any room for you to make decisions about your work and its procedures.

1   It would be more or less the same to me to have either job.
2   I would prefer job A.
3   I would prefer job B.

37.   Now let's say you have to take one of these two jobs:

JOB A	JOB B
If you take this job, you will have the same pay as you have now.	If you take this job, you will have the same pay as you have now.
In this job you will decide yourself how to do your work.	There will be hardly any room for you to make decisions about your work and its procedures.
You will fully use your skills and abilities.	There will be little opportunity for you to use your skills and abilities.
You will do something you really like.	You will not do something you really like.

1   It would be more or less the same to me to have either job.
2   I would prefer job A.
3   I would prefer job B.
*IF JOB B IS PREFERRED, GO TO QUESTION 41.

38.   Now let's say you have to take one of these two jobs:

JOB A	JOB B
If you take this job, you will have the same pay as you have now.	If you take this job, you will have 10% higher pay than you have now.
In this job you will decide yourself how to do your work.	There will be hardly any room for you to make decisions about your work and its procedures.
You will fully use your skills and abilities.	There will be little opportunity for you to use your skills and abilities.
You will do something you really like.	You will not do something you really like.

1   It would be more or less the same to me to have either job.
2   I would prefer job A.
3   I would prefer job B.
*IF JOB B IS PREFERRED, GO TO QUESTION 41.

39.   Now let's say you have to take one of these two jobs:

JOB A	JOB B
If you take this job, you will have the same pay as you have now.	If you take this job, you will have 30% higher pay than you have now.
In this job you will decide yourself how to do your work.	There will be hardly any room for you to make decisions about your work and its procedures.
You will fully use your skills and abilities.	There will be little opportunity for you to use your skills and abilities.
You will do something you really like.	You will not do something you really like.

    1   It would be more or less the same to me to have either job.
    2   I would prefer job A
    3   I would prefer job B.
*IF JOB B IS PREFERRED, GO TO QUESTION 41.

40.   Now imagine that you have to take one of these two jobs:

JOB A	JOB B
If you take this job, you will have the same pay as you have now.	If you take this job, you will have 50% higher pay than you have now.
In this job you will decide yourself how to do your work.	There will be hardly any room for you to make decisions about your work and its procedures.
You will fully use your skills and abilities.	There will be little opportunity for you to use your skills and abilities.
You will do something you really like.	You will not do something you really like.

1   It would be more or less the same to me to have either job.
2   I would prefer job A.
3   I would prefer job B.

41.   Now let's say you have to take one of these two jobs:

JOB A	JOB B
This job will permit you to have as much leisure time as you have now.	This job will permit you to have less leisure time than you have now.
It will bring you the same pay as you have now.	It will bring you 10% higher pay than you have now.
There will be little opportunity for you to use your skills and abilities.	There will be little opportunity for you to use your skills and abilities.
You will not do something you really like.	You will not do something you really like.

1   It would be more or less the same to me to have either job.
2   I would prefer job A.
3   I would prefer job B.
*IF JOB B IS PREFERRED, GO TO QUESTION 43.

42.   Now let's say you have to take one of these two jobs:

JOB A	JOB B
This job will permit you to have as much leisure time as you have now.	This job will permit you to have less leisure time than you have now.
It will bring you the same pay as you have now.	It will bring you 30% higher pay than you have now.
There will be little opportunity for you to use your skills and abilities.	There will be little opportunity for you to use your skills and abilities.
You will not do something you really like.	You will not do something you really like.

1   It would be more or less the same to me to have either job.
2   I would prefer job A.
3   I would prefer job B.

43. Now let's say you have to take one of these two jobs:

JOB A	JOB B
This job will permit you to have as much leisure time as you have now.	This job will permit you to have less leisure time than you have now.
It will bring you the same pay as you have now.	It will bring you the same pay as you have now.
There will be little opportunity for you to use your skills and abilities.	In this job you will fully use your skills and abilities.
You will not do something you really like.	You will do something you really like.

1   It would be more or less the same to me to have either job.
2   I would prefer job A.
3   I would prefer job B.
*IF JOB B IS PREFERRED, GO TO QUESTION 46.

44.   Now imagine that you have to take one of these two jobs:

JOB A	JOB B
This job will permit you to have as much leisure time as you have now.	This job will permit you to have less leisure time than you have now.
It will bring you the same pay as you have now.	It will bring you 10% higher pay than you have now.
There will be little opportunity for you to use your skills and abilities.	In this job you will fully use all your skills and abilities.
You will not do something you really like.	You will do something you really like.

    1   It would be more or less the same to me to have either job.
    2   I would prefer job A.
    3   I would prefer job B.
*IF JOB B IS PREFERRED, GO TO QUESTION 46.

45.   Now imagine that you have to take one of these two jobs:

JOB A	JOB B
This job will permit you to have as much leisure time as you have now.	This job will permit you to have less leisure time than you have now.
It will bring you the same pay as you have now.	It will bring you 30% higher pay than you have now.
There will be little opportunity for you to use your skills and abilities.	In this job you will fully use your skills and abilities.
You will not do something you really like.	You will do something you really like.

1   It would be more or less the same to me to have either job.
2   I would prefer job A.
3   I would prefer job B.

46.   And now the last choice about jobs A and B, you have to take one of
these two jobs:

JOB A	JOB B
This job will permit you to have as much leisure time as you have now.	This job will permit you to have less leisure time than you have now.
It will bring you 30% higher pay than you have now.	It will bring you 30% higher pay than you have now.
There will be little opportunity for you to use your skills and abilities.	In this job you will fully use your skills and abilities.
You will not do something you really like.	You will do something you really like.

1   It would be more or less the same to me to have either job.
2   I would prefer job A.
3   I would prefer job B.

47.   On this page are some work-related statements that people might
make. We would like you to decide whether you agree or disagree
with each of these statements depending on your personal opinions.
If you strongly agree with a statement, please circle the number 4; if
you agree somewhat with the statement, circle the number 3; and so
on.

	Strongly Disagree	Disagree	Agree	Strongly Agree
47A If a worker's skills become outdated, his employer should be responsible for retraining and reemployment.	1	2	3	4
47B It is the duty of every able-bodied citizen to contribute to society by working.	1	2	3	4

		Strongly Disagree	Disagree	Agree	Strongly Agree
47C	The educational system in our society should prepare every person for a good job if they exert a reasonable amount of effort.	1	2	3	4
47D	Persons in our society should allocate a large portion of their regular income toward savings for their future.	1	2	3	4
47E	When a change in work methods must be made, a supervisor should be required to ask workers for their suggestions before deciding what to do.	1	2	3	4
47F	A worker should be expected to think up better ways to do his or her job.	1	2	3	4
47G	Every person in our society should be entitled to interesting and meaningful work.	1	2	3	4
47H	Monotonous, simplistic work is acceptable as long as the pay compensates fairly for it.	1	2	3	4
47I	A job should be provided to every individual who desires to work.	1	2	3	4
47J	A worker should value the work he or she does even if it is boring, dirty or unskilled.	1	2	3	4

48A Imagine that you won a lottery or inherited a large sum of money and
     could live comfortably for the rest of your life without working. What
     would you do concerning working?
       1 I would stop working.
       2 I would continue to work in the same job.
       3 I would continue to work but with changed conditions.
48B __ If 1, why would you stop working and what would you miss
     __ about working?

     _____

     _____

48C __ If 2, why would you continue working in the same job?

     _____

     _____

48D __ __ If 3, what are the changed conditions and why would you
     __ __ continue working?

     _____

     _____

49. Not everyone means the same thing when they talk about working.
     When do you consider an activity as working? Choose four state-
     ments from the list below which best define when an activity is
     "working".

       A. if you do it in a working place.
       B. if someone tells you what to do.
       C. if it is physically strenuous.
       D. if it belongs to your task.
       E. if you do it to contribute to society.
       F. if, by doing it, you get the feeling of belonging.
       G. if it is mentally strenuous.
       H. if you do it at a certain time (for instance from 8 until 5).
       I. if it adds value to something.
       J. if it is not pleasant.
       K. if you get money for doing it.
       L. if you have to account for it.
       M. if you have to do it.
       N. if others profit by it.

50A If you were to start all over again, would you again choose your
     occupation or would you choose a different one?
       1 different occupation
       2 same occupation

50B[3] Would you recommend your occupation to your children for their work?
    1 no
    2 yes

50C[3] __ __ Why would you make this recommendation? _____

_____

51A Do you think that people's general attitude toward working will change in the next 10 years?
    1 no
    2 yes

51B __ __ If yes, what will be the nature and direction of change? __

_____

_____

52[3,4] If you had to choose, which would you prefer? (NOTE: NOT APPLICABLE FOR SELF-EMPLOYED OR TEACHERS.)
    1 Stay in your present organization but with a different type of job.
    2 Do the same type of work but with a different organization.

53[4] In your leisure time, how often do you do things that have nothing to do with work?
    1 never
    2 only occasionally
    3 sometimes
    4 often
    5 very often

54.[4] If your company organized group activities outside of working hours, would you participate?
    1 no
    2 maybe
    3 yes

55.[5] How often do you worry about work in your free time?
    1 never
    2 only occasionally
    3 sometimes
    4 often
    5 very often

> Now some items concerning your plans about working in the future, about what you expect will happen in the future and what you would like to see happen in the future.

56A Do you intend to change jobs   (FOR TEMPORARY
     within the next 12 months?   WORKERS, THIS MEANS
        1 no   TAKE A STEADY/FIXED JOB)
        2 yes
56B __ If yes, what are you looking for in another job? _____
     _____

57. Do you think it would be easy for you to find a similar job with
     another employer within the next 12 months? (NOTE: NOT
     APPLICABLE FOR SELF-EMPLOYED.)
        1 difficult
        2 not so easy
        3 somewhat easy
        4 easy
        5 very easy

58A Would you be willing to be retrained for a different job or occu-
     pation than you now have?
        1 under no conditions
        2 only if the economic situation forced me to
        3 under certain conditions
58B __ If under certain conditions, please specify _____
     _____

59. Do you intend to be retrained for a different job or occupation
     during the next 12 months?
        1 no
        2 yes

60. Do you intend to take part in further training related to your present
     job during the next 12 months?
        1 no
        2 yes
        3 I am already taking part

61.[6] Are you actively trying to be promoted within the next 12 months?
     (NOTE: NOT APPLICABLE FOR SELF-EMPLOYED).
        1 no
        2 yes

62A[6] Do you have any other significant plans regarding working during
the next five years?
    1 no
    2 yes
62B[6] __ __   If yes, what plans? _____
_____

63.   In the next 5 to 10 years, do you expect any societal developments
which could endanger your employment?
    1 no
    2 yes

64.   Are there any societal developments in the next 5 to 10 years which
are likley to improve your employment situation or make it more
secure?
    1 no
    2 yes

65.   In the next few years, do you expect the level of pay for your job
compared to pay for other jobs to:
    1 go down
    2 stay about the same
    3 go up

66A Compared to the present time, how important will work be to you in
the next 5 to 10 years?
    1 less important
    2 equal in importance
    3 more important
66B   __ __   What are the reasons for this? _____
_____

67.   Suppose people were able to work less hours for the same pay in the
future; which alternative would be most preferable to you? (Pick
one).
    1 more holidays
    2 less working hours per day
    3 a free afternoon every week
    4 longer periods of education before beginning to work
    5 a year off for further study about every 10 years
    6 less working hours for older workers
    7 earlier retirement

68.   If the general economic situation led to proposals to work less hours and earn proportionately less money, how would you feel about such proposals?
    1   I would be against them
    2   I don't really care
    3   I would be moderately in favor of them
    4   I would be in favor of them

> Now some final questions about you, about your background and about your family.

69.   What is your age?
    _ _   years

70.   What was the highest formal education which you completed? (Circle ONE.)
    1   primary school
    2   secondary school or further vocational training
    3   some college or similar vocational training below university level
    4   university degree

71.   Did you have a religious education?
    1   no
    2   yes

72.   To what extent are you presently associated with a religion?
    1   no contact
    2   loose contact
    3   close contact

73.   What was the highest formal education received by your parents?
73A   Father
    1   primary school
    2   secondary school
    3   some college
    4   university degree
73B   Mother
    1   primary school
    2   secondary school
    3   some college
    4   university degree

74. Concerning the community where you spent most of your childhood (to about age 14); was it primarily:
    1 city or big town
    2 village or small town
    3 rural

75. Concerning the community where you presently live; is it primarily:
    1 city or big town
    2 village or small town
    3 rural

76A Are you married and/or living with a partner in a joint household?
    1 no
    2 yes
76B   If yes, is your partner:
       1 not employed and primarily a homemaker
       2 part-time employment and homemaker
       3 employed full time
       4 other
76C __   If other please specify _____
          _____
          _____

77. How many persons do you support financially (including yourself)?
    __ __ · __ number

78. In general, how satisfied have you been with your life?

    Very   Very
    Dissatisfied 1 2 3 4 5 6 7 8 9 Satisfied

- THE END -

THANK YOU VERY MUCH.

INTERVIEWER CHECKLIST
To be completed for each respondent.

Interviewer name _____ Date of interview _____

79. Is respondent a citizen of this country?
     1 yes
     2 no

80. __ __ City in which interview was done _____

81A Was interview conducted at
     1 home
     2 workplace
     3 other
81B __ If other, please specify _____

82. Sex of respondent
     1 male
     2 female
         Target group to which respondent belongs _____

83B If self-employed, circle appropriate job type:
     1 craftsman
     2 service (non-craftsman)
     3 commercial (selling product)

84A Indicate nature and size of organization which employs the person:
     1 public
     2 private
84B Organization size at the location where the person works:
     1 under 100 employees
     2 100–299 employees
     3 300–999 employees
     4 1000 or over employees

85. Length of interview
     __ __ __ minutes

86. To what extent did the respondent understand the questions?
     1 clearly understood
     2 reasonably understood most questions
     3 had difficulty with many questions
     4 understood only a few questions

87.   Would you describe the respondent's cooperation in the interview as:
      1   high
      2   moderate
      3   low

      Interviewer comments about specific items in the interview (wording problems, understanding problems, resistance to answering) _____

      _____
      _____
      _____
      _____
      _____
      _____
      _____

      Interviewer comments about the respondent and/or the interview in general _____

      _____
      _____
      _____
      _____
      _____
      _____
      _____

Notes

[1] Questions 1 through 27 are deleted in Form C.
[2] Slightly altered in Form B.
[3] Deleted in Form C.
[4] Deleted or worded differently in Form B.
[5] Questions 54–69 not applicable for retired.
[6] Deleted in Form B.

Construction of MOW-indices

a. Non-central MOW-indices

Aggravating Work Conditions (AGGCON)

This is measured by counting the following:

Q14, dangerous job	:	(2) yes
Q15, unhealthy job	:	(2) yes
Q16, job requires too much physically	:	(3) sometimes
	:	(4) often

Quality of Work (QOFWORK)

This is measured by combining the following:

Q8, variety of work	:	(1) low
		(3) high
Q9, autonomy in work	:	(1) low
		(3) high
Q10, responsibility in work	:	(1) low
		(3) high
Q11, learning in work	:	(1) low
		(2) little
		(3) a lot
	:	(4) almost all

Q18, skill utilization

(1) very little
(2) little
(3) a lot
(4) almost all

Work Schedule (SCHED)

This is based on a combination of the codes for the following:

Q6A, work schedule

:   (1) day
    (2) night
    (3) partly day and
        partly night
    (4) shift

Q6C, work on weekends

:   (1) no
    (2) yes

Occupational Satisfaction (OCCSAT)

This includes the following questions:

Q50A, I would choose again the same occupation

:   (1) no
    (2) yes

Q50B, I would recommend my occupation to my children

:   (1) no
    (2) yes

Mobility in Work History (MWH)

The questions used are as follows:

Q21A: first job, type of job, codes between 1 and 15
Q22A1 to Q22F1: second to seventh job, type of job, codes between 1 and 15.
Q21D: first job, years working, codes between 1 and 50.
Q22A2 to Q22F2: second job to seventh job, years working, codes between 0 and 50.

Table A1 contains correlations between some of the indices and the included variables separately (r_{Iv}).

Table A1. Correlations between the a priori established indices and each (r_{Iv}) of the included variables

Index	Variables	r_{Iv}
QOFWORK	Q8	.72
	Q9	.63
	Q10	.54
	Q11	.71
	Q18	.59
AGGCON	Q14	.70
	Q15	.73
	Q16	.76
OCCSAT	Q50A	.85
	Q50B	.83
SCHED	Q6A	.71
	Q6C	.80

NOTE: Q6A was recoded to a binary variable: Q6A (1=10) (2, 3, 4 = 1).
For the a priori established indices not listed in Table A1 computation of correlation coefficients is doubtful or impossible.

b. Central MOW-indices

The following central MOW variables have been included in the analysis:

Valued working outcomes (assignment of 100 points) (Q28A).
Importance of working (7-point scale) (Q29).
Importance of certain areas in one's life (assignment of 100 points) (Q30).
Work role identification (ranking) (Q31).
Importance of work goals (combination of absolute rating and ranking) (Q32).
Social norms about working (4-point scale) (Q47).

The factor analytic procedure selected was the "PA2" method in the SPSS-package with all possible default options for the parameters of subroutine FACTOR (Nie and Hull, 1975). This implies that the factor analysis was done with:

- principal factoring
- using communality estimates as diagonal elements
- iteration for improving the estimates of communality

- selection of number of factors dependent on the eigenvalue
- the eigenvalue criterion
- varimax rotation

Two problems in connection with the factor analytic procedure requires further discussion. The first refers to the response options on valued working outcomes (Q28A) and importance of life areas (Q30). This type of response option was selected to minimize socially desirable response tendencies (see above). However, they have the disadvantage of not providing independent answers. It is clear that such answers may artificially influence the correlation matrix, and consequently the factor matrix (Fruchter, 1954, p. 201). Primarily, however, their influence will be within each question among the options presented (producing negative correlations) and there will be only a mitigated effect on the correlations with the other central MOW variables. Therefore, high interpretable loadings of single items from Q28A to Q30 on extracted factors would allow the inclusion of such an item in an index to be constructed.

The inclusion of dependent variables in a factor analysis may also lead to the generation of more (so-called incidental) factors (Thurstone, 1947, pp. 441–442). However, in the present study, attention is given to the most important, first extracted factors and therefore this will be only a minor problem.

The second problem refers to the rank order character of work role identification responses (Q31). In general it is recommended that only one type of correlation be used in factor analysis, although it is suggested that biserial or rank correlations may be used as estimates of product moment correlations (Fruchter, 1954, p. 201). It can be assumed that the ordinal scale, which was used, is the best possible approximation of the interval scale. The application of the Pearson's product moment correlation formula results in a Spearman's rank correlation coefficient for ordinal–ordinal data, and in a multiserial correlation coefficient for ordinal–interval data (Green and Tull, 1975, pp. 325–326). These correlations can be used as estimates for the product moment correlations in factor analysis.

For the index construction only variables with relatively high factor loadings were selected. In order to avoid negative index–values, standardized T-scores were computed. For computation of the T-scores, the sample "over countries over target groups" was used, with the exception of the item on "importance of work goals" (Q32). For the latter the target groups *per* country were used as samples.

The T-scores were then added and divided by the number of entries, resulting in a mean score for all indices with scale value 50.

Finally, indices were rounded off to a whole number. The general formula for index construction, therefore, was as follows:

$$I = \text{RND} \left| (T_1 + T_2 + \ldots + T_k)/k \right|$$

in which I = index constructed with k variables, $T_1, T_2 \ldots T_k$ = T-scores of variables 1, 2, . . . k, RND = rounding off, and

$$T_k = \left| (V_k - M_k)/\text{SD}_k \right| \times 10 + 50$$

in which V_k = value on variable k, M_k = mean score of variable k, and SD_k = standard deviation of variable k.

Table A2. Correlations between the indices and each of the included variables (r_{iv}) and between the indices and the sum of the included variables (r_{IV})

Index	Var.	r_{iv}	r_{IV}
CW	Q29	.82	.73
	Q30C	.68	
CONTACT	Q28A4	.76	.86
	Q31D	.72	
	Q32B	.34	
ECONOMIC	Q28A2	.61	.86
	Q31F	.62	
	Q32I	.77	
IR	Q28A6	.60	.90
	Q32E	.62	
	Q32F	.70	
	Q32H	.58	
	Q32K	.54	
OBL	Q47B	.69	.87
	Q47D	.66	
	Q47J	.71	
OPP	Q47A	.47	.94
	Q47E	.58	
	Q47G	.69	
	Q47I	.66	

c. Job Images

Preference for Intrinsic Work situations (PIW)

The index is constructed by using the following job image items.

Q33 through Q40 : (1) it is the same
(2) prefer job A
(3) prefer job B

Alternative:
Q33: Job A: pay, autonomy
    Job B: pay, no autonomy
    (same codes as above)

Q34: Job A: pay, autonomy
    Job B: 10% higher pay, no autonomy
    (same codes as above)

Q35: Job A: pay, autonomy
    Job B: 30% higher pay, no autonomy
    (same codes as above)

Q36: Job A: pay, autonomy
    Job B: 50% higher pay, no autonomy
    (same codes as above)

Q37: Job A: pay, autonomy, use skill, liking your job
    Job B: pay, low autonomy, little use of skill, disliking your job
    (same codes as above)

Q38: Job A: pay, autonomy, use skill, liking your job
    Job B: 10% higher pay, no autonomy, little use of skill, disliking
        your job
    (same codes as above)

Q39: Job A: pay, autonomy, use skill, liking your job
    Job B: 30% higher pay, no autonomy, little use of skill, disliking
        your job
    (same codes as above)

Q40: Job A: pay, autonomy, use skill, liking your job
    Job B: 50% higher pay, no autonomy, little use of skill, disliking
        your job
    (same codes as above)

Preferability for Leisure Time (PL)

This is based on the job image items (Q41–46).

Q41 through Q46: (1) it is the same
                 (2) prefer job A
                 (3) prefer job B

Alternative:

Q41: Job A: leisure, pay, little use of skill, disliking your job
     Job B: less leisure, 10% higher pay, little use of skill, disliking your job
     (same codes as above)

Q42: Job A: leisure, pay, little use of skill, disliking your job
     Job B: less leisure, 30% higher pay, little use of skill, disliking your job
     (same codes as above)

Q43: Job A: leisure, pay, little use of skill, disliking your job
     Job B: less leisure, pay, complete use of skill, liking your job
     (same codes as above)

Q44: Job A: leisure, pay, little use of skill, disliking your job
     Job B: less leisure, 10% higher pay, complete use of skill, liking your job
     (same codes as above)

Q45: Job A: leisure, pay, little use of skill, disliking your job
     Job B: less leisure, 30% higher pay, complete use of skill, disliking your job
     (same codes as above)

Q46: Job A: leisure, 30% higher pay, little use of skill, disliking your job
     Job B: less leisure, 30% higher pay, complete use of skill, liking your job
     (same codes as above).

Appendix A8

Table A8.1. Pattern of preferences and scale values for intrinsic–extrinsic job images

Pattern of Preferences	Scale Value
(3,3,3,3,3,3,3,3)	0.00
(1,3,3,3,1,3,3,3)	0.57
(1,3,3,3,1,1,3,3)	0.85
(2,3,3,3,2,3,3,3)	1.00
(2,3,3,3,2,2,3,3)	1.54
(1,1,3,3,2,2,3,3)	1.57
(1,1,1,1,1,1,1,1)	1.72
(2,1,3,3,2,2,3,3)	1.74
(2,2,3,3,2,2,3,3)	1.93
(1,3,3,3,2,2,2,2)	2.06
(2,2,3,3,2,2,2,3)	2.33
(2,2,1,3,2,2,2,3)	2.50
(1,1,1,1,2,2,2,2)	2.59
(2,2,1,1,2,2,1,1)	2.60
(2,2,3,3,2,2,2,2)	2.63
(2,2,2,3,2,2,2,3)	2.67
(2,2,1,1,2,2,2,2)	2.94
(2,2,2,3,2,2,2,2)	2.97
(2,2,2,1,2,2,2,2)	3.11
(2,2,2,2,2,2,2,2)	3.26

Table A8.2. Descriptive statistics of preferability of intrinsic work scores for combined target group samples within each country and for each target group across all countries

	Mean	Standard Deviation	Number of Cases
Country			
Belgium	2.52	0.75	880
Germany	2.81	0.58	682
Israel	2.57	0.84	834
Japan	2.47	0.84	1089
Netherlands	2.77	0.63	905
U.S.A.	2.53	0.69	847
Yugoslavia	2.67	0.64	540
Target group			
Unemployed	2.46	0.86	539
Retired	2.69	0.76	555
Chemical eng.	2.81	0.53	534
Teachers	2.96	0.49	635
Self-employed	2.91	0.56	654
Tool makers	2.48	0.72	588
White collar	2.51	0.68	685
Textile workers	2.13	0.95	554
Tempor. workers	2.55	0.65	456
Students	2.49	0.69	577

Word Definition Cluster Data

Table A9.1. Cluster solutions of representative sample of the total target group data on work definitions

Definition of work		Cluster 1 N=311 34%		Cluster 2 N=204 22%		Cluster 3 N=270 30%		Cluster 4 N=125 14%		Percentage Occurrence Overall
		%	BFR	%	BFR	%	BFR	%	BFR	
A. working place	%*	30.2		9.8		29.3		12.0		
	BFR**		1.32		0.43		1.28		0.52	22.9
B. someone tells you what to do	%	21.9		5.9		7.8		8.0		
	BFR		1.79		0.48		0.64		0.66	12.2
C. physically strenuous	%	21.9		2.9		4.4		66.4		
	BFR		1.18		0.16		0.24		3.58	18.6
D. your task	%	36.0		55.9		71.5		21.6		
	BFR		0.73		1.14		1.46		0.44	49.0
E. contribute to society	%	13.8		66.7		38.5		28.8		
	BFR		0.39		1.90		1.10		0.82	35.1
F. feeling of belonging	%	11.3		63.7		18.9		28.0		
	BFR		0.41		2.31		0.68		1.02	27.6
G. mentally strenuous	%	6.4		6.9		21.1		82.4		
	BFR		0.30		0.32		0.99		3.87	21.3
H. certain time	%	52.1		10.3		3.3		20.0		
	BFR		2.18		0.43		0.14		0.84	23.8
I. adds value	%	31.2		51.5		57.0		22.4		
	BFR		0.74		1.22		1.35		0.53	42.2
J. not pleasant	%	6.8		2.0		1.1		8.0		
	BFR		1.62		0.47		0.27		1.92	4.2
K. get money for it	%	78.5		56.9		64.4		40.0		
	BFR		1.22		0.89		1.00		0.62	64.2
L. have to account for it	%	21.9		7.8		66.3		32.8		
	BFR		0.65		0.23		1.98		0.98	33.4
M. have to do it	%	41.5		3.4		3.7		16.8		
	BFR		2.26		0.19		0.20		0.92	18.4
N. if others profit by it	%	14.5		55.4		11.9		11.2		
	BFR		0.65		2.47		0.53		0.50	22.4

* % = percentage occurrence for binary variables.
** BFR = binary frequency ratio.

NOTE: Error value = 11.9.

Table A9.2. Cluster solutions of cross-validation sample (national data, N=450)*

Definition of work		Cluster 1 $N=158$ 35%	Cluster 2 $N=122$ 25%	Cluster 3 $N=77$ 17%	Cluster 4 $N=103$ 23%	Percentage Occurrence Overall
A. working place	%**	44.9	3.6	9.1	18.4	
	BFR***	2.00	0.16	0.41	0.82	22.4
B. someone tells	%	22.8	6.2	3.9	7.8	
you what to do	BFR	1.90	0.52	0.32	0.65	12.0
C. physically	%	25.9	3.6	6.5	46.6	
strenuous	BFR	1.19	0.16	0.30	2.14	21.8
D. your task	%	43.0	67.0	51.9	50.5	
	BFR	0.82	1.28	0.99	0.97	52.2
E. contribute	%	17.7	32.1	87.0	44.7	
to society	BFR	0.45	0.82	2.21	1.14	39.3
F. feeling of	%	7.0	33.0	97.4	4.9	
belonging	BFR	0.24	1.16	3.42	0.17	28.4
G. mentally	%	10.1	12.5	20.8	64.1	
strenuous	BFR	0.41	0.50	0.83	2.57	24.9
H. certain	%	48.7	9.8	9.1	12.6	
time	BFR	2.03	0.41	0.38	0.53	24.0
I. adds	%	12.7	69.6	48.1	48.5	
value	BFR	0.31	1.69	1.17	1.18	41.1
J. not	%	10.1	1.8	0.0	2.9	
pleasant	BFR	2.17	0.38	0.00	0.62	4.7
K. get money	%	81.0	83.9	36.4	22.3	
for it	BFR	1.34	1.38	0.60	0.37	60.7
L. have to	%	25.9	44.6	9.1	28.2	
account for it	BFR	0.92	1.58	0.32	1.00	28.2
M. have to	%	31.0	0.9	5.2	21.4	
do it	BFR	1.84	0.05	0.31	1.26	16.9
N. if others profit	%	10.8	33.0	15.6	13.6	
by it	BFR	0.61	1.86	0.88	0.76	17.8

* Does not include Germany, Britain and Yugoslavia.

** % = percentage occurrence for binary variables.

*** BFR = binary frequency ratio.

NOTE: Error value = 5.6.

Table A9.3. Work definition cluster membership (percentages) by gender for national survey data

Country	Gender	Work Definition Cluster			
		Concrete	Social	Duty	Burden
Belgium	Male	28	30	26	15
	Female	31	36	21	12
Germany	Male	45	12	28	15
	Female	46	15	25	14
Israel	Male	39	33	18	10
	Female	33	36	19	12
Japan	Male	38	6	47	9
	Female	51	4	39	6
Netherlands	Male	23	27	37	13
	Female	21	29	34	16
United States	Male	29	32	22	17
	Female	29	25	29	17
Yugoslavia*	Male	16	24	52	8
	Female	14	26	53	7

* Target group data.

Table A9.4. *Distributions of work definitions clusters (percentages) by age categories for national survey data.*

Country	Age (years)	Work Definition Cluster			
		Concrete	Social	Duty	Burden
Belgium	<30	30	27	30	13
	30–50	29	35	21	15
	50>	28	36	23	13
Germany	<30	46	13	24	17
	30–50	46	11	27	16
	50>	42	16	31	11
Israel	<30	36	36	19	9
	30–50	36	36	16	12
	50>	39	31	20	10
Japan	<30	38	5	49	8
	30–50	43	4	45	8
	50>	44	7	41	8
Netherlands	<30	23	24	38	15
	30–50	24	26	38	12
	50>	18	39	28	15
United States	<30	30	32	22	16
	30–50	28	27	27	18
	50>	28	29	28	15
Yugoslavia*	<30	17	22	52	9
	30–50	14	27	52	7
	50>	16	18	61	5

* Target group data.

Table A9.5. *Distributions of work definition clusters (percentages) by educational level categories for national survey data.*

Country	Educational Level	Work Definition Cluster			
		Concrete	Social	Duty	Burden
Belgium	Primary	29	28	29	14
	Secondary	31	34	20	15
	S. College**	23	35	30	12
	University	35	26	26	13
Germany	Primary	57	13	19	10
	Secondary	45	13	26	16
	S. College	47	9	26	18
	University	28	11	45	16
Israel	Primary	49	27	14	10
	Secondary	37	37	16	10
	S. College	29	39	18	14
	University	27	36	26	11
Japan	Primary	46	15	35	4
	Secondary	48	5	39	8
	S. College	40	6	46	8
	University	31	5	56	8
Netherlands	Primary	31	33	28	9
	Secondary	25	28	35	12
	S. College	14	22	42	22
	University	14	20	59	7
United States	Primary	41	31	15	13
	Secondary	32	27	21	20
	S. College	28	31	25	16
	University	24	29	32	15
Yugoslavia*	Primary	22	18	46	14
	Secondary	16	24	52	8
	S. College	9	33	58	0
	University	7	30	59	4

* Target group data.
** Some College.

Mathematical Appendix

Quantification on Response Pattern

Factor analytic method for qualitative data (Principal components analysis in the qualitative case). The original paper by Hayashi is found in the Proc. Inst. Statist. Math., Vol. 4, No. 2, 1956, pp. 19–30, under the title *Theory and Example of Quantification (II)*. This is closely related to Guttman's 'Scale analysis (A. Stouffer ed., *Measurement and prediction*, Princeton University Press, 1952)' and quite the same at Benzécri's 'analyses des données (J. P. Benzécri *et al.*, *L'Analyse Des Données I, La Taxonomie II, L'Analyse des Correspondances*, Dunod, 1973)'.

Fundamental Theory

This is one method of classification of individuals based on the similarity of responses to questions having several categories. This method is especially important here as no other method exists for classification. The response pattern of individuals is shown in Table A13.1. We assume that individuals are interviewed with L questions and give some responses to each question. In order that individuals with similar response patterns may be listed in a certain order in the chart, so that they are located in roughly the same area of the chart as well as categories having similar characteristics, we want to classify individuals and categories simultaneously. From this, we can find the configuration for both the individuals and response categories in multi-dimensional Euclidean space, in order to be able to make inference from them. Inferences can be made easily, if we have these configurations in one-dimensional space.

This means that we can summarize the information on similarity among the individuals and among response categories on one axis. If the configurations cannot be summarized on one axis, we shall have to interpret configurations in multi-dimensional space. So, first, we will start our interpretation in one-dimensional space and then continue to multi-dimensional space.

Table A13.1. Response pattern on question items.

			A		1		2		...		L	
			B	1	2	...	K_1	K_1+1	...	...	...	R
			C	C_{11}	C_{12}	...	C_{1K1}	C_{21}	...	C_{2K1}	...	C_{l1} ... C_{lK1}
D	E	F										
l_1	s_1	1	✓			✓				✓		
l_2	s_2	2	✓			✓				✓		
l_3	s_3	3		✓			✓		✓			
.	.	.										
l_Q	s_Q	Q	✓			✓				✓		

1. '✓' sign shows the response category of an individual.
2. The categories contain neither D.K. nor 'other' responses. Those who select (D.K. or 'other' mentioned above) show no sign. Thus the number l's of responses in the question items of types are generally different.

A: item (question) B: consecutive number
C: response category D: total of signs
E: frequency F: response type (individuals)

We define $\delta_i(j)$ as

$$\delta_i(j) = \begin{cases} 1, & \text{if the } i\text{-th individual (or type) selects the } j\text{-th response category} \\ 0, & \text{otherwise} \end{cases}$$

where $i = 1, 2, \cdots, Q$ and $j = 1, 2, \cdots, R$ and

$$R = \sum_{j=1}^{L} K_j; K_j \text{ is the number of response categories in the } j\text{-th item}$$

$$l_i = \sum_{j=1}^{K} \delta_i(j);$$

$$n = \sum_{i=1}^{Q} s_i; \bar{l} = \frac{1}{n} \sum_{i=1}^{Q} l_i s_i$$

where L is the number of items, s_i is the number of respondents that fall into the i-th type and n is sample size.

We want to quantify individuals (types) and categories by assigning numerical values to them which will maximize the correlation coefficient between individuals and categories. This is the idea of simultaneous grouping of individuals and categories and also is considered to be one method of taxonomy of individuals and categories based on response patterns.

Let the types be $1, 2, \cdots, Q$ and response categories be $1(C_{11}), \cdots, K_1(C_{1K_1}), K_1 + 1(C_{21}), \cdots, R(C_{LK})$. Then we require $y_1, y_2, \cdots, y_Q$ given to types and $x_1, x_2, \cdots, x_R$ given to categories to maximize the correlation coefficient $^1\varrho$ between x and y, where

$$^1\varrho = C_{xy}/\sigma_x\sigma_y$$

$$\sigma_x^2 = \sum_{i=1}^{Q}\sum_{j=1}^{R} \delta_i(j)s_i x_j^2/(\bar{l}n) - \left\{\sum_{i=1}^{Q}\sum_{j=1}^{R} \delta_i(j)s_i x_j/(\bar{l}n)\right\}^2$$

$$\sigma_y^2 = \sum_{i=1}^{Q} s_i l_i y_i^2/(\bar{l}n) - \left\{\sum_{i=1}^{Q} s_i l_i y_i/(\bar{l}n)\right\}^2$$

$$C_{xy} = \sum_{i=1}^{Q}\sum_{j=1}^{R} \delta_i(j)s_i x_j y_i/(\bar{l}n) - \left\{\sum_{i=1}^{Q}\sum_{j=1}^{R} \delta_i(j)s_i x_j/(\bar{l}n)\right\}\left\{\sum_{i=1}^{Q} s_i l_i y_i/(\bar{l}n)\right\}.$$

And in order to maximize $^1\varrho$, it is to solve

$$\frac{\partial ^1\varrho}{\partial x_k} = 0, \quad \frac{\partial ^1\varrho}{\partial y_e} = 0 \quad (k = 1, 2, \cdots, R; e = 1, 2, \cdots, Q)$$

which implies

$$\sum_{j=i}^{R} h_{jk}x_j = {}^1p^2 \sum_{j=1}^{R} f_{jk}x_j \quad (k = 1, 2, \cdots, R)$$

where

$$f_{jk} = \begin{cases} -b_{jk}; & (j \neq k) \\ d_k - b_{jk}; & (j = k) \end{cases}$$

$$h_{jk} = a_{jk} - b_{jk}$$

$$a_{jk} = \sum_{i=l}^{Q} \frac{\delta_i(j)\delta_i(k)}{l_i} s_i$$

$$b_{jk} = \frac{1}{\bar{l}n}\left\{\sum_{i=1}^{Q} \delta_i(j)s_i\right\}\left\{\sum_{i=1}^{Q} \delta_i(k)s_i\right\}$$

$$d_k = \sum_{i=1}^{Q} s_i \delta_i(k).$$

For further convenience, the matrix representation

$$HX = {}^1\varrho^2\, FX$$

will be used in the following discussion, where the elements of the matrix H are h_{jk}, those of the matrix F are f_{jk}, and X is a column vector. Then calculate the latent vector corresponding to the maximum latent root of $^1\varrho^2$, where we can set $\bar{x} = \dfrac{1}{\ln} \displaystyle\sum_j^R \sum_i^Q \delta_i(j) s_i x_j = 0$ and $\sigma_x^2 = 1$ without loss of generality. And we obtain

$$y_e = \frac{1}{{}^1\varrho} \frac{\sigma_x}{\sigma_y} \left(\frac{1}{l_e} \sum_{j=1}^{R} x_j \delta_e(j) \right), \qquad (e = 1, 2, \cdots, Q)$$

which implies

$$y_e = \frac{1}{l_e} \sum_{j=1}^{R} x_j \delta_e(j) \quad \text{in case of } \frac{1}{{}^1\varrho} - \frac{\sigma_x}{\sigma_y} = 1.$$

This method is equivalent to that of maximizing $\eta^2 = \sigma_b^2/\sigma^2$, where σ_b^2 is between individual (type) variance and σ^2 is total variance (σ_w^2 is variance within individual (type) and is equal to $\sigma^2 - \sigma_b^2$).

We generalize this idea to multi-dimensional quantification. We want to quantify individuals (types) or categories by assigning numerical vectors to them to minimize the within generalized variance, $|W|$, with the total variance being constant. In other words, it is to minimize $|W| / |VT|$, where $|VT|$ is generalized total variance with respect to vector $^s x_i$ (or $^s y_j$) for $s = 1, 2, \cdots, S$ and for all i (or j), and S is the number of dimension of the space.

The process mentioned above is described in detail below. We consider to maximize $1 - |W| / |VT|$ under the reasonable condition that the non-diagonal elements in matrix W vanish, and this means to maximize $1 - |\tilde{W}| / |VT|$ where $\tilde{W}$ is the diagonal matrix of W. As $|\tilde{W}| / |VT| \geq |\tilde{W}| / |VT|$ and $|VT| \leq |\widetilde{VT}|$ hold, $1 - |\tilde{W}| / |\widetilde{VT}| \geq 1 - |\tilde{W}| / |VT|$, where $\widetilde{VT}$ is the diagonal matrix of VT. Thus, it is desirable to quantify the individuals and the categories (in other words, to require vector x_i, (or y_j) for all i (or j)), so as to minimize $|\tilde{W}| / |\widetilde{VT}|$, or to maximize $1 - |\tilde{W}| / |\widetilde{VT}|$. This reduces to the maximizing of

$$\prod_{s}^{S} {}^s\eta^2$$

for $^s\eta^2$ is the correlation ratio with respect to ^sx_i for all i, and which is equivalent to maximizing

$$\prod_s^S {}^s\varrho^2$$

where $^s\varrho$ is the correlation coefficient between ^2x_i and ^2x_j for all i and j.

Thus, it leads us to solve the latent equation $HX = \varrho^2 FX$, and ^sX is the latent vector corresponding to the s-th largest latent root of H. Generally speaking, the smaller S is the more desirable, (for example, S being at most three). However, we do require that the minimum dimension, or minimum S, makes $^s\varrho^2$ small.

In some cases, we make $\varrho_{sx}^2 = {}^s\eta^2$, where $s = 1, 2, \cdots, S$, without loss of generality, and when this assumption holds, it is also useful to describe some concentration ellipsoids and to classify the individuals and categories into several clusters. In the classification, some methods of statistical clustering are available with computer programs.

In order to visualize the result of above calculations, we would like to represent it in the following two-dimensional Euclidean spaces. In doing so, we take the two-dimensional vector $(^1x, {}^2x)$, for ^1x and ^2x are the corresponding latent vectors to the maximum latent root, $^1\varrho^2$, and the second maximum latent root, $^2\varrho^2$ respectively.

In the two-dimensional spaces, the nearer the points are, the more it shows that the relations in response of the categories are the closer. That is to say, in Figure A13.1 categories A and B have very close relation while A and C do not. Those who select category A(B) have a strong tendency to select category B(A) and not category C. So, the distance (far and near) between points corresponds to the similarity of categories in responses.

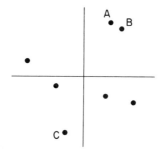

Figure A13.1

Heuristic Example

Suppose that we have Table A13.2 as the cross-tabulation from the data of a survey. In this case, $L = 4$, $K_1 = K_2 = K_3 = K_4 = 2$, $R = 8$ and $n = 2000$.

Table A13.2.

		B_1	B_2	C_1	C_2	D_1	D_2	A_1	A_2
		A_1	A_2	B_1	B_2	C_1	C_2	D_1	D_2
B_1	A_1	1000		800	200	500	500	200	800
B_2	A_2		1000	200	800	500	500	800	200
C_1	B_1			1000		700	300	400	600
C_2	B_2				1000	300	700	600	400
D_1	C_1					1000		700	300
D_2	C_2						1000	300	700
A_2	D_1							1000	
A_1	D_2								1000

Let A, B, C and D be items and suffix 1 or 2 be the category. The marginal distributions are assumed to be always equal. The cross-tabulation between any two items shows the degree of correlation between them. For example, 'A and B' have the strongest degree of positive correlation and 'A and D' have the strongest degree of negative correlation, while 'A and C' have the weakest degree of correlation, *i.e.*, no correlation in this case. The configuration of the categories in the items to reveal these interrelations are conjectured as in Figure A13.2.

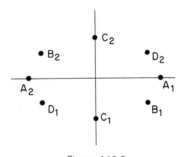

Figure A13.2

This is easily obtained by the direct observation of and intuitive mathematical reasoning from that table, because these artificial data are made to show very reasonable the simple interrelations without inconsistency. Calculation, by the method outlined in the previous section, gives Figure A13.3. This is quite similar to Figure A13.2, the intuitive expectation.

The transformation of A → B, B → C, C → D and D → A shows the counter-clockwise rotation of the configuration. This reveals that the change in cross-tabulation (for example by the transformation men-

Table A13.3.

	A_1	A_2	B_1	B_2	C_1	C_2	D_1	D_2
A_1	1000		900	100	500	500	300	700
A_2		1000	100	900	500	500	700	300
B_1			1000		600	400	400	600
B_2				1000	400	600	600	400
C_1					1000		800	200
C_2						1000	200	800
D_1							1000	
D_2								1000

tioned above) between the two items brings about the rotation of the configuration.

Next we change Table A13.2 slightly resulting in Table A13.3, keeping all marginal distributions always unchanged. Checking this table carefully, we see that the similarity between 'A and B' and that between 'C and D' are increased more than in Table A13.2 while the similarity between 'A and D' and that between 'B and C' are decreased more than in Table A13.2. In configuration of Table A13.3 it is intuitively expected that the distances between 'A and B' and 'C and D' be shorter and the distances between 'A and D' and 'B and C' be longer than in Figure A13.3. The calculation by the method reveals the structure in Figure A13.4 and the conjecture has been confirmed.

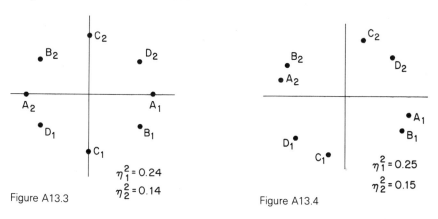

$\eta_1^2 = 0.24$
$\eta_2^2 = 0.14$

Figure A13.3

$\eta_1^2 = 0.25$
$\eta_2^2 = 0.15$

Figure A13.4

These discussions give some heuristic examples that the spacial unfolding of the table by theory, in a Euclidean space, gives the result which is intuited and interpreted from the table. We may call this spacial unfolding the 'data structure of cross-tabulations', represented by a configuration of points.

References

Adler, S., Aranya, N., & Amernic, C. (1981). Community size, socialization and the work need of professionals. *Academy of Management Journal*, **24**, 504–511.

Andrisani, P., & Miljus, R. (1977). Individual differences in preferences for intrinsic versus extrinsic aspects of work. *Journal of Vocational Behavior*, **11**, 14–30.

Aiken, M., Ferman, L., & Sheppard, H. (1968). *Economic failure, alienation and extremism*. Ann Arbor, MI: University of Michigan Press.

Allport, F. (1962). A structuronomic conception of behavior: Individual and collective. *Journal of Abnormal and Social Psychology*, **64**, 3–30.

Anderson, N. (1961). *Work and leisure*. London: Routledge & Kegan Paul.

Anthony, P. (1980). Work and loss of meaning. *International Social Science Journal*, **32**, 416–426.

Arendt, H. (1958). *The human condition*. Chicago: The University of Chicago Press.

Barfield, R. (1970). *The automobile worker and retirement: A second look*. Ann Arbor, MI: University of Michigan, Institute of Social Research.

Barfield, R., & Morgan, J. (1969). *Early retirement: The decision and the experience*. Ann Arbor, MI: University of Michigan, Institute of Social Research.

Barker, R. (1968). *Ecological psychology*. Stanford, CA: Stanford University Press.

Beales, A., & Lambert, R. (1934). *Memoirs of the unemployed*. London: Gallanez.

Bell, D. (1972). The coming of the post-industrial society, New York: Basic Books.

Berger, J., & Offe, C. (1984). Die Zukunft des Arbeitsmarktes. Zur Ergänzungsbedürftigkeit eines versagenden Allokationsprinzips. In Offe, C. "Arbeitsgesellschaft": Strukturprobleme und Zukunftsperspektiven, pp. 82–117. Frankfurt/New York: Campus.

Beveridge, W. (1945). *Full employment in a free society*. New York: Norton.

Blau, P. (1964). *Exchange and power in social life*. New York: Wiley.

Blood, M. (1969). Work values and job satisfaction. *Journal of Applied Psychology*, **53**, 456–459.

Blood, M. (1971). The validity of importance. *Journal of Applied Psychology*, **55**, 487–488.

Braude, L. (1975). *Work and wonders: A sociological analysis*. New York: Praeger Publishers.

Brenner, M. (July 1980, A–7). *Current developments*, (**24**). Washington, D.C.: The Bureau of National Affairs, Inc.

Bridgman, P. (1927). *The logic of modern physics.* New York: Macmillan.

Brief, A., & Oliver, R. (1976). Male–female differences in work attitudes among retail sales managers. *Journal of Applied Psychology*, **61**, 526–528.

Brunngraber, K. (1933). *Karl and the twentieth century.* New York: William Morrow & Co.

Buchholz, R. (1978). An empirical study of contemporary beliefs about work in American society. *Journal of Applied Psychology*, **63**, 219–227.

Campbell, J., & Pritchard, R. (1976) Motivation theory in industrial and organizational psychology. In M. D. Dunnette (Ed.), *Handbook of Industrial and Organizational Psychology*, 63–130. Chicago: Rand McNally.

Cavan, R. (1928). *Suicide.* Chicago: University of Chicago Press.

Centers, R., & Bugenthal, D. E. (1966). Intrinsic and extrinsic job motivations among different segments of the working population. *Journal of Applied Psychology*, **50**, 193–197.

Cherns, A. (1980). Work and Values: Shifting patterns in industrial society. *International Social Science Journal*, XXXII, **3**, 427–441.

Coleman, J. (1966). Foundations for a theory of collective decisions. *The American Journal of Sociology*, **71**, 615–627.

Cragin, J. (1983). The nature of importance perceptions: A test of a cognitive model. *Organizational Behavior and Human Performance*, **31**, 262–276.

Crawford, J. (1978). Career development and career choice in pioneer and traditional women. *Journal of Vocational Behavior*, **12**, 129–139.

Curle, A. (1947). Transitional communities and social re-connection: A follow-up study of the civil resettlement of British prisoners of war. Part I. Human Relations, Vol. 1, No. 1, 42–68.

Davis, J. (1980). *A national data program for the social sciences: Cumulative codebook for the 1972–1980 general social survey.* Chicago: National Opinion Research Center.

Davis, K. (1949). *Human society.* New York: Macmillan.

Dayton, N. (1940). *New facts on mental disorders.* Springfield, IL: Charles C. Thomas.

Decker, R. (1955). A study of three specific problems in the measurement and interpretation of employee attitudes. *Psychological Monographs*, **69**, (16, No. 401).

DiRenzo, G. (1967). Conceptual definition in the behavioral sciences. In G. J. DiRenzo, (Ed.) *Concepts, Theory and Explanation in the Behavioral Sciences*, New York: Random House.

Doeringer, P., & Piore, M. (1971). *Internal labor markets and manpower analysis.* Lexington, MA: D. C. Heath and Co.

Donald, M., & Havighurst, R. (1959). The meaning of leisure. *Social Forces*, **37**, 357–360.

Dooley, D., & Catalano, R. (1980). Economic change as a cause of behavioral disorder. *Psychological Bulletin*, **87**, 450–468.

Drenth, P. (1983). *Centraliteit van werken.* Inaugural Address as Rector Magnificus. Amsterdam: Free University Amsterdam.

Drenth, P. J. D., & Groenendijk, B. (1984). Work and organizational psychology in cross-cultural perspective. In: P. J. D. Drenth, H. Thierry, P. J. Willems, & Ch. J. de Wolff. *Handbook of Work and Organizational Psychology.* pp. 1197–1229. London: Wiley.

Drenth, P. J. D., & Wilpert, B. (1980). The role of "social contracts" in cross-cultural research. *International Review of Applied Psychology*, **29**, 293–305.

Dubin, R. (1956). Industrial workers' worlds: A study of the "central life interest" of industrial workers. *Social Problems*, **3**, 131–142.

Dubin, R. (1958). *The world of work*. Englewood Cliffs, NJ: Prentice Hall.

Dubin, R. (1976). Work in modern society. In R. Dubin (Ed.). *Handbook of Work, Organization and Society*, pp. 5–35. Chicago: Rand McNally.

Dubin, R., Champoux, J., & Porter, L. (1975). Central life interests and organizational commitment of blue-collar and clerical workers. *Administration Science Quarterly*, **20**, 411–421.

Dubin, R., Hedley, R., & Taveggia, T. (1976). Attachment to work. In R. Dubin (Ed.). *Handbook of Work, Organization and Society* pp. 281–342. Chicago: Rand McNally.

Dunham, R. (1977). Shiftwork: A review and theoretical analysis. *The Academy of Management Review*, **2**, 624–634.

Durkheim, E. (1893). *De la division du travail social*. Paris: F. Alcan.

Durkheim, E. (1951). *Suicide: A study in Sociology* (G. Simpson, Ed.; J. Spaulding & G. Simpson, Trans.). New York: Free Press of Glencoe (Original work published 1897).

Durkheim, E. (1960). *The division of labor in society*. New York: The Free Press of Glencoe.

Eisenberg, P., & Lazarsfeld, P. (1938). The psychological effects of unemployment. *Psychological Bulletin*, **35**, 358–390.

Embretson, S. (1983). Construct validity: Construct representation versus nomothetic span. *Psychological Bulletin*, **90**, 179–197.

Etzioni, A. (1961). *A comparative analysis of complex organizations*. New York: The Free Press of Glencoe.

Evans, A. (1975). *Hours of work in industrialized countries*. Geneva: International Labor Office.

Evans, M. (1969). Conceptual and operational problems in the measurement of various aspects of job satisfaction. *Journal of Applied Psychology*, **53**, 93–101.

Ewen, R. (1967). Weighting components of job satisfaction. *Journal of Applied Psychology*, **51**, 68–73.

Fararo, T. (1973). *Mathematical sociology: An introduction to fundamentals*. New York: Wiley.

Firth, R. (1948). Anthropological background to work. *Occupational Psychology*, **22**, 94–102.

Foreign Press Center Japan (Ed.) (1977). *The women of Japan—past and present*. Tokyo: Foreign Press Center.

Friedlander, F. (1965). Relationships between the importance and satisfaction of various environmental factors. *Journal of Applied Psychology*, **49**, 160–164.

Friedman, E., & Havighurst, R. (1954). *The meaning of work and retirement*. Chicago: University of Chicago Press.

Friedman, G. (1961). *The anatomy of work*. London: Heinemann.

Friedrichs, G., & Schaff, A. (1980). *For better or worse*. Rome: Club of Rome Report.

Friedrichs, G., & Schaff, A. (1982). Microelectronics and society. For better or for worse. Oxford: Pergamon.

Fruchter, B. (1954). *Introduction to factor analysis*. London: Van Nostrand.

Gatti, A. (1937). La disoccupazione come crisi psicologica. *Achives Italia di Psicologi*, **15**, 4–28.

Gechman, A., & Weiner, Y. (1975). Job involvement and satisfaction as related to mental health and personal time devoted to work. *Journal of Applied Psychology*, **60**, 521–523.

Gerth, H., & Mills, C. (1946). *From Max Weber: Essays in sociology*. New York: Oxford University Press.

Goldthorpe, J., Lockwood, D., Bechhofer, F., & Platt, J. (1968). *The affluent worker: Industrial attitudes and behavior*. Cambridge: Cambridge University Press.

Green, P., & Tull, D. (1975) *Research for making decisions*. London: Prentice Hall.

Guttman, L. (1941). The quantification of a class of attributes: A theory and method of scale construction. In P. Horst *et al.*, *The Prediction of Personal Adjustment* 319–348. New York: Social Science Research Council. Bulletin No. 48.

Haire, M., Ghiselli, E., & Porter, L. (1966). *Managerial thinking: An International Study*. New York: Wiley.

Hall, D. (1971). A theoretical model of career subidentity development in organizational settings. *Organizational Behavior and Human Performance*, **6**, 50–76.

Hall, D. (1976). *Careers in organizations*. Santa Monica, CA: Goodyear.

Hardin, E., Reif, H., & Heneman, H., Jr. (1951). Stability of job preferences of department store employees. *Journal of Applied Psychology*, **35**, 256–259.

Hayashi, C. (1950). On the quantification of qualitative data from the mathematics-statistical point of view. *Annuals of the Institute of Statistical Mathematics*, II.

Hayashi, C. (1956). Theory and examples of quantification (II). *Proceedings of the Institute of Statistical Mathematics*, **4**, 19–30.

Hayashi, C., Nishira, S., Suzuki, T., Muzuno, K., & Sakamoto, Y. (Eds.) (1977). Changing Japanese values-statistical surveys and analyses. *Research Committee on the Study of the Japanese National Character*. Tokyo: Institute of Mathematical Statistics.

Hearnshaw, L. (1954). Attitudes to work. *Occupational Psychology*, **28**, 129–139.

Hedges, J., & Sekscenski, E. (1979). Workers on late shifts in a changing economy. *Monthly Labor Review*, **102**, 14–22.

Heider, F. (1958). *The psychology of interpersonal relations*. New York: Wiley.

Heller, F. A. (1982a). *Competence and skill in the 1980's*. London: Work and Society Report.

Heller, F. A. (1982b). *Some theoretical problems in multi-national and cross-cultural research on organizations*. Tavistock Institute Document No. 2T 256A.

Henderson, J., & Quandt, R. (1958). *Microeconomic theory: A mathematical approach*. New York: McGraw-Hill Book Co.

Hepworth, S. (1980). Moderating factors of the psychological impact of unemployment. *Journal of Occupational Psychology*, **53**, 139–145.

Herzberg, F., Mausner, B., Peterson, R., & Capwell, D. (1957). *Job attitudes: Review of research and opinion*. Pittsburgh: Psychological Service of Pittsburgh.

Hinrichs, J. (1968). A replicated study of job satisfaction dimensions. *Personnel Psychology*, **21**, 479–503.

Holvoet, M. (1984) The construction of MOW indices and pattern variables. Ghent, Belgium: Laboratory for Applied Psychology.

Hoff, E., & Grüneisen, V. (1978). Arbeitserfahrungen, Erziehungseinstellungen, und Erziehungsverhalten von Eltern. In H. Lukesch und K. Schneewind (Eds.).

Familiaere sozialisation: Probleme, ergebnisse, perspektiven 65–89. Stuttgart: Klett-Cotta.

Hofstede, G. (1972). The color of collars. *Columbia Journal of World Business*, **7**, 72–80.

Hofstede, G. (1980). *Culture's consequences: International differences in work-related values.* Beverly Hills, CA: Sage Publications.

Hofstede, G. (1982). The cultural relativity of the quality of life concept. Paper presented at the *20th International Congress of Applied Psychology*, Edinburgh, Scotland, July.

Hofstede, G., & Perri, F. (1971). *The interpretation of job goal importance measures.* IBM Europe Personnel Research Study (11). New York: International Business Machines.

Holvoet, M. (1984). *MOW data treating.* Ghent, Belgium: Laboratory for Applied Psychology.

Horvat, B. (1979). Paths of transition to workers' self-management in the developed capitalist countries. In T. Burns, L. Karlsson, & V. Rus (Eds.). *Work and power: The Liberation of Work and the Control of Political Power.* London: Sage.

Hulin, C., & Blood, M. (1968). Job enlargement, individual differences and worker responses. *Psychological Bulletin*, **69**, 41–55.

Hulin, C., & Triandis, H. (1981). Meanings of work in different organization environments. In P. Nystrom & W. Starbuck (Eds.). *Handbook of Organization Design* Vol. 2 pp. 336–357. New York: Oxford University Press.

IDE-International Research Group. (1981). *Industrial democracy in Europe.* London: Oxford University Press.

Inglehart, R. (1977). *The silent revolution: Changing values and political styles among Western publics.* Princeton, NJ: Princeton University Press.

Inglehart, R. (1979). Wertwandel in westlichen Gesellschaften: Politische konsequenzen von materialistischen und postmaterialistischen Prioritäten. In P. Kmieciak (Ed.). *Wertwandel und Gesellschaftlicher Wandel.* Frankfurt: Frankfurt Campus.

Inglehart, R. (1982). Changing values in Japan and the West. *Comparative Political Studies*, **14**, 445–479.

Iso-Ahola, S., & Buttimer, K. (1981). The emergence of work and leisure ethic from early adolescence to early adulthood. *Journal of Leisure Research*, **13**, 282–288.

Israeli, N. (1935). Distress in the outlook of Lancashire and Scottish unemployed. *Journal of Applied Psychology*, **19**, 67–69.

Jacques, E. (1965). Preliminary sketch of a general structure of executive strata. In W. Brown and E. Jacques (Eds.). *Glacier Project Papers.* London: Heinemann.

Jahoda, M. (Sept. 6, 1979). The psychological meanings of unemployment. *New Society*, 492–495.

Jahoda, M., Lazarsfeld, P., & Zeisel, H. (1960). *Die Arbeitslosen von Marienthal.* Frankfurt/M.: Suhrkamp.

Jakubowski, T. (1968) *Meaning of work among middle-managers.* Unpublished. Amherst: University of Massachusetts.

Jurgensen, C. (1947). Selected factors which influence job preferences. *Journal of Applied Psychology*, **31**, 553–564.

Jurgensen, C. (1978). Job preferences (what makes a job good or bad?). *Journal of Applied Psychology*, **63**, 267–276.

Kahn, H., & Weiner, A. (1973). The future meanings of work: Some "surprise-free" observations. In F. Best (Ed.). *The future of work*. pp. 141–154. Englewood Cliffs, NJ: Prentice Hall.

Kahn, R. (1981). *Work and health*. New York: Wiley.

Kanungo, R. (1979). The concept of alienation and involvement revisited. *Psychological Bulletin*, **56**, 119–138.

Kanungo, R. (1982). Measurement of job and work involvement. *Journal of Applied Psychology*, **67**, 341–349.

Kaplan, A. (1964). *The conduct of inquiry*. San Francisco: Chandler Publishing Company.

Kaplan, H., & Tausky, C. (1974). The meaning of work among the hard core unemployed. *Pacific Sociological Review*, **17**, 185–198.

Karasek, R. (1979). Job demands, job decision latitude and mental strain: Implications for job redesign. *Administrative Science Quarterly*, **24**, 285–308.

Kilpatrick, F., Cummings, M., Jr., & Jennings, M. (1964). *Source book of a study of occupational values and the image of the federal service*, Washington, D.C.: The Brookings Institution.

Klein, L., (1975). Die entwicklung neuer Formen der Arbeitsorganisation. London: Tavistock Institute of Human Relations.

Klipstein, M. Von, & Strümpel, B. (1984). De Überdruß am Überfluß. München: Günter Olzog.

Kohlberg, L. (1963). The development of children's orientations toward moral order: I. Sequence in the development of human thought. *Vita Humana*, **6**, 11–33.

Kohlberg, L. (1971). From is to ought: How to commit the naturalistic fallacy and get away with it in the study of moral development. In T. Mischel (Ed.). *Cognitive Development and Epistemology*. New York: Academic Press.

Kohn, M. (1969). *Class and conformity: A study in values*. Homewood, IL: Dorsey.

Kohn, M., & Schooler C. (1983). *Work and personality: An inquiry into the impact of social stratification*. Norwood, NJ: Albex.

Korpi, W. (1978). *The working class in welfare capitalism*. London: Routledge & Kegan Paul.

Kraut, A., & Ronen, S. (1975). Validity of job facets importance: A multinational, multicriteria study. *Journal of Applied Psychology*, **60**, 671–677.

Kuethe, J., & Levenson, B. (1964). Concepts of organization worth. *American Journal of Sociology*, **70**, 342–348.

Lacy W., Bokemeier, J., & Shepard, J. (1983). Job attributes preferences and work commitment of men and women in the United States. *Personnel Psychology*, **36**, 315–329.

Lawler, E. (1973). *Motivation in work organization*. Monterey, CA: Brooks/Cole Publishing Company.

Lawler, E., & Hall, D. (1970). Relationships of job characteristics to job involvement, satisfaction and intrinsic motivation. *Journal of Applied Psychology*, **54**, 305–312.

Ledvinka, J. (1982). *Federal regulation of personnel and human resource management*. Belmont, CA: Kent Publishing.

Lipset, S. (1963). *Political man*. New York: Doubleday.

Locke, E. (1969). What is job satisfaction? *Organizational Behavior and Human Performance*, **4**, 309–336.

Locke, E. (1976). The nature and causes of job satisfaction. In M. D. Dunnette (Ed.). *Handbook of Industrial and Organizational Psychology*, pp. 1297–1350. Chicago: Rand McNally.

Locke, E., & Schweiger, D. (1979). Participating in decision-making: One more look. In B. Staw (Ed.). *Research in Organization Behavior*, Vol. I. pp. 265–339. Greenwich, CT: JAI Press.

Lodahl, T., & Kejner, M. (1965). The definition and measurement of work involvement. *Journal of Applied Psychology*, **49**, 24–33.

Luce, R., & Suppes, P. (1965). Preference, utility, and subjective probability. In R. Luce, R. Bush and E. Galanter (Eds.). *Handbook of Mathematical Psychology*, Vol. III. New York: Wiley.

Macarov, D. (1980). *Work and welfare*. London: Sage.

McClelland, D. (1961). *The achieving society*. Princeton, NJ: Van Nostrand.

McClelland, D., Sturr, J., Knapp, R., & Wendt, H. (1958). Obligations to self and society in the United States and Germany. *Journal of Abnormal and Social Psychology*, **56**, 245–255.

Maccoby, E., & Jacklin, C. (1974). *The psychology of sex differences*. Stanford, CA: Standford University Press.

MacMahon, B., Johnson, S., & Pugh, T. (1963). Relation of suicide rates to social conditions: Evidence from U.S. vital statistics. *Public Health Reports*, **78**, 285–293.

Mae, M. (1981). Japanische familien-struktur and sozialisation. In S. Yoshijima (Ed.). *Sozialisation und literatur. Ein interkultureller und interdisziplinaer versuch. Inter universitatsseminar fur Deutsche und Japanische Kultur*. Tokyo: Sansyusya Verlag.

Mahoney, T. (1979a). Another look at job satisfaction and performance. In T. A. Mahoney (Ed.). *Compensation and Reward Perspectives* pp. 322–334. Homewood, IL: Irwin.

Mahoney, T. (1979b). Organizational hierarchy and position worth. *Academy of Management Journal*, **22**, 726–737.

March, J., & Simon, H. (1958). *Organizations*. New York: Wiley.

Marx, K. (1932). Economic and philosophical manuscripts. In *Marx-Engels Gesamtausgabe* (Vol. 3). Berlin: Marx-Engels Institute (Original published 1844).

Marx, K. (1933). *Das kapital*. Zürich: Marx-Engels Gesamtausgabe, Teil II.

Maurer, J. (1968). Work as a "central life interest" of industrial supervisors. *Academy of Management Journal*, **11**, 329–339.

Miller, G. (1980). The interpretation of nonoccupational work in modern society: A preliminary discussion and typology. *Social Problems*, **27**, 381–391.

Mills, C. W. (1956). *White collar*. New York: Oxford University Press.

Morrow, P. (1983). Concept redundancy in organizational research: The case of work commitment. *The Academy of Management Review*, **8**, 486–500.

Morse, N., & Weiss, R. (1955). The function and meaning of work and the job. *American Sociological Review*, **20**, 191–198.

Mortimer, J., & Lorence, J. (1979a). Work experience and occupational value socialization: A longitudinal study. *American Journal of Sociology*, **84**, 1361–1385.

Mortimer, J., & Lorence, J. (1979b). Occupational experience and the self-concept: A longitudinal study. *Social Psychology Quarterly*, **42**, 307–323.

MOW-International Research Team (1981). The meaning of working. In C. Dlugos & K. Weirmair (Eds.). *Management under Differing Value Systems— Managerial Philosophies and Strategies in a Changing World* pp. 565–630. Berlin/New York: Walter De Gruyter & Company.

Murphy, J., & Gilligan, C. (1980). Moral development in late adolescence and adulthood: A critique and reconstruction of Kohlberg's theory. *Human Development*, **23**, 77–104.

Naoi, A., & Schooler, C. (August 24–28, 1981). *Occupational conditions and psychological functioning in Japan.* Paper presented at the annual meeting of the American Sociological Association, Toronto.

Naroll, R. (1968). Some thoughts on comparative method in cultural anthropology. In H. Blaylock, Jr. and A. Blaylock (Eds.). *Methodology in Social Research* pp. 236–277. New York: McGraw-Hill Book Co.

Nie, N., & Hull, H. (1975) *Statistical Package for the social sciences,* social education. New York: McGraw-Hill Book Co.

Nollen, S., Eddy, B., & Martin, V. (1977). *Permanent part-time employment: The manager's perspective.* Washington, D.C.: Georgetown University. (Report No. DLMA 21–11–75–16.)

Northrop, F. (1959). *The logic of modern physics.* New York: Macmillan.

Odaka, K. (1970). *The ethics of occupation.* Tokyo: Chuokoronsha.

Offe, C. 1984. "Arbeitsgesellschaft": Strukturprobleme und Zukunftsperspektiven, Frankfurt/New York: Campus.

Olafson, F. (1961). *Society, law, and morality.* Englewood Cliffs, NJ: Prentice-Hall.

Olson, M. (1965). *The logic of collective action: Public goods and the theory of groups.* Cambridge, MA: Harvard University Press.

Parker, S. R. (1965) Work and non-work in three occupations. *Sociological Review*, **13**, 65–67.

Parker, S. R. & Smith, M. (1976) Work and leisure. In R. Dubin (Ed.) *Handbook of Work, Organization, and Society* pp. 37–62. Chicago: Rand McNally.

Parnes, H., & King, R. (1977). Middle-aged job losers. *Industrial Gerontology.* **4**, 77–95.

Parsons, T. (1951). *The social system.* Glencoe, IL: The Free Press.

Parson, T., & Shils, E. (Eds.) (1952). *Toward a general theory of action.* Cambridge, MA: Harvard University Press.

Perlman, M. (1976) *Labor union theories in America.* Westport, CT: Greenwood Press.

Pharr, S. (1977). Japan: Historical and contemporary perspectives. In J. Hiele & A. Smock (Eds.). *Women: Roots and Status in Eight Countries.* New York: Wiley.

Piaget, J. (1965). *The moral development of the child.* Glencoe, IL: The Free Press. (Originally published 1932.)

Polanyi, M. (1962). *Personal knowledge: Towards a post-critical philosophy.* New York: Harper & Row.

Porter, L. (1964). *Organizational patterns of managerial job attitudes.* New York: American Foundation for Management Research.

Porter, L. & Lawler, E. (1965). Properties of organization structure in relation to job attitudes and job behavior. *Psychological Bulletin*, **64**, 23–51.

Psathas, G. (1968). Toward a theory of occupational choice for women. *Sociology and Social Research*, **52**, 253–268.

Quinn, R. (1971). What workers want: The relative importance of job facets to American workers. Ann Arbor, MI: Survey Research Center (Mimeo).

Quinn, R., & Cobb, W. (1971). What workers want: Factor analysis of importance ratings of job facets. Ann Arbor, MI: Survey Research Center (Mimeo).

Quinn, R., & Mangione, T. (1974). Evaluating weighted models of measuring job satisfaction: A Cinderella story. *Organizational Behavior and Human Performance*, **10**, 1–23.

Quinn, R., & Staines, G. (1979). *The 1977 quality of employment survey.* Ann Arbor, Mich.: Institute for Social Research, The University of Michigan, 1979.

Rest, J. (1979). *Development in judging moral issues.* Minneapolis, MN: University of Minnesota Press.

Reynolds, L. (1974). *Labor economics and labor relations (6th ed.).* Englewood Cliffs, NJ: Prentice-Hall.

Roberts, K. (1970) On looking at an elephant. An evaluation of cross-cultural research related to organizations. *Psychological Bulletin*, **74**, 327–350.

Roberts, K., & Glick, W. (1980). *Missing persons in cross-national research: Part-time workers.* Paper presented at the Academy of Management Convention, Atlanta.

Roberts, K. and Glick, W. (1981). The job characteristics approach to task design. *Journal of Applied Psychology*, **66**, 193–217.

Robinson, R., & Bell, W. (1978). Equality: Success and social justice in England and the United States. *American Sociological Review*, **43**, 125–143.

Rohner, R. (1977). Why cross-cultural research? In: L. Adler (Ed.). *Issues in Cross-cultural Research* pp. 3–12. New York: The New Academy of Sciences.

Ronen, W. (1970). Relative importance of job characteristics. *Journal of Applied Psychology*, **54**, 192–200.

Rosow, J. (March 1981). Quality of work life: Issues for the 1980. *Training and Development Journal*, 33–52.

Ross, I., & Zander, A. (1957). Need satisfaction and employee turnover. *Personnel Psychology*, **10**, 327–333.

Rousseau, J. (1916). *The social contract and discourses.* London: J. M. Dent & Sons, Ltd.

Rundquist, E., & Sletto, R. (1936). *Personality in the depression.* Minneapolis: University of Minnesota Press.

Saleh, S., & Singh, T. (1973). Work values of white-collar employees as a function of sociological background. *Journal of Applied Psychology*, **58**, 131–143.

Salz, B. (October 1955). The human element in industrialization. *Economic Development and Cultural Change*, **4**(Special supplement), 96.

Samuel, Y., & Lewin-Epstein, N. (1979). The occupational situs as a predictor of work values. *American Journal of Sociology*, **85**, 625–639.

Schaffer, R. (1953). Job satisfaction as related to need satisfaction in work. *Psychological Monographs*, **67**, (14, No. 364).

Schaie, K. (1965). A general model for the study of developmental problems. *Psychological Bulletin*, **64**, 92–107.

Schein, E. (1980). *Organizational psychology* (3rd ed.). Englewood Cliffs, NJ: Prentice-Hall.

Schmidt, F. (1974). Leisure: Meaningful activity or passive withdrawal. *Society & Leisure*, pp. 137–143.

Schmitt, N., & McCune, J. (1981). The relationship between job attitudes and the decision to retire. *Academy of Management Journal*, **24**, 795–802.

Schneider, M. (1984). Streit um Arbeitszeit. Köln: Bund Verlag.

Schöll-Schwinghammer, I., & Lappe, L. 1978. Arbeitsbedingungen und Arbeits-bewußtsein erwerbstätiger Frauen, Frankfurt/M.: RKW.

Seashore, S., & Taber, T. (1975). Job satisfaction indicators and their correlates. *American Behavioral Scientist*, **18**, 333–368.

Selye, H. (1974). *Stress without distress*. Philadelphia: J. B. Lippincott.

Sessions, F. (1978). The work ethic is alive and well. *Review of Sport & Leisure*, **3**, 112–22.

Sewell, W., Haller, A., & Ohlendorf, G. (1970). The early educational early occupational attainment process: Replications and revisions. *American Sociological Review*, **35**, 1014–1027.

Shimmin, S. (1966). Concepts of work. *Occupational Psychology*, **40**, 195–201.

Silverman, D. (1970). *The theory of organizations*. London: Heinemann.

Simon, H. (1947). *Administrative behavior*. New York: Macmillan.

Sirota, D., and Greenwood, M. (1971). understand your overseas work force. *Harvard Business Review*, **49**, 53–60.

Smith, M., & Nock, S. (1980). Social class and the quality of work live in public and private organizations. *Journal of Social Issues*, **36**, 59–75.

Soliman, H. (1970). Motivation-hygiene theory of job attitudes: An empirical investigation and an attempt to reconcile both the one and the two factor theories of job attitudes. *Journal of Applied Psychology*, **54**, 452–461.

Sorge, A., Hartmann, G., & Warner, M. (1984). Microelectronics and manpower in manufacturing, Aldershot: Gower.

Special Task Force (1973). *Work in America*. Cambridge: MIT Press.

Stafford, E., Jackson, P., & Banks, M. (1980). Employment, work involvement and mental health in less-qualified young people. *Journal of Occupational Psychology*, **53**, 291–304.

Stake, J. (1978). Motives for occupational goal setting among male and female college students. *Journal of Applied Psychology*, **63**, 617–622.

Starcevich, M. (1972). Job factor importance for job satisfaction and dissatisfaction across different occupational levels. *Journal of Applied Psychology*, **56**, 467–471.

Stearns, A. (1921). Suicide in Massachussetts. *Mental Hygiene*, **5**, 752–777.

Steers, R., & Porter, L. (1975). *Motivation and work behavior*. New York: McGraw-Hill Book Co.

Sugita, K. (1983). *L'Entreprise Japonaise*. Unpublished manuscript, Paris.

Super, D. (1970). *Work values inventory*. Boston: Houghton-Mifflin.

Super, D. (1976). *Career education and the meaning of work*. Washington: U.S. Office of Education, Government Printing Office.

Suppes, P. (1957). *Introduction to logic*. Princeton: Van Nostrand.

Takeuchi, H. (1975). Man and occupation. In R. Iwauchi (Ed.). *The Sociology of Occupation*. Tokyo: Gakubun Sha, Ch. 2.

Tausky, C. (1969). Meanings of work among blue-collar men. *Pacific Sociological Review*, **12**, 49–55.

Tausky, C., & Piedmont, E. (1967). The meaning of work and unemployment: Implication for mental health. *International Journal of Social Psychology*, **14**, 44–49.

Tawney, R. (1948). *Religion and the Rise of Capitalism*. Harmondsworth: Penguin.

Terkel, S. (1972). *Working*. New York: Pantheon.

Thompson, J. (1968). *Organizations in action*. New York: McGraw-Hill Book Co.

Thurstone, L. L. (1947) *Multiple factor analysis: A development and expansion of the vectors of mind.* Chicago: University of Chicago Press.

Tilgher, A. (1962). Work through the ages. In S. Nosow and H. Form (Eds.). *Man, Work and Society.* New York: Basic Books.

Triandis, H. (1972). *The analysis of subjective culture.* New York: Wiley.

Triandis, H., Feldman, J., & Weldon, D. (1975). Ecosystem distrust and the hard-to-employ. *Journal of Applied Psychology,* **60,** 44–56.

Trist, E. (1976). Toward a postindustrial culture. In R. Dubin (Hrsg.): *Handbook of Work, Organization and Society* (pp. 1011–1033). Chicago: Rand McNally.

Troldahl, V. C., & Carter, R. E. (1964). Random selection of respondents within households in phone samples. *Journal of Marketing Research,* 71–76.

Trommsdorff, G. (1981). *Vergleich von sozialisations bedingungen in Japan und der Bundesrepublik. Paper presented at the Tagung fur Familiensoziologie, Arnold-shain.* November.

Trommsdorff, G. (1983). Value change in Japan. *International Journal of Intercultural Relations,* **7,** 37–360.

Turner, A., & Lawrence, P. (1965). *Industrial jobs and the worker.* Boston: Harvard University Press.

U.S. Department of Labor, Bureau of Labor Statistics (1978). *Employment and Earnings.* Washington, D.C.: U.S. Department of Labor.

Udy, S., Jr. (1970). *Work in traditional and modern society.* Englewood Ciffs, NJ: Prentice-Hall.

Van Maanen, J. & Schein, E. (1979). Toward a theory of organizational socialization. In B. Staw (Ed.), *Research in Organizational Behavior.* Vol. 2 (pp. 209–264). Greenwich, CT: JAI Press.

Vecchio, R. (1980). The function and meaning of work and the job: Morse and Weiss (1955) revisited. *Academy of Management Journal,* **23,** 361–367.

Vroom, V. (1964). *Work and motivation.* New York: Wiley.

Wanous, J., & Lawler, E. (1972). Measurement and meaning of job satisfaction. *Journal of Applied Psychology,* **56,** 95–105.

Warr, P. (1978). A study of psychological well-being. *British Journal of Psychology,* **69,** 111–121.

Warr, P. (1981). Psychological aspects of employment and unemployment. *Psychological Medicine,* **12,** 7–11.

Warr, P. (1982). A national study of non-financial employment commitment. *Journal of Occupational Psychology,* **55,** 297–312.

Warr, P. (1984). Work and Unemployment. In P. Drenth, H. Thierry, P. Willems, & C. deWolff (Eds.). *Handbook of Work and Organization Psychology.* London: Wiley.

Warr, P (1985). Twelve Questions about Unemployment and Health. In B. Roberts, R. Finnegan and D. Gallie (Eds.). *New Approaches to Economic Life.* Manchester University Press.

Warr, P., & Jackson, P. (1983). Self-esteem and unemployment among young workers. *Le Travail Humain,* **46,** 355–366.

Weber, M. (1922). *Protestantische ethik und der geist des kapitalismus.* Tübingen: Mohr.

Weber, M. (1964). *The theory of social and economic organization.* New York: The Free Press.

Weber, M. (1930). *The Protestant Ethic and the Spirit of Capitalism*. London: George, Allen & Unwin.

Weick, K. (1979). *The social psychology of organizing* 2nd ed. Reading, MA: Addison-Wesley.

Weiss, D., Dawis, R., England, G., & Lofquist, L. (1964). Minnesota studies in vocational rehabilitation: XVIII. *Construct validation studies of the Minnesota importance questionnaire, Bulletin 41*. Minneapolis: Industrial Relations Center, University of Minnesota.

Weiss, D., Dawis, R., Lofquist, L., & England, G. (1966). Minnesota studies in vocational rehabilitation: XXI. *Instrumentation for the theory of work adjustment, Bulletin 44*. Minneapolis: Industrial Relations Center, University of Minnesota.

Weiss, R., & Kahn, R. (1960). Definitions of work and occupations. *Social Problems*, **8**, 142–151.

White, G. (1977). *Socialization*. London: Longman.

Wilensky, H. (1960). Work, careers and social integration. *International Social Science Journal*, **12**, 543–560.

Wilensky, H. (1961). Orderly careers and social participation: The impact of work history on social integration in the middle mass. *American Sociological Review*, **26**, 521–539.

Williamson, O. (1975). *Markets and hierarchies*. New York: The Free Press.

Wishart, D. (1978). *Clustan, user manual* (3rd ed.). Edinburgh: Program Library Unit, Edinburgh University.

Wollack, S., Goodale, J., Wijting, J., & Smith, P. (1971). Development of the survey of work values. *Journal of Applied Psychology*, **55**, 331–338.

Yankelovich, D. (1979). Work, values and the new breed. In C. Kerr & J. Rosow (Eds.). *Work in America: The Decade Ahead* (pp. 3–26). New York: Van Nostrand.

Yankelovich, D. (1981). *New rules: Searching for self-fulfillment in a world turned upside down*. New York: Random House.

Youth Bureau, Prime Minister's Office of Japan (Ed.) (1978). *The youth of the world and Japan: The findings of the second world youth survey*. Tokyo: Prime Minister's Office.

Index

Adaptation research, 41
Administrators and managers, by
    national sample, 266
Age
  birth cohort, 27–28
  chronological, 27
  distribution, workers, and life
    expectancy, 10
  and entitlement scores, by countries,
    107
  and obligation scores, by countries,
    107
  and societal norms, 105
  and work centrality levels, 86–88,
    240
  and working patterns, 186, 190–192
  and work definition, analysis,
    169–170
Aggravating work conditions, 32
  index (AGGCON), 58, 357
Agricultural workers, by national
    sample, 266
Agriculture/industry, and work
    centrality, 262
Alienation, predictor, 6
Analysis methods,
  cluster, 60
  factor analysis, 359–360
  multiple discrimination, 61
  multiple regression, 61
  word definition cluster data, 367
  see also under Appendices
Antecedents, *see under* Working
    patterns
Appendices
  construction of indices (A3.2),357–363
  interview schedule (A3.1), 325–355
  interviewer check list, 354–355
  item level response, distribution
    data,

    national samples, 265–294
    target groups, 266, 295–323
  mathematical appendix (A.13),
    375–379
  preferences and scale values (A8),
    365
  questionnaire (A3.1), 325–355
  response, distribution data (A3.0),
    265–323
  word definition cluster data (A9),
    367–371
Armed forces, by national sample, 266

Belgium,
  diversity, MOW patterns, 182
  item level response, all data,
    265–294
  samples, 52
    centrality score, 83–84, 88
    comparison, 76
    working, functions, 113
    working patterns, 179
    societal norms, 106–111
Binary frequency ratio, 171 (footnote)
Biographical variables, and working
    patterns, 185–192
  see also Age; Education; Family
    Occupation; Sex
Blacksmiths, by national sample, 266
Blue collar workers,
  all data, 265–294
  and intrinsic factors, 187
  shift work, 31
  turbulence of career, 32–33
  work definition, 171
Britain, samples
  centrality of work index, 262–263
    score, 83–84, 88
    comparison, 76

societal norms, 106–111
item level response, all data,
    265–294
working functions, 113
Buddhism, view of work, 4–5

Career perspectives, 6
Career theory,
    turbulence, 32–33
        and working patterns, 193–195
    work centrality, 34
Caterers, by national sample, 266
Centrality, cognitive,
    definition, 24
    working concepts, 25–26
Centrality of working,
    categories, 236
        and definitions, 237
    concept, 80–81
    decision orientation, 18
    definition, 17
    and hours worked, 204–206
    involvement and commitment, 89–91
    index, 59–60, 174, 251–252
        by countries, 90
        by target groups, 90
    and job tenure, 195
    as life role, 64
    measurement, 81
    MOW patterns, clusters, 214
        consequences, 216–217
    model, heuristic approach, 17–19
    peoples' characteristics, 242–244
    questionnaire, 56
    scores,
        by age group, 86, 88, 90
        commitment, 89–91
        by countries, 83–84, 90
        by sex, 87–88, 90
        by target groups, 84–86, 90
    value orientation, 19
Chemical engineers, all data, 265–294
City life, and working patterns, 186,
    188
Clerks, by national sample, 266
Collective research, 41–42
Comfort dimension, questionnaire, 119
Community,
    childhood, and working patterns, 86,
        188

importance, 71, 237
Company identification factors, 75
Construction workers, by national
    sample, 266
Contact, index, questionnaire, 59
Cross-tabulation, 221–222
Cult units, 12

Data collection, MOW study
    cross-national research, 40–42
    timetable, 39–40
Death, as consequence of
        unemployment, 6
Decision orientation, 18
Die-makers, all data, 265–294
Discrimination analysis,
    multiple, 61
    SPSS program, 61

Economic factors,
    importance, 112–113
    index, questionnaire, 59, 174
    and pattern of working, 195
    questionnaire, 118–119
'Ecosystem distrust', 7
Education,
    learning and improvement
        opportunities, 71
    and leisure, 154–155
    and obligation norm, 109
    and personal characteristics, 29
    self-direction, and centrality, 29–30
    and societal norms, 108–109
    and work centrality, 240
    and work definition, analysis, 170,
        169–170
    and working patterns, 186–188,
        190–192
Entitlement to work, see Entitlement
    norm
Entitlement norm,
    and contact orientation, 186–199
    definition, 176–178
    by countries, 95–98
    and education, 109
    evaluative standard, 21–22
    index, 59, 174
    low entitlement, MOW pattern,
        179–180

identification, target groups, 181,
    186–199
MOW patterns, clusters, 214
    consequences, 216–217
    by target groups, 98–105, 186
'Expressive' values
    and hours worked, 204–206
    identification, 176
    MOW patterns, clusters, 214
        consequences, 216–217
    target groups, 181, 196–197
    work centrality value
        definition, 176, 186–199

Family,
    background, and working patterns,
        189–190
    and leisure, 72
    quantification on response, 237
    responsibility, 27
'Future importance of work', 213,
    215

Gender, *see* Sex difference
Germany,
    item level response, all data,
        265–294
    samples, 52
        centrality score, 83–84, 88
        comparison, 76
        societal norms, 106–111
        working functions, 163
        working patterns, 179
Goals, *see* Work goals
Great Britain, *see* Britain

Health, and unemployment, 6–7
Historical note, significance of work,
    3–5
Home and community situation and
    working patterns, 186, 188
Hours worked, MOW patterns, 218
    possible reduction in, 215
    weekly, 203–205

Income, *see* Economic factors; Pay
Indices, central/non-central, 58–60

Industrial Revolution, 262
Institutional change, work as a
    variable, 7–8
Instrumental MOW pattern,
    antecedents, 186–199
    identification, 176–178
    national groups, 179
    target groups, 181, 196–197
    and unemployment, 193
    and working conditions, 196
Inter-personal contacts through
    working, 112–114
    index, 174
    MOW patterns, clusters
        consequences, 216–217
        hours worked, 204–206
Interview schedule, MOW, 325–355
    response, distribution data
        national groups, 265–294
        target groups, 295–323
Intrinsic function of working, 112–113
    index, 174
Intrinsic work situations, (PIW),
    preference, 360
Islam, view of work, 4
Israel
    item level response, all data,
        265–294
    samples, 53
        centrality score, 83–84, 88
        comparison, 76
        societal norms, 106–111

Japan
    centrality of work index, 262–263
    item level response, all data,
        265–294
    National Character Survey, 241
    samples, 53
        centrality score, 83–84, 88
        comparison, 76
        societal norms, 106–111
    Survey of National Character, 241
    working, functions, 113
    working patterns, 179
'Job image', 133–134
Judeo–Christian views of work, 4
Jugoslavia, *see* Yugoslavia, 54

Learning opportunity dimension,
    questionnaire, 119–120
    see also Education
Leisure time
    index, 60
    preferability index (PL), 361
    preference, 148–157
        effects of autonomy, 154–155
        by countries, 150, 152
        effect of education, 154–155
        by target groups, 150, 152
        sex differences, 154–155
        summary, 156
Life expectancy, and age distribution,
    10
Likert-type scales, 44
'Lottery' question, 57, 79, 89–90, 202
    by countries, 205, 237
    consequences, 215
    and MOW variables, 202–203
        differences in response, 217
    in questionnaire, 225

Materialism/post materialism, 11
Mathematical appendix, 375–379
'Meaning of working' (MOW) study
    see also Work, working
    alternative interpretations, 261–263
    antecedents
        biographical variables, 185–192
        present job, 195–199
        summary and conclusions, 199–200
        work history, 193–195
    attachment, 251–252
    centrality, *see* Centrality of working
    construction of indices, 357–358
    definitions, *see* Work, definitions
    entitlement, *see* Entitlement norm
    general structure, 248–250
    individual variability, 250
    interest and desirability, 253–255
    normative expectations, 252–253
    obligation, *see* Obligation norm
    patterns, of belief
        consequences, 201–219
        hours worked, 203–206
        MOW complexities, 212–217
        summary, 217–219
        valued outcomes, 206–212

patterns, of work
    development, indices, 174
    distribution of national samples,
        179–180
        target groups, 180–181
    identification, 175–179
    see also Entitlement/low
        entitlement; Expressive values;
        Instrumental MOW patterns
    procedure, definition and
        validation, 174–175
    summary and conclusions, 181–
        183, 255–256
    see also Centrality of work;
        Entitlement norms; Obligation
        norm
reasons for study, 1–14
subjective significance, 260–261
variables, international comparison,
    221–245
    biographical variables, 239–241
    centrality of work, 242–244
    Japan, 241
    quantification, 222–239
    summary, 244–245
Minnesota Importance Questionnaire
    (MIQ), 116, 118
Mobility in work history (MWH), 358
Mobility, index, 58
Model, heuristic approach,
    antecedents, 27–34
    concepts, relationships, 25–26
    macrosocietal influences, 34–36
    societal norms, 19–23
    summary, 37–38
    work centrality, *see* Centrality of
        work
    work goals, *see* Work goals
Money, *see* Economic factors; Pay

National groups,
    item level response distribution data,
        265–294
    see also names of participating
        countries
Netherlands,
    diversity MOW patterns, 182
    item level response, all data,
        265–294

samples, 53
  centrality score, 83–84, 88
  comparison, 76
  societal norms, 106–111
  working, functions, 113
  working patterns, 179
Norms, *see* Entitlement: Obligation:
  Societal

Obligation norms
  and education, 109
  as evaluative standard, 22
  by countries, 95–98
  and hours worked, 204–206
  index, 59, 174
  MOW patterns, clusters, 214
    consequences, 216–217
  by target groups, 98–105
Occupational satisfaction index
  (OCCSAT), 358
Occupations,
  properties, and self-direction, 30–31
  satisfaction, 213–214, 215
    index, 58
Occupational groups, *see* Target
  groups

Part-time work, 36
Pay values,
  and definition of work, 170
  and hours worked, 204–206
  index, 174, 195
  MOW patterns, 214, 218–219
    consequences, 216–217
Philosophical significance of working,
  3–5
Preferences,
  intrinsic work, 135–148
    effects of autonomy, 144–145
    by countries, 139–143
    effect of education, 144–145
    index (PIW), 360
    by target groups, 139–143
    sex difference, 144–145
  leisure, 148–157
    index (PL), 361
    see also Leisure
Prestige, and status, 112–115

Product identification factors, 75
Professions, by national sample, 266
Public *vs* private sector employment,
  197–199

Quality of work index (QOFWORK),
  357
  and MOW patterns, 198–199
Quantification on response pattern, 62,
  222–239
  results
    Belgium, 228
    Britain, 229
    Germany, 230
    Israel, 231
    Japan, 232
    Netherlands, 233
    United States, 234
  category definitions, 223
  relationships, 235–239
Questionnaires, MOW
  characteristics, 44–45
  guidelines for sampling, various
    countries, 51–55
  item level response, distribution data
    by national groups, 265–293
    by target groups, 294–323
  items and scales, 55–58
  indices, 58–60
  interview schedule, 325–355
  'lottery' question, *see* Lottery
    question
  response, distribution data
    national data, 265–294
    target groups, 295–323

'Rationale' for working, 130
Religion,
  quantification on response, 237
  role, 71
  and work ethic, 190
  and working patterns, 186–187,
    190–192
Research, current, 11–12
  cross-cultural, 12–14
  goals, 13–14
  see also Model, heuristic approach
Research, design and methods,

cross national, 40–42
    organization, 41
interview methods, 51, 55
nature of the study, 43–49
    samples, 45–49
patterns, concepts and values, 60–62
pilot studies, 49–51
questionnaires, *see* Questionnaires
samples,
    national representation, 47–49
    target groups, 45–47
Retailers and wholesalers, by national
    sample, 266
Retired people, all data, 265–294
Roman Catholic Church, dual role of
    work, 4
'Rural-urban dichotomy', 188

Sales, force, by national sample, 266
Samples,
    national groups, 47–49
        guidelines, 52–54
    target groups, 45–47
Self-employed people, all data,
    265–294
Self-expression dimension,
    questionnaire, 118
Sex difference
    and entitlement scores, by countries,
        106
    female labor force, 9
    and obligation scores, by countries,
        106
    and societal norms, 105, 106
    and work centrality levels, 87–88,
        240
    and work concepts, 28
    and work definition, analysis,
        169–170
    and working patterns, 186–187,
        190–192
Sex distribution, national groups,
    48–49
Shift work, 30–31
Skill utilization, 57
Social change, work as causal variable,
    7–8
Social contract,
    normative principles, 20–21
    obligation and entitlement, 21–23

    see also Entitlement norms;
        Obligation norms
Social institution theories, 22
Social participation, 213, 215
Social welfare systems, disincentives, 9
Societal norms, 93–110
    and age, 106–107
    analysis, 22–23
    and education, 107–109
    empirical structure, 64–65
    entitlement, 21–23, 94
    see also Entitlement norms
    location of countries, 94–98
        of target groups, 98–105
    macrosocietal influences, 34–36
    obligation, 21–23, 94
    see also Obligation norms
    principles, 20–21
    questionnaire, 56
    and sex, 106
    'space', 94
    about work, agreement, 237–238
Societal – service function of working,
    112–114
Society and work, 1–2, 8–11, 259–261
Socio-economic status, 189
Spinners and weavers, by national
    sample, 266
Stress, (aggravated work conditions),
    32
Students, all data, 265–294

Target groups,
    full list, 265
    item level response, all data, 265,
        295–323
    pilot studies, 49–51
    questionnaires, *see* Questionnaires
    selection of groups, principles and
        choice, 45–47
    sample total, and selection, 61
    sampling and interviewing, 52–55
    summary of items and scales, 55–58
    and work centrality, 241
Teachers, all data, 265–294
Technology, microelectronic
    innovations, 9
Temporary workers, all data, 265–294
Textile workers, all data, 265–294
Time at work, *see* Hours worked

Time-occupying function of working, 112–114
Toolmakers, all data, 265–294
Transfer payments, 9
.

Upbringing, and working patterns, 186, 189–190
Unemployment,
  career turbulence, 32–34
  and death, 6
  effects, 6–7
  and health, 6–7
  MOW study, 193
  societal norms, 33
  in target groups, all data, 265–294
  work outcomes, 33
  working pattern antecedents, 191–192
United States
  item level response, all data, 265–294
  samples, 53
    centrality score, 83–84, 88
    comparison, 76
    societal norms, 106–111
    working, functions, 113
    working patterns, 179
Urban life, and working patterns, 186, 188

Value orientation, 19
Valued working outcomes, see also Work, goals
  central variable, 56–57
  index, 59
  functions of working, 111–115
  and work goals, 115–128
  summary, 249–250
    goals, 129–130
    rationale, 130
Variety autonomy, 57

Wages, see Economic dimension; Pay
'White collar workers', all data, 265–294
Work, working, see also Meaning of Working (MOW) study
  'aggravated conditions', 32

index (AGGCON), 58, 357
centrality, see Centrality of working
definitions
  cluster analysis, 167–170
  by age, education and sex, 169–170
  by countries, 167
  identification, 165–166
  by target groups, 168
  by countries, 162, 163
  empirical, 166–170
  international comparison, 163
  quantification on response patterns, 235–239
  by pay, 2
  questionnaire, 161
  summary and conclusions, 170–171, 257–259
  target groups, 163–164
empirical structure, 63–77
  all countries, 74–75
  centrality of working, 64
  factor analysis interpretation, 66–74
  goals, 65
  qualitative similarities, 74–75
  societal norms, 64
entitlement, see Entitlement norm
'ethic', and religion, 190, 262
functions,
  assessment, 111–115
    by countries, 113
    rank order, 115
  list, 112
goals
  by age, 125–126
  combined national samples, 123
  by countries, 122–123
  dimensions, importance, 118–121, 130
  factor loadings, 117
  importance, degree of attainment, 65
  individual, 121
  model, heuristic approach, 24–25
  quantifications on response patterns, 235–239
  questionnaire, 57
  rank order, all countries, 115
  rationale, 130
  by sex, 125–126

summary diagram, 129
by target groups, 127–128
and valued working outcomes,
115–128
individual view, 5–7
job characteristics, 30–31
obligation, *see* Obligation norm
outcomes, importance evaluations,
24–25
rating, intrinsic *vs* extrinsic index, 60
preferences for intrinsic work,
135–148
preference for leisure, 148–157
'right to a job', 9–10
see also Entitlement norm
schedule, 31
index, 358

shift work, 31–32
socialization, models, 194–195
and society, 259–261
valued outcomes, *see* Valued
working outcomes

Yugoslavia
centrality of work index, 262
item level response, all data,
265–294
samples, 54
centrality score, 83–84, 88
comparison, 76
societal norms, 106–111
working, functions, 113
working patterns, 179